LINCOLN, THE CABINET, AND THE GENERALS

CHESTER G. HEARN

LINCOLN THE
CABINET
AND THE GENERALS

LOUISIANA STATE UNIVERSITY PRESS
BATON ROUGE

Published by Louisiana State University Press
Copyright © 2010 by Chester G. Hearn
All rights reserved
Manufactured in the United States of America
First printing

Designer: AMANDA MCDONALD SCALLAN
Typefaces: TEXT, WARNOCK PRO; DISPLAY, ROSEWOOD FILL
Printer and binder: THOMSON-SHORE, INC.

Library of Congress Cataloging-in-Publication Data
Hearn, Chester G.
  Lincoln, the cabinet, and the generals / Chester G. Hearn.
     p. cm.
  Includes bibliographical references and index.
  ISBN 978-0-8071-3637-9 (cloth : alk. paper) 1. United States—Politics and government—1861–1865—
Decision making. 2. Lincoln, Abraham, 1809–1865—Relations with cabinet officers. 3. Lincoln, Abraham,
1809–1865—Relations with generals. 4. Political leadership—United States—History—19th century.
5. Cabinet officers—United States—History—19th century. 6. Generals—United States—History—19th
century. I. Title.
  E457.45.H43 2010
  973.7092—dc22

                                                                                              2009046487

To Ann, my wife and my life,
and to Chet, Dana, Sarah, and Candace, my legacy

CONTENTS

PREFACE

Most of Abraham Lincoln's decisions involving the cabinet and his generals passed through a unique mental process. Noah Brooks, a correspondent for the *Sacramento Union,* called it "a peculiar trait of Lincoln that, in order to preclude all possibility of doubt in his own mind concerning the expediency of any contemplated act, he would state to those with whom he came in contact many doubts and objections not of his own, but those of others, for the express purpose of being confirmed and fixed in his own judgment." A keen observer of human behavior, Brooks became one of the president's closest friends and frequently visited the White House during Lincoln's squabbles with the cabinet regarding domestic, foreign, and military policy. Brooks called the tactic Lincoln's "mental habit . . . to argue . . . as though his mind were not already made up," when actually it was.[1]

When forming political and military strategies, Lincoln persistently played this "mental habit" on the cabinet. Because half his cabinet were former Whigs and the other half former Democrats, each brought to the administration biases from their former political affiliations, which led to constant haggling over policy. Every cabinet member came to the administration with an agenda. Lincoln expected this when he chose the cabinet but was disappointed when the rivalry continued. Internal clashes spilled over to the elevation of army officers. Some cabinet members preferred generals with Democratic antecedents, while others preferred Whigs. Secretary of the Treasury Salmon Chase, for instance, wanted preference given to generals from his home state of Ohio, such as Irvin McDowell and George B. McClellan.

Lincoln spent four years attempting to bring the cabinet members together in the spirit of cooperation but never completely achieved his purpose. He frequently created rifts by rejecting their advice and often made decisions without seeking their advice. For more than two years his cabinet meetings tended to be irregular and informal. Although most of the cabinet agreed on the promulgation of the Emancipation Proclamation, some members believed it went too far, while others argued it did not go far enough to liberate *all* slaves. One of the few instances in which the president followed the advice of the cabinet occurred not at the beginning of the war but in February 1865, when he considered issuing a proclamation proposing an appropriation of $400 million for the abolishment of slavery on a pro rata basis in border states and Southern states. Every cabinet member warned against infuriating the radicals in both houses of Congress and urged him to not issue the document. Surprised by the full cabinet's opposition, and perhaps deciding the members were right, he gave a deep sigh and said, "But you are all opposed to me, and I will not send the message." He picked up a pen and noted on the document, "Today these papers were drawn up and submitted to the Cabinet and unanimously disapproved by them." This may have marked the first time since becoming president in March 1861 that Lincoln, though he may not have agreed with his cabinet, followed their advice.[2]

Lincoln became president with no management experience and with less political experience than most members of his cabinet. Secretary of State William H. Seward had been governor of New York, and Secretary of the Treasury Chase had been governor of Ohio, which gave them insight into managing the offices of government. The two men, however, were political opponents with different ideas about how the national government should be run. Both Seward and Chase had presidential aspirations but lost their opportunity in 1860, when Lincoln was nominated. Although Lincoln originally wanted Seward and Chase as members of his cabinet, he did not want Simon Cameron as secretary of war or Caleb Smith as secretary of the interior but accepted them as a consequence of questionable deals made by his handlers during the nomination process. Nobody in the administration had any meaningful military experience. Postmaster General Montgomery Blair graduated from West Point in 1835 but resigned the following year to study law. Secretary of the Navy Gideon Welles, who often accused Seward of trying to run the administration, served in a minor position in the Navy Department during the Mexican conflict and was more helpful than most in getting his bailiwick organized for war. Attorney General Edward Bates, a lawyer and former Whig from Missouri, had no war experience but became instrumental as a cabinet member in defining presidential war powers, some of which are still debated today. Caleb Smith supported Seward, not the president.

The Lincoln administration might have passed with no more notice than the hapless administrations of Franklin Pierce and James Buchanan, the fourteenth and fifteenth presidents, had it not been for war. In 1861 Lincoln understood nothing about military affairs. His lone experience came in 1832, when he needed a job and served briefly as a volunteer during the Black Hawk War. With Simon Cameron running the War Department solely for the purpose of exploiting the spoils of patronage, and with ailing seventy-five-year-old General-in-Chief Winfield Scott running the army between naps, Lincoln soon disregarded everyone's advice and shouldered the responsibility for making strategic military decisions himself. Even after Edwin M. Stanton replaced Cameron as secretary of war, Lincoln continued to appoint generals and develop the strategies he wanted followed. While his plans often made better sense than the advice he received from others, poor performance by military commanders offset almost everything the president attempted to accomplish as a one-man general staff.

Ending the rebellion and reunifying the nation became the focus of Lincoln's life. While the cabinet argued, differed, cajoled, and often conspired with Congress and influential friends to get leverage with the president, Lincoln assumed the role of supreme commander, studied military tactics, and eventually created a modern command system. While Stanton administered the War Department, the president made all the strategic decisions. After the disaster at the First Battle of Bull Run and despite discord in the cabinet, Lincoln began selecting his top generals. Having assumed the role of de facto army chief, he also took responsibility for his decisions as well as the mishandling of battles fought by his generals, some of whom were incompetent and unmanageable politicians. When turning command of the armies over to Ulysses S. Grant on March 12, 1864, the president's strategy for winning the war had already been established. Even after promoting Grant, Lincoln consistently intervened on strategy to prevent the general from making mistakes.

This book adheres to the historical documents and published sources of the times. It is not about the legendary Lincoln of folk yore. It is about the determined, compassionate, complex, and self-made rustic lawyer who believed in the right of all Americans to live permanently and together in a free and unfettered society. The real Lincoln, though sometimes morbidly troubled with bouts of melancholy, gave to posterity the brilliant gift of literary expression that marked one of the extraordinary aspects of his administration. This study incorporates the relationship between Lincoln the president, the people who knew him best, and how together as cabinet members, friends, enemies, and generals, they cross-functioned during the United States's greatest calamity. In addition to the popular historical market, the book is also written for the wider scholarship enjoyed by academics.

I began work on this book about twelve years ago, when I lived in a different part of Pennsylvania than I do now. I intended to write about Lincoln's relationship with his cabinet but found the commanding generals intimately entwined with the administration and decided to write about both.

In 1995 the huge volume of research now available on the Internet did not exist, so for me long lapses occurred as I built my archive. During intervals between writing other books, I continued laboring on this work. Having moved in 1999, I can no longer find the names of all the people who aided in my research. Along with Mary Goodrich, much of my early research began in the Library of Congress, some of which is now available through the library's Web site. Holly Snyder now manages Brown University's John Hay Library, which holds the major collection of Hay's letters and diary. Some early manuscripts came from Ron Smith at the Huntington Library, Norris Foundation, in San Marino, California. In 1996, during my extended visit to the Illinois State Historical Society in Springfield, Illinois, E. Cheryl Schnirring directed me to an enormous holding of Ulysses S. Grant's and Abraham Lincoln's manuscripts. Rochester University is the main depository of William H. Seward's and Thurlow Weed's documents pertaining to the Civil War era, much of which I later found in print. Jim Moske was very helpful with research at the New York Public Library, as was Matthew Lyons at the Pennsylvania Historical Society and Doris Reed at the Dauphin County Historical Society. Evelyn Wesman at the Erie County Public Library located dozens of out-of-print books and articles, which she obtained for me on loan. To all, and others whose names I no longer remember, I render my thanks.

LINCOLN, THE CABINET, AND THE GENERALS

CHAPTER 1

"Make no contracts that will bind me"

In 1860 the Republican Party's presidential convention in Chicago's Wigwam set the stage for events that would shape, accelerate, and lay the course of America's future. Favorite sons topped the list of candidates for nomination, most notable among them the frontrunner, fifty-seven-year-old Senator William Henry Seward of New York; perhaps the most eminent Republican in the country. Seward's professional life as an attorney began in the town of Auburn, New York. Gravitating toward politics in 1830, he became a state senator and a staunch Whig. In 1838 he won the governorship of New York and won reelection two years later. His strong position on civil rights, education, and improvements in the national banking system lifted him into the U.S. Senate in 1849, and his contempt for the expansion of slavery into Western territories secured his reelection in 1855. Mentored by New York powerbroker Thurlow Weed, Seward in 1858 became the preeminent leader of the Republican Party. Although portrayed by some as shrewd, opportunistic, and somewhat cynical, Seward enjoyed a huge popular following, having built his reputation by espousing a belief in a "higher law" than the Constitution and predicting an "irrepressible conflict" wrought by slavery. Because of his reputation for expressing radical views, his strongest advocates worried about his difficulties carrying conservative states.

On October 25, 1858, Seward delivered his "Irrepressible Conflict" speech in Rochester, New York. He spoke of two radically different political systems, one dependent upon the labor of slaves and the other championing the rights and privileges of freemen. He predicted as the population in the North and South increased, both sections would steadily polarize, ultimately bringing their differences into hostile collision. "Shall I tell you what this collision means?" Seward asked his audience. "They who think that it is accidental, unnecessary, the work of interested or fanatical agitators, and therefore ephemeral, mistake the case altogether. It is an irrepressible conflict between two opposing and enduring forces, and it means that the United States must and will, sooner or later, become either entirely a slaveholding nation or entirely a free-labor nation."[1]

On June 16, 1858, Abraham Lincoln, an obscure Illinois politician, spoke before the Republican State Convention in Springfield after being nominated to run against Democrat Stephen A. Douglas for the U.S. Senate. Lincoln's brief acceptance speech launched his political career when, choosing different words, he said, "A house divided against itself cannot stand. I believe this government cannot endure permanently half slave and half free. I do not expect the Union to be dissolved—I do not expect the house to fall—but I do expect it will cease to be divided. It will become all one thing or all the other."[2]

In 1858 neither Lincoln's nor Seward's speech suggested settling differences by a clash of arms. Lincoln believed slavery must end by political compromise. Seward's use of the words *irrepressible conflict* implied a more aggressive solution favored by Republican abolitionists.

Lincoln also disagreed with Seward's position on the Compromise of 1850 when the New Yorker took the Senate floor and in his first speech said, "There is a higher law than the Constitution, which regulates the authority over the domain, and devotes it to the same noble purposes."[3] Seward meant to say the Constitution and divine law were in harmony, one with the other. Abolitionists rallied around the words *higher law*, interpreting them for public consumption to mean the Constitution was not binding to laws in discord with God. On this occasion Seward's frequent disposition for making ambiguous political statements worked both ways, and Lincoln, watching with interest from Springfield, remarked, "Insofar as it may attempt to foment a disobedience to the Constitution or the Constitutional laws of the country, it has my unqualified condemnation." Later, during the Kansas debates in 1854, Seward provoked armed collision by taunting Southern senators, declaring, "Come on, then gentlemen of the slave States. Since there is no escaping your challenge, I accept it in behalf of Freedom. We will engage in competition for the virgin soil of Kansas, and God give the victory to the side that is stronger in numbers as it is in right."[4]

Even Weed, who used his wealth, influence, and the *Albany Evening Journal* to promote Seward's political career, expressed misgivings about the "higher law" doctrine. After mentoring Seward into the governorship of New York and later the Senate—all the time coaching him in artful tactics for facing both ways on contentious issues—he worried that by winning popularity among abolitionists Seward had injured his opportunity to become president. With the nation in political turmoil, Seward, the perceived abolitionist, became the recipient of Democrat and Southern contempt. This development worried Weed because Democrats were shifting allegiance to the Republican Party. Seward had become Weed's life's work as well as his access to the ultimate power and wealth of the federal government. He discouraged Seward from running for president in 1856, holding him back because he smelled defeat and did not want the senator's candidacy in 1860 tainted by an avoidable failure. Weed's involvement, however, had already tarnished Seward. Moreover, Seward wanted the antislavery vote, not because he felt committed to emancipation but because he wanted to woo delegates from fifty-two-year-old Salmon Portland Chase of Ohio, whom he perceived as his closest competitor.

Chase shared leadership of the Republican Party with Seward, but his coalition was disorganized. Like Seward, he went to the U.S. Senate in 1848 backed by an independent Democrat/Free Soil alliance that later opposed the Compromise of 1850 and the 1854 Kansas-Nebraska Act, which divided the Great Plains into two new territories, Kansas and Nebraska, and gave inhabitants territorial discretion over slavery without repealing the Missouri Compromise of 1850.

In 1855 Chase became the governor of Ohio, promoted the antislavery movement, and trickled small sums of money into the pockets of men like fanatical abolitionist John Brown. By the time the two men met, Brown had already murdered five proslavery men in Kansas and was raising money for a raid on Harpers Ferry's federal armory. Although Chase had a reputation for changing his position on important issues, he remained an unwavering abolitionist and formed a coalition among Whigs, Know-Nothings, disaffected Democrats, and other splinter groups now calling themselves Republicans. Chase believed "if the Republican party intended in the campaign of 1860 to nominate a man whose name was a platform, he was the man."[5]

Chase unwittingly became his own campaign manager. He relied on his pristine character and a few antislavery notables who supported his nomination but provided little help. Unlike Seward, Chase had no dealmakers like Thurlow Weed.

In 1858 Lincoln believed he had no chance running against Seward and Chase, but in Bloomington he talked with Jesse Fell, recently returned from the East, who said everyone there had mentioned him as a presidential candidate. Lincoln expressed doubts but agreed to give Fell an autobiography. On the way home he encountered young Henry Villard, a reporter for the *New York Staats-Zeitung*, waiting for the same train at a flag station. Rain began falling, and the train was late, so they climbed into an empty freight car. Lincoln chatted freely about his life and prospects, while Villard made mental notes. Lincoln confided that his wife, Mary, expected him to be elected senator and then president. He paused, glanced at Villard, and said amusedly, "Just think of such a Sucker as me as President."[6]

Competition for the presidential nomination did not end with Chase and Seward. Sixty-seven-year-old Judge Edward Bates, representing the state of Missouri, also enjoyed a long, distinguished career in law and politics. The slaveholding border states liked neither Seward nor Chase. Although Bates became intrigued by the prospect for high office, he remained doubtful. In April 1859 a coalition of congressmen led by Francis P. Blair Jr., of Missouri, and Schuyler Colfax, of New York City, asked Bates to be their candidate. "Mr. Seward cannot get the nomination of his party," they said, because the New Yorker could not unite it. "His nomination," they declared, "would ensure defeat" and fragment the party.

Bates mulled over the offer, mildly resolving to "resist temptation." The judge, however, remained interested, and on February 28, 1860, the Opposition Convention composed of Whigs, slavery proponents, and antislavery men met in Jefferson City, Missouri, and unanimously named Bates their nominee.[7]

A favorite son with the most questionable credentials came from Pennsylvania. For more than twenty years Senator Simon Cameron dominated the state's politics. Contemporaries claimed he never forgot a friend or forgave an enemy. A master of quid pro quo, in 1833 he maneuvered James Buchanan into the Senate in exchange for a five-year appointment as Indian claims adjuster. Cameron's fraudulent transactions attracted Congress, which denounced him as a "swindler of Indians." The public dubbed him "the Great Winnebago," but shame never bothered Cameron. His political machine sent him to the Senate in 1845 as a Democrat and in 1858 as a Republican.[8]

In October 1859 Cameron attempted to capitalize on Lincoln's strength in the West and sent a crony to Springfield to propose a Cameron-Lincoln ticket. Cameron shrewdly believed if he carried Pennsylvania and Lincoln carried Illinois as vice president, he would be able to pull other states away from Seward and Chase. Lincoln expected nothing less from Cameron and politely declined.[9]

Lincoln suspected that Cameron no longer controlled Pennsylvania. Cameron had offered to support Andrew G. Curtin's gubernatorial election if the latter would support Cameron's presidential bid. Curtin won the election without submitting to Cameron's scheme, but Lincoln concluded, after sagaciously studying the political environment in Pennsylvania, that

Curtin's coalition controlled the state's delegates, but the first ceremonial vote would go to Cameron. Curtin opposed Cameron's dynasty and many of Seward's policies, and Lincoln knew it, but it would be politically imprudent to make an enemy of Cameron, who still had many friends in Pennsylvania. If Seward failed to win the nomination on the first ballot, to whom would Pennsylvania's delegates offer their second ballot?[10]

Cameron's ability to focus on opportunities made him a journeyman politician and a master of duplicity. He considered Seward an archrival but invited him to Harrisburg for a conference. "He took me into his house," Seward told Weed, adding, "He was for me and Pennsylvania would be. It might happen that they would cast the first ballot for him, but he was not in, etc. He brought the whole legislature of both parties to see me, feasted them gloriously, and they were . . . so generous as to embarrass me." Cameron wanted something big. The dealing had begun.[11]

Seven other names dotted the presidential docket, all with delegates committed on the first ballot. With twelve candidates competing for the presidential nomination, Lincoln's two key campaign handlers—Judge David Davis and Leonard Swett—worked tirelessly to prevent Seward from capturing the prize on the first ballot.[12]

Davis and Swett wanted Chicago to host the Republican convention, not St. Louis, Bates's hometown. The contest for site selection loomed soon after Lincoln returned to Springfield from a speaking tour through Chase country. State Senator Norman B. Judd represented Illinois on the national committee, and he naturally supported the Windy City and understood the importance of the local press. Lincoln dispatched one of his laconic messages to Judd, writing, "Our friends here, attach much more consequence to getting the National convention into our State than I did. . . . Some of them made me promise to say so to you." Judd understood his mission, and in the battle for site location his became the deciding vote.[13]

Judd's previous relations with Lincoln had been erratic. In 1855 he refused to support Lincoln, a Whig, for the U.S. Senate and backed Lyman Trumbull, a Democrat. Judd redeemed himself in 1858 by instigating the famous debates between Lincoln and Douglas. Lincoln distinguished himself by running in a close senatorial race, though he lost, and established a national reputation Judd said could not "be taken away. He hitched his own political aspirations to Lincoln's expanding reputation and provided timely guidance and encouragement to the irresolute candidate.[14]

Early in 1860 Judd formed a group of influential Illinoisans, among them Ozias M. Hatch, secretary of state, and Jesse K. Dubois, state auditor, all of whom resided with Lincoln in Springfield. Together they urged Lincoln to take his candidacy seriously and were helped by Mary Lincoln, who relentlessly pestered her husband to commit to the presidential campaign. Lincoln worried about capturing the Illinois vote because Judd had been embroiled in a political feud with Chicago's Republican mayor, John Wentworth, whose support he needed. Before leaving for New York, Lincoln asked Judd, "Can you not help me a little in this matter, in your end of the vineyard?"[15]

On February 27, 1860, at the outset of his swing through the East, Lincoln delivered his famous Cooper Union speech. The Manhattan crowd had settled their minds on "something weird, rough and uncultivated."[16] With that speech, and every one delivered later, Lincoln carefully moderated his position on national issues by differentiating them from those of Chase and Seward. He advocated the preservation of the Union and offered reasonable and legal interpretations of the Constitution and opposed higher law solutions for resolving the impasse over slavery. As an unannounced presidential candidate, his performance upset neither Seward nor Chase because he never mentioned their names. Instead, he critiqued Douglas's position on popular sovereignty and argued against "radical despoilers of the Constitution" who wished "to spit upon that old policy" or by insurrectionists like John Brown who resorted to murder. Lincoln admitted the Constitution permitted slavery, a moral wrong but legally a right. He urged Republicans to persist in excluding the practice from new territories. Disunionists had been active across the United States, and Lincoln closed by urging his audience to not "be slandered from our duty by false accusations against us, nor frightened from it by menaces of destruction to the Government. . . . LET US HAVE FAITH THAT RIGHT MAKES MIGHT, AND IN THAT FAITH, LET US, TO THE END, DARE TO DO OUR DUTY AS WE UNDERSTAND IT."[17]

Although Lincoln never expected to electrify the crowd, he came very close to doing it. His speech drew frequent applause, and his closing brought the audience roaring to its feet. Four New York papers printed the address the following day. Like many of Lincoln's speeches, it took longer for the public to digest it. Robert Lincoln spoke for the audience when he told his father, "It was the best speech I ever heard."[18]

Lincoln continued his tour to solidify his standing among Republicans. For four days he traveled with Robert, a student at Phillips Exeter Academy. The Cooper Union address preceded him. Invitations overwhelmed the weary traveler. In a letter home on March 4 the besieged speechmaker admitted being "unable to escape this toil." "The difficulty," he admitted, "was to make nine others, before reading audiences who had already seen all my ideas in print."[19]

Lincoln understood the value of making physical appearances, but he still doubted the party would accept him as a serious presidential candidate. Not until he returned to Springfield did the notion of running for president become palpable, when on April 29 he admitted to Senator Trumbull, "The taste is in my mouth a little."[20]

In 1860 presidential aspirants were prevented by tradition from campaigning on their own behalf. Nor had politics matured to the level that office seekers selected a campaign manager. Seward, however, had Thurlow Weed, a man gifted with the political instincts of a modern day handler. Lincoln had trusted advisors, Davis and Swett, who orchestrated the campaign despite rivalry from others. Lincoln tolerated the quarreling. He believed disagreements among supporters produced a healthy degree of competition and made them work harder for preferential attention. The experiment provoked Lincoln's curiosity about how men of different persuasions might work together in the White House.

Lincoln and Davis were old friends, having traveled together for many years on the circuit court. They rumbled over dirt roads in sleet and snow, sometimes stopping at farmhouses or under trees to hold court, and often "sleeping two in a bed, and eight in a room." During "court week" they drew large crowds wherever they went, enlivening taverns and presenting impromptu orations on political issues. Lincoln stood tall, lean, and rawboned in contrast to the gigantically rotund Davis. The two men became great friends. Years later Lincoln said of Davis, at the exclusion of all others, "I keep no secrets from him."[21]

Lincoln summed up his own views for nomination on April 6, 1860, when replying to a letter from Richard M. Corwine, a lawyer from Cincinnati who sought an opinion on the outcome of the forthcoming convention. Lincoln revealed a great deal about himself without saying much at all:

> Remembering that when not a very great man begins to be mentioned for a very great position, his head is very likely to be a little turned, I concluded that I am not the fittest person to answer the question you ask. Making due allowance for this, I think that Mr. Seward is the very best candidate we could have for the North of Illinois, and the very *worst* for the South of it. The estimate of Gov. Chase here is neither

better nor worse than that of Seward, except that he is a newer man. They are regarded as being almost the same. . . . Mr. Bates, I think, would be the best for the South of our State, and the worst for the North of it. If Judge McLean was fifteen, or even ten years younger, I think he would be stronger than either. I feel . . . disqualified to speak of myself in this matter.[22]

In March one resourceful supporter advised Lincoln to put ten thousand dollars into a campaign chest to promote his own candidacy. Lincoln called the proposition "an impossibility. I could not raise ten thousand dollars if it would save me from the fate of John Brown. Nor have my friends, so far as I know, yet reached the point of staking any money on my chances of success." Fund raising in 1860 stood in stark contrast to the elections of the twenty-first century.[23]

On April 23 Democrats convened in Charleston, South Carolina, to nominate the party's presidential candidate. If Douglas won the nomination, Republicans would be inclined to nominate a man from the West. Vice President John C. Breckinridge of Kentucky, a Southern states' rights advocate, also had his hat in the ring. If Breckinridge won the nomination, Republicans would likely choose an antislavery candidate such as Seward or Chase. Rumors persisted that while Northern Democrats favored Douglas, Southern Democrats preferred Breckinridge, which set the stage for a possible split in the Democrat Party. Lincoln rested his hopes on Douglas's nomination. Until Democrats selected their nominee, Lincoln's prospects remained in limbo.

At Charleston a bitter struggle erupted among Democrats over slavery in the territories. Douglas's group wanted to avoid further congressional action on territorial slave issues and abide by the decisions of the Supreme Court. William L. Yancey of Georgia demanded new laws protecting slavery in the territories, which meant those living in territories and opposing slavery would be obliged to live with it, and the government must enforce it. Douglas failed to reach a compromise, and Yancey walked out in a huff, taking with him enough delegates to prevent Douglas from obtaining the two-thirds vote needed for nomination. Yancey's action split the party, forcing Douglas's coalition to schedule a separate convention in Baltimore.

The Yanceyites moved to a new location in Charleston, called themselves "Constitutional Democrats," argued to the point of exhaustion, and decided to reconvene in June at Richmond. Some turned up in Baltimore and asked to be taken back into the fold. The Douglas men agreed but soon realized Yancey's defectors were as fanatical on the subject of slavery as before. For the sake of party harmony Douglas authorized removing his name from nomination, But his request was rejected. When voting began, some Yanceyites bolted again. The remaining delegates proceeded with the nomination of Douglas as president and Benjamin Fitzpatrick of Alabama as vice president. Fitzpatrick declined, so the national committee chose Herschel V. Johnson, a Unionist from Georgia.

The Baltimore defectors, unwilling to wait for the Richmond convention, adopted the Yancey platform and nominated Breckinridge president and Joseph Lane of Oregon vice president. On June 11 the Yanceyites in Richmond learned of the action and, having nothing better to do, ratified the nominations of Breckinridge and Lane.[24]

Adding more complications, on May 10 a splinter group of Know-Nothings and Whigs formed the Constitutional Union Party and nominated John Bell of Tennessee president and Edward Everett of Massachusetts vice president. Southern Democrats now had three choices. If they were patient over the status of slavery in the territories, they could vote for Douglas. If they were adamant about maintaining slavery in the territories, they could vote for Breckinridge. And if they disliked Douglas and Breckinridge, they could vote for Bell. The Republican nominee would never appear on a Southern ballot.

On May 9, 1860, a week before the Republican National Convention in Chicago, the Illinois Republican state convention opened its mini-Wigwam in Decatur to nominate the governor. Lincoln went to Decatur because he hoped to secure the endorsement of Illinois delegates at the national convention. Those delegates were divided, but Davis believed that Lincoln, as the state's favorite son, could secure their votes for the first ballot. Beyond that move Davis feared the national convention might nominate Seward.

Not every Lincoln supporter agreed with Davis, but they decided something dramatic must be done to improve Lincoln's visibility. Prosaic sobriquets like "Honest Abe" and "Old Abe" were not working. Richard J. Oglesby, an imaginative young politician from Decatur, aspired to correct the problem.

As the opening of the state convention approached, Oglesby visited John Hanks, a first cousin of Lincoln's mother, and together they gathered two locust rails split by Lincoln near Decatur thirty years earlier. After making a few creative modifications, Hanks burst into the convention during a lull and marched down the aisle carrying rails decorated with streamers, ribbons, and a large banner reading:

> ABRAHAM LINCOLN
> The Rail Candidate
> FOR PRESIDENT IN 1860
> Two rails from a lot of 3000 made in 1830 by
> John Hanks and Abe Lincoln, whose father
> Was the first pioneer of Macon County.

The demonstration took everyone by surprise, including Lincoln. Conventioneers cheered lustily, and with the pandemonium came demands for Lincoln to speak. Caught by surprise, the bewildered "Rail Candidate" seemed lost for words. Slightly flushed, he rose and said, "Gentlemen, John and I did make some rails down there; and if these aren't the identical rails we made, they certainly look very much like them."[25]

The ensuing turmoil startled even Lincoln. He had not come to realize his own popularity. The "rail-splitter" image fit him as a self-made laboring man, and in 1860 it connected with voters. The portrayal was also fraudulent. Lincoln avoided physical labor once he discovered ways to deploy his mental talents more profitably. Convention delegates knew him better as the man he was: an unpretentious but sagacious attorney who had served one term in the U.S. House of Representatives and who, while debating Stephen Douglas for the Senate, espoused a political philosophy that helped define the Republican Party. Although not well known outside the West, he appealed to both Eastern Whigs and anyone opposed to the expansion of slavery. He also favored economic development and protective tariffs, issues sought by the East.

As the first day of the state convention ended, Lincoln led Davis, Judd, and Oglesby to a grove near the Decatur Wigwam to discuss ways of securing the Illinois delegation at the national convention. The group studied the roster of the state's twenty-two delegates and agreed some might support Seward or Bates. They recruited attorney John M. Palmer, a persuasive delegate, to ram through a resolution in the morning "that Abraham Lincoln is the choice of the Republican party of Illinois for the Presidency, and the delegates from this State are instructed to use all honorable means to secure his nomination by the Chicago Convention, and to vote as a unit for him." The scheme worked, and Lincoln, having secured the Illinois delegation on the first ballot, returned home.[26]

Lincoln remained in Springfield during the Republican national convention. People passing through town on their way to Chicago stopped to chat with him. He presented himself as a moderate candidate, while Seward represented the extreme antislavery faction. Edward L. Baker, editor of the *Illinois State Journal,* also stopped on his way to Chicago. He carried a copy of the *Missouri Democrat* containing Seward's position on slavery. In the margin of the *Democrat* Lincoln wrote, "I agree with Seward in his 'Irrepressible Conflict,' but I do not endorse his 'Higher Law' doctrine." That message was for Baker to print, but Lincoln added another message, this one for his managers in Chicago. Well aware of Davis and Swett's penchant for bargaining, Lincoln added with underlined emphasis, "Make no contracts that will bind me," and he instructed Baker to make sure Davis and Swett read the message. The extent to which Lincoln's handlers adhered to this instruction produced a ripple effect that transcended the outcome of the convention.[27]

While Lincoln waited in Springfield, Davis took charge of the campaign at Chicago's Tremont Hotel. He assessed the political landscape and doubted whether Seward could carry Pennsylvania, Indiana, or Illinois or that Chase, Bates, or Cameron could carry their own states beyond the first ballot. Davis did worry that Weed's operatives might cut enough deals to carry Seward's nomination on the first ballot, despite the New Yorker's abundance of enemies. He believed Lincoln's best chance of winning the nomination depended on polling a strong second on the first ballot with at least one hundred votes. He circulated Swett, Browning, Judd, and a handful of others to garner support from other state delegations. To parry Weed's meddling, Judd rigged the Wigwam's seating to put the New Yorkers and Pennsylvanians at opposite ends of the hall with Illinois delegates in between.

Weed arrived on a chartered thirteen-car train filled with Seward's New York supporters, all with special tickets to the convention. Judd anticipated Weed's effort to pack the Wigwam with Sewardites and countered by printing thousands of duplicate tickets for Lincoln's friends. He passed them out, instructing the recipients to take their seats before Weed's legion arrived.[28]

In 1860 in the United States whoever controlled the White House controlled political patronage. Weed understood the game as well as any man in the country. There were thousands of federal posts to fill, and Lincoln had already received dozens of letters offering quid pro quo arrangements. He gave Davis, Swett, and Judd little latitude in the matter by instructing them to make no bargains, and the trio attempted to court delegates by persuasion, but they needed a strong voting bloc only Pennsylvania could provide.[29]

Wigwam business on Wednesday and Thursday, May 16 and 17, focused on organizing the convention and adopting a platform. A *New York Times* reporter mingled among the delegates, noting, "If it were not for the apprehensions of Pennsylvania, Seward would be nominated by acclamation." Davis and Swett observed indecisiveness among the Pennsylvanians.[30]

The night before the huge, barnlike Chicago Wigwam opened its doors for Friday's balloting, none of the 466 delegates went to bed early. They caucused, broke up, mingled, and caucused again. Around midnight a small group of Cameron's cronies—among them Judge Joseph Casey, Alexander Cummings, Judge Samuel Purviance, and John P. Sanderson—met privately with Davis and Swett. They already suspected Seward would fall short of votes and send the nomination to a second ballot. Pennsylvanians had already committed their votes to Cameron, but Sanderson and Cummings believed that if Seward failed on the first ballot, and if Lincoln did better than expected, the presidential nomination could take a new direction. Pennsylvania wanted something in exchange for their delegates, which neither David nor Swett realized were mostly controlled by Governor Curtin and not Cameron. Nor were they aware Curtin wanted no political alliances with Weed or Seward. Cameron had weeks before committed Pennsylvania's second round of votes to Seward, though he did not actually control them. Cameron's handlers, however, wanted patronage for themselves and the plush cabinet position of secretary of the Treasury for their leader.[31]

Davis telegraphed Lincoln at midnight and said an offer of a cabinet post for Cameron might swing Pennsylvania's delegation. Lincoln promptly replied, "I authorize no bargain and will be bound by none." According to Carl Sandburg, whose quotes were not always reliable, Davis reacted to such obstinacy by shouting, "Lincoln ain't here and don't know what we have to meet. So we will go ahead as if we hadn't heard from him, and he must ratify it."[32]

Although some historians question whether any deals were made, William Herndon, Lincoln's law partner, said Davis "negotiated with the Indiana and Pennsylvania delegations and assigned places in the cabinet to Simon Cameron and Caleb Smith, beside making other 'arrangements' which [Davis] expected Mr. Lincoln to ratify. Of this he [Lincoln] was undoubtedly unaware."[33]

Caleb Blood Smith of Indiana evidently sniffed opportunity on the eve of the voting. He approached Davis and Swett and said no Republican candidate could succeed at the polls without Indiana's support. Smith lacked political credentials, though he had edited a newspaper, served in Congress, and disliked Seward. Lincoln already had strength in Indiana, and Smith actually had little influence over the state's delegates. Nevertheless, Davis and Swett wanted to secure Indiana's twenty-six votes and, disregarding Lincoln's order, discussed the possibility of a cabinet post for Smith in exchange for his influence.[34]

Davis recognized the means to Lincoln's victory rested heavily on Pennsylvania. Whatever Davis pledged to Cameron's handlers they interpreted as a guarantee the Great Winnebago would be named to the cabinet as secretary of the Treasury if Pennsylvania's delegates supported Lincoln on the second ballot. Davis sealed the bargain over Lincoln's blanket objection. Had Davis accepted the "no bargains" order, Lincoln might have been forced from the race. Davis and Swett must have satisfied Casey and Purviance that a deal had been struck. Casey informed Cameron, "It [the switch to Lincoln] was only done after everything was arranged carefully & unconditionally in reference to Yourself—to our satisfaction—and we drove the Anti-Cameron men from this State into it." In a separate letter Purviance wrote, "You were pretty generally designated for Secretary of the Treasury & it seemed to be conceded you could claim & Receive what you might desire."[35]

Satisfied they could do no more, Davis and Swett went to bed to await the outcome of Friday's balloting. In September, two months before the national election, Davis summed up the Chicago deals by saying that, while he made a "personal, conditional promise," he made no bargains: "Mr. Lincoln is committed to no one on earth in relation to office—He promised nothing to gain his nomination, and has promised nothing." Whether Lincoln would agree with Davis's explanation remained to be seen, but on the hectic evening of May 17 such matters could harmlessly simmer until after November's election.[36]

On Friday, May 18, Seward's men manifested confidence. From campaign headquarters at the Richmond House they marched in step with Weed's magnificently uniformed band. One thousand caped musicians led the parade. Caps adorned with white and scarlet feathers fluttered in the Windy City's gentle breezes. By the time the procession reached the Wigwam it was filled. Barely a square foot of space remained, and only a few horn blowers squeezed inside. With ten thousand others they stood in the street. This had not been Weed's plan. His superb band could not blow horns or beat drums every time someone mentioned Seward's name.[37]

Everyone waited impatiently for nominations to begin. The process promised to be hectic. After William M. Evarts of New York nominated Seward, a tremendous roar erupted. Not all of Weed's men had been barricaded outside. Carl Schurz of Wisconsin seconded Seward's nomination, and cheers rattled the Wigwam's rafters.

When Judd placed Lincoln's name in nomination, waves of men and women rose from their seats and, "calling upon the last full measure of their lung power, fairly made the building quiver." When Caleb Smith of Indiana, himself a nominee, seconded the motion, the roar flowed through the doors and windows to be echoed by thousands packed on the grounds outside. Swett marveled at the response, writing, "Five thousand people leaped [from] their seats, women not wanting, and the wild yell made vesper breathings of all that had preceded. A thousand steam whistles, ten acres of hotel gongs, [and] a tribe of Comanches might have mingled in the scene unnoticed." New Yorkers paled at the enormous response to Lincoln's nomination.[38]

Nominations followed for Cameron of Pennsylvania, Bates of Missouri, Chase of Ohio, William L. Dayton of New Jersey, Judge McLean of the U.S. Supreme Court, and Smith of Indiana,. The weak responses made it apparent that the contest would be a two-way battle between Seward and Lincoln.

After a long roll call the secretary tabulated the first ballots and announced Seward with 173½ votes, Lincoln 102, Cameron 50½, Chase 49, Bates 48, with 43 votes going to others. Without part of Indiana's 26 votes, Lincoln would not have polled 100. Winning the nomination required 233 votes. Seward and Lincoln had a long way to go.

During the second ballot favorite sons began falling from the contest. Seward's tally jumped 11 votes, to 184½; Lincoln's climbed to 181. When the secretary announced Lincoln's gains, the Wigwam reverberated from an uproar the chairman could not silence. Delegates from Ohio and Missouri saw the tide turning against Seward. Caucuses conferred, and the third ballot began.

Lincoln gained ground. Spectators tabulated votes as they came from the floor. During the third ballot Lincoln's numbers rose to 231½, while Seward's dropped to 180. Joseph Medill of the *Tribune* saw danger in allowing the vote to go to a fourth ballot. Fully aware of Davis and Swett's willingness to cut deals, Medill turned to David K. Cartter of Ohio, who had nominated Chase, and said, "If you throw the Ohio delegation to Lincoln, Chase can have anything he wants." Medill had no authority to strike the bargain, but Cartter took the bait. He jumped to his feet and changed four votes from Chase to Lincoln.[39]

Thirty-one-year-old Murat Halstead of the *Cincinnati Commercial* wrote: "There was a moment of silence. The nerves of the thousands, which through hours of suspense had been subjected to terrible tension, relaxed, and as deep breaths of relief were taken, there was a noise in the Wigwam like the rush of a great wind in the van of a storm—and in another breath, the storm was there. There were thousands cheering with the energy of insanity."

A man on the roof watched the balloting through an open skylight. His task was to relay information to the thousands waiting outside. The moment Ohio's delegation took Lincoln over the top, the secretary on the floor shouted to the man on the roof, "Fire the salute! Abe Lincoln is nominated!" The sudden discharge of a hundred guns arranged near the Wigwam startled the crowd, but then a swelling roar of voices began flowing through the streets, and steam whistles screeched from nearby railroad yards.[40]

After Ohio made Lincoln the nominee, Seward's delegates joined the movement. The news hit the street long before the chairman announced that 354 votes had been cast for "Abraham Lincoln of Illinois . . . your candidate for President of the United States." Barely anyone noticed when the remaining delegations rose to make the nomination unanimous.[41]

At noon the Wigwam emptied into the street. Thurlow Weed buried his face in his hands. Devastated by the outcome, "he lost his habitual calm and characteristic self-possession and gave way to angry words augmented by tears."[42]

Across the nation thousands of telegraph stations began relaying the news. Frederick Seward worked at Weed's *Evening Journal.* During the afternoon he intercepted a disturbing telegram and shouted down the tube to the printing room foreman, "Abraham Lincoln is nominated for President on the third ballot." The foreman paused and hollered back, "S-a-y, what damn name was that you said was nominated President?" Employees in other Eastern presses probably asked the same question.[43]

Early Friday morning, before the balloting began, Lincoln stopped at his Springfield office and encountered Baker, who had returned from Chicago with the names of the nominees. Growing impatient for information, the two men wandered over to the telegraph office and after a long wait received results from the first ballot. Having predicted Seward would lose if he failed on the first ballot, Lincoln waited anxiously for the second ballot. When it arrived late morning, he turned to Baker, and said, "I've got him." He walked to the office of the *Journal* and found friends waiting for results of the third ballot. Charles S. Zane, the paper's editor, remained at the telegraph office to intercept the next telegram. Around noon the tally came, and Zane hand-carried it to the *Journal,* where he found Lincoln waiting and shouted, "Three cheers for the next President." A crowd quickly formed outside the *Journal.* Everyone wanted to shake the nominee's hand.

Finding himself pressed from all sides, Lincoln looked up the street toward his home and said, "Well gentlemen, there is a little short woman at our house who is probably more interested in this dispatch than I am: and, if you will excuse me, I will take it up and let her see it."[44]

After reaching home, Lincoln learned that Hannibal Hamlin of Maine, whom he had never met, had been nominated vice president. He felt obligated to discuss cabinet appointments with his running mate, not knowing his managers had already made some of those decisions for him.[45]

CHAPTER 2

"Your troubles are over now, but mine have just begun"

Having won the nomination, Lincoln felt obliged to go to Chicago to meet Hannibal Hamlin, his running mate, and to personally thank the Illinois delegates. He also wanted to unify disappointed followers of William Henry Seward, Salmon Portland Chase, and Edward Bates because he needed their support in the national election. He telegraphed his intentions to David Davis, who promptly replied, "Don't come here for God's sake. Write no letters and make no promises until you see me." So Lincoln waited, restlessly listening to the constant firing of guns in Springfield. He made brief speeches to crowds gathered outside his home on Eighth and Jackson streets and invited everyone to come inside, and most of them remained until after midnight.[1]

At 8:00 p.m. on May 19 George Ashmun of Massachusetts, heading the committee appointed to notify Lincoln of his nomination, arrived in Springfield. The group included Gideon Welles of Connecticut, Francis P. Blair Sr., of Maryland, and David Cartter of Ohio—all aspirants to cabinet posts, though in different ways. The committee strolled to Lincoln's home, a plain, comfortable, two-story house with a hallway in the center. Charles Coffin of the *Boston Journal* witnessed the formality. Struck by Lincoln's features, he wrote, "The lines upon his face, the large ears, sunken cheeks, enormous nose, shaggy hair, the deep-set eyes, which sparkled with humor, and which seemed to be looking far away, were distinguishing facial marks . . . but there was that about him which commanded instant admiration. A stranger meeting him on a country road, ignorant of his history, would have said, 'he is no ordinary man.'" After a brief acceptance speech, Lincoln's demeanor "instantly changed. A smile, like the sun shining through the rift of a passing cloud sweeping over the landscape, illuminated his face, lighting up every homely feature."

With formalities concluded, Lincoln became the affable host and ushered the committee into an adjoining room to meet his wife and slake their thirst from a pitcher of water. Lincoln's neighbors had tried to donate a "supply of needful liquors," to which he replied, "Gentlemen, I thank you for your kind intentions, but most respectfully decline your offer. I have no liquors in my house, and have never been in a habit of entertaining my friends in that way.

I cannot permit my friends to do for me what I will not myself do. I shall provide cold water—nothing else."[2]

Lincoln relaxed and resumed being what he had always been—a sagacious individual who enjoyed being with people. Carl Schurz of Wisconsin came to Springfield still distressed over Seward's loss, which some called "the ignominious slaughter of the greatest Republican leader." But he soon warmed to Lincoln's hearty nature. Later that night, while walking to the hotel, Schurz agreed with William D. Kelley of Pennsylvania, who remarked, "Well, we might have done a more brilliant thing, but we could hardly have done a better thing."[3]

For Lincoln difficult tasks lay ahead, including adjustments to his new celebrity status. Having not spoken with Davis or Swett, he knew nothing of the Chicago bargains, which neither man intended to mention until after the national election. So Lincoln fell asleep that night in May with no reservations about filling the seven important cabinet posts with men of his choosing.

During the six-month interregnum before the national election, visitors besieged Lincoln's home. Among them came Thurlow Weed, who Davis urged to stop in Springfield before returning to New York. Weed admitted being "so greatly disappointed at . . . the convention as to be unable to think or talk on the subject."

Alexander K. McClure of Pennsylvania had met with Weed, hoping to recruit his support for Lincoln, but found the powerbroker "sullen and offensive." Weed refused to talk about the contest and blamed Pennsylvania for having defeated Seward. McClure summed up the dejected New Yorker's state of mind, writing, "Weed had been defeated in his greatest effort, and the one great dream of his life had perished."[4]

Weed detrained at Springfield on May 24 still upset by what he considered a personal setback. Having spoken with his friend Henry J. Raymond of the *New York Times,* they decided to blame Horace Greeley of the more powerful *New York Tribune* for Pennsylvania's defection instead of their own lack of vigilance. On May 22 Greeley capitalized on Weed's state of mind and posted an editorial barb in the *Tribune,* writing, "The past is dead. Let the dead past bury it, and let the mourners, if they will, go about the streets."[5]

Disinclined to become one of Greeley's mourners, Weed sought ways to influence Lincoln's decisions. First he had to establish political leverage with the victors and spent six hours in Springfield chatting with Davis, Swett, and Lincoln. The discussion focused on Weed's support, not Seward. Weed returned to New York favorably impressed by Lincoln's "fitness" and agreed to "go to work with a will." Having gained Weed's support, Lincoln hoped Seward would follow.[6]

Lincoln worked from his home until his son, Willie (William Wallace Lincoln), fell ill with scarlet fever. Governor John Wood graciously offered his office in the state capitol, which Lincoln eagerly accepted. Springfield friends raised funds, with which Lincoln hired John G. Nicolay at seventy-five dollars a month to help process the mail. Letters came from everywhere, many from people wanting the nominee's autographs. F. A. Wood admitted not being a Lincoln man "but still would like to have Mr. L's autograph." To hundreds of requests Lincoln merely replied, "Well, here it is. A. Lincoln."[7]

Cameramen also flooded Springfield because newspapers wanted images. The photographs highlighted the deep crevasses on Lincoln's forehead and cheeks, the unruly hair on his head, and the facial somberness that camouflaged the bright twinkle in his eyes and the delightful animation of his voice spinning yarns. Artists worked on Lincoln's features, trying to improve his appearance so he looked more statesmanlike. The candidate appeased everyone, sometimes sitting for multiple artists and trying not to look impatient while conducting business.

Hundreds of requests poured into Springfield for Lincoln's biography. After the burden became untenable, he prepared a comprehensive campaign autobiography for John L. Scripps of the *Chicago Press and Tribune,* which other newspapers republished to reach thousands of readers across the nation.

Adversaries became active, much like party political strategists of today. In 1860 personal attacks had minimal impact because of limited media coverage. Lincoln ignored criticism except when his colleagues required a position statement. Nicolay answered most political inquiries with a form letter, stating that Lincoln's "positions were well known when he was nominated" and he did not intend "to shift or modify them." Davis and Swett beseeched Lincoln to avoid public controversies, and he followed their advice.[8]

Lincoln, the practical politician, liked the Republican platform because it appealed to diverse interest groups. A tariff plank attracted protectionists from Pennsylvania, New Jersey, and New England without alienating anti-slavery Democrats who were now Republicans. A homestead plank courted those wanting free land like one passed by the House but blocked by Senate Democrats. The platform also advocated river and harbor improvements for the Northwest, daily overland mail, a transcontinental railroad, and a relaxation of immigration and citizenship policies for the growing German population.

While Democrats clung to the retention of slavery, Republicans avoided strong statements on abolition and acknowledged the right of states to determine their own domestic institutions. Instead of tackling slavery, Republicans concentrated on promoting sectional economic interests. Although the party continued to debate issues, Republicans presented a united front. After Democrats split, Lincoln liked his chances of election even better, though rival groups within the party continued to trouble him. Although restrained by his handlers from making public statements, Lincoln did what he could to keep the party solidified through private correspondence and meetings with influential Republicans.

As days passed into months, Lincoln felt increasingly isolated from the campaign. While Republicans held gala parades, massive rallies, and torchlight processions from California to Maine, he remained quarantined in Springfield. When Douglas went on the circuit and stumped for votes in the North, Lincoln itched to do the same, but his handlers said doing so could be interpreted as "evidence of Republican alarm." On August 8 Lincoln could not avoid a Republican rally held in his hometown and spoke briefly: "It has been my purpose, since I have been placed in my present position, to make no speeches," and after two hundred words to thank the participants for support, he concluded by invoking his listeners to "kindly let me be silent."[9]

In late August, after recovering from his setback, Seward went on a five-week barnstorming tour of the West. Lincoln wanted to meet him in Chicago, but his handlers insisted he remain in Springfield. On October 1 the train stopped en route to New York, and Lincoln greeted Seward at the depot. Charles Francis Adams accompanied Seward and described Lincoln as "shy to a degree, and very awkward in manner." Adams also reported Seward ill at ease. The meeting revived bitter memories of how Weed had blocked his nomination in 1856 and convinced him that by 1860 he would be "the destined leader of his party," and this became "not only his own conviction and that of Weed, but of nine out of ten Americans."[10]

What once appeared as a political certainty became a gut-wrenching disappointment. Seward remembered the great crowd gathered before his Auburn home and the large cannon placed at the gateway to thunder a salute when the news of his nomination arrived. Stacks of wood lay piled for bonfires, bunting decorated the streets, and people waited for the telegram ushering in the greatest day in Auburn's history. Weed expected Seward to outdistance his competition on the first ballot, forcing delegates to abandon their pledges, and on the second ballot cast their votes for the true Republican leader. With Weed at the helm, Seward felt secure. Even Horace Greeley of the *New York Tribune,* who wheedled his way to Chicago as a delegate from Oregon, did not believe Seward could lose but on May 16 still hoped he would. Greeley polled the delegates and, despite his hostility toward Weed and Seward, ruefully predicted Seward's "irrepressibles" could not be stopped.

Seward remembered the messenger who came running to his home with the results of the third ballot. His face turned ashen on learning he had been whipped by the rail-splitter from Illinois. A few days later he wrote, "I had the rare experience of a man walking about town, after he is dead, and hearing what people would say of him. I confess I was not prepared for so much real grief as I heard expressed at every corner." When Henry Raymond stopped in Auburn to inquire whether Seward would be interested in a cabinet position, he responded to the question with a forcible no.[11]

The wound healed slowly. Returning to the Senate in early June gave Seward's emotional plunge a boost, but three weeks later he returned to Auburn and wrote Weed: "If I can rightly . . . remain at rest, I want to do so. I am content to quit with the political world, when it proposes to quit with me. But I am not insensible to the claims of a million friends. All that seems clear to me just now is that it would not be wise to rush in at the beginning of ·the canvass, and so seem, most falsely, to fear that I shall be forgotten. Later in the canvass, it may be seen that I am wanted for the public interest."[12]

Seward could not forget the past, but the five-week swing through the West reinvigorated his passion for politics. He shook hands with old friends and sympathizers who urged him to act in the public interest. The meeting with Lincoln, however, reopened unhealed wounds. Both men were grateful the meeting was brief. The conversation became strained when Lincoln attempted to discuss campaign strategy with the man who expected to be in his place. A *New York Herald* correspondent caustically wrote, "The meeting . . . was conventional and formal, as if each was afraid of his own virtue in the presence of the other." The train moved on, relieving both men of mutually shared discomfort. They barely knew each other, having met briefly when Lincoln was in Congress, and the Springfield discussions left each man with questions about the other.[13]

With the national election five weeks away, Lincoln returned to his office wishing the meeting with Seward had been in a more relaxed setting. A few days later a letter arrived from Auburn. "We arrived here on Saturday night," wrote Seward, "and I find no reason to doubt this State will redeem all the promises we have made." Lincoln considered the letter an offer of friendship and replied: "I am glad to have the expression of your continued confidence. It now really looks as if the Government is about to fall into our hands." Lincoln let Seward decide what he meant by the phrase "fall into *our* hands." He omitted the usual "Yours truly," signing the letter, "Most sincerely, Your friend, A. Lincoln."[14]

During the months following the Republican convention, Lincoln heard nothing from Davis or Swett regarding the Chicago "deals." Some historians believe Lincoln knew about them immediately after his nomination, but this is unlikely. Judge Samuel Purviance, however, informed Simon Cameron, "You could have been nominated for Vice-President but it would have cost you a fight & exposed you to the suspicion of having bargained for it with Mr. Lincoln's friends." Cameron promptly announced his support for Lincoln, but he experienced problems holding his coalition together, partly because of his shady reputation and partly because of his widening rift with Pennsylvania governor Andrew Curtin.[15]

Lincoln sent Davis to Pennsylvania to investigate the trouble. Perhaps to prepare Lincoln for the day the deal matured, Davis mentioned nothing about the senator's questionable character but said Cameron promised an industrious campaign in Pennsylvania. Two months of silence followed before Davis heard anything more from the conspiratorial Pennsylvanian. Cameron predicted victory "beyond a shadow of a doubt" and offered to loan several thousand dollars if Lincoln needed funds. Davis wanted votes, not more indebtedness to Cameron. Unlike Cameron, neither Caleb Smith nor Chase made efforts to promote Lincoln's election.[16]

During October Lincoln observed a growing number of young Republican "Wide-Awakes" in Springfield. They dressed in black oilcloth capes and caps and paraded torch-illuminated rails through the streets. The movement stretched across the North. Wide-Awakes organized drills, formed militia companies, hosted barbeques, and held gigantic rallies to attract Republican votes. Young Elmer Ellsworth, who studied law in the offices of Lincoln & Herndon, recruited a Zouave company called the Springfield Grays. They wore baggy, colorful uniforms patterned after the French Army Zouaves who fought in Crimea. Even Nicolay joined the Grays, became a second lieutenant, and participated in local rallies. Another group formed the Lincoln Rangers. Republicans even published their own party newspaper, the *Rail-Splitter,* which rapidly increased in circulation. Thousands of young men of foreign extraction joined the Wide-Awakes because Republicans disavowed immigration restrictions. Lincoln, being strapped to Springfield by his handlers, entirely underestimated the effort of the movement until state elections everywhere proved the power of organization.[17]

On October 10 Herndon spoke in Petersburg, Illinois, on behalf of the "rail-splitter" and "had fairly gotten into the spirit of the hour" when a clerk from the telegraph office entered the courtroom and handed him a message. Herndon expected sad news due to illness in his family but found instead a note from Lincoln: "I cannot give you details, but it is entirely certain Pennsylvania and Indiana have gone Republican." Herndon read the message aloud. "The crowd, yelled—screamed—threw up their hats—ran out the doors—made bonfires," and Herndon never finished his speech.[18]

Pennsylvania became the decisive battle for the national campaign. Alexander McClure recalled: "A party had to be created out of inharmonious elements, and the commercial and financial interests of the State were almost solidly against us." Pennsylvania's Republicans eventually raised twelve thousand dollars, but McClure noted how "the friends of Mr. Seward took no part in the great October battle."[19]

A few days before the national election, Newton "Little Newt" Bateman, state superintendent of public instruction, walked into Lincoln's office to pass time. Lincoln had once taken an important letter to Bateman for corrections. Afterward, he always introduced Bateman by saying, "This is my little friend, the big schoolmaster of Illinois." On this occasion Lincoln, who ran his own poll in Springfield, took Bateman aside and said, "There are twenty-three ministers of different denominations [in Springfield] and all of them are against me but three." He paced a few minutes in meditation before turning to Bateman: "I know there is a God, and that He hates injustice and slavery. I see the storm coming, and I know that His hand is in it. If He has a place and work for me I believe I am ready. I am nothing but truth is everything." Lincoln went to the window and stared outside. He watched the last leaves fall from trees and blow across the streets. It reminded him of every year when Election Day approached. "I may not see the end," he said reflectively, "but it will come."[20]

On the afternoon of November 6, after six months of virtual inactivity, Lincoln could not decide whether to go to the polls. Herndon was amused to find his partner unable to make a simple decision. Lincoln felt uncomfortable voting for himself, so Herndon told him to vote for state candidates. Lincoln cut his name off the top of a Republican ballot and crossed the street to the polling center at the Sangamon County Court House with Ward Lamon, Herndon, and Ellsworth. As the distinguished voter approached, a waiting crowd opened a gap. Many of them, including Democrats, removed their hats. Lincoln gave his name and deposited the ballot. He tried to escape back to the governor's room but spent the rest of the afternoon shaking hands and chatting with supporters. They followed him back to his office, where he entertained callers until polls closed.[21]

At 9:00 p.m. the telegraph office informed Lincoln of the first returns. He departed with friends and spent the next three hours lounging on a sofa listening to chattering telegraph instruments. As operators pasted the messages, Lincoln read them aloud and passed them around. Special couriers carried the telegrams outside and read them to the public. At 10:00 p.m. Lincoln learned he had won Pennsylvania. Cameron wanted credit and reported, "Penna. Seventy thousand for you. New York safe. Glory enough."[22]

At midnight Lincoln felt hungry and walked with friends to Watson's Saloon, where his wife and Republican ladies of Springfield had commandeered the establishment and prepared sandwiches and coffee. On entering, a chorus of women greeted him with "How do you do, Mr. President." Celebrations began with cheers, handshaking, and singing. Samuel R. Weed, a *New York Times* correspondent wrote, "If Mr. Lincoln left the telegraph office for the purpose of taking a little refreshment, he came as near to being killed by kindness as a man can conveniently be without serious results."[23]

Lincoln escaped from the saloon and returned to the telegraph office to await returns from New York. At 2:00 a.m. the good news arrived. "I went home," he said, "but not to get much sleep, for I then felt, as I never had before, the responsibility that was upon me. . . . This was on Wednesday morning, and before the sun went down I had made up my Cabinet."[24]

The Lincoln-Hamlin ticket eventually tallied 1,866,452 popular votes against 1,376,957 for Douglas, 849,781 for Breckinridge, and 588,879 for Bell. Lincoln captured only 40 percent of the popular vote but won 180 electoral votes against 72 for Breckinridge, 39 for Bell, and only 12 for Douglas. Every Free State voted for Lincoln but New Jersey, which split the electoral vote 4 for Lincoln and 3 for Douglas. Bell won the upper South, Breckinridge won the lower South, and Douglas won only Missouri outright and part of New Jersey.[25]

On November 7 Samuel Weed observed sadness in Lincoln's face. People came and went, and he heard the president-elect repeat several times, "Well, boys, your troubles are over now, but mine have just begun." Lincoln could not envision the magnitude of the "troubles" ahead. When he went to bed that night, he thought he had designed his cabinet, but burdens he would carry for the rest of his life were just beginning.[26]

CHAPTER 3

"They have gambled me all around"

On November 8, 1860, Lincoln took the first step in forming his cabinet by inviting the vice president–elect to Chicago. Hannibal Hamlin arrived thirteen days later, as the nation began to unravel. On November 10 South Carolina's legislature, reacting to Lincoln's election, authorized a special convention to discuss future relations with the federal government. Eight days later Georgia's legislature convened, followed by Mississippi, Florida, Alabama, Louisiana, and Texas. Lincoln could not intervene because President James Buchanan still ran government. As a consequence, Lincoln's six days with Hamlin in Chicago dealt with problems of the nation, not the cabinet.

Buchanan had no precedents to guide him through the crisis. Unable to determine if secession was unconstitutional, he did nothing to prevent it. Some members of the lame-duck Congress believed separating the South from the North an act of good riddance. Others argued against disunion with equal passion. Debate on the subject accomplished nothing. Instead of working through the crisis with a common objective, some members of Congress deferred to the untested president-elect in Springfield for guidance. Lincoln understood his election had spurred disunion, but because of his isolation during the campaign, he never became acquainted with Washington's leaders. Obliged to follow the practice of presidents before him, Lincoln made no public statements. To those who urged him to speak, he replied, "I could say nothing which I have not already said, and which is in print, and open for the inspection of all."[1]

Reacting to public pressure, Lincoln recruited his friend Senator Lyman Trumbull of Illinois to speak in Springfield and handed him two draft paragraphs. The essence of the message emphasized that "each and all of the States will be left in control of their own affairs" with the "liberty to choose, and employ, their own means of protecting property, and preserving peace and order within their respective limits, as they have ever been under any administration." Calming words coming from Trumbull did not prevent secession, but the speech put him before the public as "the President's mouthpiece in the Senate."[2]

Lincoln remained in Springfield and reserved the hours from 10:00 a.m. to noon and 3:00 to 5:30 p.m. for the reception of 160 visitors a day in the governor's room at the capitol. The room held a dozen people—twenty if standing. As they appeared at the doorway, Lincoln would say, "Get in, all of you." Most of them shook his hand and left. Journalists wanted something to tell the press; politicians wanted to discuss cabinet selections, and others sought patronage. Lincoln dealt with the groups affably. He discussed any subject but secession. After two weeks the fifty-one-year-old president-elect showed signs of fatigue. Henry Villard of the *New York Herald* observed the change and on November 19 wrote, "Mr. Lincoln's personal appearance is the subject of daily remark, among those who have known him formerly. Always cadaverous, his aspect is now almost ghostly."[3]

Bundles of correspondence arrived, and each day the pile grew. Nicolay became swamped, so the president-elect hired John Hay, an 1858 graduate of Brown University who worked in the law office next door to Lincoln & Herndon. As assistant secretary, Hay processed requests for autographs. The spoils system flourished, and Lincoln could not escape from the overwhelming heap of patronage requests. Pubic offices were regarded as rewards to faithful party workers. At one point Lincoln compared himself to "a man so busy in letting rooms in one end of his house that he cannot stop to put out the fire . . . burning in the other."[4]

Lincoln received a letter from eleven-year-old Grace Bedell of Westfield, New York, suggesting he grow a beard because "all the ladies like whiskers" and would "tease their husbands to vote for you." Lincoln chuckled and replied in his own handwriting, "As to the whiskers, having never worn any, do you not think people would call it a piece of silly affect[at]ion if I were to begin it now?" After the election Lincoln followed Miss Bedell's advice. Friends were surprised to see stubble on his face, and for several days he looked grotesque.[5]

When meeting with Hamlin and Republican leaders in Judge Ebenezer Peck's home in Chicago, Lincoln mentioned his cabinet selections and why he wanted them. On the night after the election he could not sleep and wrote the names on a blank card. Conspicuously missing were Caleb Smith and Simon Cameron, but Lincoln always intended to find a position for Chase:[6]

> Lincoln   Judd
> Seward   Chase
> Bates   [Montgomery] Blair
> [William L.] Dayton   Welles

Fifteen people wanted a cabinet post, but only four of them appeared on Lincoln's list. Neither Seward nor Bates had applied, and no one besides

Lincoln had mentioned Judge Dayton of New Jersey. David Davis and Leonard Swett were not invited; Trumbull attended but knew nothing about the
deals. Lincoln wanted to balance the cabinet geographically with Republican
Whigs and former Democrats. He authorized Hamlin to choose for New
England but insisted he select "a man of Democratic antecedents." Lincoln
preselected the others—Seward for New York, Dayton for New Jersey, Judd
for Illinois—and for the border states he chose Bates for Missouri and Montgomery Blair for Maryland. Lincoln knew little about these men. He wanted
at least one personal friend in the cabinet and chose Judd.

The conferees agreed on Seward as secretary of state, the top cabinet
post to be settled first. Conscious of Seward's distress after having lost the
nomination, Lincoln worried he might not accept. To avoid a snub that
might reflect harmfully on the new administration, Lincoln gave Hamlin
the sensitive mission of meeting with Seward before making the offer.[7]

Hamlin waited until Congress reconvened to carry out his mission. On
December 13 he fell in step with Seward on Pennsylvania Avenue and, on
reaching his hotel, invited the New York senator to his rooms for a private
talk. Different versions of the conversation exist. Gideon Welles recorded
Seward as having claimed "he was tired of public life and that he intended
to resign his seat or decline reelection and retire," repeating several times
he would "not go into the Cabinet of Mr. Lincoln." Hamlin, however, quoted
Seward as having said, "If that is what you have come to talk to me about . . .
we might as well stop here. I don't want the place, and, if I did, I have reason
to know that I could not get it. Let us have no more talk about it."[8] Seward's
response delighted Hamlin, who personally believed having Weed's alter ego
in the cabinet would be dangerous. Hamlin told Seward the matter would
be dropped, but Lincoln had given him two letters, both dated December
8, with instructions to show them to Seward one at a time. The first letter
read: "With your permission, I shall, at the proper time, nominate you to the
Senate, for confirmation, as Secretary of State for the United States. Please
let me hear from you at your earliest convenience." Hamlin knew the content
of the letter and handed it to Seward expecting it would be politely refused.
But Seward turned "pale with excitement" and opened the envelope with
trembling hands.[9]

The short, concise letter seemed cold, and after digesting the blunt offer
Seward dismissed it as a disingenuous formality meant for him to decline.
He had many enemies in New York, which accounted for his statement to
Hamlin about quitting public service. Trumbull had been stopped by William
Cullen Bryant, editor of the *New York Evening Post,* and other Seward detrac-

tors as he passed through the city on the way to Washington. He received an earful of warnings about Seward's connection with Weed, whose alleged corruption of the state legislature tarnished Seward. Trumbull disliked Seward and Weed and advised Lincoln that New Yorkers wanted "honest men with clean hands" in the cabinet. After Trumbull's warning, Lincoln prepared a second more gratifying letter for Hamlin to hand Seward. After the senator absorbed Lincoln's second message, his whole outlook changed:[10]

> In addition to the accompanying and more formal note, inviting you to take charge of the state department, I deem it proper to address you this. Rumors have got into the newspapers to the effect that the department, named above, would be tendered to you, as a compliment, and with the expectation that you would decline it. I beg you to be assured that I have said nothing to justify these rumors. On the contrary, it has been my purpose, from the day of the nomination in Chicago, to assign you, by your leave, to this place in the administration. . . . I now offer you the place, in the hope that you will accept it, and with the belief that your position in the public eye, your integrity, ability, learning, and great experience, all combine to render it an appointment pre-eminently fit to be made.

Turning to Hamlin, Seward said, "This is remarkable. I will consider the matter, and, in accordance with Mr. Lincoln's request, give him my decision at the earliest practicable moment." Seward wrote Lincoln asking for "a little time to consider whether I possess the qualifications and temper of a minister and whether it is in such capacity that my friends would prefer that I should act if I am to continue at all in the public service"—which meant he wanted time to confer with his wife and Weed.[11]

Weed had different ideas about forming the cabinet, and so did Seward. Both wanted an all-Seward, all-Whig cabinet with one or two friendly Whigs from the South. Seward also wanted to control the administration with his own plan—one unpopular with "irrepressibles" in Congress—for forestalling conflict with the South. He now understood his worth. For accepting the high title of secretary of state, Seward believed he held bargaining chips and urged Weed to win concessions by going to Springfield and placing them on the table. Welles called the scheme to sidetrack a constitutionally elected president the "Albany program."[12]

On December 20 Weed collected Davis and Swett in Bloomington before proceeding to Springfield. Weed assumed his most gracious demeanor to begin the first of several six-hour conversations with Lincoln, who had chosen Blair, Chase, Judd, and Welles, all one-time Democrats, for cabinet posts. Weed argued there were many qualified Republicans ready to serve and suggested Marylander Henry Winter Davis in place of Blair, especially given that Davis was a cousin of Judge Davis, to whom Lincoln owed his nomination. For Massachusetts, Weed suggested Charles Francis Adams for the Treasury, partly because Adams and Seward were close friends but mostly because Seward despised Chase. When Lincoln balked on Davis and Adams, Weed suggested three Southerners. No Southern state carried Lincoln's name on the ballot, so why, he asked, should he reward them with cabinet posts. He also mentioned the "making of the cabinet, now that he had to do it, was by no means as easy as he had supposed" and found "great men scarcer than they used to be."

Weed further objected to Lincoln's choices because in his opinion four former Democrats against only three former Whigs (Bates, Dayton, and Seward) skewed the cabinet, rendering it unmanageable. He doubted whether Seward would like the arrangement. Lincoln replied, "You seem to forget that *I* expect to be there; and counting me as one, you see how nicely the cabinet would be balanced and ballasted."[13]

The conference gave Weed an opportunity to study Lincoln's political sagacity, which he found far more advanced than anticipated. He departed from Springfield with a greater respect for the president-elect but without concessions. Lincoln did present Weed with three draft resolutions he believed would mollify the South and asked that Seward introduce them to the Senate. The drafts contained proposals forbidding alteration of the Constitution by Congress to interfere with slavery in the states; a revision to the fugitive slave law granting a jury trial to fugitives; and another from Congress making states repeal personal liberty laws in conflict with the Constitution. Lincoln closed by adding, "The Federal Union must be preserved."[14]

Weed departed from Springfield with a preview of the cabinet. Although he disagreed with four choices, he assured Lincoln that Seward would accept the State Department. He also banked on having several weeks with Seward's help to change Lincoln's mind and replace Blair, Chase, and Welles with Seward's friends. One matter became agonizingly clear: control of the Republican Party had passed from Seward to Lincoln.

Seward joined Weed at Syracuse for a report on the Springfield sessions. He studied Lincoln's three proposals and agreed to put them before the Senate, but the cabinet unhinged him. He hesitated to accept the State Department because he believed Blair, Chase, and Welles would not support him and create disharmony. Weed argued that having the top post in the administration was better than having none. Days passed in Springfield without word from Seward, and Lincoln found forming a cabinet more troublesome than anticipated.[15]

Seward introduced Lincoln's three proposals to the Senate, and Thomas Corwin, speaker of the House, agreed to do the same. None survived. After reporting defeat to Lincoln, Seward said he expected the Deep South to secede even if every proposal had passed.[16]

Seward's prediction came as no surprise. President Buchanan had already instructed Major Robert Anderson at Charleston, South Carolina, "to surrender Fort Moultrie if attacked." "If that is true," Lincoln snapped, "they ought to hang him."[17]

Lincoln recruited Elihu Washburne to take a message to General-in-Chief Winfield Scott imploring him to "either *hold,* or *retake,* the forts" as conditions allow. Scott had made the same recommendation, but Buchanan refused to act. Lincoln now faced another critical issue he could do nothing about.[18]

Lincoln could not wait indefinitely for Seward's decision. Bringing Weed to Springfield had been meant to clear the air, and if afterward Seward declined the top cabinet post, Lincoln would be disappointed but not without options. A week before Weed's visit, friends of "the Blairs" began lobbying Lincoln for a cabinet post for Montgomery Blair. For two generations the Blairs had been a powerful influence in politics. Francis P. Blair Sr., paternal head of the family, never held public office, but from 1830 to 1854 he edited the *Washington Globe*—a powerful Democratic organ—and became Andrew Jackson's right-hand man. He once owned slaves but believed the Union took precedence over sectional interests. He bolted from the Democrats over the Kansas-Nebraska Act, aligned himself with Republicans, and supported Lincoln. He raised two sons, Francis P. "Frank" Blair Jr. and Montgomery Blair. The three became known as "the Blairs" because the interests of one Blair became the interests of all of them.

After graduating from Princeton, Frank Blair earned a law degree at Transylvania College in Kentucky and later settled in Missouri, where he became the most powerful Republican in the state. He formed the Free-Soil Party in Missouri, organized the state's Wide-Awakes, backed Bates for president before backing Lincoln, and in 1860, at the age of thirty-nine, began serving a second term in the House of Representatives. Lincoln did not consider Frank Blair for the cabinet because he had already pre-chosen Bates. This left Montgomery Blair of Maryland.[19]

In exchange for support the Blairs expected patronage. Rather than approach Lincoln directly, they worked through intermediaries. On November 15 Preston King wrote Senator Trumbull, Lincoln's point man in Washington, "Our friends the Blairs would like to have Judge Montgomery Blair made Attorney General."[20]

Forty-seven-year-old Montgomery Blair held worthy credentials. After graduating from West Point in 1835 and serving in the Seminole War, he resigned his commission to study law. He settled in Missouri as a Democrat, became a U.S. district attorney, mayor of St. Louis in 1842–43, and judge of the common pleas court in 1845–49. He moved to Maryland in 1853, established a prosperous law practice, and became nationally known arguing the *Dred Scott* case before the Supreme Court. He became a Republican and at the Chicago convention swung Maryland's delegates to Lincoln. Friends and family now came to collect. Making Blair attorney general also made sense, but Lincoln had a problem. He had decided to make Bates secretary of state if Seward declined or attorney general if Seward accepted.[21]

On December 11, Frank Blair arrived in Springfield to promote his brother as attorney general. Frank wanted to be speaker of the House and hoped to gain leverage by having Montgomery in the cabinet. Lincoln remained unresponsive because he had not heard from Seward or spoken with Bates, which made the Blairs nervous. They probed Trumbull, who posted a feeler to Lincoln proposing Montgomery Blair as secretary of war. On December 24 Lincoln broke his silence and advised Trumbull, "I expect to be able to offer Mr. Blair a place in the cabinet; but I can not, as yet, be committed on the matter, to any extent whatsoever."[22]

On December 13, the same day Hamlin tendered the top position to Seward, Lincoln decided to speak with Bates. The sixty-seven-year-old judge had been a slaveholder in Missouri, a powerful politician, a member of Congress on the Whig ticket, and later a Republican. When President Millard Fillmore offered Bates the post of secretary of war, he turned it down. Lincoln thought Bates might decline a post again but felt obliged to ask.

Aware of Bates's notorious ego and disdain for Seward, Lincoln offered to meet with him in St. Louis, but Bates "saw an unfitness in *his coming to me, and that I ought to go to him.*" Two days later Bates arrived in Springfield and found Lincoln mobbed by visitors at the capitol. Being unable to conduct a private conversation without interruption, they withdrew to Bates's hotel.[23]

Bates found Lincoln troubled by Seward's silence because the president-elect believed the New Yorker deserved "first place" in the cabinet. Seward's refusal, said Lincoln, could lead to "a dangerous if not fatal rupture of the party." Bates disagreed, calling Seward's appointment risky. "It would exasperate the feelings of the South," he warned, "and make conciliation impossible, because they consider Mr. S[eward] the embodiment of all they hold odious in the Republican party." He also said "it would alarm and dissatisfy that large section of the Party which opposed Mr. S[eward]'s nomination, and now think that they have reason to fear that, if armed with the power of that high place, he would treat them as enemies" and greatly weaken the administration.[24]

Having already offered the secretary of state post to Seward, Lincoln extended the offer to Bates if the New Yorker declined. If Seward accepted the State Department, Bates would be named attorney general. Bates agreed to accept either department, giving Lincoln a fallback position should Seward defect. Lincoln, however, expected Seward to accept secretary of state, thus accomplishing what he had intended by having Bates as attorney general.

Bates wanted a statement issued, so on December 18 Lincoln informed the *St. Louis Daily Missouri Democrat:* "We have the permission of both Mr. Lincoln and Mr. Bates to say that the latter will be offered, and will accept, a place in the New Cabinet, subject of course to the action of the Senate. It is not yet definitely settled which department will be assigned to Mr. Bates." Not everyone welcomed the announcement. Although nobody debated Bates's spotless integrity, he had become an indolent vestige of the past, and those who knew him well believed he should have remained in retirement.[25]

As late December approached, Lincoln reminded Hamlin to select a former Democrat to serve in the cabinet. Hamlin liked Charles Francis Adams, son of one American president and grandson of another. The choice would please Seward, but Adams was a Whig. Lincoln gave Hamlin a list of three former Democrats—Amos Tuck of New Hampshire, Governor Nathaniel Banks of Massachusetts, and Lincoln's original choice, Gideon Welles of Connecticut. By December 24 he had lost patience and wrote Hamlin, "Which of them do the New England delegations prefer? Or shall I decide for myself?"[26]

Hamlin moved with alacrity. Massachusetts lobbied for Banks, but Hamlin disliked him. Tuck had wanted a cabinet position and in early December still did. Hamlin chose Welles, however, perhaps because he knew Lincoln preferred the unassuming politician and former editor from Hartford, Connecticut. The vice president–elect promptly replied to Lincoln that he had "no hesitation in saying that . . . Mr. Wells [*sic*] is the better man for New England."[27]

Fifty-eight-year-old Gideon Welles fit neatly into Lincoln's balanced cabinet. For many years Welles had served as Hartford's postmaster before abandoning the Democrats to help establish the Connecticut Republican Party. As a delegate to the Chicago convention, he opposed Seward and came to Springfield with the committee formally notifying Lincoln of his nomination. During the Mexican War Welles had served as chief of the Naval Bureau of Provisions and Clothing, gaining exposure in naval affairs. As state comptroller of public accounts, he had better experience than most politicians managing public funds. He had no skeletons in his closet and was respected for his honesty. Welles also had the support of James Dixon, the Republican senator from Connecticut and a colleague of Hamlin. Lincoln needed a postmaster general and a secretary of navy to fill his cabinet, and Welles knew something about both.[28]

Two days after the national election the Cameron deal made in May surfaced. Because Pennsylvania Republicans remained bitterly divided between the Curtin and Cameron factions, Lincoln decided to exclude both from the cabinet rather than alienate either group and decided to appoint William L. Dayton of New Jersey, which had tariff interests in common with Pennsylvania. John Sanderson and Joseph Casey, both having acted as Cameron's managers in Chicago, suspected Lincoln was not "fully acquainted . . . with the understanding." On November 10 they arrived in Springfield with Davis and Swett to collect. Casey refrained from discussing the bargain, returned to Pennsylvania empty-handed, and told Cameron if he wanted a cabinet post to go to Springfield. Cameron refused to make the trip without an invitation because "it was incomprehensible to him, who was always the lord with suppliants eagerly grasping for the crumbs from his table, to picture himself a solicitor at the feet of the mighty Lincoln whom, secretly . . . he held very much in contempt." Instead, correspondence from Pennsylvania began pouring into Springfield extolling the virtues of Cameron as a cabinet choice.[29]

On November 27 Casey wrote Swett asking that Lincoln be made aware of the bargain before cabinet appointments were announced. Swett could no longer conceal the arrangement and sent Casey's letter to Lincoln, enclosing his own letter to Cameron stating that the president-elect could not be bound by pledges made by himself or Davis.[30]

Lincoln did nothing, nor did he hear from Cameron. On December 20, when Weed visited Springfield, Lincoln broached the subject of adding Cameron to the cabinet. Weed distrusted Cameron, who had promised, but later reneged, to back Seward's nomination. He suggested a trustworthy Republican from a slave state as an alternative, so Lincoln dropped the matter.[31]

Cameron's claim emanating from the Davis-Swett bargain tortured Lincoln most. He sent Swett to Pennsylvania to confer with Cameron. During Swett's absence more correspondence from powerful forces supporting Cameron as Treasury secretary flooded Lincoln's daily mail. On December 30 Cameron and Sanderson arrived in Springfield and said they had come at the request of Swett. Lincoln spent two hours in cordial conversation without ever getting to the point.[32]

In the morning Lincoln sorted through sixty letters collected from Pennsylvanians urging Cameron's appointment to the cabinet. They included delegates to the Chicago convention, congressmen, journalists, and former governors—all with political ties to the Pennsylvania senator. Letters from detractors, though fewer, mentioned Indian scandals, bribery, influence peddling, and larceny, raising serious questions about Cameron's fitness to serve in government. Because favorable letters outnumbered negative ones, combined with Swett and Davis's involvement, Lincoln relented. In an ego-inflating note before Cameron returned to Pennsylvania, Lincoln confidentially offered him the Treasury or the War Department, adding, "Which of the two, I have not definitely decided. Please answer at your own earliest convenience."

Cameron gleefully departed, stopped in Harrisburg on his way to Washington, and, instead of remaining silent, told his friends he would be appointed Treasury secretary. Newspapers reported the statement, which took Cameron's enemies by surprise, and fresh bundles of negative correspondence inundated Lincoln's mail.[33]

On December 31, the day Cameron departed for Harrisburg, Lincoln received a formal letter of acceptance from Seward. Feeling more at ease, he invited Chase to Springfield to discuss the Treasury Department. Chase had just been elected to the U.S. Senate and was mildly miffed because Lincoln had not contacted him sooner. Like Cameron, he also had a deal to collect, but Davis and Swett never mentioned it because they knew Lincoln wanted Chase for the cabinet and would eventually contact him.[34]

Chase arrived the night of January 4 and checked into the Chenery House. He attracted attention, being "tall, broad-shouldered, and proudly erect" with "features strong and regular . . . a picture of intelligence, strength, courage and dignity. He looked as you would wish a statesman to look." Although slightly shorter than Lincoln, Chase's smooth and unblemished complexion stood in stark contrast to Lincoln's wrinkles.[35]

After morning pleasantries Lincoln asked Chase if he would "accept the appointment of Secretary of the Treasury without, however, being exactly prepared to make you that offer." Chase refused to jeopardize his Senate seat without a firm offer. He disliked being second to Seward, whom he personally loathed. He feared Seward would attempt to dominate the administration. He also hoped Lincoln would ask him to serve as a personal favor, implying he did not come to Springfield seeking a cabinet position. Chase's bruised ego rubbed both ways. If he rejected Lincoln's offer, he would jeopardize "a distinguished and patronage-rich" opportunity to better position himself for another run at the presidency. Lincoln offered more bait, suggesting that if Seward later rejected the state department, Chase could have it.[36]

Chase believed Lincoln might offer him the State Department post because Seward's acceptance had not been publicized. He also thought the Treasury had been offered to Cameron. When considering what Chase knew before reaching Springfield, he could not avoid being flabbergasted when offered the Treasury Department on a "maybe basis" instead of the State Department.

Because Cameron could not keep his mouth shut, combined with an instant uproar from his enemies over the appointment, Lincoln on January 3 wrote a curt letter to the Pennsylvania troublemaker, saying, "Since seeing you things have developed that make it impossible for me to take you into the Cabinet." He asked Cameron to telegraph immediately "declining the appointment." Lincoln explained the situation to Chase but never received a declination from Cameron.[37]

Chase liked Cameron no better than Seward, which raised questions about Lincoln's political judgment. He eventually developed a deeper appreciated of what Lincoln was trying to accomplish from Springfield in the face of a national crisis about which he could do nothing. As Chase's ego thawed, he found more in common with Lincoln, and the notion of working in partnership with him became more attractive. When Chase departed from Springfield on January 7 with Lincoln's conditional offer, he understood why the Treasury could not be officially tendered until later. He talked to his friends, pretending to be ambivalent about joining the cabinet, but he wanted the Treasury Department position if for no other reason than to oppose Seward.[38]

Although favorably impressed by Chase's grasp of national affairs, Lincoln could do nothing until he resolved the Cameron imbroglio. He wrote to Senator Trumbull, "Gen. C[ameron] has not been offered the Treasury, and, I think, will not be. It seems to me not only higher priority, but a *necessity*, that Gov. Chase shall take that place." The Cameron arrangement exasperated Lincoln. He wanted a way out of the mess but fretted over what Pennsylvanians might say if he excluded Cameron altogether. Lincoln admitted he could put Cameron in the war office, "But then comes the fierce opposition of his having any Department."[39]

In mid-January Lincoln met with Gustave Koerner and Judd and said, "I am in a quandary. Pennsylvania is entitled to a Cabinet office, but whom shall I appoint?" Judd and Koerner replied, "Not Cameron!" adding he would corrupt any office he held. "I know, I know," Lincoln replied, "but can I get along if that State should oppose my administration?" Lincoln believed Cameron's friends were more powerful than they actually were, and Cameron hoped to restore power relinquished to Curtin by distributing Treasury Department patronage. Lincoln finally decided to send Judd to Washington to convince Cameron to retain his seat in the Senate and asked Trumbull to help. But with rumors spreading of Chase's appointment to the Treasury, Cameron refused to decline a cabinet post and . stepped up pressure on Lincoln by circulating the December 31 letter promising him a post while concealing the January 3 letter rescinding it.

On January 12 Sanderson arrived in Springfield with Senator Edgar Cowan of Pennsylvania to bargain on behalf of Cameron. Swett had spoken with Cameron and reported him offended by Lincoln's second letter. Sanderson protested Chase's appointment, calling him a low tariff man unacceptable to Pennsylvania. Lincoln mentioned the War Department in his December 31 letter, but Cameron wanted the patronage-rich Treasury Department. Lincoln made no promises and sent Sanderson and Cowan back to Cameron with a letter apologizing for any harsh words, adding, "If I should make any cabinet appointment for Penn[sylvania] before I reach Washington, I will not do so without consulting you."[40]

Meanwhile, three men from the anti-Weed delegation, after conferring with Chase, arrived in Springfield. Lincoln received them cordially, listened to their arguments for appointing Chase immediately, but politely informed them he would make no more cabinet decisions until reaching Washington. This had not been his intention, but Cameron's refusal to remain in the Senate left Lincoln little choice.[41]

Lincoln stumbled on another problem issuing from the Chicago deals when Judge Davis, without giving any reason, told him that Caleb Smith also wanted a cabinet post. Lincoln preferred Smith's rival, Schuyler Colfax, who had supported Bates at the convention and afterward worked for Lincoln's election while Smith did nothing. Lincoln intended to save a post for Judd, but then Cameron's deal surfaced and now Smith's deal. On January 18 Smith wrote Davis to remind him of their agreement and protested the possibility of Colfax obtaining *his* cabinet seat. Smith deserved no consideration, which gave Lincoln another reason to avoid cabinet discussions until Inauguration Day. "They have gambled on me all around," he grumbled. "Bought and sold me a hundred times. I cannot begin to fill the pledges made in my name." For the next six weeks Lincoln parried a quagmire of cabinet applicants, making no decisions and leaving all contenders but Seward and Bates in perpetual limbo.[42]

The president-elect's wavering on appointments made Lincoln look indecisive, and powerful influences interceded. The anti-Weed clique in New York wanted Seward dethroned and recruited Horace Greeley to step up adverse publicity in the *New York Tribune.* When Greeley spoke, people listened, and it did not matter whether or not they agreed. The outspoken publisher fervently extolled the virtues of Chase, urging him to take the State Department or if not, the Treasury Department.

Washburne read the *Tribune* and on January 10 wrote Chase, "Cameron will *not* have a place in the cabinet. The idea prevails here . . . that you have been offered the Treasury, but many fears are expressed that you will not accept. . . . The country demands your services in the Treasury department. . . . I tell you it is *now* a necessity that you should go into the cabinet if Lincoln has tendered you a place." On January 22 New York congressman Francis E. Spinner added his two cents, writing Chase, "Intrigues are again in progress to place a particular man [Cameron] at the head of the Treasury Department. The country is alarmed at the mere suggestion. Now it is believed that the President elect has offered you the place, and you have declined it. For God's sake . . . reconsider this, and save the party." Friends fueled Chase's ego, and by mid-January he relented and admitted to a friend that if the Seward-Cameron influence prevailed, he would have to "lay personal considerations to myself aside" and accept a cabinet offer, if tendered.[43]

Lincoln received both pro-Chase correspondence from reliable sources and bundles of anti-Cameron letters. He had no reservations about Chase's qualifications, but Cameron, despite an army of loyal supporters, immensely troubled him. He invited objective comments on Cameron's character, and on February 5 William Cullen Bryant of the *New York Evening Post* responded: "Cameron has the reputation of being concerned in some of the worst intrigues in the Democratic party. At present, those who favor his appointment in this State are the men who last winter so shamefully corrupted our Legislature. If he is to have a place in the Cabinet at all, the Treasury department is the last of our public interest that ought to be committed to his hands."[44]

Bryant's missive should have doomed Cameron, but the crafty Pennsylvanian refused to be dismissed. He continued to wave Lincoln's December 31 letter about the state as if nothing had changed. Lincoln could not shed Cameron, and the end of January found the cabinet no closer to finalization than it had been in December. Herndon watched his partner's frustration grow, writing, "Lincoln is in a fix. Cameron's appointment . . . bothers him. If Lincoln do[es] appoint Cameron, he gets a fight on his hands, and if he do[es] not he gets a quarrel deep-abiding, & lasting. . . . Poor Lincoln! God help him!"[45]

Davis, who had fashioned the deal with Cameron's handlers, now went to Weed for help. Before leaving for Albany, he mailed a confidential letter to Cameron: "Every effort that mortal man could make has been made by me—Keep the spirits of your friends up. *Don't relax effort until the end.* . . . Write me at Albany if necessary, care of Thurlow Weed."[46]

Unaware of the agenda Davis intended to discuss with Weed, Lincoln decided privately that the War Department would go to Cameron and the Treasury Department to Chase. His one concern was whether the Senate would oppose Cameron and create a national scandal over the appointment.[47]

Lincoln also had traveling on his mind. On February 11 the presidential train prepared to leave Springfield. He and Mary packed their belongings for a long circuitous train ride interrupted by frequent speechmaking stops before reaching Washington, D.C. Lincoln personally planned the tour, but his arrival in the nation's capital would be unlike anything anticipated on his itinerary.

CHAPTER 4

"I can't afford to let Seward have the first trick"

When Lincoln entrained for Washington on February 11, 1861, South Carolina, Mississippi, Florida, Alabama, Georgia, Louisiana, and Texas had already seceded from the Union. Delegates met in Montgomery, Alabama, and on February 8 adopted a provisional constitution creating the Confederate States of America. The convention elected Jefferson Davis of Mississippi president and Alexander H. Stephens of Georgia vice president. Each state seized federal mints, forts, arsenals, customhouses, and any asset labeled U.S. government. When Lincoln bid good-bye to Springfield only two Southern forts remained in Federal control: Fort Sumter in Charleston's harbor and Fort Pickens at Pensacola, Florida.

In December President Buchanan absolved himself of the greatest issue since the formation of the republic with a long-winded annual message to Congress. He shed the problem by sending General Duff Green to Springfield to invite the president-elect to Washington to negotiate a settlement with the South. In Green's view only Lincoln could "prevent a civil war."[1]

Lincoln rejected the invitation unless secessionists agreed to suspend "all action of dismemberment from the Union." He said, "No State can in any way lawfully get out of the Union without the consent of the others; and it is the duty of the President . . . to run the machine." On learning rebels had seized Federal forts, he told Trumbull to make it known forts will "be retaken after the inauguration."[2]

The House of Representatives created a Committee of Thirty-three (one member from each state) to deal with the crisis. The Senate formed a Committee of Thirteen for the same purpose. Senator John J. Crittenden devised a plan to extend the Missouri Compromise line through the territories and strengthen the enforcement of the Fugitive Slave Act. Virginia tried to hold a peace conference in Washington. None of the measures worked, and Lincoln, though invited to participate in discussions, refused to take part in "another round of bribes to secessionists." When asked his opinion on secession, he replied: "The right of a State to secede is not an open or debatable question. It was fully discussed in Jackson's time, and denied not only by him, but by the vote of Congress. It is the duty of a President to execute the laws and maintain the existing Government. He cannot entertain any proposition for dissolution or dismemberment." Lincoln told friends in the Senate that he opposed "compromise on the question of *extending* slavery" in the territories, and said, "Stand firm. The tug has to come, & better now, than any time hereafter."[3]

Beset by threats of war and unresolved cabinet issues, Lincoln offered a short farewell address to friends gathered at Springfield's depot. "Here I have lived from my youth until now I am an old man," he said somberly. "Here the most sacred ties of earth were assumed; here all my children were born, and here one [Edward] of them lies buried. To you, dear friends, I owe all that I have, all that I am." His words struck reporters as a eulogy, as if he never expected to return. Lincoln was not an old man. On the following day, February 12, he turned fifty-two, a good age to become president.[4]

The president-elect's private three-car train provided accommodations for about thirty personal friends, political associates, reporters, military staff, Lincoln's son Robert, and Nicolay and Hay. Judd came to aid on cabinet matters, and Davis planned to join the train at Indianapolis. Lamon and Ellsworth acted as bodyguards. Major David Hunter, Captain John Pope, and Captain George W. Hazard provided the military escort. A fourth officer, Colonel Edwin V. Sumner, missed the train and joined later. Others planned to detrain at Indianapolis so Mary Lincoln and the boys, Willie and Tad, could join the excursion. Two reporters, Henry Villard of the *New York Herald* and Edward L. Baker of the *Illinois State Journal,* made the trip to keep the public informed.

Lincoln made five speeches before reaching Indianapolis, where he stopped for the night and gave three more speeches. On February 12 he traveled to Cincinnati for more speeches. In the morning he addressed the Ohio legislature at Columbus and made another speech from the steps of the state capitol. On the same day the Electoral College met in Washington and legalized Lincoln's election as the sixteenth president of the United States.[5]

The presidential train pulled out of Columbus in the morning and arrived at Pittsburgh behind schedule, during a heavy rainstorm. That night, from the balcony of the Monongahela House, Lincoln spoke briefly to a field of umbrellas. When a battalion of Cameron's supporters appeared, Davis pulled them aside, warned them not to press their demands, and said that in eight days Lincoln would be prepared to meet with them at Harrisburg.[6]

On February 15 the presidential caravan backtracked to Cleveland, where Lincoln planned to spend the night. On the way to the Wedell House, David Cartter, who had swung the final four delegates nominating Lincoln for president, appeared at the president-elect's side and clung like a leech.

Cartter dealt those votes in exchange for giving Salmon Chase a cabinet post and now wanted one for himself. Having grown tired and hoarse, Lincoln turned the Ohio aspirant over to Davis. Cartter, still searching for another opportunity to plead his case, decided to accompany the train to Buffalo.[7]

The morning train started for Buffalo with six intermediate stops, including one at Westfield, New York. Lincoln stopped the train and asked for Grace Bedell, "if she was among the crowd," and then told the story of how he came to grow a beard. Lifted to the platform, Miss Bedell received a kiss from the bewhiskered president. Asked how she liked the beard, laughter from the crowd drowned out her answer.[8]

Former president Millard Fillmore met Lincoln at Buffalo and escorted him to the American House for another exhausting reception. From the balcony Lincoln spoke in a raspy voice before a huge crowd that could not hear what he said but cheered anyway. He rested a day before continuing to Albany. Judd mingled and eavesdropped on Davis's discussions with Pennsylvanians, writing Trumbull, "I believe I know what will happen . . . if the Treasury is offered to Gov. Chase he must accept."[9]

Weed hosted Lincoln at Albany, probing to learn anything new about the president-elect's cabinet selections. Lincoln remained unresponsive, so Weed took Lamon aside and asked where the president planned to stay in Washington. Lamon said Trumbull and Washburne had rented a private home. Weed knew the senators were pressing for the appointment of Chase, so he telegraphed Willard's Hotel and reserved rooms for the presidential party. He convinced Lincoln that as a public man he must stay in a public place and arranged for Davis and Lamon to occupy nearby rooms. Weed understood the value of influence. Davis had been conniving to put Cameron in the Treasury Department, and Lamon and Caleb Smith were personal friends.

On February 20, after receiving his fill of pro-Cameron and anti-Chase advice at Albany, Lincoln arrived in New York City, where anti-Weed Republicans attempted to dissuade him from selecting Cameron and Seward and urged him to appoint Chase. If Lincoln had free time, Weed filled it with entertainment from Sewardites. "To the impartial observer," wrote Harry Carman, "it appeared as if the Davis-Weed-Cameron–Caleb B. Smith interest was in the ascendant in the President-elect's affections."[10]

At 4:00 p.m. on February 21 Lincoln's entourage detrained at Philadelphia's Kensington depot, where a carriage conveyed the family through a cheering crowd of 100,000 people to the Continental Hotel. After Cameron's lieutenants cornered Lincoln in the lobby, twenty policemen pulled him free and took him to his rooms, where five more Cameronites waited. Lincoln brusquely confirmed what he had said before—that no decision on appointments would be made until he reached Washington. Having grown weary of being harassed by Cameron's collaborators, he gave them a scare, suggesting he might retain some cabinet holdovers from Buchanan's administration. Cameron received a full report of Lincoln's comments along with a subtle warning that if he failed to obtain a cabinet post, he could blame himself.[11]

S. M. Felton, president of the Philadelphia, Wilmington & Baltimore Railway, shouldered the responsibility of conveying Lincoln's entourage to Washington, D.C. On hearing of a plot to kill the president-elect, Felton hired detective Allan Pinkerton of Chicago to investigate the threat. Pinkerton had formed the country's first broad-based detective agency and lived the hectic life of fictional sleuth Sherlock Holmes. Pinkerton's operatives confirmed that thugs intended to assassinate Lincoln when the train stopped in Baltimore. That evening Judd urged Lincoln to not lose another hour and to leave secretly for Washington. Lincoln refused. He had a morning engagement to speak at Independence Hall and another later in the day at Harrisburg.

During the evening reception Judd took Lincoln by the arm to meet Frederick Seward, who had arrived from Washington with a letter from his father. Seward wanted to speak privately, so Lamon escorted him to the president-elect's room. An hour later Lincoln came down the hallway, greeted young Seward, and read the note. The letter contained information supplied by General Scott corroborating Pinkerton's claim that assassins planned to kill Lincoln during the switching of trains at Baltimore. Lincoln suspected Pinkerton had started the rumor, so he asked several questions. Because Seward had never heard of Pinkerton, Lincoln finally admitted "there may be something in it."[12]

Seward looked for Lincoln at breakfast but learned he had gone to Independence Hall to deliver an address celebrating Washington's Birthday and the unfurling of a new thirty-four-star flag recognizing Kansas statehood. Commenting on the freedoms provided in the Declaration of Independence, Lincoln said, "If this country cannot be saved without giving up that principle . . . I would rather be assassinated on this spot than surrender it." Seward thought the statement "had a deeper meaning than his audience guessed."[13]

During the speech Lamon took Seward aside and said the president-elect agreed to pass through Baltimore at a different hour. Judd had spent the night with railroad officials arranging for Lincoln to make a hasty trip to Harrisburg and then leave suddenly at 6:00 p.m. on a special train having one passenger car, one baggage car, and an exclusive right of way to Philadelphia. Felton arranged to have linemen cut telegraph wires to conceal Lincoln's departure from Harrisburg and delayed the regular night train from Philadelphia to Baltimore until Lincoln returned. Seward took an earlier train to inform his father that Lincoln would arrive with Lamon at the Washington depot before daybreak.[14]

Lincoln spoke briefly to the Pennsylvania state legislature at Harrisburg and spent the rest of the afternoon sequestered in rooms at the Jones House. Colonel Sumner took Judd aside and called Lincoln's plan to enter Washington incognito an insult to military officers assigned to protect him. While Sumner argued over who would escort Lincoln to Washington, Davis and Judd guarded the doors and fended off efforts by Cameron's operatives to get inside. When Judd decided only Lamon, who was heavily armed, would accompany Lincoln, Sumner insisted that he go, too. After a hurried supper Lincoln donned a different hat and coat and with Lamon at his side ducked into a closed carriage. Judd distracted Sumner as the carriage sped for the depot. "A madder man," said Judd, "you never saw."[15]

Lincoln returned to Philadelphia wearing a shawl, as he often did, around his shoulders. This gave rise to *Vanity Fair*'s caricature of him being dressed in a "Scotch plaid cap and a very long military cloak." Joseph Howard Jr. of the *New York Times* admitted inventing the tale "to get up some sort of story for his paper." When Lincoln and Lamon reached Philadelphia, they found Pinkerton waiting with the latest report. There were now fifteen thousand desperadoes waiting to stop the train as it entered the city in the morning.[16]

Lincoln ignored the report and at 11:00 p.m. entered a sleeper car provided by Pinkerton. The train reached Baltimore in the early hours, and at 6:00 a.m. Lincoln pulled into Washington's fogbound depot. Washburne, acting as a reception committee of one, recognized Lincoln immediately, grasped his hand, and said, "Abe, you can't play that on me." The greeting caught Lamon and Pinkerton off guard, but Lincoln waved them off, saying, "This is only Washburne!" The four men checked into Willard's and were later joined by Seward, who had overslept. News of Lincoln's arrival took Washington by surprise. Within hours the first office seekers began descending on Parlor No. 6, the president-elect's rooms.[17]

Having settled on Bates, Seward, Welles, and Smith, and despite opposition from the Weed-Cameron coalition, he still wanted Chase. He narrowed his choice of postmaster general to Montgomery Blair or Winter Davis, both of Maryland, but he could not decide what to do with Cameron. Weed and Seward still wanted Davis instead of Blair, Banks instead of Welles, and Cameron instead of Chase, thereby eliminating their enemies from the cabinet.

On the afternoon of February 23, eight hours after Lincoln arrived in Washington, Blair Sr., accompanied by his son Montgomery, called on Lincoln. Father Blair came with two missions: to nail down his son's cabinet position and to articulate his disdain for Weed. Judge Davis opposed Blair and promptly reported the visit to Weed, who suddenly materialized in Washington to block Blair's appointment. Lincoln listened but settled on Montgomery Blair.[18]

As March approached, Lincoln finally grappled with the problem of the Treasury, which Cameron lusted for and which Chase had neither accepted nor declined. Out of time and patience, Lincoln decided on the last day of February to offer Chase and Cameron cabinet positions. He called Cameron to his room and offered him the Interior Department. Cameron fumed because he wanted to head the Treasury. Lincoln said the Treasury was going to Chase. Fearing Lincoln might offer him nothing, Cameron settled for the War Department. A day later he made unauthorized announcements to the press that Seward would be secretary of state, Chase secretary of the Treasury, with himself as secretary of war.

On March 2 Seward supporters called on Lincoln to challenge the incongruity of having their man and Chase sitting on the same cabinet. Lincoln said he admired both men and the country would be better served by having their mutual talents in the cabinet. The debate continued, and Lincoln, showing signs of exasperation, picked up a piece of paper and said, "I had written out my choice here of Secretaries in the Cabinet after a great deal of pains and trouble; and now you tell me I must break the slate and begin all over!" After pausing to let his statement take effect, he asked the delegation if they would prefer Chase for the Treasury, William Dayton as secretary of state, and Seward as minister to England. The alternative shocked the delegation. They withdrew to consult in private with Weed and Seward. One observer reported seeing "more cursing than consultation going on just now."[19]

The delegation, having been outmaneuvered, advised that Chase would go into the cabinet as Treasury secretary with or without Seward in the State Department. This forced Seward to play his last card. He sent Lincoln a note stating "circumstances" had occurred since accepting the state portfolio rendering it now necessary to "withdraw that consent." Lincoln knew the "circumstances" was a ploy to keep Chase out of the cabinet in exchange for

Seward's return. He waited two days, giving Seward time to reconsider the consequences. Monday morning, as the March 4 inauguration procession formed outside Willard's Hotel, Lincoln handed Nicolay a note for Seward: "The public interest, I think, demands that you should [reconsider]; and my personal feelings are deeply enlisted in the same direction. Please consider and answer by 9 o'clock A.M. to-morrow." In the margin of the draft he scrawled for Nicolay's eyes only, "I can't afford to let Seward have the first trick."

After the inauguration Seward met Lincoln at the White House for a confidential discussion. The following day he withdrew his letter and once again accepted the State Department, writing to his wife, "At all events I did not dare go home, or to England, and leave the country to chance." In Seward's opinion the president and the cabinet could not function without him.[20]

Another important change occurred on Inauguration Day. Democrats held a majority in the Senate and were presided over by John C. Breckinridge of Kentucky. At 1:00 p.m. Republicans took control of the Senate presided over by Hannibal Hamlin. Secessionists departed, leaving Lincoln with an upper chamber he knew would support his cabinet nominations. When the Senate convened the following morning, he laid before it the following names:

> William H. Seward of New York, Secretary of State
> Salmon P. Chase of Ohio, Secretary of the Treasury
> Simon Cameron of Pennsylvania, Secretary of War
> Gideon Welles of Connecticut, Secretary of the Navy
> Caleb B. Smith of Indiana, Secretary of the Interior
> Montgomery Blair of Maryland, Postmaster General
> Edward Bates of Missouri, Attorney General

Lincoln had never confirmed a cabinet post with Chase, nor had Chase agreed to one because none had been formally offered. The confusion ended on March 6, when Chase accepted the Treasury post and resigned his seat in the Senate. He wrote to Lincoln, "My distrust in my own judgment in this decision, and of my ability to perform adequately the duties about to devolve on me, is very great; but trusting to your indulgence and humbly invoking divine favor and guidance, I will give my best endeavors to your service and our country's." Lincoln noticed the striking difference between Chase's humble acceptance and the antics perpetrated by Seward and Cameron. Chase knew little about Lincoln, yet in January he decided the president-elect was "*a man to be depended upon.*"[21]

The new Republican Party was a mix of conflicting political philosophies, which few but Lincoln understood when organizing the cabinet. The only issue on which everyone agreed was opposition to the expansion of slavery. Other issues made it impossible for Lincoln to select a cabinet of like-minded men without risking a fatal split in the party. Had Seward, Chase, or Bates become president, they would only have selected cronies. Lincoln once said, "By no act or complicity of mine, shall the Republican party become a mere sucked egg, all shell and no principle in it." Without Lincoln the Republican Party might never have survived.[22]

The cabinet was unique in American history, an experiment carefully designed by the president. Few politicians expected it to succeed, and everyone regarded Lincoln as a novice. The president did not expect his cabinet to work in harmony, but he needed advice. To get it meant manipulating the rivalry among the cabinet members with more dexterity than their collective efforts to manipulate him.

As the cabinet began to function, it predictably divided with Seward-Cameron-Smith on one side and Chase-Welles-Blair on the other. Bates became an observer. Lincoln expected two coalitions to form, and it happened quickly. They all forgot a president could dictate his cabinet's policy-making decisions. Nicolay and Hay remarked, "In weaker hands such a Cabinet would have been a hot-bed of strife; under him it became a tower of strength." But on March 5 neither the cabinet nor the president anticipated an administration drenched in bloodshed.[23]

The first crisis occurred when swarms of office seekers descended on Washington and beat a path to the White House seeking patronage. Alarmed by the influx, George Julian of Indiana wrote, "There was no pause in this business. . . . The pressure was so great and constant that I could scarcely . . . cross the street." To Henry Villard, Lincoln remarked, "Yes, it was bad enough in Springfield, but it was child's play compared with the tussle here. I hardly have a chance to eat or sleep. I am fair game for everybody of that hungry lot."[24]

Office seekers either called at the White House or pestered a cabinet member. Lincoln could not shed them because many were friends and acquaintances. Even though he announced appointments were to be filled by department heads, he felt obligated to find work for those who had supported him. He arranged with Seward to send Judd to Berlin, Charles Francis Adams to London, Dayton to Paris, Gustave Koerner to Madrid, and Cassius Clay to Russia and made room for scores of others.[25]

Cabinet members selected their own aides. Seward made his son Frederick assistant secretary of state, but he also retained a few Southerners loyal

to the Union, such as the indispensable veteran William Hunter, who had
first been appointed chief clerk by John Quincy Adams and held that position ever since.[26]

Chase looked for competence. Having little background in finances, he
chose men with experience. He named George Harrington, a veteran from
previous administrations, assistant secretary because Harrington knew how
to create a financial program for a nation threatened by war. He named Elisha
Whittlesey first comptroller because the Ohioan had served with distinction
under former presidents. Chase also retained several qualified Democrats.
He did load the Department of the Treasury with political friends, but even
they, for the most part, were men of intelligence with good credentials.

Cameron lived up to his reputation for peddling spoils by inundating
the War Department with friends. The top position of chief clerk went to
his faithful crony, John P. Sanderson, one of his dealmakers. Cameron dismissed qualified employees from subordinate positions and replaced them
with chums whose activities traced back to the scandalous Indian transactions. Apart from Cameron's unsavory reputation, he was a practical man
with wide political connections, which in an emergency could be useful to a
president.[27]

Weed's efforts to control patronage failed. Chase would not allow him to
select port collectors, and Blair would not yield to Weed's advice on naming
New York postmasters. Blair named John A. Kasson, an Iowan and close
associate of his brother, first assistant postmaster general and put friends
into other districts. The ever-watchful Horace Greeley, aware of Weed's dis-
gruntlement and Blair's distribution of patronage, wrote, "The thieves hunt
in gangs and each helps all the rest. Three quarters of the post-offices will go
into the hands of corruptionists."[28]

Welles tapped William Faxon, who had helped organize the Republican
Party in Connecticut, as the navy's chief clerk. Bates hired his son Richard
as a payroll clerk in the Justice Department and appointed Titian J. Coffey assistant attorney general. As a young man, Coffey had studied law in
Bates's office. Caleb Smith filled the Interior office with pals, one being John
P. Usher, whom he named assistant secretary. In addition to being Smith's
closest confidant, Usher had worked diligently in Indiana for Lincoln's election. Smith spoke for the entire cabinet when he complained to a friend, "I
am annoyed by the applications for Clerkships. The number is ten times
greater than all the Clerkships in the Department . . . but no one seems
to look over Mason and Dixon's line to the terrible and with lightning-like
velocity spreading fire of hellish treason."[29]

The massive influx of patronage seekers clouded the greater problems rumbling in the Deep South. Anyone listening to the debate in the Senate on March 3 might have gleaned an accurate picture of the oncoming struggle. Problems began on January 5, 1861, when the Buchanan administration dispatched the steamship the *Star of the West* on a secret mission to Charleston for the purpose of provisioning and reinforcing Fort Sumter. The government also issued instructions to Major Robert Anderson, the fort's commander, to fire on any South Carolina batteries engaging the ship. The message, however, traveled by regular mail and reached Charleston after the relief vessel arrived off the harbor. It made little difference. Northern newspapers had already reported the mission to the public. When on January 9 the steamer began moving into the harbor, South Carolinians fired the first shots from Morris Island. Lacking orders, Anderson held his fire. The *Star of the West* turned about and headed back to sea.[30]

The incident festered until March 3, when Louis Wigfall of Texas, delivering a farewell speech in the Senate, said, "The *Star of the West,* flying your flag, swaggered into Charleston harbor with supplies for Fort Sumter. South Carolina struck her between the eyes, and she staggered back; and now, what do you propose to do about it?" After minutes of silence Andrew Johnson stood, eyes aflame, and replied, "I will tell the senator from Texas what I would do about it. I speak only for myself. But if I were President, as James Buchanan today is, and as Abraham Lincoln to-morrow will be, I would arrest the senator and his friends on the charge of high treason; I would have them tried by a jury of their countrymen, and, if convicted, by the eternal God, I would hang them!" For Lincoln tomorrow had come, and for the rookie president and his cabinet the business left unresolved in Charleston Harbor became a slow fuse burning steadily toward a massive powder keg.[31]

CHAPTER 5

"If this must be done, I must do it"

On his first full day of work Lincoln found a message on his desk from the outgoing secretary of war, Joseph Holt. Major Robert Anderson reported having provisions for six weeks and said Fort Sumter could not be approached without first neutralizing Charleston's batteries. President Buchanan had never mentioned Sumter's condition, so Lincoln summoned Holt and asked for particulars. Holt said Anderson's situation "takes the Department by surprise, as his previous correspondence contained no such intimation." Lincoln conferred with seventy-five-year-old General Winfield Scott, who rambled through Fort Sumter's problems and finally said, "Evacuation seems almost inevitable."

On March 6 Lincoln called his first cabinet meeting, which Edward Bates described as "uninteresting." Lincoln had never conducted a business meeting. A cabinet provided him with a chain of command, which meant he would have to learn to delegate. Meanwhile, office seekers continued to distract him from the business of governing.[1]

Three days later he presented the Sumter problem to a shocked cabinet, which asked whether the garrison could be reinforced. Lincoln referred the question to Scott, who requested "a fleet of war vessels and transports, 5,000 additional regular troops, 20,000 volunteers," and "six to eight months" to assemble them. Scott said funds would have to be authorized by Congress, which was no longer in session. He said the time for rescuing the fort had "passed away nearly a month ago" and surrender or starvation was merely "a question of time." He did not know how many regulars were in the army, nor had Cameron thought to ask, but in March 1861 the army consisted of 1,100 officers and 15,250 enlisted men scattered mostly among frontier outposts.[2]

Lincoln wanted to hold Sumter, but he also wanted "the Administration to get in working order." According to Gideon Welles, the president "was adverse to offensive measures and anxious to avoid them." Before adjourning, Lincoln invited Brigadier General Joseph G. Totten, chief of engineers, to present options considered by the Buchanan administration. Then he asked each cabinet member, "Assuming it possible to now provision Fort-Sumter [*sic*] . . . is it wise to attempt it? Please give me your opinion, in writing."[3]

Lincoln received mixed advice. William Henry Seward advised against a relief expedition, predicting it would "probably initiate civil war." Salmon Chase disagreed with Seward, saying relief of Sumter would not "produce such consequences" but cautioned against provoking a conflict requiring money to enlist an army. Simon Cameron agreed with Seward and repeated Scott's position. Welles labeled any effort to relieve Sumter "unwise." Caleb Smith believed a relief effort might be successful but disapproved of it. Montgomery Blair wrote, "The evacuation of Fort Sumpter [*sic*] . . . will convince the rebels that the administration lacks firmness" and urged the fort be provisioned "to maintain the authority of the United States." Bates said the federal government had the legal right to maintain the fort, but he would rather evacuate it than be an instrument in fomenting civil war. Lincoln counted Seward, Cameron, Welles, Smith, and Bates as against a relief expedition, with Chase weakly and Blair strongly in favor of it.

Chase continued to mull over the problem. He decided the nation should first enforce its dominion everywhere but recognize secession in the break-away states as "accomplished through the complicity of the late administration." He also believed the government should stop the spread of secession elsewhere because the Confederacy would tire of its experiment and rejoin the Union. Such wishful thinking demonstrated how poorly Chase understood the determination of Jefferson Davis. Had Blair known Chase's inner thoughts, he would have shamed them. Blair knew Confederate leaders had clearly organized a government and believed the North lacked the courage to interfere with secession. The evacuation of Sumter, said Blair, would support that belief, and no expense should be spared to defend the fort.[4]

Lincoln spoke privately with other officers who disagreed with Scott. Blair's insistence the fort be provisioned came from an earlier idea presented by former navy lieutenant Gustavus Vasa Fox, Mrs. Blair's brother-in-law. Having once surveyed Charleston Harbor, Fox said shallow draft vessels could pass over the bar at night, run to Sumter with reinforcements and supplies, and return to sea before daylight. Buchanan had flatly rejected Fox's plan. Scott disparaged the scheme because it was a navy plan. Because Blair, the only West Point man in the cabinet, promoted the plan, Lincoln listened.[5]

To Cameron's preference for evacuation, Lincoln said "to so abandon that position . . . would be utterly ruinous," warning, "It would discourage friends of the Union, embolden its adversaries, and go far to insure [Confederate] recognition abroad; that in fact would be our national destruction consummated." This, Lincoln ruled, cannot be allowed.[6]

The Fox plan became the only alternative to the Seward-Cameron evacuation proposal. Fox had spent nineteen of his thirty-nine years in the navy before resigning to engage in more lucrative civilian pursuits. He was energetic, enormously resourceful, even-tempered, and immensely persuasive. While commanding steamships, he became intimately acquainted with Charleston's harbor, the arrangement of Fort Sumter, and the location of shore batteries prior to 1856. Navy men believed Fox's plan would have succeeded in February, before more batteries were added. Although Scott disagreed, Fox said with enough ships and men, he could still reinforce Sumter and land enough provisions to keep the fort succored for two months. This would give the president more time to bargain with the South.[7]

Lincoln wanted to know more and authorized Cameron to send Fox to Charleston to speak with Major Anderson and Governor Francis W. Pickens. Fox asked a Charleston friend, Commander Henry J. Hartstene, to make arrangements for meeting with both men. Fox reached Charleston the night of March 20 and explained his mission to Hartstene. Together they met with the governor and Brigadier General Pierre G. T. Beauregard, who commanded Charleston's defenses. Believing Fox had come to arrange Sumter's evacuation, Beauregard permitted him to go to the fort with Hartstene as escort. That night Fox spent two hours with Anderson, who thought any relief of the fort by sea would fail. The major also expected to be out of provisions by April 15. As Fox prepared to leave, he heard boats moving about below but could not see them. This confirmed his impression that a night relief operation could succeed.[8]

Anderson thought about Fox's plan and on the following day wrote the War Department, "I have examined the [landing] point alluded to by Mr. Fox last night. A vessel lying there will be under the fire of thirteen guns from Fort Moultrie." Anderson suggested a better location but warned that a ship drawing ten feet would require forty feet of staging.[9]

Lincoln remained undecided. Seward, who advocated evacuation, said he could save the Union by peaceful policies. Because Sumter was "practically useless," he would not want to "provoke war in any way now." He wanted nothing done to irritate Charleston's governor because he believed a strong Union party still existed in South Carolina.[10]

On March 25 Lincoln sent Stephen A. Hurlbut of Illinois, a former Charleston lawyer, to confer with James Petigru, a South Carolina Unionist, to test whether Seward's statements were true. Hurlbut traveled as a private citizen but was accompanied by Lamon. While Lamon hobnobbed with secessionists at the Charleston Hotel, Hurlbut stayed in the house of his sister and visited old friends and former neighbors. Governor Pickens treated Lamon as the president's official "messenger," spoke with him privately, and allowed him to visit Fort Sumter. On returning, Hurlbut advised Lincoln: "[Petigru] is now the only man in the city of Charleston who avowedly adheres to the Union . . . I have no hesitation in reporting . . . that separate nationality is a fixed fact." Lamon quoted the governor as saying, "Nothing can prevent war except the acquiescence of the President . . . and his unalterable resolve not to attempt any reinforcement of the Southern forts." Both reports contradicted Seward's advice.[11]

On March 26 Beauregard asked Anderson to surrender and avoid war, promising "transportation out of this harbor for yourself and command." He also demanded the fort be turned over with all ammunition and guns in working condition. Anderson snubbed the general's offer and replied, "I shall never, so help me God, leave this fort alive."[12]

Sumter's fate continued under discussion for three weeks without a plan. Seward's assessment of Union sentiment in South Carolina had been wrong, and Lincoln doubted whether the situation was different anywhere in the South. The fate of Fort Pickens at Pensacola also came into play. When Lincoln first discussed Sumter with the cabinet, Bates pressed him to reinforce Pickens and suggested the entire coast from South Carolina to Texas be guarded by the "entire power" of the navy. The problem was not new. On March 5 Lincoln issued verbal orders to reinforce all forts still in Federal hands but learned four days later Cameron had done nothing. On March 11 he put the order in writing. Welles sent the seven-gun USS *Mohawk* and a troop transport to Fort Pickens, assuming that would be enough.[13]

On March 28 Lincoln hosted the first state dinner at the White House, after which he invited the cabinet into a private room. Clearly annoyed, he said Scott had just advised Cameron to evacuate forts Pickens and Sumter. Scott went too far, writing, "Our Southern friends are clear the evacuation of both the forts would instantly soothe and give confidence to the eight remaining slaveholding States, and render their cordial adherence to this Union perpetual." Lincoln recognized Seward's influence, and Cameron made no comment. After a long silence Blair spoke. He angrily denounced Scott for mixing politics with professional duties, spurned his advice, and aimed his remarks mainly at Seward, whose peace policy he aggressively criticized.[14]

Unsolicited advice came from other sources. Neal Dow, Republican leader from Maine, said his state would approve evacuation because "it is undoubtedly a Military *necessity*. . . ." Stephen Douglas thought Anderson should be withdrawn because South Carolina was entitled to Fort Sumter. But on March 28, a few hours before the state dinner, Trumbull had introduced a resolution to the Senate to make it "the duty of the President to use all the means in his power to hold and to protect the public property of the United States."[15]

Lincoln suspended the meeting until the following day. According to Montgomery Meigs, the president could not sleep. Fox had returned confident Sumter could be reinforced and supplied by night. The time had come for the president to act. He could not count on the cabinet to work in concert. The full weight of governing descended on him. Meigs called Lincoln's task "the last hope of free government on the earth."[16]

Jefferson Davis and Governor Pickens had discussed Sumter with the same indecisiveness as Lincoln. On March 1 Secretary of War Leroy P. Walker thought Sumter should "be in our possession at the earliest possible moment" and said the South's "first blow must be successful." Two days later Beauregard reached Charleston and said Sumter, if reinforced by Federal troops, would become "a perfect Gibraltar." He asked for time to add batteries before reducing the fort.[17]

In early March three Southern commissioners—former congressman Martin J. Crawford of Georgia, Mobile newspaperman John Forsyth, and Louisiana governor Andre B. Roman—arrived in Washington, D.C. Secretary of State Robert A. Toombs had sent them to buy time, spy on the Lincoln administration, and seek recognition for the South. Barred by ordinary diplomatic channels from speaking directly to Lincoln or his cabinet, they recruited Senator William M. Gwin of California, a Southern sympathizer and Seward's liaison. Before becoming secretary of state, Seward had remained close to the secession movement and proclaimed his personal policy of peace and conciliation. Gwin assured Davis that under Seward's guidance Lincoln would seek a peaceful settlement. When the administration failed to recognize the Southern envoys, Gwin appeared at the State Department and told Seward to receive the commissioners or Sumter would be attacked.[18]

Seward dodged the issue, and Gwin lost his effectiveness as an intermediary. According to Gwin, Seward was to be the administration's "ruling power," and the commissioners wondered why no reaction had occurred after threatening to attack Sumter. They cheered up, based on State Department rumors, when the *New York Herald* announced Sumter would be evacuated "within ten days." Toombs took advantage of the rumor and ordered the commissioners to include in their demands the evacuation of Fort Pickens. Seward rebuffed a visit from their secretary, saying he did not recognize the Confederate States as an independent nation and would not communicate with them. The commissioners decided not to advise Toombs of Seward's message but lingered in Washington to gather intelligence.

Seward fell into the commissioners' game when he engaged John A. Campbell, an associate justice of the Supreme Court, as a peace intermediary. Campbell agreed with Seward's peace plan, sympathized with the South, and acted as a double agent. After meeting the commissioners, Campbell told Seward it was not right to reject them. Seward replied it was "impossible to receive . . . them personally" but that Sumter would be evacuated and collision avoided, though "no change is contemplated at present in respect to Pickens." Campbell informed the commissioners and then sent the same information to Jefferson Davis. Seward also gave Campbell a written memorandum: "The President may desire to supply Sumter, but will not do so without giving notice to Governor Pickens." Campbell relayed the information to the commissioners, adding that he doubted Sumter would be reinforced. The commissioners finally returned to Richmond because Campbell, though he continued to keep them informed, was now in direct communication with President Davis.[19]

On March 29 Lincoln reconvened the cabinet and read the members' opinions regarding forts Sumter and Pickens. This time the vote was four to two favoring reinforcement. Cameron avoided the meeting. Welles and Bates joined Chase and Blair on reinforcing both forts. Bates thought Southern ports should be "closed" to commerce by ships of the navy. Chase advocated holding both forts, arguing that evacuating one but holding the other would still lead to war. If war was the consequence of protecting Federal property, then let the South initiate the first blow. Welles favored provisioning Sumter but thought adding troops would appear warlike. He agreed that Pickens should be made impregnable and naval forces should be increased on the southern coast. Blair condemned Scott's unsolicited political views and threatened to resign if the president listened to the general's advice. He said Sumter should be resupplied immediately. "South Carolina is the head and front of this rebellion, and when that State is safely delivered from the authority of the United States it will strike a blow against our authority from which it will take us years of bloody strife to recover."[20]

With Cameron absent, Seward and Smith remained the only holdouts. Seward still insisted Sumter be evacuated, but he favored strengthening Pickens. He ignored Chase's point that strengthening Pickens would lead to war just as quickly as defending Sumter. Smith also missed the point, arguing "Major Anderson's command be unconditionally withdrawn" but all other forts defended and Southern ports "blockaded." Smith could not explain how his proposal, with a blockade added, would not lead to war.[21]

Lincoln took interest in the shifting attitudes of the cabinet. He had already met with Fox and decided to reprovision Sumter using a plan similar to the one proposed in February. As the cabinet meeting concluded, Lincoln sent orders to Welles and Cameron to launch the expedition no later than April 6.[22]

On January 21 Buchanan had sent the *Brooklyn* to Fort Pickens with reinforcements, but the infantry never went ashore. On March 12 Lincoln ordered Scott to land the troops, but nothing happened. Instead, Captain Henry A. Adams arranged an unauthorized truce with General Braxton Bragg, the Confederate commander, and used the arrangement as a reason to detain the troops. A second relief operation sailed from New York on March 16, but Adams blocked it from going ashore.[23]

When Lincoln authorized the Sumter expedition on March 29, he believed Pickens was safe, but in early April he learned the troops were still on ships. Nevertheless, he told Fox, who was in New York preparing the Sumter mission, to proceed on schedule. Fox confirmed he would sail on April 9, which gave Lincoln time to cancel the expedition, but he kept the date because Sumter would be out of provisions. On April 6, at Seward's request, he dispatched Robert Chew of the State Department to inform Governor Pickens that supply ships were being sent but there would be "no effort to throw in men, arms, or ammunition," unless the enemy resisted.[24]

While Fox organized the Sumter expedition, Seward staged a theatrical drama with the War Department to secure Fort Pickens. Having done everything possible to sacrifice Sumter, he now authored a scheme to assault Pensacola, Florida, as if this would somehow not be construed by the South as warring. Ignoring General Scott, Seward wanted the president to hear from a qualified officer recently back from the Gulf of Mexico and brought Captain Meigs of the engineer corps to the White House. When Lincoln asked whether Pickens could be held, Meigs said, "Certainly, if the navy would do its duty." The president asked who should command Pickens, and Meigs said he could but not as a captain. Seward turned to the president and said, "Captain Meigs must be promoted."[25]

Lincoln ordered Scott to support the Pickens program, so Meigs returned to the White House with Seward to discuss plans with the general. Scott approved the expedition, but Meigs required help from the navy. In his haste to get the operation to sea, Seward neglected to inform Welles about it. Meigs, however, discussed the plan with his next-door neighbor, navy Lieutenant David Dixon Porter, who believed by quick action Pickens could be saved and the Pensacola Navy Yard recaptured.[26]

Fort Pickens stood on Santa Rosa Island at the eastern entrance to Pensacola Harbor: two Confederate forts occupied the western entrance, protecting Pensacola's navy yard and Bragg's headquarters. Only forty-six federal soldiers and thirty ordinary seamen occupied Fort Pickens. Bragg could send several thousand rebels against the fort at any time. The Meigs-Porter plan called for a transport to land troops at Pickens while a Union warship steamed boldly past Confederate batteries to take position inside the bay, thereby preventing Bragg from mounting an amphibious assault against Pickens.

On April 1 Seward brought Meigs and Porter to the White House for a meeting. Meigs explained his plan to put six companies of soldiers ashore at Pickens, and Porter suggested using the eleven-gun steamer USS *Powhatan* for the expedition because it had been decommissioned. Seward thought Porter should command the *Powhatan* and suggested the mission be kept secret. "But what," Lincoln asked, "will Uncle Gideon say?" Seward warned of leaks in the Navy Department and replied, "I will make it all right with Mr. Welles. This is the only way, sir, the thing can be done."[27]

Lincoln asked what orders were needed, and Porter, according to his account, retired to another room to write them. He relieved Captain Samuel Mercer of command of the *Powhatan,* put himself in charge, and ordered Commodore Samuel L. Breese at the Brooklyn Navy Yard to arm and provision the ship for an undisclosed mission. "She is bound on secret service," Porter added, "and you will under no circumstances communicate to the Navy department the fact that she is fitting out." Lincoln signed the orders, but he turned to Seward and said, "See that I don't burn my fingers."

Porter and Meigs departed for New York, but Seward, after promising "to make it right with Mr. Welles," did nothing. After trying to block Welles's appointment to the cabinet, he now exercised unauthorized license in directing the affairs of the navy. His meddling in the Pickens expedition created ten days of chaos and almost ended Porter's career.[28]

Confusion began immediately. Unaware of Seward's interference, Welles issued orders for Captain Mercer to fit out the *Powhatan* for the Sumter expedition. Meanwhile, Porter arrived at the navy yard with orders from Lincoln. Captain Andrew Hull Foote thought it odd Welles had never mentioned releasing the ship to Porter. Thinking an error had been made, he prepared to telegraph Welles for clarification when Porter interceded.

"If you must telegraph," he said, "send a message to the President or Mr. Seward." He reminded Foote the president's orders specifically excluded the Navy Department.

Meigs arrived to confirm Porter's orders, but Foote remained troubled. On April 4 Foote sent an unclear message to Welles mentioning only Meigs and referred to "certain preparations" being made to place "things" on board vessels "going to sea." Welles thought Foote's allusion to "preparations" meant the Sumter expedition and that Meigs was part of it, and he urged Foote to hurry.[29]

Foote made another attempt to invite Welles's curiosity: "I am executing orders received from the Government through a Navy officer as well as the Army officer." Welles knew of no orders from the government, suspected Southern sympathizers of plotting to steal the ship, and immediately tele- graphed Foote to "delay the *Powhatan* for further instructions." Foote sent the order to Porter, who replied, "We are telegraphing Mr. Seward. Meigs thinks Mr. Welles telegram is bogus. Would he . . . dare countermand an order of the president? I will be at the yard at six o'clock in the morning."[30]

Late on April 5 Meigs informed Seward that Welles was diverting the *Powhatan* for the Sumter expedition. At 11:00 p.m., with his project at risk, Seward stormed into Welles's room at Willard's Hotel, shook the slumbering secretary awake, and waved in his face the telegram from Meigs. He accused Welles of obstructing the Pickens expedition and insisted that the navy sec- retary retract it immediately. Wiping sleep from his eyes, Welles demanded an explanation. Seward replied, "It related to the *Powhatan* and Porter's command." Welles retorted, "Porter has no command." The discussion became heated, so Welles dressed and suggested calling on the president. Lincoln was astounded by the late visit. Thinking Seward had cleared *Pow- hatan's* mission with Welles, Lincoln admitted the ship had been diverted. Welles went to his office and returned with a handful of messages showing orders to Breese, Foote, and Mercer. Lincoln agreed that Sumter was more important than Pickens and directed Seward to "return the *Powhatan* to Mercer without delay."

Although not prone to making apologies, Seward admitted he had learned a lesson "from this affair, and . . . had better confine his labors to his own department." Lincoln took responsibility and said "it was careless- ness, heedlessness on his part." Welles went back to bed furious with Seward but hoped some good would come from it. Seward kept the problem alive, however, by waiting until morning to cancel Porter's mission.[31]

Early the next morning Meigs sailed with four companies of infantry and waited off Staten Island for Porter. Two hours later Porter sailed from Brooklyn. As the *Powhatan* steamed out of sight, Foote received Seward's message to Porter: "Give the *Powhatan* up to Captain Mercer." Foote sent Lieutenant Francis A. Roe on a fast steamer to overhaul Porter and return the gunboat. Reaching Porter at the Narrows, Roe handed him Seward's order, which Porter read and handed back, replying "I received my orders from the President and shall proceed and execute them." On April 12 Porter and Meigs reached Fort Pickens, put infantry and artillery ashore, and successfully defended the fort against an enemy assault.[32]

Seward's interference stemmed from a belief that Lincoln could not run the administration without him. Cameron claimed Seward was also trying to run the War Department and threatened to arrest Meigs. Welles said, "It was a misfortune of Mr. Seward . . . that he delighted in oblique and indirect movements . . . to control and direct the war and navy movements, although he had neither the knowledge nor the aptitude that was essential for either." Welles claimed Seward's "craving desire" to control the administration never changed, which again became apparent on April 1, when Seward sent an astonishing memorandum to Lincoln titled, "Some Thoughts for the President's Consideration." The first sentence read, "We are at the end of a month's administration, and yet without a policy, either domestic or foreign." Seward plunged ahead with suggestions about how to run the government.[33]

The administration actually had no stated policy, only Lincoln's inaugural address. Carl Schurz expressed public sentiment best, writing the president, "Any distinct line of policy, be it war or recognition of the Southern Confederacy, would be better than this uncertain state of things." Seward deeply believed the president needed advice, and in many respects he was right. He also suspected the president did not understand Washington politics and stepped forward to save the country from disaster. He abhorred disunion, regarding "civil war as the most disastrous and deplorable of national calamities."[34]

After the Senate adjourned on March 28, Seward felt freer to assert himself because his critics had left town. By setting himself up as Lincoln's "premier," he turned Welles, Chase, and Blair against him. The first setback came when Lincoln disregarded his advice and ordered Sumter provisioned, and then Welles caught him meddling in naval affairs. Seward's own bailiwick required attention because his foreign policy "resembled a reckless invention of a mind driven to extreme measures." England, France, and Spain wanted to intervene in Mexico; rebels overthrew the Dominican government; and Jefferson Davis planned to open diplomatic relations with Europe. If the State Department did not soon devise its own policies, the old principles of the Monroe Doctrine would be undone. To prevent this outcome, Seward recklessly recommended war be declared against France and Spain if "satisfactory explanations are not received" as a way to mitigate problems with the South.[35]

Seward's "Thoughts" might have led to his departure from the cabinet. Instead, Lincoln coddled Seward and tolerated his suggestion that "some member of the Cabinet" be designated to decide national policy, and once adopted, "debates on it must end, and all agree and abide." Seward volunteered to be that man, carefully adding, "I neither seek to evade nor assume [this] responsibility." Lincoln patiently rejected the offer, replying without rebuke, "If this must be done, I must do it." On the day Seward submitted his "Thoughts" and received the president's answer, the secretary of state's premiership ended.[36]

Until the night Seward confessed his intrusion into naval affairs, Welles and Fox expected the Sumter expedition to arrive on schedule. Lincoln said if the effort to "send bread to Anderson" drew fire, the South would be unable to convince Europe the Union started the war. On April 6 Chew departed for Charleston to inform Governor Pickens a supply vessel was coming, but Porter disappeared with the *Powhatan* and set the Sumter expedition back four days.[37]

Chew delivered Lincoln's message to the governor on the eighth, not knowing Seward had upset the schedule. Beauregard stopped mail from going to the fort, and with communications cut, rebel intermediaries told Major Anderson that Washington had abandoned the fort. Lincoln, however, had written Anderson under Cameron's signature, and the message reached the fort hours before Beauregard terminated communications. The letter promised that a relief expedition would arrive on the eleventh or twelfth and asked Anderson to hold out, but if attacked in force and "capitulation becomes necessary, you are authorized to make it."[38]

Relieving the fort on April 11 might have produced a better outcome had Seward not snatched the *Powhatan* from the navy and if Lincoln had not sent Chew to Charleston to keep a promise made by Seward. On April 10 Confederate war secretary Walker authorized Beauregard to demand the surrender of the fort "and if this is refused," he said, "proceed . . . to reduce it." Beauregard asked Hartstene whether Union ships could relieve the fort at night and received an affirmative answer. Davis said the South could not afford to allow the expedition to succeed.[39]

Davis considered the Confederacy independently sovereign, permanently dissolved from the Union, with every right to resist an invading expedition, even though its purpose was humanitarian. On April 11 Beauregard sent three officers under a flag of truce to demand Sumter's surrender. Anderson replied, "I will await the first shot, and if you do not batter us to pieces we will be starved out in a few days." Anderson kept one eye on the Atlantic, watching for the overdue relief ships, and the other eye on Charleston's batteries.[40]

Anderson's reference to being soon starved out prompted Beauregard to advise Walker of the fort's condition. Walker told Beauregard to ask Anderson when he intended to evacuate. He answered, "By noon on the 15th." A three-day delay did not satisfy Beauregard. At nightfall he advised Anderson that Sumter would be fired upon at 4:20 a.m. on April 12.[41]

At dawn a signal shell arced across the harbor from James Island, after which thirty guns and seventeen mortars opened on Fort Sumter. At 7:00 a.m. Anderson replied in kind. Eight hours later three Union ships appeared off the bar. The relief ships had arrived but too late. The firing continued until dark with little damage to the fort. On April 13 Beauregard renewed the bombardment, while Anderson's garrison ate the last pork and rice. While Union sailors watched from sea, Anderson shot the last cartridges, spiked the guns, destroyed everything of military value, and surrendered.[42]

The expeditionary force's late arrival traced directly back to Seward's orders, which had forced Welles to assemble a squadron of different ships. He had also given Captain Mercer authority to "repel by force" any interference by the rebels. The *Pawnee* and *Pocahontas* were posted at Norfolk, and the *Powhatan* and *Harriet Lane* were located at New York. Welles instructed all four warships, along with Fox's transports, to rendezvous on the morning of April 11 ten miles east of Charleston's lighthouse. All of Welles's carefully worded instructions to relieve Fort Sumter malfunctioned when Porter took the *Powhatan* to Fort Pickens.[43]

At 2:00 p.m. Mercer arrived and explained the diversion of the *Powhatan* to Fox. Thirty minutes later Anderson lowered Fort Sumter's flag. Commander John P. Gillis of the *Pocahontas* sent a boat under a flag of truce and negotiated the evacuation of the fort. On April 14 the transfer of men began. "With colors flying and drums beating," Anderson saluted the flag, stepped with his garrison onto the steamer *Isabel,* and bade farewell to Fort Sumter.[44]

The surrender of Fort Sumter and the reinforcement of Pickens marked the first six weeks of Lincoln's administration. They also marked the end of

Seward's efforts to conciliate the South. Lincoln had spoken to the South in his inaugural address: "In *your* hands, my dissatisfied fellow countrymen, and not in *mine,* is the momentous issue of civil war. The Government will not assail *you.* You can have no conflict without being yourselves the aggressors."[45]

Some contemporaries blamed Lincoln for tricking South Carolina into starting the war. Orville Browning talked to Lincoln ten weeks later and quoted the president as saying, "The plan succeeded. They attacked Sumter—it fell, and thus, did more service than it otherwise could." Yet some facts remain. Lincoln proposed sending supplies without reinforcing the fort and advised Governor Pickens the expedition was humanitarian. Whatever Lincoln meant, or what Browning intended to mean by quoting Lincoln as saying the "plan succeeded," one matter is clear: in Charleston Harbor on April 12, 1861, General Beauregard fired the shots that launched the American Civil War.[46]

Often accused of having no policy, the president now had one everyone understood. His patent reply when asked about his policy had been "My policy is to have no policy," which many believed he meant. He preferred peaceful ways to restore the Union, but he vowed not to surrender the forts, which he knew might lead to war. He also promised not to be the first to spill blood. Sumter gave Lincoln political value, not military value. One can say he baited South Carolina into firing the first shots. If so, the cabinet became the muddling instrument for achieving it. Sumter also gave Lincoln a policy everyone understood.[47]

CHAPTER 6

"The president is the best of us"

The Confederate shelling of Fort Sumter unified the North and created a common cause for the cabinet—to preserve the Union. Lincoln acted with unprecedented swiftness, almost as if the Sumter affair fit neatly into his plans. On April 15, one day after the fort's surrender, Lincoln issued a proclamation calling for seventy-five thousand ninety-day militia. The document commanded treasonable elements to disperse within twenty days and stated that the first objective of the Union would be to repossess Federal property seized by the Confederacy. He reconvened Congress on July 4 in extra session to "consider and determine" what measures were required to ensure the public safety.[1]

The cabinet met at 10:00 a.m. and remained in conference until nightfall. People came and went, warning rail and telegraph communications would be cut and Washington isolated. Salmon Chase and Simon Cameron asked for a half-million troops, but William Seward argued for 75,000, the number General Winfield Scott said would be enough to end the war in ninety days. Montgomery Blair flatly disagreed and said Seward could not shake his policy of reconciliation. Stephen Douglas, who on March 15 had shouted in the Senate, "War is disunion. War is final, eternal separation," lobbied for 200,000 volunteers. Orville Browning suggested 300,000, and Horace Greeley thought a half-million volunteers would have responded to Lincoln's call had he asked. Douglas returned to Illinois and worked assiduously with Western Democrats to support the president. On June 3, soon after declaring, "The shortest way to peace is the most stupendous and unanimous preparation for war," Douglas passed away in Chicago.[2]

Regardless of the number of troops authorized, Cameron faced a gigantic task. Southern sympathizers surrounded the capital, disloyal elements infested the city, and the man in charge, General Scott, was too feeble to take the field. The White House remained open and without security, there were always strangers seeking patronage camped in the hallways leading to the president's office, and any one of them could have been an assassin. The lack of security prompted Lincoln to remark if he were General Beauregard, he would take Washington.[3]

Had 500,000 men volunteered, they could not have been armed, clothed, or paid. Cameron assumed the title "general" without knowing anything about war and lamented, "Oh it was a terrible time. We were entirely un-prepared. . . . There were very few people who believed the war would last for more than a few weeks [but] we had no guns, and no ammunition." The treasury was empty but for a small loan arranged by Chase.[4]

The North enjoyed the advantage of population with 20 million inhabit-ants compared with the South's 6 million whites and 3.5 million slaves. The Union also enjoyed an enormous advantage in industrial output, railways, and individual wealth. The South, however, was better prepared for war. The government controlled state militias and had 82,000 one-year volunteers enrolled. The men were already formed into regiments and armed with weapons seized from Federal arsenals. Reacting to Lincoln's proclamation, Jefferson Davis increased the number of men under arms to 150,000. The South also had the best products of West Point to lead the army.[5]

Cameron proposed a strategy calling for the capture of Southern coastal cities, but the cabinet preferred Scott's constrictive blockade, dubbed the "Anaconda plan" because it squeezed the Confederacy into submission from all sides. Bates agreed with Scott's plan and endorsed a blockade of Southern ports, command of the Mississippi, protection of Washington, control of the Harpers Ferry armory, and reinforcement of the navy yard at Norfolk, Virginia. Scott's plan put a heavy load on Gideon Welles, whose ninety-ship navy was scattered and partly out of commission.[6]

Lincoln tried in his proclamation to put the coming conflict into perspec-tive. Expectations of a short war troubled him. "People of the seceded States, like those of the loyal ones, are American citizens, with essentially the same characteristics," he said. "We must make up our minds that man for man the soldier from the South will be a match for the soldier of the North and *vice versa*."[7]

Chase believed cabinet members were overly conservative, dangerously engaged in their own ambitions, or hopelessly incompetent. Doubting whether Cameron could organize the war effort, he inserted himself into the department as the secretary's guiding influence. Cameron accepted Chase's help, which included issuing orders, consulting on strategy, and planning battles. Chase influenced decisions in which neither he nor Cameron had any experience, such as determining military appointments and selecting generals. Although Chase claimed he "never undertook to do any thing in [Cameron's] department, except when asked to give help," the War Depart-ment became Chase's second job.[8]

Raising a militia of 75,000 became Cameron's task. He assigned quotas to states and told governors where to assemble the regiments for deployment.

A typical regiment consisted of 37 officers and 743 men. Cameron requested 94 regiments, 5 major generals, 17 brigadier generals, and 73,369 officers and men. Twenty regiments came from border states: Virginia (3), North Carolina (2), Tennessee (2), Arkansas (1), and 4 each from Maryland, Kentucky, and Missouri.[9]

Governor John Letcher of Virginia replied, "Your object is to subjugate the Southern States, and [your] requisition will not be complied with." The following day Virginia joined the Confederacy. Blair anticipated the defection and, acting unofficially on behalf of Cameron, offered Colonel Robert E. Lee command of the Union army. Two days later Lee resigned.[10]

On May 6 Arkansas seceded, followed a month later by North Carolina. Governor Isham G. Harris of Tennessee refused to supply "a single man for purpose of coercion, but 50,000, if necessary, for the defense of our rights and those of our Southern brethren." Eastern and western Tennessee remained strongly divided, and it took Harris until June 8 to pull the state out of the Union.[11]

Border states fumed at the order. Beriah Magoffin of Kentucky said the state "will furnish no troops for the wicked purpose of subduing her sister Southern States." Kentucky remained loyal, but part of the state supported the South. Cameron promised Governor Thomas A. Hicks that Maryland militia would only be used to protect Washington. Governor Claiborne F. Jackson of Missouri called Cameron's request for militia "illegal, unconstitutional, and revolutionary . . . and cannot be complied with."[12]

Forty-eight hours after Lincoln's call for troops, Governor John A. Andrew of Massachusetts activated four regiments and informed Cameron that half would come by rail through Baltimore, a city of 200,000, and half by steamer. Brigadier General Benjamin F. Butler, a politically powerful Massachusetts Democrat with a penchant for acting independently, commanded the troops.[13]

Secessionists demanded the Maryland legislature be called into session, but Governor Hicks feared rebellious leaders would take the state out of the Union. Colonel Edward F. Jones, by marching the Sixth Massachusetts Regiment through Baltimore against the governor's wishes, provoked a crisis. "Plug-ugly" hoodlums disputed the regiment's one-mile march through the city to the Washington terminal. When they fired on the column, the Sixth Massachusetts returned fire, killing nine hoodlums but carrying four corpses of its own. Rioters howled for secession and threatened new demonstrations if more Yankees passed through town. Learning another regiment was on the way, Hicks ordered railroad bridges dismembered between Harrisburg, Philadelphia, and Baltimore.[14]

The loss of bridges disturbed Cameron. Having invested in the Northern Central, which ran between Harrisburg and Baltimore, Cameron counted on making money during the war, giving him an incentive to do everything possible to keep Maryland in the Union. Lincoln wrote Hicks and promised to keep Union troops out of Baltimore. With Baltimore calmed, Hicks returned to Annapolis, Maryland's capital, and discovered several ships offshore with Butler's Eighth Massachusetts in one group and Marshall Lefferts's Seventh New York in the other. Hicks told Butler to go away. He appealed to Lincoln, insisting "no more troops be ordered or allowed to pass through Maryland."[15]

Surrounded by Maryland and Virginia, Washington felt like a city under siege. Hundreds of army and navy officers resigned their commissions and joined the Confederacy. Clerks followed with their families. The cabinet declared the exodus good riddance, but in the city prices rose, and businesses closed. After the Sixth Massachusetts reached the city, Lincoln began looking for Lefferts's regiment. On April 23 he spoke to the Massachusetts men and said, "I begin to believe that there is no North. The Seventh Regiment is a myth. You are the only real thing." John Hay remembered Lincoln returning to the White House muttering, "Why don't they come! Why don't they come!"[16]

During an April 23 cabinet meeting Bates asked why Virginia and Maryland caused so much trouble when "we hurt nobody; we frighten nobody; and do our utmost to offend nobody." Chase replied, "Let me beg you to remember that the disunionists have anticipated us in everything, and as yet we have accomplished nothing but the destruction of our own property." He urged Lincoln to let Scott use the army to keep the rebels from taking over Maryland.[17]

Butler ignored Governor Hick's request not to land troops, but his transport went aground off Annapolis. With Lefferts's help, Butler moved his men ashore, repaired an old locomotive, and on April 24 began feeding troops into Washington. Rather than go himself, Butler waited at Annapolis for more regiments and sent them by rail to the capital. Scott approved Butler's methods and put him in charge of the Department of Annapolis, which consisted of an area twenty miles on both sides of the tracks running to Washington.[18]

With Butler using Annapolis as a staging area, Hicks moved the state legislature to Frederick. Scott predicted the state would secede. As an extra precaution, Lincoln authorized Scott to suspend the privilege of the writ of habeas corpus if Maryland threatened any part of the military line between Pennsylvania and Washington.[19]

Suspending the writ of habeas corpus allowed the government to arrest and hold without a warrant anyone suspected of aiding the Confederacy. Arrests were made. John Merryman went to prison for being an officer in a secessionist drill company. He obtained a writ of habeas corpus from Chief Justice Roger B. Taney, which entitled him to a fair trial in a civil court or release from imprisonment. Lincoln asked Bates if Taney could supersede the executive. Bates replied, "No judicial officer had the power to take a prisoner or soldier out of the hand[s] of the Pres[ident], by Habeas Corpus." Lincoln denied the writ, and Taney said the president had overstepped the law. Having sworn Lincoln into office "to faithfully execute" the laws, Taney also expected him to obey them. Lincoln was too busy to engage in a debate over presidential war powers and ignored Taney's rebuke. Because the action continued to fester, Lincoln reiterated Bates's position on habeas corpus when Congress reconvened on July 4.[20]

General Scott's fears of Maryland's secession were overblown. Unrest in Baltimore subsided, bridges and telegraphs were repaired, Unionists dominated the majority, and efforts by secessionists to create alliances with Virginia were unearthed and suppressed. On May 4 Lincoln told three visiting Marylanders the full force of the Union would be exerted on states in rebellion. This convinced Maryland's delegation that secession would not be worth the cost.[21]

Lincoln meant what he said. Scott authorized Butler to post two regiments at the Relay House, nine miles north of Baltimore, to protect train movements. Butler took the Sixth Massachusetts to the Relay House and after a week of idleness decided to pay Baltimore an unauthorized visit. On the night of May 13, aided by thunderstorms, he moved troops into the city. The same unit had been mobbed by plug-uglies four weeks earlier. They raided Baltimore's arsenal, and as wagons packed with weapons exited the city, crowds threatened to riot. Butler's invasion occurred on the day Maryland's legislature adjourned and revived the secession movement Governor Hicks had just suppressed. Butler received a rebuke from Scott, but public opinion in the North endorsed the raid. Butler ignored Scott's scolding because Lincoln had sent his name to the Senate for promotion to major general. Disgusted by Butler's shenanigans, Scott transferred him to Fort Monroe, Virginia, where he expected the general to cause less trouble.[22]

During the April 15 cabinet meeting, Bates predicted Virginia would secede and said, "Harpers Ferry and Gosport ought to be protected, if possible." On April 16 Scott mentioned something should be done to reinforce Norfolk and Harpers Ferry and then did nothing. Welles had planned to send 250 additional sailors to the Gosport yard at Norfolk but redirected them to the Sumter expedition. Cameron and Scott became immersed in the protection of Washington and for several days forgot Harpers Ferry. There had been too much focus on forts, too many distractions caused by patronage seekers, and no experience preparing for war.[23]

Secretary Welles clearly understood the importance of Norfolk, the Union's most important naval base, but he expected a stronger defensive effort from an old and weary commandant, Charles S. McCauley. On April 19, two days after Virginia seceded, McCauley allowed Southern officers professing loyalty to persuade him to abandon the base. McCauley issued orders to torch the yard and ten ships. Even though some vessels were old, Welles needed them for blockade duty, especially the steam-powered USS *Merrimack*, which McCauley ineffectually scuttled.

Because McCauley failed to supervise the demolition work, the dry dock remained undamaged. On April 21, after McCauley departed, Virginia militia occupied the base and rescued 1,200 cannon and 2,800 barrels of gunpowder. Weeks later the same guns appeared at Charleston, Mobile, New Orleans, and Vicksburg. The loss of Norfolk bred far-reaching consequences. Besides losing a powerful warship, the Union navy suffered its most humiliating loss of the war and gave the Confederates ordnance they could never have produced.[24]

Among cabinet members only Bates and Blair worried about the Harpers Ferry armory. On April 17 General Scott made a vague reference to sending troops but deferred the decision to Cameron. The secretary ignored the armory until April 18, when First Lieutenant Roger Jones, whose company guarded the facilities, warned of attack and requested reinforcements. No one responded. That night Virginia militia drove Jones's detachment out of Harpers Ferry and captured more than fifteen thousand firearms and all the musket-producing machinery. Virginians shipped everything to Richmond, where the machinery became the core of the Confederacy's weapons industry. The South now had rifles, cannon, gunpowder, and ships to enhance its war-waging capabilities.[25]

Since March 16 Bates had been studying the legality of a naval blockade. When the cabinet met on the twenty-ninth, he recommended deploying a strong naval force along the rebel coast "sufficient to *command it*" and "close" enemy ports. Nothing happened until April 17, when Jefferson Davis issued a proclamation inviting "private armed vessels" to apply for letters of marque and reprisal. Davis intended to wage war against Union shipping, and any Southern mariner willing to risk his ship could become a privateer and collect a 20 percent commission on the value of Union prizes.[26]

Lincoln bristled at Davis's rashness and on April 19 countered with a

proclamation establishing a blockade of Southern ports and said any privateer molesting "a vessel of the United States, or the persons or cargo aboard
her," would be punished as a pirate. Davis called Lincoln's proclamation absurd because Welles had only ninety vessels to blockade thirty-five hundred
miles of coast. Of those only forty-two ships were actively in use. Under
the Declaration of Paris of 1856, which President Buchanan never signed,
a blockade to be binding must be effective. Davis called Lincoln's decree a
"paper blockade" in violation of international law and expressed astonishment over it being "issued by authority." He voiced outrage over the threat
to punish privateers, which had been an effective countermeasure among
seafaring nations for hundreds of years.[27]

Davis's rejoinder received unexpected support from Welles, who like
Bates believed Southern ports should be "closed," not blockaded. Under
municipal law Union ships would be legally empowered to seize any vessel entering a closed port and prosecute offenders as smugglers. Welles
convinced most of the cabinet that the United States would look ridiculous
to the world if it announced a blockade of its own ports. Lincoln listened
to academic discussions between closing ports versus blockading ports
but never changed his mind. Either action would obstruct the South from
importing arms and exporting cotton. Lincoln and Seward understood the
risk of alienating England and France by shutting down European cotton
mills. Both men expected Europe would give belligerent status to the Confederacy but not recognition. Welles lost the argument and had to build a
navy swiftly.[28]

The blockade also put a burden on Seward, who had wasted time trying
to "guide" Lincoln instead of managing his own affairs. He now had serious
diplomatic issues. Holdovers from Buchanan's administration still occupied
ministerial posts in Europe, and Seward thought some of them were "absolutely disloyal."

After failing to obtain a cabinet position for Charles Francis Adams,
Seward appointed him minister to Great Britain. Adams had no diplomatic
experience, but he came from a family of two American presidents. Equally
as brilliant as his forefathers, Adams carried to London a low opinion of
Lincoln's executive ability and great admiration for Seward. Eight years after
the war Adams still believed, and said outright, "Mr. Lincoln could not fail
soon to perceive the fact that, whatever estimate he might put on his own
natural judgment, he had to deal with a superior in native intellectual power."
Adams never observed the squabbles in the cabinet or the patience Lincoln
exerted in order to instill unity among the rivals.[29]

Adams reached London on May 13, the same day Queen Victoria issued Britain's proclamation of neutrality. His first mission had been to prevent England from using the word *neutrality* on the premise of not applying to factions within a legitimately recognized government rebelled. Seward's claim of the Confederacy being a "pretended new state . . . existing in pronunciamento only" made no impression on Lord John (later Earl) Russell, the British foreign secretary. Russell, an astute individual, genuinely tried to make sense out of the American rebellion. France followed Great Britain's lead and issued a similar proclamation. Louis Napoleon III followed the usual practice of waiting to see what England did before announcing the same policy for France.[30]

It was fortunate Russell never saw Seward's May 21 unamended Dispatch No. 10 to Adams. The paper provides insight into the president's editing of Seward's international correspondence. He changed several words and, according to historian J. G. Randall, "transformed a bellicose and threatening dispatch" accusing England of provoking the rebellion. After shaving the confrontational language, Lincoln told Seward to instruct Adams to use the dispatch as a confidential guide and never show it to Russell.[31]

England's annoyance over trade traced to Lincoln's proclamation blockading the entire South instead, as Welles and Bates suggested, of closing specific Southern ports. Seward favored a blockade because he clearly understood international guidelines already existed but also because the decision fell within the powers of the State Department. As Welles and Bates predicted, England and France recognized the blockade as a condition of war, not rebellion.

Blockades were designed to isolate and weaken an enemy by allowing the interdiction of neutral merchantmen to determine whether the ships carried contraband. If bound for a blockaded port, ships could be seized and brought before a prize court for adjudication. By virtue of a blockade promulgated by the Union, on one hand, and privateering authorized by the Confederacy, on the other hand, England and France had two choices: they could recognize the Confederate government as a nation at war or take a half-step, declare neutrality, and recognize both parties as belligerents. Being prudent diplomats, Lord Russell and Napoleon III agreed to a policy of neutrality and went the "belligerent" route.[32]

Lincoln had his own diplomatic problems at home. After Virginia seceded, he lost Arkansas, North Carolina, and Tennessee. The crucial states, after Maryland remained loyal, became Kentucky and Missouri, where proslavery elements carried political clout. Kentucky connected geographically to Tennessee and Virginia but shared northern boundaries on the Ohio River with Illinois, Indiana, and Ohio. Lincoln could not afford to lose control of the river or the state of his birth. He thought of losing Kentucky as losing "the whole game." If Kentucky joined the rebellion, so might Missouri. With "these all against us," said Lincoln, "We would as well consent to separation at once, including the surrender of this capital."[33]

Despite being a slave state, Kentucky always enjoyed friendly relations with its Northern neighbors, but Cameron's call for troops infuriated secessionists. When Henry Clay died in 1852, Kentucky lost its strongest Unionist. Senator John J. Crittenden attempted to fill the void, but nobody could replace Clay. Governor Beriah Magoffin informed Cameron he would resist "to the death, if necessary," from being "subjugated to an antislavery government." Magoffin attempted to obtain arms from Jefferson Davis but failed. He then failed in an attempt to gain unfettered control of the state's public credit. Unable to join the Confederacy and opposed to joining the Union, Magoffin adopted a policy of quasi-neutrality, but he made every effort to support the South by inveigling former vice president John C. Breckinridge and Inspector General Simon B. Buckner to organize a pro-Confederate military force.[34]

Indiana governor Oliver P. Morton watched the activity across the Ohio River and reported his concerns to Cameron: "The people entertain no doubt that Kentucky will speedily go out of the Union. They are in daily fear that marauding parties from the other side of the river will plunder and burn their towns." Thirty-four-year-old Major General George B. McClellan, commanding the Department of Ohio, sent spies into Kentucky and warned the administration, "From reliable information I am sure the Governor of Kentucky is a traitor. Buckner is under his influence, so it is necessary to watch them." Archibald Dixon preferred neutrality, writing, "Let us not fight the North or the South. . . . If we must fight, let us fight Lincoln and not our government."[35]

The Constitution provided no guidance on states declaring neutrality, but Lincoln had insight into Kentucky politics. His brother James, an attorney, lived in Louisville, as did Joshua Speed, an old friend he completely trusted. Both men suggested letting Kentucky's policy of neutrality run its course, thereby giving devoted Unionists time to strengthen support within the state. Earnest men in Kentucky perceived armed neutrality as a practical farce but used it "as an artful contrivance to kill secession." In late April Congressman Garrett Davis traveled to Washington to ask how the government intended to treat Kentucky. Lincoln replied that "though he had the unquestioned right at all times to march the United States troops into and over any and every State . . . if Kentucky made no demonstration of force against the United States, he would not molest her."[36]

Lincoln let Kentucky's neutrality policy stand under its own weight, knowing it could not last. It helped keep Maryland and Missouri in the Union and bought precious time for the administration. Kentucky eventually enacted a pro-Union military bill, created a Home Guard, and stopped the governor's funding of Buckner's rebellious State Guards. The final blow came when the legislature forced State Guards and Home Guards to swear allegiance to the state and the Union. A neutrality clause in the bill prevented arms from being used against either the North or the South "unless to protect Kentucky against invasion." Kentuckians, thinking they could live in a sanctuary surrounded by war, soon come to grips with reality, but the temporary expediency of neutrality kept the state in the Union.[37]

The border slave state of Missouri, home of Bates and Frank Blair Jr., presented a political problem not unlike Kentucky. While Kentucky controlled traffic on the Ohio River, Missouri controlled traffic on the Mississippi. Unfamiliar with Missouri politics, Lincoln relied on Bates for advice and Blair for political help. During the 1860 election Missouri demonstrated its tangled politics by casting 58,801 votes for Douglas, 58,372 for Bell, 31,317 for Breckinridge, and only 17,028 for Lincoln. Lincoln's support came mainly through the efforts of Frank Blair, who held a seat in the House of Representatives, but the governorship went to Democrat Claiborne F. Jackson.[38]

Like Magoffin, Jackson became conspiratorial and encouraged secessionists to raid the St. Louis arsenal, but they found it well defended. The group moved operations outside the city and named its base Fort Jackson. Blair used his influence to put Captain Nathaniel Lyon, a man thoroughly opposed to slavery, in charge of the arsenal. Lyon tried to quash the secession movement before it attracted more volunteers, but the local commander, Brigadier General William S. Harney, had many slaveholding friends and prevented Lyon and Blair from unifying the state's Union sympathizers. Equilibrium between the two factions existed until Cameron requested four regiments. At Blair's suggestion Cameron relieved Harney and replaced him with Lyon. When Jackson refused to provide four regiments to defend the Union, Cameron ordered Lyon to recruit them.[39]

Cameron's directive led to a collision between Lyon's force at the arsenal and Brigadier General Daniel M. Frost's secessionists at Fort Jackson. On April 17 Governor Jackson asked Jefferson Davis for artillery. Six days later

Davis sent two twelve- and two thirty-two-pounders and urged Jackson to capture and secure the St. Louis arsenal. Blair did not wait for Davis's artillery to arrive. Without authority from Cameron or Scott, he instructed Lyon to capture Fort Jackson. Lyon's successful attack on May 10 led to riots. Jackson formed a special military force and put it under the command of former governor Sterling Price. Cameron sent General Harney back to St. Louis to work out a détente with Price similar to the neutrality agreement in Kentucky. The Blairs undermined Harney's return and on May 16 succeeded by having him relieved for the second time in four weeks. The influence of the Blairs cannot be underestimated. Frank Blair, when writing Cameron, always demanded an answer "at once" or "immediately."[40]

Lincoln rejected the truce between Price and Harney, which led to internecine war in Missouri and disaffection among the populace for years to come. Like Kentucky, Missouri remained in the Union but contributed many regiments to the Confederacy.

On May 3 the president issued a new proclamation calling for 42,034 volunteers to serve three years and 18,000 sailors to bolster Welles's blockade. The order swelled the army to 156,861 men, half of them three-month volunteers, and 25,600 sailors. He did not wait for congressional authorization, nor did he instruct Cameron to irritate the border states by demanding new quotas.[41]

Response to the proclamation swamped the War and Navy departments, created massive confusion, confounded Cameron, and overwhelmed gout-ridden Scott. Lincoln now understood what must be done, and he relentlessly pressured Cameron, Chase, and Welles to get the war machine functioning before Congress reconvened in July. Stretching presidential powers to the utmost, he authorized Chase to raise $16 million and ordered Welles to purchase and arm fifteen steamships to keep water communications open with Washington.[42]

During the weeks following the Sumter expedition, Assistant Navy Secretary Gustavus Fox grumbled to Montgomery Blair that diverting the USS *Powhatan* had damaged his reputation. Lincoln felt partly responsible for the mission's failure and observed that Welles needed help, so to satisfy Blair he asked Welles to appoint Fox chief clerk in the Navy Department. Welles already had William Faxon, a department veteran familiar with the duties of the office. Although he acknowledged Fox's good credentials, Welles argued that Faxon deserved the post. In an effort to placate everyone, Welles told Lincoln he would reinstate Fox to his former rank of lieutenant in the navy, and the president agreed. Thinking the problem solved, Welles promised Faxon the chief clerk's post.[43]

Welles's plan pleased Faxon but disappointed Fox, who rejected the commission because he wanted the clerkship. Blair claimed Fox's talents would be lost to blockade duty at a time when Welles needed men of knowledge and experience to guide the country through war. Lincoln decided Blair might be right and revisited the matter with Welles.[44]

Lincoln's change of mind annoyed Welles because hours earlier he had promised the position to Faxon. Lincoln and Blair held another discussion and mutually decided Fox should join the Navy Department as assistant secretary, thereby enabling Faxon to serve as chief clerk. Lincoln spoke with Welles and explained that while the secretary and the chief clerk were both landlubbers, Fox understood naval operations. He suggested splitting duties. While Welles and Faxon managed contract, administrative, and budgetary matters, Fox could run fleet operations, much like a modern chief of naval operations. Had Welles been an arrogant man, he might have resented having Fox thrust into his bailiwick, but the secretary knew the Navy Department needed help. Fox's appointment could not be approved until Congress convened on July 4, so on May 8 Fox became chief clerk. Faxon assured Welles he would continue serving in any position the secretary wished. Welles promised to make it right, and when Fox was confirmed as assistant secretary, Faxon moved into the chief clerk's office. Six years later Fox told Welles, "When Faxon and I were together there were really two Asst. Sec'y's, a civil and a naval one."[45]

Many of Lincoln's friends believed the onset of war would have a telling effect upon the president's endurance. Much to Seward's surprise, Lincoln showed no strain. The president worked through day-to-day problems despite being constantly beset by office seekers, defections, cabinet scuffles, and shortages of everything from money, troops, ships, and weapons to competent generals to run the war. There had been no serious fighting, but Lincoln saw it coming. As the first three months of the administration came to a close, Seward penned a reflective letter to his wife, writing, "Executive skill and vigor are rare qualities. The President is the best of us: but he needs constant and assiduous cooperation." Although Seward occasionally forgot those words, he had finally found a greater power than himself.[46]

CHAPTER 7

"The fat is all in the fire now"

In late April Lincoln began pressuring Secretary of War Cameron to produce a plan for using the seventy-five thousand men of the three-month
militia before their enlistments expired. After creating an army, Cameron
had given no thought to using it. General Winfield Scott emphasized defense
and recommended Washington, D.C., be protected. Surplus troops could be
organized into brigades for recapturing Harpers Ferry or Norfolk. Cameron
agreed, although Harpers Ferry and Norfolk had already been gutted of
military stores.[1]

On April 27 Scott placed Brigadier General Joseph K. F. Mansfield in
charge of Washington's defenses and six days later ordered him to seize and
fortify nearby Arlington Heights. Despite rumors of hostile forces about
to strike Washington, Mansfield ruminated over how to carry out Scott's
instructions. When a small enemy force appeared in Alexandria, Lincoln
observed from his office windows a rebel flag flying over the town. He turned
to Colonel Elmer Ellsworth and said such arrogance should not be permitted
in the backyard of the nation's capital.[2]

Scott sent Ellsworth's New York Zouaves to Alexandria to tear down the
flag, while another force under Brigadier General Samuel P. Heintzelman
captured Arlington Heights. At 2:00 a.m., May 24, the movement began in
moonlight. While seven regiments crossed from the Aqueduct Bridge at
Georgetown and the Long Bridge at Washington, Ellsworth's regiment went
by steamer and disembarked unopposed at Alexandria. The only mishap
occurred when Ellsworth entered Alexandria's Marshall House to tear down
the rebel flag with his own hands. He ascended the winding stairs to the roof,
cut the halyards, and started back down. At a doorway James T. Jackson, the
hotel's proprietor, sprang from concealment and emptied a double-barreled
shotgun into Ellsworth's chest. As the colonel toppled backward, Private
Francis Brownell shot and bayoneted Jackson.

Ellsworth's death brought war and bereavement home to Lincoln. The
colonel had been Lincoln's companion since the chaotic days in Springfield,
and he had intended to present the offensive rebel banner, now stained with
his own blood, to the president. He did not expect to die. Lincoln placed
Ellsworth's body in the East Room to lie in state where the cabinet, diplo-

mats, and military personnel could pay their last respects to a young man loved by all.[3]

Before the funeral Senator Henry Wilson entered the White House and found the president in the library staring across the Potomac toward Alexandria. At first Lincoln did not move; then he turned abruptly, saying, "Excuse me, but I cannot talk." Wilson thought the president had lost his voice, when to his surprise "the President burst into tears, and concealed his face in a handkerchief." Lincoln composed himself and said, "I will make no apology, gentlemen, for my weakness; but I knew poor Ellsworth well. . . . [His] unfortunate death . . . was so unexpected . . . that it quite unmanned me." He later expressed his remorse to Congress, writing, "The people of Virginia have thus allowed this giant insurrection to make its nest within her borders; and this government has no choice left but to deal with it, *where* it finds it."[4]

Having secured Washington, Cameron turned his attention to Harpers Ferry, where General Joseph E. Johnston's rebels had dismantled the Baltimore & Ohio Railroad and left nothing of value behind. Scott gave the task of recapturing the town to sixty-nine-year-old Major General Robert Patterson, commanding the Pennsylvania militia. Patterson predicted the first great battle of the war would be fought at Harpers Ferry with decisive results. A few days later he entered Harpers Ferry and found it abandoned. Johnston had retired to Winchester, a maneuver Patterson completely misread, claiming the enemy had "fled . . . in confusion."[5]

Scott questioned Patterson's analysis and ordered him to fortify Harpers Ferry. Cameron never understood the situation. Johnston abandoned Harpers Ferry because he considered it indefensible and wanted to be closer to rail connections at Strasburg, which led to Manassas. Scott ordered Patterson to remain at Harpers Ferry to await an attack that never came. Meanwhile, Johnston kept a force in the area to check Patterson's movements, and Scott unwittingly kept Patterson out of position to participate in the first great battle of the war.[6]

Scott's plans also ran afoul the day he put Ben Butler in charge of Fort Monroe. Butler protested the assignment, but Cameron and Scott wanted him out of the way. On May 24, two days after Butler arrived at Fort Monroe, a sentry captured three runaway slaves. Butler put them to work in the fort and a day later received a visit from Confederate major John B. Cary, who demanded the slaves. Butler replied that unless the owner swore an oath of allegiance to the United States, he would retain the runaways as "contraband of war."[7]

Lincoln deliberated over how to respond to Butler's unilateral policy of emancipation. Republicans endorsed the action, even though Butler was a

Democrat, and "contraband" became a new appellation for runaway slaves. The press praised Butler, and even Scott approved, dubbing the action "Butler's fugitive slave law." Lincoln discussed the matter with the cabinet and decided Butler might be right. Cameron wrote Butler, "Your action in respect to the Negroes who came into your lines . . . is approved," and agreed to Butler's proposal to employ fugitives and pay for their labor and maintenance. From Baltimore, Major General John A. Dix disagreed with the policy and advised Cameron, "We are neither negro stealers, nor negro catchers, and . . . we should send them away if they come to us." So for several weeks Butler operated one policy and Dix another.[8]

By July 30 Butler had nine hundred fugitives employed. His action stunned the South, stirred the political pot, and created an ongoing debate in the cabinet. Lincoln finally asked Congress for legislation ratifying Butler's action. On August 6, the last day of the special summer session, Congress passed the first Confiscation Act. Among other articles the act deprived masters of slaves used to support the rebellion. The wordage closely resembled the language Butler had adopted in his original explanation to Scott.[9]

After being shuttled into a command he disliked, Butler set out to redeem himself as Scott's number one general. Runaways seeking sanctuary informed him of a Confederate outpost at Big Bethel, Virginia. On June 10 Butler sent twenty-five hundred infantry by two different roads to capture the rebel camp. When converging at a crossroad, the two columns fired into each other before realizing the error. Considerably shaken by the mistake, the Federals plodded forward and encountered a lightly defended enemy battery backed by twelve hundred Confederates. They stopped to maneuver, parried for an hour, suffered seventy casualties, and returned to Fort Monroe with exaggerated reports of the enemy's strength. Butler's first tactical strike had suffered an embarrassing setback, and though it came as no surprise to Scott, the defeat raised questions about Butler's ability to command troops.[10]

When Congress convened in special session on July 4, 1861, Lincoln sent a message explaining the course pursued at Sumter and blamed the South for initiating hostilities. He also explained his proclamations for the defense of the Union. He avoided using the words *Confederate States of America* unless they were preceded by *so-called* and referred to the conflict as a "rebellion" or "insurrection" instead of a war. He also coached the cabinet to adopt the same practice. The message set the tone of the administration for the next four years.

Lincoln clung to his belief that the American experiment of free government must not fail because of some inherent defect. The whole concept of democracy was on trial. Suppressing the rebellion had a greater purpose, not of war but of a "People's contest," which, "on the side of the Union it is a struggle . . . to elevate the condition of men—to lift artificial weights from all shoulders; to afford all an unfettered start, and a fair chance in the race of life." He explained why a free government must succeed in preventing the dissolution of the nation. It would be "a great lesson of peace," he said, "teaching men that what they cannot take by an election, neither can they take it by a war—teaching all, the folly of being the beginners of war." The theme became Lincoln's life. Secession could never become a legal right.

Lincoln redefined presidential war powers by making the prosecution of the war an exclusive function of the executive branch. He had already exercised that prerogative by increasing the size of the army and navy, extending enlistments to three years, authorizing loans, purchasing weapons and ships, declaring a blockade, and suspending the writ of habeas corpus. "These measures, whether legal or not," he explained, "were ventured upon under what appeared to be a popular demand, and a public necessity; trusting, then, as now, that Congress would ratify them." He believed "nothing has been done beyond the constitutional competency of Congress," and the statement went unchallenged by most everyone but Chief Justice Roger B. Taney, who opposed Lincoln's suspension of the writ.[11]

On July 5 a clerk drolly read to Congress one of the most important messages of the century, which became buried in the *Congressional Globe.* No one listened closely because Congress, now in Republican control, had become a "War and Union" party willing to pass the president's war requests. Lincoln asked for 400,000 men and $400 million to be placed under the control of the executive. He said the conflict would be "a short, and a decisive one." To ensure a quick and successful campaign, Congress upped the ante by appropriating $500 million for an army and navy of a half-million men.

Orville Browning may have been the only senator who understood Lincoln's message. Having stopped at the White House on other business, the Illinois statesman sat through a recital by the president. Two years later at Gettysburg, Lincoln articulated the same theme in fewer words, and this time the message took root, sprouted, and became a national treasure.[12]

Aside from mild arguments from border state members, Congress passed bills retroactively approving Lincoln's temporary usurpation of legislative powers. Senator John Crittenden of Kentucky, who strongly supported Lincoln, put a resolution on the Senate floor blaming "the disunionists of the Southern States" for the conflict and declared the right of the government to "maintain the supremacy of the Constitution, and to preserve the Union." The resolution passed without debate on the day after the war's first great battle at Bull Run. Such harmony would not last, but Lincoln had obtained the powers he needed to prosecute the war and was disinclined to give them back.[13]

Congress adjourned without discussing the appointment of army officers. Lincoln asked Cameron for help, and the befuddled secretary referred the problem to his venerated military expert, General Winfield Scott, whose seniority list contained regular army veterans who had fought fifteen years ago in the Mexican War. For the first appointments to major general Scott chose Mansfield, age fifty-eight, and Robert Patterson, age sixty-nine. Lincoln picked thirty-four-year-old George B. McClellan, a major general in the Ohio militia who had acted swiftly to safeguard western Virginia, and Benjamin Butler, age forty-three, who had rescued Washington during the chaotic days following Fort Sumter.[14]

None of the generals became directly involved in the first major battle of the Civil War. That task fell to forty-one-year-old Irvin McDowell, a regular army veteran who had graduated from West Point in 1838. As a staff officer in the adjutant general's office in Washington, McDowell had not served in the field for thirteen years. Under Scott he developed a reputation for being censorious and a voracious eater. Cameron assigned McDowell to a geographical area covering part of Virginia and Maryland. Having been a major for the past five years, McDowell was not prepared for the "on to Richmond" push when on May 14 Cameron made him a brigadier general. Scott put him in charge of a massive military buildup composed of three-month volunteers for offensive operations against General P. G. T. Beauregard's army at Manassas.[15]

McDowell's appointment had more to do with Chase than Cameron. Having wormed his way into Cameron's confidence, Chase became the war secretary's trusted advisor. Cameron's inability to act decisively made him receptive to Chase's help. Seward, also critical of the War Department, wrote to his alter ego Thurlow Weed, "It is the President, General Scott, and I against the two C's [Chase and Cameron]." Seward overstated the situation, but Chase clearly wanted Ohio men like McDowell and McClellan chosen for generalships. He also wanted Cameron's friendship. The politically powerful Pennsylvanian fitted neatly into Chase's future presidential plans, which never stopped percolating.[16]

Chase coached McDowell, helping him prepare a strategy to screen Washington while making military thrusts at Richmond. After driving twenty thousand Confederates out of Manassas, McDowell would take control of the Orange & Alexandria Railroad and move swiftly south. Scott approved the plan, giving McDowell the most difficult assignment in the Union army—organizing a field army to win a battle everyone expected to be the first and only major engagement of the rebellion.[17]

McDowell believed his Chase-assisted strategy would win the war, but he did not expect to fight that summer. He would be the first general in American history to command thirty thousand men, none of whom were trained. His staff lacked experience, and maps of Virginia were outdated. Nor did Scott want to fight, fearing too much bloodshed might destroy the nearly nonexistent Union sentiment in the South. Lincoln ignored Scott. He wanted the rebels whipped that summer.[18]

McDowell proposed a sensible maneuver to flank the Confederates out of Manassas and drive them back to Fredericksburg. McDowell knew Johnston also commanded twelve thousand troops in the Shenandoah Valley and warned, "There is nothing to hinder their coming," unless Patterson's force at Harpers Ferry kept them occupied. Having no control over Patterson, McDowell relied on Scott to issue the orders. Scott, however, waited nearly three weeks, until July 13, to contact Patterson.[19]

Lincoln made the decision to launch an offensive not because of public pressure but because he believed fifty thousand untrained Federal troops could defeat thirty thousand untrained Southern troops. Like McDowell, he expected Patterson's twenty thousand Pennsylvanians to make a decisive difference. The original plan, later refined by Scott, included the capture of Richmond. Lincoln believed it could be done before the South became stronger. He expected the campaign to go as planned, and the cabinet expected the South to quit after the first major military defeat.[20]

During a meeting with Scott and McDowell, Lincoln designated July 9 for the advance on Manassas. McDowell protested, arguing it was wrong to insist he organize, discipline, march, and fight all at the same time. Recruits were still arriving, none had been trained, some did not know how to fire a musket, and planning had outpaced logistics. Lincoln agreed to a week's delay but said, "You are green, it is true; but they are green, also, you are all green alike." He did not want Beauregard to get stronger and told McDowell to stop stalling. Delays had already caused problems. Leaks appeared in the press, forewarning Beauregard of McDowell's plans. To make matters worse, Patterson moved to attack Johnston at Winchester, inexplicably stopped nine miles short, and went no farther. Johnston ignored Patterson and began shuttling reinforcements to Manassas.[21]

On July 16 McDowell issued marching orders and told his commanders it would be unacceptable "to fall back." Washington spectators followed in carriages as 35,732 Federals moved at a snail's pace to Fairfax Courthouse and pushed Confederate outposts back to Centreville.

On July 18, as General Daniel Tyler's first division advanced, the enemy retired across Bull Run—a winding, shallow stream with several fords. Instead of pressing forward, Tyler stopped and waited for McDowell. He reported roads too narrow to move his force against the enemy's fortified left flank, so McDowell lost another day revising his orders. Meanwhile, Patterson did nothing, and Johnston's army began arriving on the Manassas Gap Railroad. When McDowell finally advanced, Beauregard had as many men as McDowell.

Three days later the public watched as McDowell launched a massive attack on Beauregard's left flank. Because of poor roads, poor staff preparation, and poor communication, the unsynchronized attack faltered and during the afternoon disintegrated from enemy counterattacks. Union soldiers threw down their weapons, fled back across Bull Run, stampeded the spectators, and some soldiers never stopped running until they reached the Potomac. McDowell rallied briefly at Centreville and led the troops back to Washington. Had Patterson checked Johnston's army at Winchester or had McDowell attacked on July 20 instead of waiting another day, the battle might have resulted in a defining Union victory instead of a dismal failure.[22]

By midday on July 21 encouraging telegrams from Fairfax Station, four miles from the front, began arriving at the White House. At three o'clock Lincoln wanted an expert analysis and went with Cameron to Scott's office, found the general asleep, and shook him awake. Scott read the messages, said all was well, predicted McDowell would win, composed himself for another nap, and at 4:00 p.m. Lincoln returned to the White House.[23]

At 5:15 p.m. one of Scott's aides appeared with a telegram from the battlefield written an hour earlier confirming that McDowell had "driven the enemy before him." Scott seconded the report, assuring the president that by evening, certainly no later than "to-morrow noon," Beauregard would surrender. That said, the president ordered his carriage and cheerfully took the family for their customary evening drive.[24]

At 6:00 p.m. Seward entered the White House looking "pale and haggard" and said he must speak to the president. "Gone for a ride," Nicolay replied. Seward asked for news from Centreville, and the secretary read the latest optimistic telegram. "Tell no one," said Seward. "That is not true. The battle is lost. McDowell is in full retreat and calls for General Scott to save the capital. Find the President and tell him to come immediately."

The news astounded Lincoln. He reached the War Department at 7:00

p.m. and read, "General McDowell's army in full retreat through Centreville. The day is lost. Save Washington and the remnants of this army. . . . The routed troops will not reform." Lincoln returned to the White House an hour later and never went to bed. At 2:00 a.m. General Scott urged the president to send his family north. Mary refused to go, and Lincoln told Scott to not worry—the Confederates would stay where they were.

Nicolay remained by the president's side during the night but later returned to his desk and summed up the day, writing, "The fat is all in the fire now, and we shall have to crow small until we can retrieve the disgrace somehow." A few days later he heard someone tell Lincoln that Johnston had reported the Confederates "more disorganized by victory than the United States by defeat." Lincoln grumbled, "Ah, I see. We whipped the enemy and then ran away from him."[25]

On July 23 the president rode with Seward to Arlington to visit McDowell. According to one observer, Lincoln told McDowell, "I have not lost a particle of confidence in you," to which the general replied, "I don't see why you should, Mr. President." This was not the answer Lincoln expected. He later stopped at Fort Corcoran and met with Colonel William T. Sherman of the Sixty-ninth New York State Militia. Sherman spoke plainly, blaming the defeat on undisciplined citizen soldiers who were becoming so "mutinous" he threatened to shoot them "if they dared to leave camp without orders." Lincoln would not forget men like Sherman.[26]

The visit made a deep impact on Lincoln. He returned to the White House convinced the job had become too big for McDowell. He also formed doubts about Scott, who seemed overly anxious to exonerate himself by pinning the blame for the Bull Run disaster on the president. Blair had no confidence in Scott and warned Cameron to take charge of the War Department or accept the consequences for whatever went wrong. Cameron's limitations on military matters shined brightly on July 22, when Colonel J. E. Kerrigan of the Twenty-fifth New York Volunteer Infantry Regiment warned there were seven thousand confused men at Alexandria without officers and asked for guidance: "Please tell me what I shall do with my regiment." Cameron never replied.[27]

Lincoln decided to ease Cameron out of the War Department, but his immediate problem was finding someone to command the army. Only one general had led a successful campaign. General McClellan's mini-engagements in western Virginia had checked the rebels and paved the way for Unionists to organize an independent state. On July 22 Lincoln summoned McClellan to Washington to take command of a new army composed of three-year regiments. Three-month militia, their enlistments up, returned home, and General Patterson went with them.[28]

Lincoln made several changes. Major General Nathaniel Banks replaced Patterson as commander of the Department of the Shenandoah at Harpers Ferry, Brigadier General William S. Rosecrans replaced McClellan in western Virginia, Major General John A. Dix took command of the Department of Maryland in Baltimore, and McClellan replaced McDowell at Washington. Chase approved of McClellan's elevation because the general came from Ohio. John T. Morse Jr. wrote, "In the procession of admirers which heralded the advent of this military savior none blew a more confident trumpet than did Secretary Chase."[29]

In response to Lincoln's summons McClellan rode sixty miles on horseback to the nearest train station. He detrained on July 26 and called on Scott before going to the White House. Lincoln invited him to attend a cabinet meeting but excluded Scott. The omission appealed to McClellan's sense of importance but annoyed the venerated army chief. Over the next few days McClellan fantasized that the president, cabinet, and Scott all deferred to his superior wisdom on how to save the Union. "By some strange operation of magic," he wrote his wife, "I seem to have become the power of the land." Power appealed to "Little Mac," who the press hailed as "the Young Napoleon."[30]

McClellan's credentials for leadership ranked among the best in the army. Born in Philadelphia to a wealthy family, he went to West Point and in 1846 graduated second in his class. After earning two brevets for distinguished service in the Mexican War, the army sent him to Europe during the Crimean War to study tactics. In 1857 he resigned his commission to become chief engineer and vice president of the Illinois Central Railroad. In 1860, as president of the Ohio & Mississippi Railroad, he moved to Cincinnati, where in 1861 Governor William Dennison appointed him major general of the Ohio volunteers. By July, Little Mac had become the only officer in the army showing promise on the battlefield, though his western Virginia campaigns were minor affairs and modest victories.

On July 23 Lincoln prepared a "Memoranda of Military Policy Suggested by the Bull Run Defeat," setting a broad policy and establishing new military objectives. He wanted Manassas captured and held; railways and communications reopened between Washington and Harpers Ferry; Memphis captured on the Mississippi; and an expedition from Cincinnati mounted to protect a strong Unionist element in eastern Tennessee.[31]

McClellan understood railroads and waterways, and Lincoln expected him to be useful, but the general regarded everyone as military inferiors. During the Illinois senatorial campaign in 1856 McClellan met Lincoln, pegged him as a good storyteller, and voted for Douglas. Five years later his opinion of the president remained unchanged. Lincoln now had his general, and McClellan an opportunity to demonstrate his worth.

Little Mac had competition. On July 3 Lincoln picked a counterpart for the West, forty-eight-year-old Major General John C. Frémont, known nationally as the "Pathfinder" for his 1840 trailblazing expedition across the Rocky Mountains. Frémont was a handsome and charismatic Westerner who in 1856 became the first presidential candidate of the Republican Party. He seemed well suited for building a Western army, but Bates believed Frémont had the potential of becoming a military despot and a threat to civil authority. Frémont surrounded himself with foppish Hungarian and German staff officers bedecked in fancy uniforms. They paraded around St. Louis headquarters and prevented people arriving on legitimate business from speaking to the general.[32]

Taking charge in July, Frémont found the state in turmoil, with Lyon in possession of Jefferson City and marching on Springfield. Confederate resistance stiffened, and Frémont faced full-scale war. While Bates tried to preserve peace in Missouri, Frémont let Lyon turn the state into a battleground. On August 10 Lyon led his ill-prepared force into an impetuous battle at Wilson's Creek and lost his life rallying his defeated command. When Bates learned the details, he wrote Chase, "The very heart of the state is broken. All confidence is destroyed." Bates was so disgusted with Cameron that he appealed to Chase for reinforcements.[33]

On August 14, after Lyon's defeat, Frémont attempted to quell disorder by declaring martial law. As guerrilla raids spread through the state, he created an uproar by proclaiming that civilians found "with arms in their hands" or "engaged in treasonable correspondence" would be summarily shot, their property confiscated, and their slaves liberated. In other words, military force could be used against the civilian population, which ensured that those harmed would be barred from reconciling their complaints in civil courts.[34]

Many senators endorsed Frémont's action. Charles Sumner of Massachusetts and Zachariah Chandler of Michigan, both representing the growing number of radicals in the Senate, wanted emancipation immediately, and the entire character of the conflict changed to a war of abolition. Radicals believed emancipation would so disrupt the economy of the South that the Confederacy would implode. With the border states in mind, Lincoln listened but urged patience.[35]

Frémont's proclamation ran contrary to Lincoln's inaugural policy of not interfering with slavery. After Butler permitted fugitives to seek asylum at Fort Monroe, Lincoln let his policy be modified by the Confiscation Act, passed on August 6, which established a judicial process for seizing slaves supporting the rebellion. Frémont's policy went beyond emancipation by threatening to shoot civilians bearing arms. Aghast at the general's recklessness, Lincoln sent Blair and Meigs to St. Louis with orders for Frémont to amend his proclamation. "Should you shoot a man, according to the proclamation," said Lincoln, "the Confederates would very certainly shoot our best man . . . in retaliation; and so, man for man, indefinitely." Frémont disliked being rebuked. Stronger policies, he stated, were needed in Missouri to curb raids; martial law and emancipation were "right and necessary."[36]

Frémont sent his wife to Washington to argue his case. Jessie Benton Frémont, daughter of Missouri senator Thomas Hart Benton, booked a room at Willard's on September 10 and sent her card to the White House demanding an interview. Lincoln replied, "Now, at once," and at 9:00 p.m. Mrs. Frémont entered the executive mansion and followed the doorman to the Red Room. Lincoln refused her a chair and stood while she presented her husband's letter. He read the letter without comment and allowed her to speak, which she did with passion. When she asked why Blair had been sent to St. Louis, Lincoln merely replied as "a friend and adviser." Mrs. Frémont knew better because, she said, "when the Blairs go into a fight, they go in for a funeral." Frank Blair, a colonel in Frémont's army, had been arrested for preferring corruption charges against the general. Mrs. Frémont decided she disliked the president as much as she disliked the Blairs. To her arguments Lincoln replied, "It was a war for a great national idea, the Union, and . . . General Frémont should not have dragged the Negro into it." The comment irked Mrs. Frémont, who threatened that her husband might "set up [a government] on his own." Speaking of this interview later, Lincoln said, "She taxed me so violently with many things that I had to exercise all the awkward tact I [had] to avoid quarreling with her."[37]

Jessie Frémont did her husband great harm. Lincoln questioned whether Frémont could be trusted to command in the West. He could not have generals redefining civil law or deciding questions of policy that were exclusive prerogatives of the president. He ordered the general to retract certain sections of the proclamation to make them "conform to, and not to transcend," the provisions in the Confiscation Act.[38]

Bates wanted Frémont removed before the general completely destroyed civil control, and Cameron, a master of corruption himself, confirmed the

presence of fraudulent activity in Frémont's department. On September 13
Cameron arrived at St. Louis with orders for the general's dismissal. On discovering the purpose of the visit, Frémont pleaded for patience, promising
a victory. Cameron kept the order in his pocket and years later still had it.
When Frank Blair learned Cameron had "*flummoxed* on the Frémont business," he became furious, writing, "Who can believe him?" For two months
Bates had raged against Frémont. During a cabinet meeting on October 22
he furiously insisted Frémont be removed "instantly."[39]

Lincoln began to wonder whether there were any generals in the Union
army he could trust. On October 24, after conferring with his cabinet, he ordered Cameron to relieve Frémont and transfer the command to fifty-nine-
year-old Major General David Hunter, who was already in Missouri. Hunter,
however, was part of Scott's old guard, high in seniority, and of questionable
ability. The book had not completely closed on Frémont, who would appear
on another field, but John Hay accurately summed up Frémont's potential
when he wrote, "I think he has absolutely no military capacity."[40]

On November 9, 1861, Lincoln dissolved Frémont's department and
put forty-six-year-old Major General Henry W. Halleck in charge of the
Department of the Missouri and moved Hunter into Kansas. Best known
for his "gigantic intellect," Halleck graduated from West Point third in the
class of 1839 and soon became a recognized expert in military theory and
fortifications. He fought in the Mexican War, wrote books, became a lawyer,
and served as secretary of state for California before returning to the army.
Halleck restored discipline and efficiency in a command badly mishandled
by Frémont. Halleck's officers included a little known brigadier general, Ulysses S. Grant, who gave Halleck the nickname "Old Brains," a sobriquet with
dual interpretations. Halleck would become another of Lincoln's disappoint-
ments, but as the close of 1861 approached, the president believed with Halleck in the West and McClellan in the East the war could be won in 1862.[41]

CHAPTER 8

"The bottom is out of the tub"

General George McClellan reached Washington, D.C., on July 26, 1861, and made an immediate impression. Hailed as the savior of the country, the young, handsome general looked the part, and when he told his wife he had "become the power of the land," he believed it. While designing a ring of interconnected fortifications around Washington, he began forming a new army from thousands of three-year volunteers. McClellan asked for 273,000 troops, 100 field batteries (600 guns), 28 cavalry regiments, and 5 engineer regiments. On August 20 the force became the Army of the Potomac, swelling in size from 50,000 in July to 168,318 officers and men in October.[1]

The administration provided McClellan with the best arms, artillery, and equipment at the expense of unfilled requisitions for General Halleck's army in the West. The public adored watching the magnetic Young Napoleon ride from camp to camp with a military staff bedecked in natty uniforms yet untarnished by the smoke of battle. The Washington establishment loved McClellan, not because of what he had done but because of what everyone expected him to do. Little Mac knew how to attract attention. He staged massive troop reviews with Lincoln, the cabinet, and members of Congress at his side. Sitting erect in the saddle beside the president, McClellan looked elegant, while Lincoln looked ungainly, and Little Mac knew it. Letters from the public predicted the general's ascent to the presidency, even a dictatorship. "I would cheerfully take the dictatorship and agree to lay down my life," he wrote home, "when the country is saved." British reporter William Howard Russell, however, noted that McClellan seemed not to be "a man of action, or, at least, a man who intends to act as speedily as the crisis demands."[2]

McClellan's popularity peaked in October, and regression began. The press accused the general of wasting the fall instead of marching on Richmond. Radicals in Congress goaded McClellan to take the field before the rebels became stronger. Beauregard still occupied Manassas, and even Lincoln, after providing all the tools of war, could not give his general the pugnacity, which had to come from the man himself. Instead, McClellan blamed his inactivity on his superior, writing, "Gen. Scott is the most dangerous antagonist I have."[3]

The McClellan-Scott spat involved a difference of opinion: McClellan said Washington was vulnerable; Scott said it was secure. By mid-August Little Mac had twice as many men as Beauregard, but he insisted Beauregard had more. He blamed the disparity on the president and the "old general." When in October Lincoln pressed for action, McClellan informed his wife of "becoming daily more disgusted with this administration—perfectly sick of it." He avoided the president by being "too busy" to see him. On October 10, when attending a cabinet meeting, he claimed to be "bored and annoyed," adding, "There are some of the greatest geese in the cabinet I have ever seen—enough to tax the patience of Job." McClellan's friends were all Democrats. They urged the general to save the country from its incapable rulers.[4]

Some of Lincoln's allies, among them Zachariah Chandler and Lyman Trumbull, had aligned themselves with the "Jacobin club," the radical movement in the Senate. On October 26 they called to "worry the administration into battle," claiming McClellan had been taking too good care of himself by doing nothing. Lincoln defended McClellan's "deliberateness" but admitted being perplexed by the general's inaction. Later he walked to army headquarters to discuss the matter and found the general gone, but he overheard others talking about the importance of clearing the enemy out of Manassas "at once." Lincoln asked Colonel Thomas M. Key about McClellan's idleness. Key replied, "The General is troubled in his mind. I think he is much embarrassed by the radical difference between his views and those of General Scott." Lincoln expected to hear more on the matter soon.[5]

When radicals tried to goad the general into taking the field by questioning his loyalty, Little Mac acted swiftly. He blamed Scott for feeble-mindedness and obstructing military efforts. The senators returned to the White House and demanded Scott's removal. On November 1 Lincoln accepted Scott's resignation and named McClellan general-in-chief. In addition to the Army of the Potomac, Little Mac now controlled Don Carlos Buell's Army of the Ohio, Halleck's Army of the Missouri, and everything else. The new general-in-chief informed Lincoln, "I feel as if a great weight were taken from my shoulders today. I am now [directly] in contact with you, and the Secretary [of War]." Lincoln replied, "Call on me for all the sense I have . . . the supreme command of the Army will entail a vast labor upon you." McClellan replied, "I can do it all." The general had once called the president "an idiot" but softened the insult with further description, "a well-meaning baboon"; now he intended to override executive interference.[6]

During a cabinet meeting to discuss Scott's replacement, Bates observed

Lincoln's hesitation to turn the army over to McClellan. He reminded the president that the *"general chief—*or *chief general—*is only *your lieutenant.* You are the constitutional 'Commander in chief,' and may make any general you please." McClellan admitted being uncomfortable around Bates, an "old fool" who always studied him without saying much."[7]

McClellan continued to wear two faces, one to his wife and the other to those who gave him power. Having seduced Cameron, he attempted to do the same with Blair, Chase, and Seward, with "whom all the greater war questions [were] to be settled." McClellan called Seward the "meanest" man in the cabinet and "a meddling, officious incompetent little puppy because the secretary asked probing questions. He liked Blair and Chase because they supported the removal of Scott. Chase had reservations, but he recognized Little Mac had become the "people's choice." As soon as Lincoln signed the order, Chase wrote, "McClellan is commander-in-chief, let us thank God and take courage."[8]

McClellan seldom dealt directly with Welles, who Lincoln jocularly called "Father Neptune," but the navy had been upstaging the army. Commodore Silas H. Stringham led a successful amphibious operation and in August captured Hatteras Inlet, North Carolina. Two months later Commodore Samuel F. DuPont led another amphibious operation and captured Port Royal and Beaufort, South Carolina. The two expeditions made national news. Because most of the credit had gone to the navy, McClellan had little good to say about Welles, referring to him as "weaker than the most garrulous old woman you were ever annoyed by." Criticizing someone else always made McClellan feel better.[9]

Nobody wanted McClellan to succeed more than Lincoln. For two weeks he walked every night with Seward and Hay to army headquarters hoping for good news, but none came. On November 13, finding McClellan gone, they went to the general's home on H Street. A servant answered the door and said McClellan was attending a wedding, so they waited in the drawing room. An hour later the general arrived, learned the president was waiting, walked past the drawing room without looking inside, and disappeared upstairs. Thirty minutes later, thinking his presence had not been announced, Lincoln sent the servant to get the general, who had gone to bed. Lincoln overlooked the affront but made no more visits to McClellan's home. Although Lincoln later quipped he would "hold McClellan's horse if he would only bring us success," the general's snub marked the beginning of the president's exasperation with his newly appointed general-in-chief. He agreed, however, not to allow "points of etiquette and personal dignity" to get in the way of winning the war.[10]

For Lincoln and his cabinet the trials and turmoil of civil war were just beginning. On November 8, 1861, Captain Charles Wilkes, commanding the USS *San Jacinto*, fired a shot across the bow of the British mail steamer and stopped the RMS *Trent* in the Bahamas Channel. Wilkes sent a boarding party to arrest James M. Mason of Virginia and John Slidell of Louisiana, Confederate commissioners bound, respectively, for England and France. Despite furious objections from British officers, Wilkes's boarding party removed the commissioners and their secretaries as contraband of war and deposited them in Boston's Fort Warren.

Although Wilkes had acted without authority, jubilation spread in the North from people starved for good news. Hailed as a national hero, Wilkes received praise from Welles, Congress, the press, and the public. Fallout began a few days later. England accused Seward of authorizing the *Trent* affair and issued an ultimatum to release the commissioners. Prime Minister Lord Palmerston sent eight thousand troops to Canada and placed an embargo on shipments of war materials to the United States. The ultimatum thrust Lincoln and Seward into an untenable position. While freeing the commissioners might cause political harm at home, keeping them could draw England into the war. Charles Francis Adams wrote from London, "War with the United States seems imminent. It may spread itself all over Europe."[11]

Dampening a volatile situation without appearing incompetent fell mainly on Lincoln rather than Seward. He predicted that Mason and Slidell would "prove to be white elephants," and if the British demanded their release, "we must give them up." Bates rendered his opinion, writing, "Not only was it lawful to seize the men, but, I think, the ship itself was subject to confiscation." Bates had his facts wrong but not the British. Under international law Wilkes had rights as a belligerent to search the *Trent* for contraband but no right to make an arrest at sea. Bates acquainted himself with international law and in late December admitted Wilkes had committed a serious mistake and amends must be made.[12]

Because Seward disliked the British and tended to be confrontational, Lincoln developed a working relationship with Charles Sumner, a Harvard-trained chairman of the Senate Foreign Relations Committee. Having traveled the world, Sumner understood the culture of Great Britain and France. Lincoln and Sumner were quite different. Sumner had no sense of humor, tended to be prudish, and probably never understood a joke. Lincoln found humor in everything, and his allegorical yarns mystified the senator. Sumner lived by conventional standards while Lincoln, being unconventional and seen to be running a loose operation, appalled the senator. Yet they found admirable traits in each other, and Sumner became so important on foreign policy that Seward accused Lincoln of trying to run the administration with two secretaries of state.[13]

On December 25 Lincoln called a cabinet meeting to discuss Seward's reply to England. Anticipating a need to tone down Seward's message, he invited Sumner, who had contacted John Bright and Richard Cobden, two liberal British leaders friendly toward the United States. By then international clamor had subsided, and England was as anxious to settle the *Trent* affair as the administration. Although Lincoln had once considered arbitration, he and the cabinet unanimously agreed to admit Wilkes had acted improperly and to release the rebel commissioners. Seward composed a letter that chastised the British for recklessly impressing American sailors in past wars before apologizing for violating British maritime rights. Chase agreed the letter must be sent but grumbled, "It is gall and wormwood to me. Rather than consent to the liberation of these men [Mason and Slidell], I would rather sacrifice everything I possess."[14]

The peaceful outcome of the dispute gratified both sides of the ocean, including France, which stood ready to go to war against the United States if Britain did. On January 10 Adams carried Seward's apology to the British foreign office. "The current which ran against us with such extreme violence six weeks ago now seems," he said, "to be going with equal fury in our favor." He warned, however, if by the first of May "we shall have made no decided progress towards a [victorious] result, we may was well make up our minds to disbelieve in our own power to do it at all. Foreign nations will come to that conclusion if we do not."

While dodging war with Britain provided a diplomatic success, the impression of avoiding war with the South heaped pressure on the administration. Lincoln's annual message to Congress on December 3, 1861, contained a bundle of cabinet reports but made no promises for ending the war. The oversight raised concerns among congressional leaders.[15]

Congress viewed the administration as a mess. McClellan's mighty army had not budged, war expenses had ballooned beyond comprehension, the Treasury was empty, and reports of War Department corruption had mushroomed into a national scandal. Congress decided to assert legislative power and formed committees to investigate everything from the conduct of the war to Kentucky-born Mary Lincoln's rumored disloyalty to the Union.

When an earlier congressional committee began digging through contracts issued by the War Department, Lincoln expected the investigation to lead to trouble because of Cameron's involvement. John Nicolay had been watching the unfolding drama and made a notation referring to Cameron as "utterly ignorant" of department management in addition to being "selfish and openly discourteous to the President." The committee issued a scathing report listing dozens of scandals involving army contracts. Cameron had engaged unscrupulous Pennsylvania middlemen who acted as army agents and did nothing but collect outrageous commissions. They purchased unusable rifles, pistols rejected by the Ordnance Department, old and diseased horses tagged for the glue factory, and beef at twice the market price. Cameron also arrange for soldiers arriving from New York to be rerouted through Harrisburg so the Northern Central Railroad, commonly called the Cameron road, could pocket the revenue. The report did not directly incriminate Cameron but emphasized his inability to manage. The department's scandalous activities disenchanted investors in U.S. bonds, and New York bankers informed the president that $100 million sought by Chase could not be raised at reasonable rates unless Cameron was replaced.[16]

On December 1 Cameron finally tested the president's patience for the last time. In preparing his annual address, Lincoln asked each cabinet member for a report, which he intended to massage before submitting it to Congress. Instead of following orders, Cameron sent copies to strategically located post offices with instructions to mail them the day Lincoln's message went to Congress. Cameron's report called for three million troops and announced that former slaves should be inducted into the army. Cameron expected the public to accept the report as having been endorsed by the president. The printer, however, noticed the slave clause, considered the political impact, and took a copy to the White House. Lincoln read the passage in question and exclaimed, "This will never do! Gen. Cameron must take no such responsibility. That is a question which belongs exclusively to me!" Chase agreed with the clause and urged the president to let it stand. Lincoln ignored Chase and ordered Blair to recover all copies from the post offices. When Cameron protested, Lincoln silenced him.[17]

Chase had suggested the controversial clause, and Edwin McMasters Stanton, the former attorney general in Buchanan's administration, made the insertion when hired by Cameron to write the report. Whether deliberate or not, Stanton prepared the downfall of his client. Every cabinet member but Chase demanded Cameron's removal. They called the slave-arming proposition an effort to divert attention away from corruption in the War Department. Seward wanted to dispose of Cameron because of the war secretary's alliance with Chase. Even Caleb Smith, who seldom spoke, attacked Cameron for mentioning slavery. Despite Blair's efforts to recover the mail, copies reached New York before the amended report went to Congress. This pleased Cameron, who became defiant over Lincoln's alterations. On the same day Congress heard the president's annual address, Cameron's uncut version appeared in the press. He bluntly told the president, "The copies I have sent out will stand." Relations between Lincoln and Cameron had always been troubling. They now reached a climax.[18]

For weeks Lincoln had been studying charitable ways to remove the man who embodied his greatest liability without irritating Pennsylvania voters. The opportunity came in early January, when Cassius Clay, ambassador to Russia, resigned. Knowing of Chase's relationship with Cameron, Lincoln authorized him to broach the matter with the secretary. Because the Russian post reported to the State Department, he also inducted Seward. Chase and Seward usually held opposing views, but they supported the transfer of Cameron to Russia and independently recommended filling the vacant post with Stanton. Although Lincoln preferred filling the post with Joseph Holt of Kentucky, who had served briefly as Buchanan's secretary of war, he hoped naming Stanton might achieve harmony between Chase and Seward.[19]

Lincoln's announcement of the change caught all but Seward and Chase by surprise. The suddenness shocked Cameron, whose official notification arrived on January 11, 1862. Lincoln accepted Cameron's resignation— though the secretary had not resigned—and offered him the portfolio of minister to Russia. According to Alexander McClure, who observed the letter opening, Cameron howled, wailing that his ejection meant "personal as well as political destruction," and "wept bitterly over what he regarded as a personal affront from Lincoln." Cameron's cronies visited Lincoln the following morning and asked him to replace the letter with a kinder and gentler one. Lincoln complied because he had never intended to insult Cameron and retro-dated the second letter. The public never saw the original.[20]

By replacing Cameron with Stanton—a forty-seven-year-old short, stocky, imperious, but brilliant Washington attorney—Lincoln believed the new secretary would blend well with Seward and Chase, although Stanton was fundamentally a Jacksonian Democrat who had once defended the rights of slaveholders. Lincoln had collided with Stanton in 1855, when both men were involved in patent litigation during the McCormick reaper case. Although Lincoln received a thousand-dollar fee, Stanton led the defense team and snubbed Lincoln during the trial. After taking one look at Lincoln in his unkempt clothes, Stanton asked patent lawyer George Harding, "Why did you bring that d——d long armed ape here; he does not know anything and can do you no good." Lincoln returned to Springfield insulted and irritated. Despite the unpleasant experience, he respected Stanton's ability.[21]

Although seven years had passed since the McCormick case, Stanton still questioned Lincoln's ability. He enjoyed meddling in Cameron's affairs and contributed to the secretary's ejection—which may have been his objective. On January 15, 1862, he traded in a practice netting fifty thousand dollars a year for a cabinet post paying eight thousand dollars. Ten months earlier Lincoln had said, "Mr. Stanton, as you know, had been serving conspicuously in the Cabinet of Mr. Buchanan, faithful among the faithless. There is a common appreciation of his ability and fidelity, and a common expectation that I will take him into my Cabinet, but you know that I could not possibly pursue that course in view of his personal treatment of me." After months of watching Cameron mismanage the War Department, Lincoln took the same friend aside and said, "I have made up my mind to sit down all my pride—it may be a portion of my self-respect—and appoint him to the place."[22]

Despite personal differences, Stanton and Lincoln shared common traits. Both men exercised a consuming passion for the preservation of the Union. Although they would often disagree on methodology, both of them were fundamentally honest. Although never patient, Stanton was an excellent administrator and just what the War Department needed. Stanton's tendency to be aggressively assertive, ingratiate himself to those in power, and push underlings around caught Welles's attention. He believed McClellan would have been a better secretary of war than a general, and his opinion, though never tested, may have had merit.[23]

As secretary of war, Stanton was entirely different than Cameron. At the first official meeting with the officers of the army, he looked directly at McClellan and said, "It is my work to furnish the means, the instruments, for prosecuting the war for the Union and putting down the rebellion against it, and mine to see that you use them." The statement stung McClellan's tender ego, prompting him to write, "Without any reason known to me, our relations . . . completely changed. Instead of using his new position to assist me he threw every obstacle in my way. I soon found it impossible to gain access to him." Access to Stanton was never the problem. McClellan avoided him.

Stanton sized up the situation quickly, writing, "This army has got to fight or run away; and while men are striving nobly in the West, the champagne and oysters on the Potomac must be stopped."[24]

Stanton faced many problems besides McClellan. The newly composed Joint Committee on the Conduct of the War, organized by radicals investigating the disasters at Bull Run and Ball's Bluff, encumbered the administration. On January 20 he went before the committee to form alliances with its members and promised to prosecute the war "with all possible dispatch." He won over Ben Wade, Zachariah Chandler, Andrew Johnson, and several other senators. Committeeman George Julian was "delighted" with the meeting and expressed "perfect confidence in [Stanton's] integrity, sagacity, and strong will." Stanton's public relations effort netted immediate dividends, loosening legislative impediments on important appropriations needed to support the war.[25]

Stanton also had to deliver on his promises. He moved his long, high desk into a room open to the public, stood behind it while he worked, upbraided contractors for sloppy workmanship, and chastised military officers applying for undeserved promotion. Within a month he brought order to the War Department, cleaned up Cameron's messes, completely wore himself out, and suffered a slight stroke. He soon returned, his capacity for work undiminished, and began looking for ways to push McClellan's vaunted Army of the Potomac on to Richmond.[26]

The Committee on the Conduct of the War also put pressure on McClellan, who was recovering from typhoid fever. On January 6 Lincoln rejected Senator Wade's demand to replace McClellan. He urged the general to go before the committee "the earliest moment your health will permit—today, if possible," and explain his plans. McClellan refused to discuss plans with anyone, including the president and cabinet, and he also refused to discuss them with his own generals. Because he trusted no one, he never appointed a second in command. When a frustrated Congress summoned McClellan's division commanders to appear before the committee to explain the general's plans, the officers said nothing because they knew nothing. The standoff between McClellan, the administration, and Congress continued. General Meigs wrote, "President comes to me much depressed re[garding] inactivity of army and McClellan's sickness. The people are impatient; Chase has no money, and he tells me he can raise no money; the Gen. of the Army has typhoid fever. The bottom is out of the tub. What shall I do?" Meigs felt inadequate. He could give sympathy but not advice.[27]

By replacing Cameron with Stanton, Lincoln expected improvements.

At first McClellan regarded Stanton as his friend and counselor. The working relationship ebbed as the secretary applied pressure and worsened as Stanton began denying the general's requests for more men or more time. According to McClellan, Stanton behaved like everyone else in the cabinet, diminishing in stature from being the savior of the administration to being "the most unmitigated scoundrel I ever knew, heard or read of." But in February 1862, after Stanton took office, McClellan agreed to a spring campaign. Once again the public began speaking optimistically of one final battle to end the war. After waiting so long for the Army of the Potomac to go on the offensive, they expected nothing less.[28]

CHAPTER 9

"I can't spare this man; he fights"

Winter cast a pall over the administration. Lincoln wanted the Confederates driven out of Manassas, and on December 1, 1861, he wrote General McClellan, urging a campaign before the end of the year. Ten days later the general curtly replied, claiming Joe Johnston's Confederates could meet the Army of the Potomac with equal forces. "I have now my mind turned towards another plan of campaign," he replied, "[not] at all anticipated by the enemy, nor by any of our own people." At the time, McClellan commanded 150,000 men, Johnston 45,000. Lincoln did not ask about the plan because McClellan went to bed with typhoid fever, and the war machine in Washington ground to a standstill.[1]

The cabinet wondered why Lincoln tolerated the general's arrogance. Bates blamed it partly on the cabinet, writing on New Year's, "It is not *an* administration but the separate and disjointed action of seven independent officers, each one ignorant of what his colleagues are doing. It seemed as if all military operations were to stop, just because Genl McClellan is sick." Bates reminded Lincoln that as commander in chief, "it was not his *privilege* but his *duty* to command; and *that* implied the necessity to *know* the true condition of things." He thought the president was "an excellent man . . . but he lacks *will* and *purpose,* and, I greatly fear he has not *the power to command.*" Lincoln admitted being baffled by McClellan's behavior.[2]

To educate himself in military matters, Lincoln started reading books on tactics and, as his knowledge increased, began probing generals with penetrating questions. On January 10 he considered leading the army himself and summoned generals Irvin McDowell and William B. Franklin to the White House. According to McDowell, Lincoln said, "If General McClellan did not want to use the army he would like to borrow it, providing he could see how it could be made to do something." McDowell said an energetic movement against the rebel flanks would force the enemy to fight in the open and would succeed. Franklin preferred to move on Richmond by a water route, which unintentionally disclosed a proposal McClellan had refused to share with the administration. Lincoln instructed both generals to agree on a movement and return in forty-eight hours with a decision.[3]

McDowell and Franklin returned to the White House on the twelfth and found Seward, Chase, and Meigs with the president. Franklin now agreed with McDowell's Manassas plan, so Lincoln gave the generals another day to design the attack. When McDowell and Franklin returned the next day, McClellan arrived looking fit and obviously annoyed. McDowell presented his proposal to Lincoln and the others—Blair, Chase, Meigs, and Seward—after which McClellan brusquely said, "You are entitled to have any opinion you please." All but Blair approved the plan, and McClellan spoke angrily of the inadequacy of his forces and condemned McDowell's plan as a blunder "so clear a blind man could see it." Disgusted, Chase asked McClellan bluntly what he intended to do with the army and when he intended to do it. McClellan ignored the question, saying Buell must move first in Kentucky. He then threatened to cancel the transfer of Butler's troops to Louisiana, which would have quashed Commodore David G. Farragut's expedition against New Orleans. Lincoln asked McClellan if he had "any particular time fixed" for an offensive campaign, and the general said he did. "I think the meeting had better break up," said Seward. "I don't see that we are likely to [get] much out of Gen. McClellan." Had McDowell's plan been executed, which happened to be the same plan Lincoln suggested to McClellan six weeks earlier, the campaigns of the Army of the Potomac would have been remarkably different and likely more successful.[4]

Lincoln and the cabinet waited two weeks for McClellan's timetable. Frustrated by the general's stalling, Lincoln issued General War Order No. 1 on January 27 calling for a "general movement of land and naval forces" no later than February 22. This included the movement of the three main armies under McClellan's command. Lincoln wrote the order without consulting anyone then read it to the cabinet, telling McClellan, Stanton, and Welles he expected his instructions to be followed. He failed, however, to get through to McClellan.[5]

The order created new problems for McClellan. General Buell hesitated to advance into eastern Tennessee, and Brigadier General George H. Thomas's command stopped at Cumberland Gap. Buell said he preferred engaging the enemy at Bowling Green, Kentucky, which would provide a platform for operations against Nashville. Although disappointed by these developments, Lincoln wanted action and accepted the new plan. Liberating eastern Tennessee's Unionists from rebel control made political sense, but occupying Nashville made military sense. McClellan had held Buell back for two months before Lincoln interceded. Although Buell complained that he could not "seriously engage the enemy," two weeks later Bowling Green fell, and on February 25 Buell entered Nashville against light resistance.[6]

On February 6 Halleck wrote from St. Louis, "I was not ready to move," but on that day General Ulysses S. Grant captured Fort Henry and four days later attacked Fort Donelson. New Madrid and Island No. 10 fell, and on March 3 Commodore Andrew Foote took possession of Columbus, Kentucky.[7]

While operations in the West progressed, Lincoln could not pry a timetable from McClellan for using the Army of the Potomac. On January 31 he issued Special War Order No. 1 directing McClellan to provide protection for Washington and attack Manassas no later than February 22. Little Mac insisted he had a better plan. He would assault Richmond by moving down the Potomac in transports and up the Rappahannock River to Urbanna. On February 3 Lincoln presented McClellan with five points of argument asking why the Urbanna plan was better than the Manassas plan. The general issued a lengthy response opposing the Manassas plan because of "insufficient force" and "determined resistance" by the enemy. He praised his own plan as the shortest and swiftest route to Richmond, insisting it could be achieved by "one march from West Point [on the York River] . . . and thence by two marches to Richmond." McClellan, however, had never ordered a thorough reconnaissance of Manassas, and the huge rebel force existed only in his imagination.[8]

Lincoln erred by giving McClellan an opportunity to defend the Urbanna plan. Had the Army of the Potomac advanced as Lincoln ordered, McClellan might not have won the war, but he would have gained at slight cost a sweeping victory. Lincoln left himself with three options: he could order the Manassas attack, accept the Urbanna plan, or find another general. Little Mac, however, pledged, "I will stake my life, my reputation on the result—more than that, I will stake upon it the success of our cause."[9]

Lincoln felt uncomfortable demanding his general-in-chief to execute a military operation under protest, and no general but McClellan had the adoration of the Army of the Potomac. This left the Urbanna plan. The president made one last attempt to change McClellan's mind and asked him to conduct a council of war. Twelve generals attended. Four voted against the Manassas plan, one voted for it with conditions, and the other seven generals sided with McClellan. Stanton remarked, "We saw ten generals afraid to fight." During the session Lincoln was not in command of his emotions. His son Willie, who had been ill, died on February 20. During the death watch Lincoln told Stanton, "We can do nothing else than accept their plan and discard all others. We can't reject it and adopt another without assuming all the responsibility in the case of the failure of the one we adopt."[10]

February 22 came and went without the Army of the Potomac advancing from Washington. McClellan took credit for Halleck and Buell's advances in the West and seemed undisturbed they accomplished so much while he accomplished so little. Lincoln began to question McClellan's competence in other areas. He wanted Harpers Ferry occupied and the bridge over the Potomac rebuilt so the Baltimore & Ohio could resume operations to the West. McClellan ordered special boats made to carry bridge-building materials up the Chesapeake and Ohio Canal. After discovering the boats were six inches wider than the locks, McClellan abandoned the project. Lincoln flew into a rage. John Nicolay's daughter Helen later recalled, "This is almost the only time in all my father's notes that he mentioned seeing the President shaken out of his usual calm."[11]

The canal boat fiasco added to a growing number of warnings from anti-McClellan radicals who suspected the general of disloyalty. Lincoln doubted the allegations but on March 8 summoned McClellan to the White House to air his concerns over the protection of Washington. When he mentioned being warned by credible sources that the general's Urbanna plan "was conceived with the traitorous intent of . . . giving over to the enemy the capital and the government, thus left defenseless," McClellan bolted from his chair and said he would allow no man to call him a traitor. Equally agitated, Lincoln said his statement was not intended as an accusation. He merely repeated what others had said and "did not believe a word of it." Lincoln still wanted the Manassas plan, which would have protected Washington, but McClellan missed the point.[12]

In a second directive issued that day, Lincoln ordered McClellan to launch the Urbanna-Richmond campaign no later than March 18, leaving Washington "entirely secure." McClellan resented being told what to do and on March 9 asked Stanton to suspend part of the president's order. Stanton replied, "I think it is the duty of every officer to obey the President's orders, nor can I see any reason why you should not obey them." McClellan continued to argue with Stanton about leaving so many troops to guard Washington, which was the price McClellan paid for rejecting the Manassas plan.[13]

On March 8, during the reorganization of the Army of the Potomac into corps, the CSS *Virginia,* a powerful ironclad converted from the remains of the USS *Merrimack,* steamed out of Norfolk and created mayhem in Hampton Roads, destroying two Union ships and grounding the forty-four-gun USS *Minnesota.* The administration worried the monstrous ironclad would ascend the Potomac and attack the capital or go to sea and dismantle the blockade. McClellan used the threat as a valid reason to delay his movement to Urbanna. Lincoln looked to Welles, hoping the navy could provide a solution. Welles remained calm and said the USS *Monitor* was en route to Fort Monroe. This did not quiet Stanton, who spoke of catastrophic disasters occurring everywhere, but he seemed pleased about one issue and said, "McClellan's mistaken purpose to advance on the Peninsula must be abandoned." Seward relaxed after Welles told the men the *Virginia*'s draft would prevent it from ascending the Potomac, but when the Fort Monroe telegraph went dead, Stanton periodically went to the window and looked down the Potomac to see if the iron menace was steaming upriver toward the White House.[14]

Being a man of action but fundamentally a landlubber, Stanton listened closely when Commander John A. Dahlgren proposed sinking sixty rock-filled canal boats across Kettle Bottom Shoals near the lower Potomac. Welles called the idea absurd, but the president ordered it done. On March 9 Stanton, Seward, and Dahlgren went downriver to watch the boat-sinking effort. Later Fort Monroe's telegraph resumed communications and confirmed Welles's prediction: the USS *Monitor* had intercepted and repulsed the CSS *Virginia*. Weeks later Lincoln went down the Potomac with Stanton and other officials and passed a long line of rock-filled boats resting against the shore. "That is Stanton's navy," he said, pointing to the boats, "Welles . . . opposed to the scheme, and it has proved that Neptune was right. Stanton's navy is as useless as the paps of a man suckling a child."[15]

Because the *Monitor* fought the *Virginia* to a draw but did not sink the Confederate ship, Stanton continued to worry the rebel ironclad might break out of Hampton Roads and threaten McClellan's campaign. Shipping tycoon Cornelius Vanderbilt came to Washington and suggested chartering the *Vanderbilt*, the strongest and swiftest merchant steamer in the Western Hemisphere. He offered to strengthen its bow with timbers and iron plates and place it at Fort Monroe with orders to run down the *Virginia*. Stanton asked the cost, and Vanderbilt said he would do everything at his own expense. He also told Stanton the same offer had been rejected by Welles. Stanton saw an opportunity to run his own navy, approved the project, and chartered two more steamers with reinforced bows. All three ships remained idle at Fort Monroe until the rebels scuttled their ironclad. Stanton's attempt to run the navy as well as the army, however, did not end.[16]

The clash of ironclads on March 9 turned out to be a good day for the navy but not good for McClellan. Federal scouts reported Confederate fortifications at Manassas abandoned and filled with Quaker guns (wooden imitations of cannon). Johnston's army had quietly slipped away on February 22, raising questions about the reliability of McClellan's intelligence network.

The general blamed the cabinet for leaking the Urbanna plan, but Johnston admitted having no knowledge of the operation. McClellan now faced the prospect of fighting a reinforced rebel army on the Peninsula, proving Lincoln was correct by wanting McClellan to attack the Confederates at Manassas. Johnston remarked that McClellan "seems not to value time especially." By shifting to the Rappahannock, Johnston vastly improved his maneuverability and undermined the Urbanna movement, forcing McClellan to plead for more time.[17]

The general then made another puzzling decision. Instead of taking the Army of the Potomac to Manassas when Confederates were there, he issued orders on March 10 for a general movement toward Centreville to confirm the enemy's withdrawal. The entire army marched to the old Bull Run battlefield, found nobody there, realized the enemy never had more than forty thousand troops (about a third of McClellan's estimate), and marched back to Washington. McClellan never explained why he waited for Manassas to be evacuated before ordering an advance except to say he used the exercise as a dress rehearsal for the upcoming campaign. McClellan could no longer use Urbanna, which was fifty miles from Richmond. He now had to go farther down the Chesapeake and land at Fort Monroe, which added another thirty miles. Had he marched from Manassas, the distance to Richmond would have been ten miles shorter, with better roads. McClellan's tardy expedition to and from Manassas cost him command of the Union army.[18]

On March 11 Lincoln called Chase, Seward, and Stanton together and read War Order No. 3, which relieved McClellan of all responsibilities but the Army of the Potomac. Lincoln consolidated Buell's operations in the West under Halleck's department and, to appease the radicals, established a Mountain Department in western Virginia under General Frémont. All departments reported to Stanton. Lincoln excluded Blair from the meeting because he knew the postmaster general would object to reinstating Frémont. Stanton disagreed with the president's decision and merely said, "If Gen. Frémont has any fight in him he shall have a chance to show it and I have told him so." Stanton understood very little about warfare and soon became swamped with administrative problems related to military operations.[19]

Lincoln's reorganization met with most of the cabinet's approval. Even McClellan, who some thought and others hoped would resign, accepted his demotion with dignity and wrote Lincoln, "I shall work just as cheerfully as ever before." Bates doubted McClellan's sincerity. He also disapproved of Lincoln's unwarranted courtesy toward the general. In his opinion Lincoln had failed as commander in chief. "The very best of them [the generals]," said

Bates, "until very lately, never commanded more than a battalion. If therefore, they presume to quarrel with the orders of *their superior* . . . they ought to be dismissed." Bates disliked Banks, Frémont, Halleck, and McClellan and believed many junior officers would make better field commanders. Commenting on McClellan's pointless expedition to Manassas, Bates said, "Upon the whole it seems as if our general went with his finger in his mouth on a fool's errand, and that he has won a fool's reward." "But after all," he noted acerbically, "[he] did actually capture one rebel captain and five privates."[20]

Having at last obtained McClellan's commitment to launch a campaign, Lincoln refused to change generals. He had provided the Young Napoleon with the best-equipped and trained army on the planet, and he expected the general to use it and bring home a victory. During a conversation with Browning, Lincoln expressed his one reservation, admitting that McClellan had "the capacity to make arrangements properly for a great conflict, but as the hour for action approached he became . . . oppressed with the responsibility and hesitated to meet the crisis." The general's recent burst of energy, however, made Lincoln hopeful.[21]

On March 17 McClellan embarked the first of 121,500 soldiers, 14,592 animals, 1,150 wagons, 44 batteries, 74 ambulances, and tons of equipment on 113 steamers, 188 schooners, and 88 barges. Until World War II the project ranked as the greatest amphibious operation in American history.[22]

On April 1 McClellan sailed to his new headquarters at Fort Monroe. In a letter home he wrote, "I did not feel safe until I could fairly see Alexandria behind us, [as I might] be sent for from Washington. Officially speaking, I feel very glad to get away from that sink of iniquity." The general had reasons to "get away." Stanton discovered McClellan had left only nineteen thousand troops to defend Washington, not forty thousand. He ordered headcounts taken and confirmed the report. McClellan had scattered the other twenty thousand troops across northern Virginia. Because McDowell's corps had not embarked, Stanton retained it. McClellan watched part of his army stripped from the campaign, and if he needed an excuse for failing, he now had one, at least from his perspective.[23]

McClellan reached Fort Monroe on April 2 with fifty-eight thousand men available, but he seemed unable to get his army in motion. Nicolay noted the growing impatience at the White House, writing, "Gen. McC. is in danger. Not in front but in rear. The President is making up his mind to give him a peremptory order to march. It is disgraceful to think how the little Confederate squad at Yorktown keeps him at bay." McClellan broke no records for speed. Five days later Bates wrote, "Poor McClellan! I think he has committed a blunder, fatal to his reputation, in attempting to conquer . . . Richmond through that narrow peninsula."[24]

With McClellan's expedition under way and with Halleck's operations moving smoothly in the West, a general feeling persisted among the public that the war may be short after all. In February, after capturing Fort Henry, General Grant said, "I shall take and destroy Fort Donelson on the 8th." Although he was detained by floodwaters, Grant kept his word on the sixteenth. He captured fifteen thousand prisoners; collected a huge haul of weapons, horses, and supplies; and coined the phrase *unconditional surrender*. The press made a fanciful play on the general's initials and dubbed him "Unconditional Surrender Grant." Unconditional surrender was what the president wanted, not unauthorized political deals made by military commanders. Lincoln nominated Grant major general, the Senate confirmed the promotion, and the entire military establishment recognized the possibility of promotion by merit.[25]

Differentiating Grant from McClellan's generals, Lincoln said, "I cannot speak so confidently about the fighting qualities of the Eastern men . . . [but] if the Southerners think that man for man they are better than . . . Western men generally, they will discover themselves in a grievous mistake." Former secretary of war John B. Floyd, who had served in the Buchanan administration, escaped from Donelson. Stanton knew Floyd personally and said, "I am sorry he got away. I want to catch and hang him."[26]

With Western armies collecting laurels, Halleck expected to be named supreme commander of the West, though he never strayed far from St. Louis. Because Grant had earned his promotion, he thought Buell and John Pope should be elevated. Having captured Bowling Green on February 14 and Nashville two weeks later, Buell deserved consideration. Pope had opened the central Mississippi by capturing New Madrid and Island No. 10. Brigadier General Samuel R. Curtis also belonged on the promotion list for winning battles at Pea Ridge and Elkhorn Tavern. So on March 11 Lincoln rewarded Halleck by putting him in charge of the Department of the Mississippi and ten days later elevated Buell, Pope, and Curtis to major general. Halleck then pointed to Memphis, his next target.[27]

Fifty-nine-year-old General Albert Sidney Johnston ranked among the South's best generals. Despite his highly regarded reputation, he abandoned Nashville when attacked by Buell and began transferring troops from Kentucky, Tennessee, and Mississippi to General Beauregard, who had been sent west to build a new army. Had Buell moved with alacrity after securing Nashville, he could have captured Memphis virtually unopposed. Instead, Halleck allowed Buell to remain idle and sent Grant up the Tennessee River to destroy Confederate communications. Halleck thought Grant had moved too slowly and put Major General Charles F. Smith in charge of the expedition. He recognized his mistake and on March 17 put Grant back in command. Halleck's indecision caused ten days of unrecoverable delay. When Grant returned, he found both halves of the army nine miles apart on opposite sides of the flooded river and ordered them consolidated at Pittsburg Landing.[28]

On March 16 Halleck urged Buell to move his idle force out of Nashville "as rapidly as possible" and join Grant at Savannah. Grant advised Buell the army was at Pittsburg Landing, not Savannah. For two weeks Buell remained confused by his orders. He decided to follow Halleck's instructions, and on April 5 the first elements arrived at Savannah. Halleck seemed not to appreciate the danger of having half of the army on the west side of the river and half on the other side. Grant knew Confederate forces were strengthening at Corinth, so he went to Savannah and told Brigadier General William Nelson, "I will send boats for you . . . sometime early next week. There will be no fight at Pittsburg Landing; we will have to go to Corinth, where the rebels are fortified." Grant was about to suffer one of the most impressive lessons of his military career.[29]

Delays imposed by Halleck and by Buell allowed Johnston and Beauregard to consolidate forty thousand troops at Corinth and, on the night of April 5, placed them two miles from Pittsburg Landing. Federal reconnaissance failed to observe the movement, and Grant told his division commanders the rebels were still at Corinth. Five of Grant's divisions camped on a triangular plateau with no defense against attack except for a weak line of pickets a mile away. At 5:00 a.m. the Confederate line moved forward, brushed away Union pickets, and slammed into a Federal regiment that put the entire Union front on alert. Minutes later forty thousand Confederates faced off against thirty-three thousand Federals in a determined slugfest around a patch of ground occupied by Shiloh Church.[30]

Johnston fell leading a Confederate brigade, but Beauregard, entrusted with the assault, continued to press against the Union center. He cut gaps in the Union line, isolating patches of Federal troops. The assault created breaches through which Confederates poured, routing Federals and driving some to the banks of the river. Grant knew he was in trouble and sent a message to Buell, "If you will get upon the field, leaving all your baggage on the east bank of the river, it will . . . possibly save the day for us."[31]

Beauregard intended to destroy the transports and force Grant to surrender. Instead, Grant forced the Confederates into difficult terrain. The rebels held the battlefield, but Federals controlled the central position, the supplies, and the communications. Grant's army remained better unified because thousands of Confederate stragglers deserted their units to plunder Union camps for food and booty. At sunset prospects of a Southern victory diminished as Buell's leading elements began disembarking at Pittsburg Landing.

At 7:30 a.m. on April 7 Grant counterattacked from the right and Buell from the left. The two generals had no battle plan other than to drive the enemy from the field. In a bitterly contested struggle that seesawed around Shiloh Church and lasted until three that afternoon, the Confederates grudgingly gave ground and fell back to Corinth. Both sides suffered more than ten thousand casualties. Two days later Grant decided to pursue Beauregard. He asked for reinforcements, and on April 15 Halleck sent General Pope's twenty thousand–man army from Island No. 10. Halleck decided to take field command and arrived with Pope.[32]

Despite his rank and reputation, Halleck's credentials as a field commander had never been tested. Stanton was uncertain what to expect and merely said, "I have no instructions to give you. Go ahead." Halleck reorganized the army at Pittsburg Landing into three corps, Grant taking the first, Buell the second, and Pope the third. Halleck, however, disliked Grant because he failed to file timely reports, ignored red tape, and liked whiskey. After days of snooping, Halleck decided that Grant, by incompetence or drunkenness, was responsible for Shiloh's staggering losses. He later discovered the rumors were false and put Grant in the useless position of being second in command and pulled Major General George Thomas out of Kentucky to command the First Corps. Grant threatened to resign, but General William Tecumseh Sherman talked him out of it.[33]

Halleck's comments about Grant's performance at Shiloh, together with an unsupported rumor that the general had been absent without leave, reached the White House. Lincoln asked Stanton whether "any neglect or misconduct" of Grant contributed to the worst bloodbath of its kind since the beginning of the war. Halleck refused to assign blame because Grant won the battle. Halleck admitted there were officers "utterly unfit" for command but said the casualties resulted from superior "numbers and bravery" of the enemy. To a friend, however, Halleck confided having never seen a general more deficient in organizational skills than Grant. On skills for conducting operations in the field, Halleck would soon prove to be among the greatest blunderers of all.[34]

Lincoln ignored the rumors and retained confidence in Grant. He did not care if his generals ignored red tape. Alexander McClure stopped at the White House and suggested Grant be removed because the country was against him. Lincoln thought for a spell, gathered himself up in a chair, and said, "I can't spare this man; he fights." McClure later wrote, "The only man in all the nation who had the power to save Grant was Lincoln, and he decided to do it."[35]

In late April, after gathering 100,000 men at Pittsburg Landing, Halleck prepared for his big push on Corinth. The original Union strategy had been to capture Memphis and secure more of the Mississippi, but the concentration of Confederate forces at Corinth changed Halleck's plans. Lincoln waited for operations to commence, but Halleck behaved like McClellan when aggressiveness counted. For four weeks he advanced "provokingly slow," averaging a mile a day and entrenching at every stop. On May 25 he began arranging artillery to bombard Corinth. Four nights later Beauregard's 50,000-man army slipped away from Corinth and crossed the Tuscumbia River. Halleck decided to consolidate his gains in Tennessee and remain on the defensive, and every passing day added to Lincoln's frustration.[36]

While Halleck's army crawled snail-like toward Corinth, Farragut's squadron of oceangoing warships bumped over the bars at the mouth of the Mississippi, ran a gantlet of fire from Forts Jackson and St. Philip, fought a flotilla of Confederate gunboats, and on April 25 captured New Orleans. Welles's navy continued to deliver on promises, while Stanton's army lagged behind. As biographer Benjamin P. Thomas observed, "Like all Americans, Stanton had to be educated in how to fight this war."[37]

When Stanton joined the cabinet, he expected the navy to submit to the War Department. All Welles asked of Stanton was to be notified whenever the army needed the navy. Stanton, however, had not learned from Seward's mistakes. If Welles did not cooperate, Stanton believed it would be acceptable for him to take matters into his own hands.[38]

After the capture of Island No. 10, Stanton turned his attention to Memphis, which he wanted as a base on the Mississippi River for supplying Halleck's army. Before Stanton became secretary of war, Charles Ellet, a civil engineer with no military training, approached Welles and asked the navy to buy a squadron of fast river steamers fitted with ironclad bows for operations on the Mississippi. Welles rejected the offer because Ellet wanted to operate the rams as privateers. Ellet took the scheme to Stanton, who observed an opportunity to make Welles look bad. Stanton approved the scheme and authorized Ellet to build the rams and forward the bills to the War Department.[39]

By the end of April Ellet had purchased two tenders and refitted seven riverboats with iron bows. Welles refused to provide naval officers, so Stanton made Ellet a colonel and put him in charge of recruiting men for the Ram Fleet. Stanton claimed bragging rights after Ellet took the rams downriver to Fort Pillow, steamed through Welles's riverine squadron, rammed the Confederate River Defense Fleet, and captured Memphis. Welles made no comments until several weeks later, when the Ram Fleet began looting towns and plantations. To avoid further embarrassment, Stanton pitched the unit to the Navy Department, and Lincoln made Welles take it. The surrender of Memphis on June 6, however, revealed a serious flaw in Halleck's reconnaissance operations. A small Union force could have captured Memphis a few days after the Battle of Shiloh because Beauregard had removed the troops from the city and brought them to Corinth.[40]

After occupying Corinth on June 10, Halleck seemed incapable of organizing aggressive operations. His inactivity in the West became as annoying to the administration as McClellan's stalling in the East. Lincoln still had an opening for a general-in-chief, which he had stripped from McClellan prior to the Peninsular campaign, but he bided his time, hoping Halleck would work with Farragut to open the Mississippi while McClellan swept into Richmond.

CHAPTER 10

"If I could save the Union . . ."

While Halleck's huge army stagnated at Corinth, McClellan's equally huge army dallied on Virginia's peninsula, between the York and James rivers. On April 3 the Young Napoleon had fifty-eight thousand troops and one hundred guns ready to move against Yorktown and another fifty thousand troops in transit. Major General John B. Magruder, with only eleven thousand Confederates, posted half his troops at Yorktown and strung the other half across thirteen miles of the lower peninsula. Infused with wishful thinking, McClellan confided to his wife, "I hope to get possession of Yorktown day after tomorrow. The great battle will be (I think) near Richmond, as I have always hoped and thought. I see my way very clearly, and . . . will move rapidly."

The general's energetic campaign ended the following day, when Magruder staged a theatrical show of resistance. Instead of pressing the attack, McClellan put the Confederates under siege and, instead of flanking the position with his vastly superior forces, wasted exactly one month. Lincoln observed McClellan's stalling and on April 9 wrote, "Once more let me tell you, it is indispensable to *you* that you strike a blow. *I* am powerless to help this. You will do me the justice to remember I always insisted that going down the Bay in search of a field, instead of fighting at or near Manassas, was only shifting, and not surmounting, a difficulty—that we would find the same enemy, and the same or equal entrenchments, at either place." The president promised to send Franklin's division from McDowell's corps, adding, *"But you must act."* McClellan disliked presidential interference and wrote his wife, "I was much tempted to reply that he had better come and do it himself." When on May 3 Magruder withdrew unnoticed to Williamsburg, McClellan lost another day getting his army in motion.[1]

McClellan blamed his ineptitude on others. He criticized the administration for insufficient support and the navy for not silencing Yorktown's batteries. With more than 100,000 troops on the peninsula, McClellan needed no reinforcements to defeat Magruder, and the navy did all it could.[2]

Magruder admitted his lines could have been pierced at any time, later reporting, "But to my utter surprise he permitted day after day to elapse without an assault." Union generals were astonished by McClellan's cautiousness. Congressmen John A. Gurley of Ohio condemned McClellan as a "traitor" who intended "to have his own army beaten." He quoted a conversation between Little Mac and a local physician, during which the general allegedly said, "The South was right and he would never fight against it." When Bates learned of the comment, he branded McClellan as not a traitor, "only a foolish egot."[3]

Unaware McClellan was now moving forward, Stanton invited Lincoln and Chase to accompany him to Fort Monroe to determine whether the general's constant demands for reinforcements were justified. Arriving on May 6, they were greeted by seventy-three-year-old General John E. Wool, who said McClellan had reached Williamsburg and was marching on Richmond. Having little to do, Lincoln's party toured Hampton Roads and learned from Commodore Louis Goldsborough that the CSS *Virginia* lay berthed at Sewall's Point, across from Fort Monroe.[4]

Lincoln wanted to see the *Virginia* and asked Goldsborough to shell the batteries at Sewall's Point. Moments later the ironclad, belching black smoke, swung into Hampton Roads and steamed toward the Union ships. Goldsborough withdrew the wooden gunboats but not the *Monitor.* To everyone's disappointment the *Virginia* circled and returned to Sewall's Point.

Lincoln, Chase, and Stanton returned to Fort Monroe and decided to give the war effort a boost by capturing Norfolk. Wool provided charts but insisted it would not be possible to land troops because of shoals. Late that night Chase used a tugboat for soundings and located a stretch of deep water near shore. With a bright moon overhead, Lincoln and Stanton took the tug into the shallows, while the USS *Miami* stood by with guns registered on Sewall's Point. The president could not resist going ashore and enjoyed a brief walk on the beach.

After proving troops could be landed, Lincoln issued orders through Stanton for two infantry brigades and a cavalry company from Wool's garrison to attack Sewall's Point. On the night of May 9 a five thousand–man expedition went ashore with Chase and Wool. The Federals entered Sewall's Point unchallenged and continued on to Norfolk, where Chase met a delegation from the city carrying a white flag. Lincoln came ashore, accepted Norfolk's surrender, and toured the area in a carriage. At dusk the presidential party returned to the *Miami,* leaving Chase to comment, "I think it quite certain that if he [Lincoln] had not come down, [Norfolk] would still have been in possession of the enemy and the *Merrimac* as grim and defiant and as much a terror as ever." On the following morning Confederates set fire to the *Virginia* and blew up the ship.[5]

Although insignificant compared with the army's greater task, the destruction of the *Virginia* and the occupation of Norfolk cleared the lower river of rebels and opened the way for McClellan later to move his supply base to the James River. According to Wool, the Army of the Potomac was making exceptional progress, so Lincoln, Chase, and Stanton returned to Washington satisfied with their effort to support McClellan's campaign.

McClellan's month-long siege of Yorktown gave General Joe Johnston time to move 40,000 troops from the Rappahannock to Williamsburg. He stalled McClellan's lethargic advance and slowly withdrew to the south bank of the Chickahominy River. As McClellan approached Richmond, his returns showed 100,000 men available for duty, but he claimed having only 70,000 effectives. Allan Pinkerton's spies shattered McClellan's nerves by doubling the actual size of Johnston's force to 120,000.[6]

McClellan slowed his advance and demanded the return of McDowell's corps. Lincoln refused but, after conferring with Stanton, decided that because McDowell's force was already near Fredericksburg, he could bolster McClellan's strength by having McDowell march on Richmond and merge with the right wing of the Army of the Potomac. To this logical compromise McClellan complained to his wife, "Those hounds in Washington are after me again. Stanton is without exception the vilest man I ever knew or heard of."[7]

On the eve of the first battles for Richmond, McClellan still wanted to argue with the president over the organization of the army. Bates commented, "I do believe the Gen[eral] has such a morbid ambition of originality that he will adopt no plan of action suggested by another. He must himself *invent* as well as execute every scheme of operations." McClellan objected to McDowell's direct approach on Richmond and insisted the corps return to Washington and be transported by boat to the peninsula so "my authority over McDowell may be clearly defined." It was McClellan's way of saying he wanted McDowell's corps but not McDowell.[8]

Ever since Lincoln ordered McClellan to form his divisions into corps, the general had wanted to impose his will on the president and shape the army differently. He now used Lincoln's edict as an excuse to delay operations and asked permission to reorganize the army as he wished. The president knew Little Mac merely wanted to "pamper one or two pets and to persecute and degrade their supposed rivals," and though exasperated by the general's demands, he authorized McClellan to adopt whatever chain of command he wanted and press forward. McClellan did want to promote two friends, Porter and Franklin, to corps command, and he personally disliked Sumner, Heintzelman, and Keyes because they had opposed his Urbanna plan. The five-corps structure should have improved communications because Mc-Clellan seldom spoke with Sumner, Heintzelman, or Keyes.[9]

On May 23 Lincoln and Stanton rescinded a junction of McDowell's corps with the Army of the Potomac because Stonewall Jackson's Shenandoah Valley army struck General Banks's corps at Front Royal and drove the Federals back to Maryland. Instead of McDowell marching to aid McClellan, Jackson marched to aid Johnston. Matthew F. Steele, commenting on Stanton's role in diverting part of McDowell's corps to the Valley, wrote, "by his obstinacy and ignorance of the science of war he probably set back the fall of Richmond and the Confederacy [by] three years." Despite McClellan's chronic mismanagement of troops, had McDowell's corps struck Richmond's defenses from the north at the same time the Army of the Potomac struck Johnston's army from the east, it is difficult to see how the Confederate capital could have escaped seizure.[10]

On May 21 McClellan established an extended line on Virginia's Chickahominy River, the right wing being seven miles and the left wing twelve miles from Richmond. Ten days passed while engineers built bridges. McClellan moved the left wing across the Chickahominy, putting it in an exposed position on the south side of the river. After advising the president on May 26 he was "quietly closing in upon the enemy preparatory to the last [final] struggle," five days of inactivity followed. Johnston decided McClellan would never attack and on May 31 struck Keyes's corps at Seven Pines. McClellan had 100,000 men available to oppose Johnston's 62,000, but the Union line stretched for twelve miles through wooded, rain-drenched, and unmapped country. In a battle of errors committed on both sides, Johnston suffered a serious wound, and the Confederates withdrew to their original position. The Prince de Joinville, one of McClellan's advisors, wrote, "[The] Federals had had the defensive battle they desired; had repulsed the enemy . . . gained nothing by their success [and] missed a unique opportunity of striking a blow." When McClellan reported having "gained a glorious victory," Stanton accepted the news with suspicion but dispatched a message complimenting the general for the army's success.[11]

After the Battle of Seven Pines, McClellan renewed his demands for reinforcements. Stanton doubted whether the general needed more troops but agreed to send fifteen fresh regiments, Brigadier General George A. McCall's ten thousand–man division, and five batteries of artillery—in all twenty-four thousand troops to offset five thousand casualties suffered at Seven Pines.[12] This left McClellan with only one excuse, the weather, and even that improved. "I shall be in perfect readiness to move forward and take Richmond the moment McCall reaches here," wrote the general.

Johnston had not let weather delay his May 30 attack at Seven Pines, nor had Grant during his campaigns in the West, but rain stopped McClellan. On

June 20 the Army of the Potomac reported 156,838 troops. The weather was hot, the roads now dry, but McClellan still stalled. Lincoln asked McClellan when he intended to fight. Little Mac replied, "A general engagement may take place at any hour," but he left the decision to "Providence." McClellan was too busy changing his base to the James River to think seriously about fighting.[13]

After Johnston's disabling wound at Seven Pines, Robert E. Lee took command of Richmond's defenses. McClellan told Lincoln not to worry because Lee was "*too* cautious and weak under grave responsibility . . . yet is wanting in moral firmness when pressed by heavy responsibility & is likely to be timid & irresolute in action." McClellan accurately described himself, not Lee. His twenty-five days of ineffectual maneuvering enabled Lee to pull reinforcements from other fields, extending his army to 80,762 troops. Lee had the advantage of better maps and better cavalry. From June 12 to 15 Major General James E. B. "Jeb" Stuart unnerved McClellan by riding completely around the Army of the Potomac. Lee also brought Jackson from the Shenandoah to attack McClellan's right flank. McClellan discovered the movement and warned Porter, whose corps on the north side of the Chickahominy lay separated from the main army.[14]

McClellan decided June 26 would be the day for "our final advance," but on the twenty-fifth Lee struck Porter's right flank at Mechanicsville. Porter commanded the best disciplined corps of regulars in the entire Union army and repulsed the attack. That night McClellan visited Porter and found him anxious to strike Lee at first light while the main body of the army assaulted Richmond. McClellan turned indecisive and returned to headquarters. At 4:00 a.m. Porter received instructions to withdraw to the rear and await attack. Astonished by the order, Porter predicted McClellan would never go on the offense. Had McClellan taken Porter's advice and vigorously attacked in the morning, Richmond might have fallen before the Confederacy became any stronger. Instead, McClellan carried out plans to change his base to the James River, fended off Lee's attacks for the next five days, conducted a well-executed withdrawal, hunkered down under the protective guns of the Union navy at Harrison's Landing, and left a record of unsurpassed cautiousness. When the Committee on the Conduct of the War investigated the campaign, it found that McClellan never appeared on the field to take command of troop movements and left all decisions other than withdrawal to his corps commanders.[15]

On June 29 at Savage's Station, McClellan lost an opportunity to face the army about and possibly win the campaign by being aggressive. Instead, he panicked and blamed the president for being "ungenerous when I said my force was too weak. . . . The Government must not and can not hold me responsible for the result." To Stanton he wrote, "If I save this army now, I tell you plainly that I owe no thanks to you or to any other person in Washington. You have done your best to sacrifice this army." The words were so insubordinate that Edwards S. Sanford, military supervisor of telegrams, omitted them on the copy sent to Stanton.

After that outburst no other general would have held his commission for another twenty-four hours, but Lincoln envisioned the army's capitulation. McClellan then sent Brigadier General Randolph B. Marcy, his father-in-law, to worry the administration. Drawn into the fiction, Lincoln wrote, "Save your army at all events. Will send reinforcements as fast as we can." Stanton immediately pulled troops from Halleck (25,000), McDowell (5,000), and everywhere else they could be found. After asking for 20,000 troops and being promised 50,000, McClellan then asked for 100,000. Lincoln told a visitor to the White House if he could give McClellan 100,000 men, he would do so and tell the general to go to Richmond tomorrow, "but when to-morrow came," Lincoln added glumly, "[McClellan] would telegraph that he had certain information that the enemy had 400,000 men, and that he could not advance without reinforcements."[16]

After bottling up McClellan at Harrison's Landing, Lee began withdrawing troops to attack General Pope's Army of Virginia, which had assimilated McDowell's corps near Fredericksburg. This gave McClellan an opportunity to advance on Richmond, but he stayed put and continued berating the administration as "dolts . . . bent on my destruction." McClellan knew his army was safe but would not admit it. July also marked the beginning of the general's quest for a political career, and he might have been more successful had he captured Richmond. Instead, he turned his self-imposed defeat into a publicity campaign to save the army. When he wrote Lincoln, "I would be glad . . . to lay before your Excellency . . . my views as to the present state of military affairs throughout the whole country," McClellan was reaching for something far beyond the Army of the Potomac.[17]

Disturbed by McClellan's behavior, Lincoln embarked on the USS *Ariel* and on July 8 arrived off Harrison's Landing. McClellan came on board and presented his "Harrison Bar Letter," which contained his personal views on military and political affairs. Lincoln did not come for political advice. He read the letter without comment, stuffed it in his pocket, and focused the conversation on ways to end a costly and unproductive campaign. When McClellan insisted the rebels were poised to attack, Lincoln convened the corps commanders. Sumner, Heintzelman, and Franklin said the enemy had withdrawn; Keyes agreed, warning Lee would advance on Washington; and Porter thought Richmond should be attacked. When Lincoln asked if the army could be withdrawn safely, Keyes and Franklin said it could, but others wanted to stay and fight. McClellan objected to Lincoln's questions but saved his comments for his wife, accusing the president of being "quite incapable" of understanding "the magnitude of the crisis."[18]

Lincoln returned to Washington perplexed by an unaccountable disappearance of half of McClellan's army. On July 13 he advised the general that 160,000 men had been sent to Virginia, but McClellan claimed having only 86,500 present. Where, asked Lincoln, were the others? "If I am right," he said, "and you had these men with you, you could go into Richmond in the next three days." McClellan never responded, claiming to "be on the brink of eternity."[19]

Lincoln remained distressed because McClellan would only respond with demands for reinforcements. As July wasted away, McClellan's generals lost faith in their leader and believed the army should return to Washington. Lincoln wanted an expert opinion, so he brought Halleck to Washington as general-in-chief and put Grant in charge of operations in Mississippi and Tennessee.

Halleck arrived in Washington on July 23 and two days later met with McClellan at Harrison's Landing. He asked the general's plans, and McClellan said he would cross the James River and attack Petersburg. Halleck vetoed the idea and said the troops should be consolidated with General Pope's Army of Virginia and reorganized to operate against Richmond by way of Manassas. McClellan objected, so Halleck gave him two options: attack Richmond or withdraw from the James. McClellan said he would attack Richmond. The day Halleck returned to Washington, the Young Napoleon demanded reinforcements. Halleck replied, "I have no reinforcements to send you." McClellan wrote his wife, "Halleck is turning out just like the rest of the herd."[20]

McClellan can be partly excused for believing that Lee had 200,000 men. The misinformation came from Pinkerton, but as other historians discovered, evidence suggests the spymaster usually told McClellan what he wanted to hear.[21] For McClellan the campaign had ended. Lincoln and Stanton tried to support McClellan, but they made a fundamental mistake, even when they knew better, by allowing the Army of the Potomac to go to the peninsula. McClellan's defeat presented Lincoln and the cabinet with a grim reminder that the rebellion had not been crushed. There had been no major Union victories since spring, and the initiative for war in Virginia had reverted back to the Confederacy.

McClellan's extravagant campaign in Virginia had emptied the Treasury. Chase said he could not raise money if McClellan remained in command. Since February he had partly financed the war by printing "greenbacks," legal tender notes of $5 or more, and by issuing $500 million in 5–20 year bonds, which could only be sold at discount. Neither Chase nor Lincoln believed greenbacks were constitutional, but nobody challenged the practice, so the Treasury kept the printing presses rolling. When Lincoln inquired into ways of reducing the government's indebtedness, Chase suggested cashiering Banks, Buell, Butler, and McClellan. He also suggested emancipating the slaves, believing the act would revive confidence in the government and bolster the Treasury.[22]

Ben Butler inadvertently began advancing emancipation in May 1861, when he characterized slaves as contraband. Congress legalized Butler's action on August 6 by enacting the first Confiscation Act. Twenty-four days later General Frémont embarrassed the administration by taking emancipation a step farther, proclaiming that slaves captured from persons supporting the rebellion would be confiscated and "hereby declared freemen." Lincoln revoked Frémont's proclamation because it overstepped the Confiscation Act. Radicals approved Frémont's emancipation program, but months passed before Congress enacted a second confiscation measure.[23]

In his 1861 annual message to Congress, Lincoln broached the subject of purchasing and colonizing slaves "at some place, or places, in a climate congenial to them." He disliked returning slaves to their masters but did not want them living in idleness around army camps. Moreover, he did not want to contend with mass emigrations into the "Negrophobic" North. He asked Congress to consider a new law expanding emancipation while avoiding extreme measures. Because slavery still existed in border states, he drafted two bills for "compensated gradual abolishment." Put to test in the Delaware legislature, the answer came back that "when the people of Delaware decide to abolish slavery within her borders they would do so in their own way." When Congress reconvened on March 6, 1862, Lincoln asked for a resolution to provide subsidies to any state adopting "gradual abolishment of slavery." After the border states refused, Congress took a mini-step and on April 16 passed an act compensating emancipation in the District of Columbia at $300 per slave and provided $100,000 for expenses to cover voluntary emigration to Haiti or Liberia.[24]

Advocates of colonization also existed in the South, the idea having been debated for more than a decade. Blair Sr. promoted a solution, going so far as to suggest either "deportation or extermination." Montgomery Blair preferred colonization to ethnic cleansing, although he believed the two races could never live together peacefully. Welles preferred assimilation to deportation. Chase thought colonization might work but wanted his opinion to remain private. Lincoln delegated the project to Secretary of the Interior Caleb Smith, which virtually ensured its death even though Smith backed colonization.[25]

Stanton joined the cabinet later and became an emancipationist mainly because he wanted to induct blacks into the army. As the availability of white volunteers declined, the enormous pool of black refugees swelled. For many years blacks had served on ships, but the army had no clear policy. Officers could put them to work, as Butler did, or return them to their owners. After General David Hunter took command at Hilton Head, he issued a proclamation on May 9, 1862, abolishing slavery in Florida, Georgia, and South Carolina. Lincoln flexed his constitutional power over Chase's objections and replied, "No commanding general shall do such a thing, upon *my* responsibility, without consulting me," and revoked Hunter's order. Stanton came to believe the real issue of the war centered on the slavery question. With Lincoln unwilling to act on emancipation, Stanton worked behind the scenes with Congress to enact a second confiscation act freeing all fugitive, captured, and abandoned slaves owned by rebels but excluded the border states. Signed into law on July 17, 1862, the act defined Confederates as traitors, ordered the confiscation of their slaves and property, and empowered the president to employ blacks in the armed services as he wished. Lincoln was unready to use blacks to kill whites, which had more volatile ramifications than emancipation itself, but he approved their use as noncombatants. He signed the legislation without completely agreeing to enforce it.[26]

Lincoln had been privately studying the emancipation issue for months. On July 13, while riding to a funeral for Stanton's infant son, he turned to Seward and Welles and suddenly said that after giving considerable thought to emancipation, he had "about come to the conclusion that it was a military necessity absolutely for the salvation of the Union, that we must free the slaves or be ourselves subdued." Welles recalled, "This was . . . the first occasion when he had mentioned the subject to anyone." While Chase talked of emancipation as a matter of principle, Lincoln became convinced the real issue involved a national policy on freedom and adopted that course rather than Chase's.[27]

After signing the second Confiscation Act, Lincoln called a cabinet meeting to discuss a draft of the Emancipation Proclamation. The document came as a surprise because he composed it in the telegraph office, at the desk of chief telegrapher Thomas T. Eckert, where he could concentrate without being interrupted. Eckert said the president "would look out the window a while and then put his pen to paper, but he did not write much at a time. He would study between times and when he had made up his mind he would put down a line or two, and then sit quiet for a few minutes." This continued for several weeks. Eckert hid the document until July 22, when Lincoln took it to the White House. Subject to remarks from the cabinet, he projected January 1, 1863, as the date for declaring "all persons held as slaves within any state or states, wherein the constitutional authority of the United States shall not then be practically recognized, submitted to, and maintained, shall then, henceforward, and forever, be free."[28]

At first the cabinet failed to grasp the significance of the draft, so Lincoln read it again. Chase admitted it reached farther than he expected and agreed with Stanton that blacks should be armed as a national policy, but he felt district commanders in the field should decide whether black regiments were warranted and, if so, form them discreetly. Given that loyal blacks in the navy wore uniforms, Welles believed any free person should be entitled to wear one. He also thought slaves emancipated in the South should all become legally free and entitled by military necessity to the privilege of joining the armed forces. Smith opposed emancipation but remained silent because Lincoln never listened to his advice.[29]

Blair and Seward cautioned against emancipation but for different reasons. Blair worried about offending the border states as well as the impact on the fall elections. Bates came from a border state and gave "unreserved concurrence" to the abolishment of slavery. Seward agreed with emancipation but questioned the timing. McClellan's failure on the peninsula had aggravated foreign relations in Europe because cotton shortages were causing massive unemployment in textile mills. "Foreign nations," Seward warned, "will intervene to prevent the abolition of slavery for the sake of cotton." He also worried emancipation could turn the war for the Union into a class war and said emancipation on the heels of a defeat hinted of desperation. "I suggest, sir," said Seward, "that you postpone its issue until you can give it to the country supported by military success."[30]

Stanton vigorously disagreed with Seward. He wanted Lincoln to issue the proclamation immediately, noting on his tablet, "The measure goes beyond anything I have recommended." After instigating the second Confiscation Act, Stanton went a step farther. He quietly approved of Butler's scheme in New Orleans to reorganize noncombatant laborers into black infantry regiments whether the administration agreed or not. Stanton selected colorful Zouave uniforms for his "sable arm." Later, meeting with Joseph Holt, Stanton forcibly commented, "The war could never be successfully closed for the government, without the employment of colored troops in the field." Bates, the only other member of the cabinet who agreed completely with Stanton, thought the proclamation should be promulgated immediately.[31]

Lincoln followed Seward's advice and decided not to issue the proclamation on the heels of McClellan's defeat. He inserted the draft proclamation in a drawer of his desk, locked it, and waited for the next military success.

A few days later the press excoriated Lincoln for not enforcing Stanton's surreptitiously inspired second Confiscation Act. Horace Greeley inserted an open letter in the *New York Tribune* sullying the president for not taking immediate action to implement the act. He closed his fiery editorial saying, "[What] your countrymen require of you is a frank, declared, unqualified, ungrudging execution of the laws of the land." Lincoln replied:

> My paramount object in this struggle *is* to save the Union, and it is *not* either to save or to destroy slavery. If I could save the Union without freeing *any* slave, I would do it; and if I could save it by freeing *all* the slaves, I would do it; and if I could save it by freeing some and leaving others alone, I would also do that. What I do about slavery and the colored race, I do because I believe it helps to save the Union; and what I forbear, I forbear because I do *not* believe it would help to save the Union. I shall do *less* whenever I . . . believe what I am doing hurts the cause, and I shall do *more* whenever I . . . believe doing more will help the cause.[32]

Greeley disliked the answer, but the nation approved. It clarified exactly where Lincoln stood on the issue of the war and slavery. Weed told Seward it would "clear the air" and give the president stronger "ground to stand on." Indeed it did, though others still pressed for its release. "What good would a proclamation from me do," Lincoln asked, "especially as we are now situated? I do not want to issue a document that the whole world will see must necessarily be inoperative, like the Pope's bull against the comet! Would *my word* free the slaves, when I cannot even enforce the Constitution in the rebel states?" The dilemma continued, and so did the pressure. War governors warned they could not meet draft quotas if the president refused to act against slavery. From abroad came more warnings. The annual crop of cotton had been picked, and Europe wanted it. Only a strong stand on emancipation, they said, could stave off recognition. To a group of Chicago Christians lobbying for emancipation, Lincoln replied, "It is my earnest desire to know the will of Providence in this matter. And if I can learn what it is I will do it!" Later, during a cabinet meeting on the matter, Welles remembered Lincoln saying he had made a vow, a covenant, "If God gave us a victory in the approaching battle, he would consider it an indication of Divine will, and that it was his duty to move forward in the cause of emancipation." When the way was unclear in his mind, Lincoln shifted part of the burden, letting God decide the question of being for or against slavery.[33]

Days passed, and Lincoln tried to remain patient, as if waiting for an omen. The summer campaign had not ended. While McClellan's Army of the Potomac sweltered in the heat of the James River, Pope's Army of Virginia began moving toward Culpepper. Into Pope's army went McDowell's corps, Banks's corps, and elements from Frémont's corps. With Lee's army pinned between McClellan on one side and Pope on the other, the prospect of squeezing Richmond into submission still seemed possible. All depended on McClellan's willingness to take the offensive, and Lincoln waited for the one important battle to change the course of the war. As July drifted into August, the wait ended, but not on Lincoln's terms.

CHAPTER 11

"In my position I am environed by difficulties"

As the 1862 fall elections approached, disagreements over emancipation remained contentious, threats of foreign intervention intensified, and with half the summer wasted, Lincoln needed a victory in Virginia. Peace Democrats threatened to gain strength in November, and dissident Republicans challenged the handling of the war because they feared losing their seats in Congress. The president endured growing pressure from radicals, though he felt they were wrong or simply too impatient. He elevated General Pope to command the Army of Virginia partly as a concession to Senator Benjamin F. Wade's Committee on the Conduct of the War, but according to Welles, the whole idea of bringing Pope east resulted from "an intrigue of Stanton's and Chase's to get rid of McClellan." Welles believed Stanton hated McClellan and any other general would have been an acceptable alternative. Lincoln liked Pope, a robust forty-year-old Western general and a devoted antislavery Republican. At New Madrid and Island No. 10, Pope had helped secure the upper Mississippi. According to Halleck, Pope had performed well at Corinth, even though Halleck had not.[1]

Lincoln continued searching for generals who would fight. Pope came from Kentucky, graduated from West Point in 1842, served gallantly in the Mexican War, and earned a reputation for being energetic and courageous. Because of Pope's knowledge of military affairs, Lincoln used him as an advisor during McClellan's Richmond campaign. Others pegged Pope as an impetuous, loud-mouthed braggart whose abrasive personality made him one of the most detested officers in the army. Historian Joseph P. Cullen quoted one Western general as saying, "I don't care for John Pope one pinch of owl dung."[2]

When Pope took command of the Army of Virginia he tactlessly addressed his command, bragging, "I have come . . . from the West, where we have always seen the backs of our enemies; from an army whose business it has been to seek the adversary and to beat him where he was found; whose policy has been attack and not defense." After his statement reached the Army of the Potomac, General Fitz John Porter remarked, "I regret . . . that Gen[eral] Pope has not improved since his youth and has now written himself down [as] . . . an ass." The storm of ridicule amazed Pope. It lasted as long as he commanded the Army of Virginia and kept him from gaining his troops' confidence. McClellan encouraged the criticism because he considered Pope a rival and a potential successor.[3]

Nor did Lincoln see Pope's astounding military edicts threatening to destroy Southern homes, arrest male noncombatants, confiscate household supplies, expel those who refused to take the oath of allegiance, and impose the death penalty for the commitment of minor offenses. After General Lee learned of Pope's pronouncements, he vowed to expel him.[4]

During August there were two armies in Virginia, one under McClellan and the other under Pope. Halleck commanded both but could get neither to fight. Halleck reported to Stanton, who looked for ways to move the Army of the Potomac back to Washington so he could get rid of McClellan. Stanton wanted to consolidate the two armies and put Halleck in command. McClellan believed that on returning to Washington both armies would be unified under his command. Stanton planned not to let that happen. Halleck became uneasy over McClellan's status, believing Lincoln and Stanton, having exhausted their patience, wanted him to "do what they were afraid to attempt" so he could take the blame. "I am almost broken down," Halleck lamented to his wife, "I can't get General McClellan to do what I wish." Lincoln felt constrained from taking any action. With one eye on Pope and the other on McClellan, he waited for favorable developments.[5]

On August 8 Pope put his 46,858-man army on the road to Charlottesville. A brigade from General Banks's Second Corps marched in the van. The following morning, five miles south of Culpeper, Virginia, Banks collided with Stonewall Jackson's 24,000-man corps near Cedar Mountain. Banks may have won a decisive victory had he ordered up reserves. Instead, he threw 8,000 men at the Confederate right, bent it back until it almost broke, and then withdrew at dark, leaving the field to Jackson. When two days later Jackson's force withdrew to Gordonsville, Pope boasted, "The enemy fled from the field." Halleck issued a congratulatory message, saying, "Your troops have covered themselves with glory," and concealed the bungled battle because he wanted to keep Pope's army out of McClellan's hands.[6]

On August 13, as McClellan withdrew from Harrison's Landing, Lee moved Longstreet's corps to Gordonsville. He wanted to destroy Pope before McClellan's army reached Washington. Pope discovered Lee's plans and fell back. Halleck anticipated a trap and ordered McClellan to send reinforcements to Pope "immediately." Three days later Halleck telegraphed Pope, "Beware of a snare."

No day passed without Halleck prodding McClellan to hasten to Washington, and no day passed without Little Mac repeating his reasons for not complying. In an effort to energize McClellan, Halleck promised him command of operations in Virginia, even though he knew it was contrary to Stanton's wishes. Halleck sent General Ambrose Burnside to assure McClellan the evacuation was not a plot to get rid of him but was meant to encourage him to move with speed.[7]

During the third week of August Halleck relaxed when Pope crossed to the north side of the Rappahannock River and assimilated Burnside's Ninth Corps. McClellan arrived at Aquia Creek, asked Halleck for Pope's location, but also asked if he was to command both armies as promised. Halleck did not know Pope's whereabouts but dodged McClellan's question on who was in command. Halleck had been preoccupied by Buell's refusal to advance into eastern Tennessee and Lincoln's threat to fire the general for refusing to obey orders. Halleck persuaded the president to give Buell one more chance, and Lincoln said Buell must win or go. On August 27 Halleck still had not heard from Pope, and his ignorance of the situation was about to a take a huge toll on his credibility.[8]

On August 25, reinforced by Burnside and McClellan, Pope had seventy-five thousand men and Lee fifty-five thousand. Jackson crossed the Rappahannock in the morning and two days later, after marching fifty-nine miles, destroyed the Federal supply depot at Manassas. The raid surprised Pope, who misread Jackson's movement and did nothing until Confederates appeared in his rear. With Jackson's corps at Manassas and Longstreet's corps twenty miles west, Pope wasted a rare opportunity to strike Jackson while impeding Longstreet. Jackson posted his corps in a strong position on the Union flank and so thoroughly confused Pope that the latter lost track of the Confederates until August 28, when his army collided with Jackson at Groveton on the old Bull Run battlefield. Pope was still studying how to force Jackson into the open when on August 29 Longstreet's corps arrived. The next day Pope hammered away at the rebels, unaware he was facing both Longstreet and Jackson. That afternoon he dispatched an exultant message to Halleck stating he had fought a terrific battle and driven the enemy from the field. Lincoln went to army headquarters and found Halleck brimming with confidence, claiming, "The greatest battle of the century was now being fought." On August 31, after McClellan reported Pope's defeat, Lincoln did not wait for confirmation from Halleck. At 8:00 p.m. he summoned Hay and said, "Well, John, we are whipped again." On September 1 Lee struck Pope's flank and drove the Army of Virginia reeling back to Washington. Lincoln acknowledged what he had suspected for months: that Northern generals appeared to be markedly inferior to Southern generals.[9]

During the Second Battle of Bull Run neither Pope nor Halleck grasped what was happening. For four days Lincoln tried to understand the situation at Manassas while watching Halleck buckle from strain. When McClellan reported Franklin's and Sumner's corps ready to move, Halleck did not know where to send them. Nor could he define McClellan's authority. When the general demanded an answer, Halleck curtly replied, "I have no time for details. You will, therefore, as ranking general in the field, direct as you deem best; but at present orders for Pope's army should go through me." How Halleck expected McClellan to "direct as best" from Alexandria without knowing Pope's situation provides an example of how Old Brains, the master tactician, reacted to crisis.[10]

Halleck had options. He could reinforce Pope with McClellan's force, put Little Mac in charge of the battle, order Pope and McClellan to attack separately, or do nothing. He did nothing. Stanton stepped in and issued orders stating that Burnside at Falmouth was in command of his own corps except the part sent to Pope; McClellan was in command of the Army of the Potomac except the part sent to Pope; Pope was in command of the Army of Virginia and all troops attached to him, with Halleck in command of all. Stanton did not see Halleck's telegram to McClellan the night of August 31, 1862, which read, "I beg of you to assist me in this crisis with your ability and experience. I am entirely tired out." McClellan told him to order the troops back to Washington and requested a meeting in the morning. Halleck agreed and ordered McClellan to take command of Washington's defenses but not Pope's army.[11]

With growing trepidation Lincoln observed Halleck's inability to take charge of anything. When Pope reported from Centreville of "able to hold his men," Lincoln said, "I don't like that expression. I don't like him to admit his men are 'holding.' He must hurt this enemy before it gets away . . . Pope must fight them."[12]

On the morning of September 2 the president went to Halleck's home to encourage aggressiveness but was told that McClellan's officers refused to cooperate with Pope. He took Halleck to the home of McClellan, who denied the accusation but promised to rectify the problem if true. Lincoln began reading dispatches in Halleck's possession and found one particularly callous statement attributed to McClellan about abandoning Pope and letting him "get out of his own scrape." The comments came from Army of the Potomac officers and not from McClellan, so Lincoln verbally directed McClellan to take command of Pope's forces as they entered the city.[13]

Lincoln's reinstatement of McClellan to command drew sharp criticism. Stanton and Chase protested in writing and obtained signatures from Bates and Smith. Welles agreed with the document but refused to sign it. Chase provided a space for Blair's signature but not for Seward's. Stanton disclaimed any responsibility for Lincoln's order and condemned McClellan as incapable of executing offensive warfare. Chase became furious, describing discussions with the president on McClellan's status as "useless" and a "national calamity." He said, "McClellan ought to be shot." Stanton thought McClellan should be retained in rank but left "without anything to do, with no men or orders . . . to gnaw a file." Lincoln replied, "McClellan knows this whole ground; his specialty is to defend; he is a good engineer, there is no better organizer. [He] can be trusted to act on the defensive; but he is troubled with the 'slows.'" Knowing Lincoln would not listen, Stanton returned to the War Department in a state of morbid depression. Lincoln suffered a bout of melancholy because all his hopes for a successful summer campaign ended with another gloomy disaster.[14]

On September 4 Pope appeared before the president and cabinet to read his report. It was more an indictment against McClellan than an account of Bull Run. It also ended the careers of McDowell and Porter, whom Pope wrongly accused of disobeying orders. After Pope left the room, the cabinet agreed to suppress the report because publication would cause "war among the generals, who were now more ready to fight each other than the enemy." On the fifth, acting under Lincoln's orders, Halleck abolished the Army of Virginia and sent Pope back west, where he held minor commands for the remainder of the war.[15]

A few days later, while walking with Welles, Lincoln explained his actions. "I must have McClellan to reorganize the army and bring it out of chaos," he said, "but there has been a design, a purpose in breaking down Pope, without regard of consequences to the country. It is shocking to see and know this; but there is no remedy at present, McClellan has the army with him." Lincoln ignored the allegation that McClellan had intentionally withheld troops to destroy Pope. The general had never learned how to act decisively in a crisis and merely behaved normally.[16]

There was never a moment when Lincoln or any cabinet member expected Washington to be attacked. The president told McClellan to reorganize the army quickly and repeatedly said, "We must hurt this enemy before it gets away." Even Welles, who had developed an acute ability to predict the intentions of the enemy, never considered Washington in danger. "They may venture to cross the upper Potomac," he declared, "but they will not venture to come here." Two days later Jackson's corps passed through Leesburg, and fifty-five thousand rebels began wading across the upper Potomac, singing "Maryland, My Maryland."[17]

Lee's invasion of Maryland upset Lincoln's plan of only using McClellan temporarily to reorganize the Army of the Potomac. Action had to be taken to check the enemy's advance. The president sent for General Burnside, the only other general in the East who had exercised independent command, and offered him the Army of the Potomac. Burnside declined, saying McClellan should lead the army. This left the president no choice. Expecting Stanton to object, Lincoln did not consult him and merged the Army of Virginia into the Army of the Potomac and put McClellan in command. The president's decision revitalized army morale. Stanton quickly fell in line, admitting, "The best defense . . . is to strengthen the force now marching against the enemy under General McClellan."[18]

McClellan moved into Maryland with more than ninety thousand troops and on reaching Frederick stumbled upon a war-winning stroke of good fortune. At the abandoned rebel campsite an Indiana private found three cigars wrapped in a copy of Lee's Special Order No. 191, dated September 9. Lee had divided his force, sending Jackson to Harpers Ferry while Longstreet's corps marched west to Boonsboro. Realizing Lee's orders were genuine, McClellan crowed, "Here is a paper with which if I cannot whip Bobbie Lee I will be willing to go home." He telegraphed the president, writing, "I have all the plans of the rebels, and will catch them in their own trap if my men are equal to the emergency." Stanton remained circumspect, questioning whether McClellan would be up to the task. Welles predicted McClellan would move too cautiously, noting that "Stanton is cross and grouty. A victory for McClellan will bring him no joy, though it would gladden the whole country."[19]

Instead of moving promptly, McClellan waited until morning and advanced slowly. On September 14 Longstreet delayed the Federals at South Mountain until reinforcements drove the Confederates across Antietam Creek. At South Mountain, Lee merely fought a delaying action, but McClellan believed he had won a great victory and informed Halleck the enemy was retreating "in a perfect panic." From McClellan's telegrams one might assume Lee's army had been smashed, but Lincoln remained circumspect. To keep the general focused, he replied, "God bless you, and all with you. Destroy the rebel army, if possible."[20]

On September 17 McClellan advanced in strength but a day late. With an enormous advantage in numbers he occupied the superior position. With better coordination he could have clamped the enemy in a vise. The disjointed attack allowed Lee to hold out until elements from Jackson's corps

arrived from Harpers Ferry. McClellan made the error of withholding reserves to cover, if defeated, his retreat. Instead of winning a stunning victory,
the bloodiest one-day battle of the war ended in a draw. The following night
Lee withdrew to Virginia.

Certain of having won a great victory, McClellan made no effort to pursue the enemy. The army stayed put, exactly as the general wished. When
Halleck issued orders to advance, McClellan resorted to his patent excuses of
having fatigued troops, no supply wagons, not enough ammunition, and not
enough men. Using two special trains on tracks cleared of traffic, Stanton
sent ammunition, artillery, and a fresh division of infantry. The effort proved
fruitless. McClellan fretted too much over the "risks of defeat." His concept
of victory was foiling the Confederate offensive and saving Maryland and
Pennsylvania, not the destruction of Lee's army. The cabinet resumed heated
discussions on McClellan's lack of aggressiveness, and according to Welles,
there was "no abatement of hostility" toward the general.[21]

On September 20 Lincoln pulled the Emancipation Proclamation from his
desk, changed a few words, and two days later called a cabinet meeting. On
reintroducing the proclamation, he said, "I think the time has come now. I
wish it were a better time. I wish that we were in better condition." Having
made a pledge to his Maker, Lincoln intended to keep the promise. "I do
not want your advice about the main matter," he said, "for that I have determined for myself," but he agreed to accept comments on phraseology. Some
of the arguments for and against the proclamation remained unchanged,
and being six weeks from the national election caused more consternation.
Even Lincoln questioned whether the document would gain favorable public
approval, but he told the cabinet, "I must do the best I can and bear the
responsibility of taking the course which I feel I ought to take." When Blair
repeated his warning of border state repercussions, Lincoln replied, "We
must make the forward movement. They would acquiesce, if not immediately, soon; for they must be satisfied that [slavery] could not survive the
rebellion." Having disagreed with most of Lincoln's policies, Caleb Smith
merely grunted his disapproval. Lincoln closed the meeting, announcing that
on January 1, 1863, "all persons held as slaves within any state" or section of
a state in rebellion "shall be then, thenceforward, and forever free."[22]

Two days later serenaders appeared at the White House to celebrate the
announcement of the proclamation. Still troubled his decision might divide
the fragile coalition of Republicans, war Democrats, and border state leaders,
Lincoln intended to remain silent, but called to speak, he remarked, "I can

only trust in God I have made no mistake." The crowd shouted, "No mistake. Go ahead, you're right." Lincoln replied, "It is now for the country and the world to pass judgment on it . . . I will say no more upon this subject. In my position I am environed by difficulties." Those difficulties included peace Democrats laboring to unify the party, win seats in border states, and find a strong nominee to run against Lincoln in 1864. Referring to slaveholders, Lincoln remarked to Hay, "This was a most wonderful history of an insanity of a class that the world [has] ever seen. If the slaveholders had staid in the Union they might have kept life in their institution for many years to come. That what no party and no public feeling in the North could ever have hoped to touch they . . . madly placed in the very path of destruction."[23]

The proclamation quieted Lincoln's critics in the North. Even fiery editors like Horace Greeley offered words of uncustomary praise. When Hannibal Hamlin wrote from Bangor, Maine, expressing his "sincere thanks for your Emancipation Proclamation," Lincoln replied, "I wish I could write more cheerfully. The North responds to the proclamation sufficiently in breath; but breath alone kills no rebels." With securities declining in value and with voluntary recruitment dropping, the president's call for another 600,000 troops caused critics to ask when the endless drain of American blood would stop.[24]

Jefferson Davis called the proclamation an effort to foment slave insurrection and urged Southerners to fight harder for independence. He predicted the extermination of slaves or the exile of the whole white population from the Confederacy. Davis rallied support, including Southern Unionists and some border state men who had once believed Lincoln would leave slavery alone.[25]

Distressed by sluggish recruitment, on September 24 Lincoln issued a second proclamation suspending the writ of habeas corpus. The document allowed arbitrary arrests of any person "discouraging volunteer enlistments, resisting military drafts, or guilty of any disloyal practice affording aid and comfort to the Rebels" and made offenders subject to martial law and liable to trial in military courts. The document carried sinister undertones impinging on civil liberties and censorship of the press. Although Lincoln only intended to define the War Department's role in enforcing the Militia Act of July 17, 1862, it did expose the public to overly zealous military arrests and to some degree muffled criticism of the administration. Caleb Smith, who thought like border state men, resigned from the cabinet. His departure displeased no one.[26]

When news of the Emancipation Proclamation reached the Army of the Potomac, McClellan regurgitated his contempt for the document, informing his wife it was "almost impossible to retain [his] commission and self-respect at the same time." He had to win a battle so Lincoln could issue the proclamation, and the irony maddened him. Nor did he approve of Lincoln's suspension of the writ of habeas corpus. Angered by both proclamations, he invited his generals to dinner to ask whether they would follow him in opposing emancipation. Astounded by the question, the generals told him to support Lincoln and confirm his support to the troops. McClellan obliged and sent a copy of his circular to Lincoln. The president studied the document and found a disturbing sentence, which read, "The remedy for political errors, if any are committed, is to be found only in the action of the people at the polls." Democrats interpreted the wordage as McClellan's bid for the presidency.[27]

Emancipation Proclamation business also brought Allan Pinkerton to Washington. Instead of spying on the enemy, McClellan sent him to spy on the administration. Lincoln concluded that McClellan's chief of intelligence intended to pry information from the government and instead used his cross-examination skills to pry information from Pinkerton. He learned more from Pinkerton than the detective intended to disclose, including a long list of unanswered questions such as why McClellan had failed to attack Lee after the Battle of Antietam, when he had nearly a three-to-one troop advantage. Through this interview Lincoln concluded that Antietam was not the great victory McClellan claimed but another in a series of lost opportunities. He learned nothing from Pinkerton to suggest disloyalty on McClellan's part, but he formed the opinion that some officers in the Army of the Potomac were not committed to destroying the Confederacy. Tipped off by Pinkerton's unguarded comments, Lincoln initiated his own investigation of McClellan's officers.[28]

Four days later Lincoln began hearing rumors the government needed a dictator instead of a president. One source came from Halleck's office. When asked why the "rebel army had not been bagged," Major John J. Key replied, "That is not the game. The object is that neither army shall get much advantage of the other; both shall be kept in the field until they are exhausted; when we will make a compromise and save slavery." Lincoln learned Key's brother, Thomas, served as judge advocate and political advisor on McClellan's staff. On September 27 Lincoln summoned Major Key to the White House for an explanation. Key admitted making the remark but pleaded loyalty. Lincoln said if a "game" existed to have the army not "take advantage of the enemy when it could, it was his object to break it up." He dismissed Key from the army, knowing the action would ripple back to the Army of the Potomac. McClellan ceased pondering the possibility of challenging

Lincoln's proclamations when Montgomery Blair reminded him of what had happened to Major Key.[29]

After the Pinkerton and Key interviews, Lincoln entrained for Sharpsburg, Maryland. At sunrise on October 3 he climbed a hill with Ozias Hatch and, looking down on the vast Federal camp, said, "This is General McClellan's bodyguard." He visited the wounded and spent the rest of his time trying to coax McClellan into fighting. Lincoln returned to Washington only after the general agreed to pursue Lee. A few days later he grumbled, "[I] came back thinking he would move at once. But when I got home, he began to argue why he ought not to move. I peremptorily ordered him to advance. It was 19 days before he put a man over the river." Halleck transmitted Lincoln's order and directed McClellan to cross the Potomac and drive the enemy. Instead, the Young Napoleon enraged Stanton with new demands. While at Antietam, Lincoln made one important observation. He now realized the army was with him, and he could remove McClellan without repercussions.[30]

McClellan misread the purpose of the president's Antietam visit. He expected better treatment from Stanton and Halleck but did not get it. He also expected to be made general-in-chief or otherwise resign. Meanwhile, Stanton howled for McClellan's removal, but Lincoln told him to be patient. Stanton became distraught and told Chase he was ready to resign. Chase said if Stanton went, he would go, and if they both went, then everyone should go. Chase complained of having forty-five million dollars in unpaid bills and no money. Welles heard the rumors and said Stanton and Chase "no more intend resigning than the President or Seward." Some members of the Senate advised Lincoln to fire them both, especially Chase, whom they pegged as "the most sinister of all the cabinet."[31]

McClellan continued building a case for his own destruction. Newspapers called him the "Great American Tortoise." Stanton became so incensed by McClellan's demands that he failed to notice the general had finally exhausted the president's patience. Six weeks after being ordered to pursue Lee, McClellan crossed the Potomac. When he allowed Lee to retire across the Rappahannock unmolested, Lincoln decided to remove him but only after the fall elections.[32]

In 1860 Democrats lost both houses of Congress, but in 1862 they expected to gain seats. They rallied around McClellan, who had gained political strength without accomplishing much on the battlefield. After Antietam, McClellan had been flexing his political muscle instead of his military might.

He believed he had saved the Union twice and the nation should repay him by removing obstacles in his way. On October 31 he wrote his wife, "I think it will end in driving Stanton out. . . . If I can crush him I will—relentlessly and without remorse." In an effort to hurry Stanton's downfall, McClellan called on the press to condemn the war secretary.[33]

On November 5 Lincoln tallied party losses, admitting Republicans had suffered at the polls partly because of his policies, partly because Democrats would not support his administration because it was too radical, and partly because some Republicans withdrew support because it was not radical enough.[34]

What annoyed the public and politicians alike were the slothful military movements of McClellan and Buell. With elections over, Lincoln did what the cabinet had demanded for months. He directed Halleck to remove McClellan "forthwith, or as soon as he may deem proper," and replace him with General Burnside. The order came with a twist. Lincoln let Old Brains decide when to relieve McClellan but took responsibility for the order whenever it was issued. Stanton would not wait and told Halleck "forthwith" meant immediately because McClellan's removal was "a matter of absolute necessity." Halleck agreed, confiding to his wife, "In a few more weeks, he [McClellan] could have broken down the government." Years later Stanton admitted his own reputation hinged on McClellan's success or failure. Soon after taking office, he realized if the general remained in command longer, efforts to reunify the nation would be "wasted in inconclusive maneuverings," leading eventually to war-weariness and Southern independence.[35]

Lincoln explained McClellan's dismissal in one word—slow. The general had been too slow on the Virginia peninsula, too slow helping Pope at Manassas, too slow at Antietam, and too slow afterward. Lee could accomplish in one day what took McClellan weeks. Lincoln said the general would never catch Lee and would not fight unless attacked. When Blair Sr. asked for an explanation, Lincoln replied, "I said I would relieve him if he let Lee's army get away from him, and I must do so. He has got the 'slows,' Mr. Blair."[36]

The president shared in the blame for missed opportunities. He knew the country could not afford commanders like McClellan but could not find a replacement. He wanted a fighter and chose Burnside without understanding that some generals are better corps commanders than army commanders. Stanton doubted whether Burnside, who was Lincoln's and Halleck's choice, would perform any better than McClellan.

During the autumn of 1862 Lincoln made other changes. He had already cashiered Frémont and for many weeks had been pressing Buell to advance on

Chattanooga and Knoxville, Tennessee. Buell's progress resembled another campaign dominated by the "slows." As Buell's army plodded east, Confederates under General Bragg and General E. Kirby Smith invaded Kentucky. Buell cut his campaign short and marched into Kentucky with more than fifty thousand men. On October 8, 1862, he struck Bragg's thirty thousand Confederates and drove them out of the state. Bragg fell back and reoccupied Nashville. Buell failed to pursue the enemy, so Lincoln began looking for another general. Halleck repeated what Lincoln had once said to McClellan, writing, "[Buell] does not understand why we cannot march as the enemy marches, live as he lives, and fight as he fights, unless we admit the inferiority of our troops and our generals." Halleck warned Buell the administration would not tolerate more delays and urged him to go on the offensive. Buell proved to be as obstinate as McClellan when it came to obeying orders.[37]

On September 24 Grant had placed forty-three-year-old General William S. "Old Rosy" Rosecrans in charge of the Army of the Mississippi. Rosecrans had fought two partly successful battles, one at Iuka on September 19 and the other at Corinth on October 3–4. Lincoln thought he had found a fighting general and on October 24 replaced Buell with Rosecrans. He gave Old Rosy the same orders as Buell but a few days later complained to Stanton, "Gen. Rosecrans [is] still at Corinth."[38]

Rosecrans graduated from West Point in 1842 fifth in a class of fifty-six and served twelve years in the regular army before taking a higher-paying civilian job. He served under McClellan in western Virginia, later under Pope and Halleck, and eventually under Grant. He fought some of his battles independently, which attracted Lincoln's attention. Stanton did not oppose Rosecrans's appointment, although he preferred George Thomas, a Democrat like himself. Halleck preferred Rosecrans, and so did Chase, who always supported Ohio Republicans regardless of their ability. Lincoln no longer listened to military advice from his cabinet. The war was on his back. He would fight it his way whether anyone agreed or not.[39]

Lincoln also ordered Banks to New Orleans to replace Butler, who lavished in corruption. Butler could not mount a military campaign because he did not know how, but as a Democrat he still carried immense political power. Banks, a political general also lacking military skill, was nonetheless a Republican Lincoln trusted. Unlike Butler, Banks would fight, though he never learned how to handle troops or direct field operations. Lincoln misjudged Banks's generalship, but he liked the man's administrative ability. He told Halleck to order Banks up the Mississippi to join forces with Grant, capture Vicksburg, and then proceed up the Red River and invade Texas.

Two weeks later Banks was still in Washington requisitioning supplies and horses. Lincoln confronted Stanton, asking why Banks had not sailed for New Orleans. When Halleck presented the general's requisitions for supplies and animals, Lincoln gasped and sent Banks a McClellan-like letter prodding him to leave immediately. "The simple publication of this requisition," he warned, "would ruin you."[40]

The final months of 1862 marked a period of some of the president's greatest mistakes. One involved Major General John A. McClernand, a Democrat and fellow townsman who in September came to Washington with a plan to raise another army, descend the Mississippi, and capture Vicksburg. The task had already been assigned to Grant, but because McClernand promised to raise thousands of volunteers, which the army desperately needed, Lincoln approved the plan because it sounded feasible and would encourage political support from Democrats.

McClernand's training as a lawyer enabled him to write creative battle reports, making him appear as a skillful tactician when he was actually more like Butler and Banks. Lincoln envisioned a massive pincers movement on Vicksburg with Grant striking from the rear, the Union navy striking from the river, Banks advancing from the south, and McClernand advancing from the north. Lincoln believed, as did Stanton, that McClernand surpassed Grant as a military tactician, which attests to the inability of the president and the secretary of war to evaluate smooth-talking politicians with stars on their shoulder straps. Stanton wanted to see what a nonprofessional soldier could do, so in October Lincoln authorized McClernand to build his army and by doing so may have set back the capture of Vicksburg by several months. Halleck, always skeptical of amateur generals, knew nothing of the president's special arrangement with McClernand until December.[41]

A few days after replacing Buell, Rosecrans moved eastward, and Grant commenced operations against Vicksburg. Banks sailed for Louisiana, and Burnside headed south. McClernand prepared to descend the Mississippi River with an independent command to join Grant. Halleck made it unclear whether McClernand or Grant would head operations at Vicksburg. Lincoln expected good results on all fronts. With his confidence revived, he made frequent visits to the telegraph office, expecting to hear good news from his generals. He was unprepared for the outcome.[42]

CHAPTER 12

"If there is a worse place than Hell, I am in it"

Lincoln chose Ambrose Burnside, a thirty-eight-year-old poker player with the flourishing sideburns, because he thought the general would fight better as an independent commander than a corps commander serving under McClellan. Burnside had twice refused command of the Army of the Potomac, which Lincoln interpreted as coming not from a man lacking confidence but from one who valued his friendship with McClellan more than he valued his own promotion. After Burnside made a misstep at Antietam, his relationship with McClellan cooled. Lincoln never knew of the problem. Burnside, however, participated in battles; McClellan never did. The men adored the sight of McClellan prancing about on his horse during reviews, but they never saw him rallying troops or facing fire on a battlefield.[1]

Although a brilliant organizer and administrator, the Young Napoleon was not a warrior. Burnside knew something about fighting, but his mind worked slowly. On November 7, 1862, it became Burnside's turn to breathe life into the 120,000-man Army of the Potomac by scoring a victory before winter brought campaigning to an end. After being superseded by Burnside, McClellan informed his wife, "They have made a great mistake. Alas for my poor country!"[2]

A congenial man with a powerful build, Burnside stood six feet tall. He exuded confidence in social gatherings, and people mistook his affability for wisdom. His distinguishing feature, heavy whiskers flowing from his jowls, compensated for his barren pate. He could look dashing and brave, which he was, and also intelligent, which he was not. He had graduated in the middle of the West Point class of 1847, but as one observer noted, "When he first talked with you, you would think he had a great deal more intelligence than he really possessed. You had to know him some time before you really took his measure." Burnside disliked problems requiring dexterous decision making and preferred being told what to do. As General Meade observed, "Burn" made a good subordinate commander, but he did not have the brains to command a large army. Burnside understood his limitations. Lincoln should have paid more attention instead of mistaking the general's impressive veneer for the man inside. Despite rumors of mutiny, most soldiers hailed McClellan's dismissal as necessary. "We are well pleased with

Burnside," one private said, "our soldiers will fight as well under B. as McC." For the common soldier the issue had never been one of fighting well but of being led well.[3]

Burnside understood the administration wanted action. On November 8 he told Major General Darius N. Couch his promotion had been a mistake. Two days later Major General Oliver O. Howard called at headquarters and found the commander depressed. Unable to sleep, Burn showed signs of physical and emotional fatigue from trying to produce a quick plan to advance on Richmond.[4]

McClellan's original plan, approved by the president, called for the army to cross at the upper fords, interpose between General James Longstreet's corps at Culpeper and Jackson's corps in the Shenandoah Valley, and defeat each before assaulting Richmond. Burnside abandoned the plan and drafted one designed to avoid fighting. By moving the army east to Fredericksburg, he planned to cross the Rappahannock River on pontoon bridges and move directly on Richmond. Halleck knew Lincoln wanted a battle, so on November 12 he visited Burnside to set matters straight. After a laborious two-day session with Burnside barely able to keep awake, Halleck returned to Washington thinking the general had reverted to McClellan's plan. Burnside returned to headquarters confused and reverted to his original plan. Montgomery Meigs and Herman Haupt had accompanied Halleck, but on the trip back to Washington neither man could remember what had been decided. Haupt, however, had endorsed Burnside's plan, so Halleck decided it must have been the plan agreed to.[5]

When Halleck reported that Burnside would cross the Rappahannock at Fredericksburg and strike south for Richmond, Lincoln said the army should cross at the upper fords and strike Longstreet before worrying about Richmond. Halleck insisted Burnside's plan had merit. Disappointed by Halleck's response, Lincoln glumly approved the plan, warning if Burnside moved slowly, Lee would place forces opposite Fredericksburg and block the crossing.[6]

Burnside wasted no time putting the army in motion. On November 14 he compressed six corps into three grand divisions. The First and Sixth corps formed William Franklin's Left Grand Division; the Third and Fifth corps made Joseph Hooker's Center Grand Division; and the Second and Ninth corps became Edwin V. Sumner's Right Grand Division. Early the next morning, and under the watchful eyes of Confederate scouts, Sumner's right wing led off for Falmouth, Virginia. Halleck inadvertently destroyed Burnside's opportunity for surprise. He forgot Burnside had specifically asked to have pontoons rushed to Falmouth for bridging the four hundred-foot-wide

river. Finding no pontoons at Falmouth, Sumner waited, instead of crossing
unopposed on two bridges at Fredericksburg.[7]

Perturbed by inaction, Lincoln steamed down the Potomac and on November 26 met Burnside at Aquia Creek. During the meeting the pontoons
arrived. Longstreet's corps also arrived and occupied the heights across the
river, which meant Jackson's corps would follow. Lincoln no longer agreed
with Burnside's plan and suggested landing a corps on the south bank of the
Rappahannock at Port Royal and using gunboats on the Pamunkey River
to divert Lee's right flank. The strategy made sense, but Lincoln wanted a
second opinion and hauled Burnside to Washington. Old Brains opposed the
plan because time would be lost transporting reinforcements. He thought
Burnside should attack immediately. Halleck forgot that Banks's corps was
still in Washington, having never shoved off for New Orleans. Burnside sided
with Halleck and rebuffed Lincoln's plan because good fighting weather
would end with the onset of winter. Before turning Burnside loose, Lincoln
made it clear he wanted the army's "crossing of the river to be nearly free
from risk." During Burnside's absence Stonewall Jackson's corps filed into
defensive positions on Longstreet's right.[8]

A month had passed since Burnside took command. Against his
122,000-man army on the north side of the Rappahannock, Lee had arranged
his 78,500-man army in strong defensive positions on the other side of the
river. Burnside had an option. He could go into winter quarters and wait for
spring, or he could launch a frontal attack across the swollen Rappahannock
because he said he would, even though conditions had drastically changed.

Burnside waited until December 11 before issuing the first in a series of
confusing orders putting five brigades across the river along a ten thousand–
yard front. Lee's forces, holding natural defensive positions on hills overlooking Fredericksburg, watched as Yankees laid pontoons and struggled
across the river against Confederate sharpshooters. Lee wanted the Federals
to cross and foolishly assault his defenses, which Burnside appeared determined to do. Burnside's only chance for success was to break the Confederate line at some point. Instead, he ordered a poorly synchronized assault on
December 13 and lost 12,700 killed and wounded without ever penetrating
Lee's defenses.[9]

Before the battle opened on the Union left, Burnside began to doubt
the merits of his plan and became nervous. He read the same doubts in
the eyes of his corps commanders. Some of the generals expected him to
fail, and some of Little Mac's friends did not object to helping. Nothing
demonstrated Burnside's defective generalship more than the day of battle.

Generals waited in "sleepless anxiety" throughout the night of December 12 waiting for Burnside's battle plan.

When orders arrived in the morning, Franklin found them too vague to follow, so he spent the morning slugging away at Jackson's corps without doing any damage. General Sumner's one joy in life was fighting, but after receiving his orders, he went directly to Burnside's headquarters and said, "General, I hope you will desist from this attack. I do not know of any general officer who approves of it, and I think it will prove disastrous to the army." On the Union right, near headquarters, Hooker severely criticized a frontal attack on Marye's Hill, and after it failed, he said, "There has been quite enough bloodshed to satisfy any reasonable man, and it is time to quit." Hooker disliked Burnside and later testified, "Finding I had lost as many men as my orders required me to lose, I suspended the attack." Later Burnside considered relieving Sumner, arresting Hooker, and putting Franklin in charge of the army. He then changed his mind and talked incoherently about leading a suicidal charge across the river, but his generals talked him out of it. After blaming everyone else for a poorly executed assault, he finally found reasons to blame himself.[10]

Early on December 14 Lincoln received fragmentary reports from Burnside and suspected something had gone wrong. Later that evening correspondent Henry Villard arrived at the White House with shocking details. The president heard nothing official until the following day, and the reports were even worse than Villard's account. On December 18 General James S. Wadsworth visited the White House and quoted the president as saying, "If there is a worse place than Hell, I am in it." The wrath and sadness sweeping the North fell mainly on Lincoln and Stanton for replacing McClellan with a general who never wanted the job. The public never knew Lincoln had instructed Burnside to strike quickly, if at all, or that Halleck had failed to deliver pontoons on time.[11]

Unlike McClellan, who never accepted blame for anything, Burnside manly shouldered responsibility for the Fredericksburg fiasco. Learning the public blamed the administration for forcing him to fight against his will, he asked permission to come to Washington. Lincoln replied, "Come, of course, if in your judgment it is safe to do so." On December 20 Burnside checked into a hotel and sent his secretary, David R. Larned, to the White House to make an appointment. Larned found the president in bed unable to sleep, so Lincoln said he would see Burnside at once. The general arrived at midnight and told Lincoln he intended to publish a letter taking full blame for Fredericksburg. Burnside's offer came as a great relief to Lincoln because it muffled the glut of anti-administration editorials flooding the press. Lincoln later said no general other than Burnside had ever relieved him of responsibility for a military setback.[12]

Two days later the president sent a sympathetic dispatch to the Army of the Potomac, complimenting them for showing "the qualities of a great army, which will yet give victory to the cause of the country." Burnside, however, was still trying to mount an offensive. On December 29 Lincoln learned the overly aggressive general was planning another harebrained effort to cross the river seven miles below Fredericksburg. He also knew most of the generals wanted Burnside removed. To prevent another failure, he telegraphed Burnside, "I have good reason for saying you must not make a general movement . . . without letting me know." Flabbergasted, Burnside sailed for Washington to ask the meaning of the order. Lincoln spoke of dissension among the officers. He mentioned no names and asked Burnside to be patient. With the generals against him, Burnside returned to headquarters and advised Lincoln that the army should be commanded by someone else and offered to "retire to private life."[13]

Lincoln knew he must replace Burnside; until then he wanted no more hapless campaigns. Hooker had once been considered as McClellan's successor, but he had openly criticized Burnside for incompetence, calling his movements "absurd." Hooker had also labeled the administration "imbeciles" and said nothing would go right until the country had a "dictator, and the sooner the better."[14]

After the president refused to accept Burnside's resignation, Stanton fumed, and Halleck fussed. Lincoln told Halleck to visit Burnside, study his plans for crossing the Rappahannock, and approve or reject them. Halleck said he would advise Burnside but not tell him what to do. Lincoln replied, "Your military skill is useless to me, if you will not do this." Halleck objected to the tone of Lincoln's reply and asked to be relieved. Lincoln had enough problems without losing Halleck, who, if nothing else, provided a buffer between himself and the generals. Lincoln withdrew his letter, and Halleck did the same.[15]

Instead, Halleck brought Burnside to Washington to confer with Lincoln and Stanton. No decisions were reached, and Burnside returned to the field. Annoyed by the meeting's inconclusive outcome, Burnside asked Halleck whether he should bother planning another campaign. Old Brains replied, "It will not do to keep your large army inactive," and told Burnside to "decide upon the time, place, and character of the crossing which you may attempt." The president endorsed Halleck's ambiguous reply, adding, "Be cautious."[16]

Lincoln recognized the irony of replacing McClellan, who could lead the army but not fight, with Burnside, who would fight but could not lead the army. Lincoln's endorsement, however, encouraged Burnside to seek redemption by giving the president, whom he personally admired, a stunning victory. On January 21 Burnside ignored warnings from Franklin and Hooker that the enemy was too strong and army morale too low, and with ominous obstinacy he issued orders for the next foredoomed enterprise. The skies opened, torrents of rain fell, the roads became a sea of bottomless mud, and wagons and artillery sank to their axles and stuck fast. The expedition failed, and the men joked about "Burnside's Mud March" as they slogged back to camp.

Feeling despondent, Burnside prepared orders to dismiss Hooker for demoralizing the army and proposed relieving Franklin and others for being uncooperative. On January 24 he arrived at the White House for approval. Armed with a letter of resignation, Burnside gave the president the choice of accepting one or the other. Lincoln let the general down easily. He refused Burnside's resignation, gave him a thirty-day leave, and transferred him to the Department of the Ohio.[17]

The next issue involved Burnside's successor. Public opinion favored Hooker, whose indiscrete statements regarding Burnside and the administration had not gone unnoticed by the president. Having been with the Army of the Potomac since its formation, Hooker had fought well but always openly criticized the mistakes of others. Lincoln believed Hooker had the confidence of the men and the experience to lead the army, but he also expected the general to be more aggressive than McClellan and less reckless than Burnside. He made the decision without conferring with Stanton or Halleck, and on January 25 "Fighting Joe" Hooker became the third commander of the Army of the Potomac. Lincoln gave him good advice. Alluding to the general's earlier comment that "both the Army and the Government needed a Dictator," Lincoln said, "Of course it was not for this, but in spite of it, that I have given you the command. Only those generals who gain successes, can set up dictators." Knowing he had Hooker's full attention, he said, "What I now ask of you is military success, and I will risk the dictatorship." He promised to give Hooker full support but warned, "Beware of rashness." Hooker enjoyed a three-month reprieve from action while preparing for his first test as the Army of the Potomac's chieftain. Lincoln could change Hooker's responsibilities, but could he change the general's attitude?[18]

The carnage at Fredericksburg focused public attention on the military failings of the administration. Radicals in Congress had waited for an opportunity to flex legislative muscle, and Fredericksburg provided the impetus. For several months Salmon Chase had been railing against the practices of the administration, blaming Secretary of State Seward in particular, and finally convinced his radical friends that the secretary of state, who originally opposed the war, caused all the calamities.

In 1861 Lincoln's efforts to balance the cabinet began when he chose Seward, who represented conservative elements in the Republican Party, and Chase, who represented radical elements in the party. Each man exerted himself with equal energy and public devotion, but their attitudes toward the president differed. Seward performed his duties by putting the country first and did so without ulterior ambitions beyond the scope of his departmental responsibilities. After the Fort Pickens episode he became too engrossed in diplomacy to spend time on political combinations. After the 1862 elections, when the next presidential nomination became a subject of speculation, Seward recognized Lincoln as the most able and qualified man to continue as president and gave him full and unreserved support. Chase, however, still believed a great mistake had been made in 1860, when Republicans nominated Lincoln. Despite outstanding work as Treasury secretary, Chase felt alone in the cabinet. He regarded the president and the cabinet as inferiors and unwise guardians of the public welfare. He fervently believed disasters occurred whenever others rejected his advice and that good fortune followed when everyone agreed with him. Chase's correspondence often mentioned his efforts "to rescue the President and the rest of the Cabinet from the consequences of their own errors." He cultivated close relations with generals having grievances against the administration, and if they had political connections, he comforted them even though they had performed poorly in the field. He once said to Hooker, when the Peninsular campaign failed, "General, if my advice had been followed, you would have commanded [the army] after the retreat to James River, if not before." Having been lately elevated to command the army, a few months were required to determine whether Hooker would perform any better than McClellan or Burnside.

Chase's private correspondence harshly criticized Lincoln's policies. He declared "the rebellion would be ended now" had McClellan followed *his* policies instead of the president's. He opposed Lincoln's early policy on slavery, writing, "I am just as sure the masses will and the politicians must come . . . to opinions expressed by me." He described those who agreed with him as "well-read and extremely intelligent" and admitted avoiding anyone who differed with him. When a reporter accused the president and other cabinet members of mismanagement, Chase offered no defense for his colleagues, replying, "I am not responsible for the management of the war and have no voice in it, except that I am forbidden to make suggestions; and do so now and then when I can't help it."

The president knew his Treasury minister was running an underground campaign against him because Chase had spoken with Thurlow Weed, who informed Seward, who told Lincoln. The president had immense respect for Chase's capacity and overlooked, as he did with everyone, personal slights. Chase, however, considered Seward "a man without gall" and believed a time would come when the two would openly collide over their differences.[19]

The gradual ripening of hostility toward Seward became manifest in Congress after Chase convinced the radicals that Seward's "backstairs influence" had led to Lincoln's military and domestic mistakes. With ripple effects from Fredericksburg heading the news, Senator Morton S. Wilkinson believed "the country was ruined and the cause lost [but] the Senate might yet save it." Championing Chase's line of reasoning, he said the secretary of state "exercised a controlling influence on the mind of the President" and that "no improvement could be expected . . . so long as Mr. Seward remained in the Cabinet." With Wilkinson's backing, Chase convinced Senate radicals to author a resolution calling for Seward's removal. The first resolution failed, but the second, calling for a partial reconstruction of the cabinet, was adopted. On December 19, 1862, the Senate formed a committee to carry the resolution to the president. Seward, having been tipped off by Senator Preston King, said, "They may do as they please about me, but they shall not put the President in a false position on my account." He immediately tendered his resignation and that of his son Frederick, the assistant secretary of state. Believing the issue settled, Seward began packing his personal belongings for the trip back to Auburn, New York.[20]

King also warned Lincoln of the committee's purpose. The president foresaw a possible collapse of the government and became more upset than at any time during the war. Bates recorded Washington rumors, writing, "The town all in a buzz—all the Cabinet to resign." In a brief conversation with Illinois senator Orville Browning, Lincoln asked, "What do these men want?" Answering his own question, he said, "They wish to get rid of me, and I am sometimes half disposed to gratify them."[21]

The eight-member Senate committee arrived at the White House at 7:30 p.m. and found the president relaxed, with no signs of the underlying anxiety suppressed beneath his outward cordiality. Every cabinet member attended but Seward. Embarrassed by the subject matter in which he had a hand, Chase attempted to skip the meeting, but Lincoln insisted he come. The president still had friends in the Senate and knew Chase had told Chandler the cabinet existed only in name, met infrequently, issued no reports, held no regular discussions, reached no conclusions, and implied the only voice Lincoln heard was Seward's.[22]

Jacob Collamer of Vermont presented the committee's resolutions, and Lincoln, after reading them, asked each senator for comments. James W. Grimes, Charles Sumner, and Lyman Trumbull attacked the administration's war policies in general and Seward in particular, demanding that Seward leave but the others stay. Collamer and William P. Fessenden spoke less forcibly, and the other three senators refrained from speaking at all. Having inspired the treachery, Chase became noticeably uncomfortable when asked for his views because he could not speak openly against Seward or the administration without looking foolish. When questioned whether the cabinet was divided on policy, Chase flabbergasted the committee by admitting that "there had been no want of unity in the cabinet, but a general acquiescence on public measures." He mildly complained of having too few cabinet meetings, but Lincoln had earlier explained the "necessities of the times . . . prevented frequent and long sessions." Visibly upset, Chase protested having not come to be "arraigned." It was a harsh lesson. He could not serve as advisor to congressional radicals as a member of the cabinet without being disloyal to one and loyal to the other.[23]

To end the meeting, Lincoln took a formal vote, asking the senators, "Do you, gentlemen, still think Seward should be excused?" Grimes, Sumner, and Trumbull, along with Samuel Pomeroy of Kansas, said yes. Ira Harris of New York voted no, and Collamer, Fessenden, and Jacob M. Howard abstained. At midnight, as the senators departed, Welles reported the meeting concluded "in a milder spirit than it met." Trumbull, however, took Lincoln aside and said privately that Chase had spoken in a quite different tone when they last discussed Seward. Lincoln, of course, already knew this.[24]

Rumors of Seward's resignation spread through the city. Radicals predicted more resignations, perhaps a thorough housecleaning, and began speculating on replacements. Democrats rejoiced, anticipating political gains in 1864 and perhaps a presidency for their new leader, General George B. McClellan.

Before the cabinet convened in the morning, Welles met with Lincoln and offered to counsel Seward on retracting his resignation. Lincoln accepted the offer, and Welles went to the secretary's home and found him deeply depressed and partly packed. He repeated the president's statements to the Senate committee without directly accusing Chase of complicity.

Because Lincoln had specifically told Welles he did not want Seward's resignation, the troubled secretary said that "if the President and country required of him any duty in this emergency he did not feel at liberty to refuse it." Welles returned to the White House and found Stanton and Chase with the president. Lincoln asked Welles if he "had seen the man." Welles nodded and said, "he assented to my views." Neither Chase nor Stanton understood the conversation.

Lincoln turned to the Treasury secretary and said, "I sent for you because this matter is giving me great trouble." Chase admitted being "painfully affected by the meeting last evening, which was a total surprise to him," and said he had written his resignation. "Where is it?" the president demanded. Chase removed a sealed letter from his pocket and said, "I brought it with me." Lincoln reached an arm out and said, "Let me have it." Chase hesitated, unwilling to let go, but Lincoln snatched the letter from his hand and read it. Turning toward Welles in triumph, he waved Chase's resignation and said, "This cuts the Gordian knot. I can dispose of this subject now without difficulty. I see my way clear. The trouble is ended." Stanton misread Lincoln's reaction and offered to resign on the spot. Lincoln replied, "You may go to your Department. I don't want yours." He raised Chase's letter and said, "This is all I want."[25]

When Chase returned to his office, he found John Nicolay with a letter from the president addressed to both himself and Seward requesting they withdraw their resignations. Shortly afterward, Chase received a note from Seward stating he had rescinded his resignation. Chase seemed unable to admit to himself that his cabal had backfired, and he kept Lincoln waiting over the weekend for an answer. On December 22, after having clumsily injured his own credibility, Chase made a weak effort to justify his behavior and then agreed to remain in office. His friends in the Senate remained cordial and were glad he stayed with the Treasury, but as a leader of their radical persuasions, Chase had irreparably damaged his prestige. Later Browning asked Collamer how Chase, a man of integrity, could have made such scurrilous statements about Seward. Collamer replied, "He lied."[26]

Lincoln survived his severest test as president unaided by the advice of others. He turned the greatest threat to his administration into an overwhelming defeat of cabinet discord, at the same time setting Congress straight on the hazards of pursuing its members' misconceptions. He told radicals that further attacks on Seward would lead to the departure of Chase, and he told Seward's friends that attacks on Chase would weaken the secretary of state. Perhaps at no time during his two-year administration had Lincoln more clearly demonstrated his talents as chief executive. The Seward-Chase episode, rather than destroying the cabinet, solidified it. On the day Chase submitted his resignation and Seward withdrew his, Lincoln knew he had won. Having balanced the policy differences between Seward and Chase, he told Senator Ira Harris, "I can ride on now. I've got a pumpkin in each end of my bag."[27]

No one understood the value of Chase more than Lincoln. After Fredericksburg he needed Chase managing the Treasury as urgently as he needed Seward in the State Department. The national debt on July 1, 1861, topped $90 million, with a balance of $2 million in the Treasury. On July 17 Congress authorized the borrowing of $250 million, which included a $20 million direct tax on states. Chase based his requests on an army of 300,000 men, which soon doubled. By the end of 1861 the cost of financing the war rose to $50 million a month, and during the December session of Congress Chase asked for $200 million more. When he suspended payments in specie on February 25, 1862, and authorized greenbacks as legal tender, there was still too little money in circulation. Chase considered the legal tender bill unconstitutional, but in 1862 it served as an expedient and prevented a national financial crisis. "It is true," Chase said in 1862, "that I came with reluctance to the conclusion that legal tender . . . is a necessity, but I came to it decidedly, and I support it earnestly."[28]

The Army of the Potomac, the most expensive on the continent, consumed money voraciously. Troops had not been paid and contractors were peddling receivables at discounts. The federal debt rose to $300 million, and daily expenditures topped $2 million. Chase said $150 million in greenbacks would keep the country running, but in June he asked Congress to approve $150 million more. By July 1, 1862, the federal debt had risen to $524 million and twelve months later approached a billion. Gold acted as the inflation monitor, jumping from $17 an ounce in July 1861 to $72.50 after the passage of the legal tender bill, eventually peaking at $185.[29]

Chase adopted novel ways to liberate the government from impoverishment. Loans, bonds, notes, and greenbacks all contributed to maintaining solvency, but he soon found troves of counterfeit banknotes. State banks compounded the problem by issuing their own currency. Travelers found the contents of their wallets changing value every time they crossed state lines.

In December 1861 Chase worked with two members of the Ways and Means Committee to establish a national banking bill. In 1862 the Third Legal Tender Act flooded the market with another $150 million in greenbacks and $50 million in fractional currency. Chase wanted the committee to set monetary policy in accordance with fluctuating market values. Lincoln backed the establishment of federally chartered banks and said so in his annual message to Congress. On February 12, 1863, the National Banking Act passed by two votes in the Senate, and on February 20 it passed by a vote of seventy-eight to sixty-four in the House. Currency of the new federally chartered banks was backed by holdings in government bonds, and though far from perfect for suppressing inflation, public confidence in the new banking system made it possible to pay for the war. On May 12, 1863, Chase reported, "There is not an unpaid requisition in my Department." Among those who suffered from the unstable currency, however, were soldiers. They received greenbacks in pay without a commensurate adjustment to the purchasing power of the currency.[30]

The National Banking Act was regularly amended and, though never perfect, stands as one of the outstanding efforts of statesmanship emanating from the war. During the Buchanan administration the Treasury had borrowed money at 12 percent. Once Chase obtained full command of monetary policy through the National Banking Act, the Treasury financed the war at 6 percent or less. To Chase's credit, Lincoln exercised less scrutiny over the Treasury than any other department. Chase eventually exercised a small amount of latitude in the design of the Treasury notes: "I had put the President's head on the higher priced notes, my own, as was becoming on the smaller ones."[31]

Chase never forgot how the president first lured and then exposed him to his greatest political blunder or how afterward Lincoln let it pass as if nothing had happened. Unlike Chase, Seward's faith in Lincoln's ability as a truly gifted executive came with the president's lesson in interpersonal management. He knew he had the president's confidence and goodwill, and he no longer questioned who was in charge. He became more sensitive about what he said and meddled less in the affairs of his colleagues, except to give advice when asked.[32]

Lincoln also benefited from the experience. The open meeting with the cabinet and the Senate committee revealed his own shortcomings. His cabinet meetings became more businesslike, and he dealt more openly with the concerns of radicals and conservatives in Congress. On December 23, 1862, he held a cabinet meeting to ask for constitutional advice on a bill creating the new state of West Virginia. Chase, Seward, and Stanton recommended the bill be signed; Bates, Blair, and Welles answered in the negative. Caleb Smith had retired to a judgeship in Indiana and had not yet been replaced by John P. Usher of Indiana, the assistant secretary of the interior, and this created a tie. Lincoln requested comments in writing and received long, elaborate arguments. He took the cabinet's opinions under consideration, and though he still questioned the constitutionality of the act, on December 31 he exercised his super-vote, saying, "I think I cannot do less and live," and signed the bill.[33]

The president also held a cabinet meeting before signing the final version of the Emancipation Proclamation. With fingers stiff from shaking hands with guests attending the annual New Year's Day reception at the White House, he reached for the document and said, "Now, this signature is one that will be closely examined, and if they find my hand trembled, they will say 'he had some compunctions.' But, any way, it is going to be done." Lincoln took the pen, steadied his arm, and signed the proclamation, saying, "I never, in my life, felt more certain that I was doing right, than I do in signing this paper."[34]

With the problems of 1862 behind him, and with the hopes of 1863 ahead, Lincoln felt refreshed and ready. He would no longer be pushed around by anybody, nor would he allow anyone to criticize a member of his cabinet. When David Dudley Field and George Opdyke of New York came to the White House to renew efforts to remove Seward, claiming to "be willing to see the country ruined if they could turn out Seward," Lincoln reacted uncharacteristically. "For once in my life," he told John Hay, "I rather gave my temper the rein and I talked to those men pretty damned plainly." Hay said Opdyke seemed "cool" upon departing, causing Lincoln to snort, "I may have given him reason."[35]

Having matured as an executive, Lincoln still faced grave problems in the year ahead. As Bates noted, "We have not suppressed the rebellion. The hand of God is in this thing."[36]

CHAPTER 13

"My God, my God, what will the country say"

Ink had barely dried on the Emancipation Proclamation when reports of the Battle of Stone's River began trickling into the War Department's telegraph office. For several weeks Lincoln had watched for positive news from General Rosecrans. On December 5, 1862, Henry Halleck expressed the president's impatience, writing, "If you remain one more week at Nashville, I cannot prevent your removal." Rosecrans replied, "If my superiors have lost confidence in me, they had better at once put someone else in my place. . . . To threats of removal . . . I am insensible." Halleck became more conciliatory but made it clear that Lincoln wanted the rebels driven from middle Tennessee because Southern sympathizers in England would use the January session of Parliament to put pressure on the prime minister to intervene. If Union forces occupied middle Tennessee, pro-Confederate parliamentarians would be unable to claim the South was winning the war. Referring to Lincoln, Halleck added, "You can hardly conceive his great anxiety about it."[1]

On December 26, as Rosecrans's army marched into middle Tennessee, General Bragg's Confederates began moving west to attack Nashville. On the last day of December the two armies collided at Stone's River. Bragg struck Rosecrans's right wing, bent it back, but could not break it. On New Year's Day, while Lincoln hosted the annual reception at the White House, Rosecrans's and Bragg's armies stared at each other from across the West Branch of Stone's River and did nothing. On January 2 Confederates unsuccessfully assaulted the Union left and retired to their original position. Rosecrans claimed victory because Bragg withdrew, but he neither hurt the enemy nor gained middle Tennessee. Like McClellan, he succeeded by fighting defensively. Lincoln could not evaluate the battle from Washington, but after the recent debacle at Fredericksburg, he took Rosecrans at his word, telegraphing, "God bless you and all with you!"[2]

Rosecrans's account of Stone's River contained distortions, but Lincoln valued any good military news coming his way. As weeks passed into months, he came to understand the incompleteness of the Rosecrans victory. Instead of pursuing the rebels and fighting, Rosecrans wintered at Murfreesboro. On February 17 Lincoln gave Rosecrans a nudge, instructing him to stop "defensive" measures and launch "counter-raids." Rosecrans never responded. Instead of taking action against the enemy, he fretted over the president's insinuations.[3]

In January Lincoln pointed to Rosecrans as a general with a future but two months later realized Stone's River had been a draw. Meanwhile, Rosecrans accused Halleck of intentionally withholding men and supplies to force him to fight. Then he accused Stanton of doing everything possible to make him fail. Neither accusation made sense. Halleck explained that Stanton merely wanted to encourage aggressiveness and would grant a major generalship in the regular army to the first man to win the next important victory. Rosecrans fumed, saying he felt degraded by an administration "auctioneering" commissions to officers in an effort to force them to fight before they were ready. Rosecrans looked foolish. The same offer went to all generals, who went about the business of war without comment.[4]

On March 16 Rosecrans sent his list of grievances directly to the president. Lincoln addressed the general's complaints with characteristic patience. Among the requests Rosecrans wanted his promotion to major general retro-dated to rank Grant. Lincoln said doing so would only hurt others, adding, "The world will not forget that you fought the battle of 'Stones River' and it will never care a fig whether you rank Gen. Grant on paper, or he so, ranks you." Lincoln's message failed to assuage Rosecrans's state of mind, nor did his closing remark: "You wrong both yourself and us, when you even suspect there is not the best disposition on the part of us all here to oblige you." The words might better have been cast to the wind. Having assumed a McClellan-like posture, Rosecrans stepped up requests for reinforcements and supplies. Halleck said he received more demands from Rosecrans than all the generals in the field combined.[5]

Nothing Lincoln said changed Rosecrans's opinions about Stanton and Halleck, but the general refused to let his name be used against the president. Radicals who doubted Lincoln's ability to win in 1864 sent an emissary to Tennessee to explore Rosecrans's political ambitions. The general dismissed the agent and advised him to return to his friends and assure them Lincoln was the right man "in the right place."[6]

The president, however, suspected Rosecrans may be the wrong man to have in the right place for launching an offensive against Chattanooga. Spring bloomed, roads dried, and Rosecrans languished behind Murfreesboro's fortifications. Grant had spent the winter assiduously but unsuccessfully trying different stunts to break through the confounding topography around Vicksburg. Lincoln asked Rosecrans to help Grant by attacking Chattanooga, which he explained would draw troops from Mississippi to defend Tennessee, thus preventing reinforcements from reaching Vicksburg. Rosecrans replied, "I will attend to it."[7]

Rosecrans did nothing, but on April 30 Grant moved troops across the Mississippi River below Vicksburg and began a roundabout campaign that eventually developed into a two-month siege. On June 2 Halleck advised Rosecrans that General Joseph Johnston had detached forces from Bragg to attack Grant's rear. "If you can do nothing yourself," Halleck explained, "a portion of your troops must be sent to Grant's relief." Rosecrans replied, "We have begun a movement," but again he did nothing.[8]

Lincoln could not comprehend Rosecrans's logic, nor could Halleck, who asked for an explanation. Rosecrans met with his generals and replied, "Not one thinks an advance advisable until Vicksburg's fate is determined," adding that "fighting two immense and decisive battles at the same time" was contrary to "a great military maxim." If Old Brains understood nothing else about fighting, he understood military theory and threw Rosecrans's remarks back in his face, writing that the axiom applied to one army dissipating its strength by fighting several battles and did not apply to two armies fighting separate battles. "If you are not strong enough to fight Bragg with part of his troops absent, you will not be able to fight him after . . . Vicksburg is over and his troops return to your front." Besides, Halleck cautioned, "councils of war never fight."[9]

Halleck erred by giving Rosecrans a lesson in textbook warfare without telling him what to do. Lincoln ordered Halleck to demand a deadline. On June 16 Rosecrans promised to advance in five days. Eight days later Halleck received a telegram, "The army begins to move at 3 o'clock this morning." During the next nine days Rosecrans maneuvered Bragg out of middle Tennessee and into Chattanooga. Bragg's army, however, had not been damaged, and Rosecrans would later pay a price for avoiding a fight.[10]

During the winter of 1863, while Grant slugged away at Vicksburg and Rosecrans marked time at Murfreesboro, Lincoln monitored General Joseph Hooker's activities along the Rappahannock. With some misgivings he had given "Fighting Joe" an opportunity to succeed where McClellan, Pope, and Burnside had failed. Hooker's sprawling encampment of 120,000 magnificently trained and equipped troops had for two months amused themselves with snowball fights, letter writing, and card playing. As the weather warmed, Hooker turned his attention to Halleck's orders, which read, "In regards to the operations of your army, you can best judge when and where it can move to the greatest advantage, keeping in view always the importance of covering Washington and Harper's Ferry."

On April 19 Hooker reviewed Slocum's Twelfth Corps at Falmouth and remarked, "If the enemy does not run, God help them." Ten days later he entertained a party of officers in his tent and gloated, "I have the finest army the sun ever shone on. I can march this army to New Orleans. My plans are perfect, and when I start to carry them out, may God have mercy on General Lee, for I will have none." Hooker, however, remained indecisive. To engage Lee's army he had to cross the river somewhere other than Fredericksburg.[11]

Lincoln sensed Hooker's indecisiveness and traveled to Falmouth, accompanied by his wife, son Tad, Bates, Noah Brooks, and two friends. They spent three leisurely days at Hooker's headquarters, while Lincoln talked with Fighting Joe. Hooker exposed a worrisome trait, habitually making allusions to "When I get to Richmond" and "After we have taken Richmond." Lincoln remarked to Brooks, "That is the most depressing thing about Hooker. It seems to me he is overconfident." Before leaving Falmouth, the president summoned Darius Couch, second in command, to review Burnside's mistakes at Fredericksburg and McClellan's mistakes from earlier campaigns. After learning neither general had committed his reserves, Lincoln closed the discussion, saying, "Gentlemen, in your next battle, *put in all your men.*"[12]

Lincoln disliked Hooker's allusions to Richmond and told him to concentrate on destroying Lee's army. On April 11 Hooker sent his chief of staff, Major General Daniel F. Butterfield, to Washington to explain a plan resembling a compromise between McClellan's original strategy and Burnside's later version of crossing the Rappahannock below Fredericksburg. Hooker believed by using the upper fords and turning the enemy's left, he could defeat Lee. He would send his cavalry into Lee's rear to destroy communications with Richmond, cross with the army, force Lee to fight in the open, trap the Confederates between the infantry and the cavalry, and destroy the rebel army. Hooker did not discuss the plan with his generals because he wanted the president's endorsement first.

Lincoln approved the plan because it avoided a frontal attack and focused on destroying Lee's army. Hooker launched his plan on April 13 by sending Major General George Stoneman's 10,000-man cavalry up the Rappahannock to cross the river and assault Lee's communications. Rain fell in torrents, flooded the river, and rendered the fords impassable. The all-important initial movement of Hooker's campaign bogged down for two weeks. Stoneman never crossed the river until the twenty-ninth, the same day the infantry movement began.[13]

Lincoln paid close attention to Hooker's timetable because he wanted to avoid another disaster. On April 14 he reacted to Stoneman's delay, grumbling, "He is not twenty-five miles from where he started [with] sixty to go." Heavy rains were falling when Hooker received Lincoln's cheerless message, "I greatly fear it is another failure already." Dissatisfied with progress, Lincoln asked the general to meet him at Aquia. Despite flooded rivers, Hooker must have convinced the president that Stoneman's raid was still executable because he never canceled it.[14]

As more rain fell, Hooker modified his plan. He decided to threaten Lee's right flank by crossing at Fredericksburg while three corps marched thirty miles upriver to cross the upper fords and pounce on the Confederate left. On April 27 Hooker shared his plans with the president after putting the army in motion. Likewise, he did not completely inform his generals of the change until days later. He believed anything said would fall within hours into Lee's hands. Lincoln promised to keep Hooker's plans to himself, and Halleck did not learn until April 30 that the Army of the Potomac had crossed the Rappahannock.[15]

Having crossed the river unfettered by enemy resistance, Hooker resorted to boasting. To reporters at headquarters he said, "The rebel army is now the legitimate property of the Army of the Potomac. They may as well pack up their haversacks and make for Richmond." Lincoln would have considered the statement a sign of trouble. He did not want the rebel army to pack up their haversacks and make for Richmond. He wanted Lee destroyed. Hooker had won the initiative, but like the flawed generals of the Army of the Potomac, he lost it by losing his nerve.

On May 1 Hooker's army moved into an unmapped wilderness area of tangled woods and baffling roads. By sending Stoneman's cavalry on a wild-goose chase, he deprived himself of scouts. On May 2, as Hooker advanced, Stonewall Jackson marched his corps from the hills overlooking Fredericksburg and struck Hooker's right flank, while Lee engaged the Union center. The unexpected attack startled Hooker, but the Federals held and re-formed, which put Union forces in good position to launch a counterattack and win a victory. When on May 3 an exploding shell knocked Hooker temporarily senseless, he lost confidence and ordered a withdrawal. On May 4–5, despite objections from his generals, Fighting Joe recrossed the river.[16]

Lincoln heard nothing for six days. For security reasons Hooker said he would forward no messages without having something decisive to report.

Certain a battle was under way, Lincoln waited nervously. While Hooker nursed his concussion, no one communicated with Washington. At Falmouth, General Butterfield had heard nothing about the outcome of the battle but thought Lincoln deserved an update, so on May 3 he informed the president, "A battle is in progress" and "in an hour or two [victory] will be a fixed fact." Puzzled by the message, Lincoln asked, "Where is General Hooker? Where is Sedgwick? Where is Stoneman?" Butterfield realized his mistake, said nothing, and deferred to Hooker, who had recovered his senses. In a sophomoric attempt at ambiguity, Hooker reported the "desperate fight . . . resulted in no success to us." He said General John Sedgwick had taken no part in the engagement but urged the president to "not despair of success." Hooker could not explain the whereabouts of Stoneman's cavalry because it had completely vanished.[17]

Twenty-four hours passed before the War Department received a newspaper account confirming Hooker's defeat. Lincoln telegraphed Falmouth, "We have news here that the enemy has reoccupied heights above Fredericksburg. Is that so?" Hooker replied, "I am informed that it is so, but attach no importance to it." Welles found Lincoln pacing the telegraph office and impatiently waiting for more information. Two days passed without word from Hooker, but on May 6 Lincoln received a telegram from Butterfield reporting the army was pulling back across the Rappahannock and taking defensive measures. By evening Hooker confirmed he had crossed to the "safety" of the north bank. The news stunned Lincoln. Returning to the White House, he found Noah Brooks waiting and said, "My God, my God, what will the country say. What will the country say!" Hooker's mistake of going into battle with only three of his seven corps annoyed Lincoln most. With Rosecrans and Grant on the move in the West, Lincoln had all but wept for a victory in the East.[18]

Realizing he could no longer rely on Hooker for straight answers, Lincoln departed with Halleck for Halleck's headquarters. The president expressed more concern about the morale of the army than the causes of defeat, which he already understood. The generals wanted Fighting Joe replaced by George Meade, who wanted no part of the scheme, and Couch said he could no longer serve under Hooker. The revolt disturbed Lincoln. It reminded him of Burnside's troubles, and he worried the generals might not fight.[19]

Lincoln spoke privately with Hooker to determine whether the general had a plan because, remembering Burnside, he wanted nothing done in desperation or rashness. Observing that Hooker had not recovered from his defeat, Lincoln decided it would be best if Fighting Joe strengthened the army and avoided major engagements. Tipped off that Hooker was planning a Burnside-like advance, Lincoln brought him to Washington and said, "I shall not complain if you do no more for a time than to keep the enemy at bay and out of mischief . . . and to put your own army in good condition again." Hooker departed for Virginia, and the president resumed the search for a new commander, but nobody wanted the job.[20]

Hooker took Lincoln's advice and did little. Soon he would look across the river and find the Confederates gone.

With the settlement of the *Trent* affair in 1862, foreign relations became William Seward's full-time job. Lincoln gave his foreign minister a simple five-word directive—"One war at a time." His instructions to Seward often conflicted with those given to Gideon Welles.

Wanting Confederate cotton, English firms fitted out hundreds of blockade-runners. One trip to a Confederate port with a cargo of munitions and back again to Europe laden with cotton could pay for building the ship and still leave a tidy profit for the owner. Welles ordered the navy to interdict any ship suspected of carrying contraband and either bring the prize into port for adjudication or release it. Ever since the blockade-running business began, Union warships had been stopping suspicious steamers and inspecting cargoes in compliance with maritime rules.

Naval operations sometimes conflicted with Seward's efforts to keep England and France out of the war. In February 1863 Charles Wilkes, the same captain responsible for the *Trent* affair, captured the British merchant steamer *Peterhoff* off St. Thomas in the West Indies. The ship carried contraband for Matamoras, a Mexican port used by the South to bring arms across the Rio Grande to Brownsville, Texas. The *Peterhoff* case might never have bloomed had someone other than Wilkes boarded the vessel and claimed it as a prize. The case became historic because it established the principle of "continuous voyage," which gave a belligerent "the right to seize cargo destined only nominally for a neutral port and plainly intended for an enemy."[21]

The issue concerned the ownership of the mail, not the cargo. Seward entered into the dispute when Welles refused to surrender the mailbags. He sided with the British, but Welles remained obdurate, claiming the right to seize everything on a ship carrying contraband. The mail lay impounded in New York's district court, and the only question concerned the legality of keeping it. Lincoln asked Seward whether holding the mail of a captured ship engaged in smuggling was legal and received a vague but negative reply, which Welles flatly contradicted. The subject had been discussed earlier, and Welles believed his position had already been confirmed months ago.

For several weeks Seward and Welles jockeyed for the president's support. Welles put aides to work searching old records to substantiate his view and soon dragged Senator Charles Sumner, the chairman of the foreign relations committee, into the debate. Without conferring with Bates, Seward went directly to District Attorney Delafield Smith at New York and told him to give up the mails. Bates discovered Seward's meddling, rescinded the order, and instructed Delafield to hold the bags. Chase examined the issue and agreed with Bates and Welles. Lincoln found himself in the middle, besieged from both sides. While Seward worried the president about the possibility of war, Sumner called fears about going to war over mailbags absurd.

The unresolved mailbag question continued for more than two months and involved the president, the cabinet, the Senate, and British minister Lord Richard Lyons. On April 30 Sumner appeared at the White House and told Lincoln that Lord Lyons had never demanded the mails not be opened, to which Lincoln curtly replied, "I shall have to cut this knot."[22]

The so-called *Peterhoff* case came to a head on May 15 when Lord Lyons, probably at Seward's request, delivered a letter demanding the mailbags. Welles still wanted the issue adjudicated according to "law and usage" because the navy had been removing mail from blockade-runners since the beginning of the war. Lincoln said, "We were in no condition to plunge into a foreign war on a subject of so little importance," and ordered the mails returned to England. Lincoln's decision, though he knew Welles was right, prevented a small incident from getting out of control. Instead of trying to win a legal point, he directed his efforts toward improving relations with Great Britain. He said small international squabbles might best be settled by small concessions, especially because Europeans would regard the news from Chancellorsville as another victory for the South.[23]

During the early months of 1863 Lincoln became concerned about his sagging popularity. He lost support from moderate Republicans, whose centrist views brought them closer to the antiwar philosophy of peace Democrats, also known as "Copperheads" because they wore badges inserted with a copper penny. Such a consolidation of political power could bring peace and permanent disunion and would likely dissolve the Republican Party.

Newspapers fashioned public opinion faster than comments coming from the White House, and after Congress adjourned, the press kept running. Lincoln had friendly publishers such as Henry J. Raymond of the *New*

York Times, but he also had enemies. Powerful newspapermen like Horace Greeley could take strong positions on an issue one day and a few days later change their minds. Greeley had been an outspoken advocate of the Emancipation Proclamation, but in 1863 he was willing to fling it away in exchange for mediation of the war with England or France, the two nations most dependent on slave labor for cotton. Greeley was so convinced of his own influence that he told Raymond he would "drive Lincoln" to accepting mediation. Greeley had no business becoming directly involved with foreign envoys promoting peace, especially knowing France had designs on Mexico. When Seward recommended prosecuting Greeley under the Logan Act, which prohibited subversive activities, Lincoln vetoed the suggestion because he believed Greeley's meddling to revoke the Emancipation Proclamation would eventually do more to sustain the war than end it.

The Emancipation Proclamation purchased political capital for Lincoln and the pro-Union cause in Great Britain. He believed once the people of England understood the Civil War focused on freedom, they would be more willing to suffer to support it. In a letter to the unemployed "Workingmen of Manchester, England," Lincoln asked for patience and shifted the blame for the cotton shortage from the blockade "to the actions of our disloyal citizens." He "deeply deplored" the sufferings of all workingmen but said he could not allow a government "built upon the foundation of human rights" to be overthrown by one based exclusively on human slavery. Lincoln gave no reasons for the two-year delay before issuing the proclamation.[24]

Greeley's domestic ravings caught the attention of peace Democrats and gave them a powerful voice to harass the administration. No aspect of the 1862 election, other than the war, had caught the attention of the public more than the suspension of the writ of habeas corpus, which allowed arbitrary arrests and threatened to stifle the press. So Greeley, feeling threatened, picked a new quarrel with the president.

Gains in 1862 elections encouraged Democrats to attack Lincoln's suspension of the writ of habeas corpus while demanding both mediation on the war and the release of political prisoners. Protests against the habeas corpus issue were not new, only now more vociferous and pervasive. Even Welles doubted the constitutionality of the president's proclamation, writing, "I question the wisdom . . . of a multiplicity of proclamations striking deep on great questions." Greeley and the peace Democrats, however, created a puzzling irony by calling themselves the protectors of civil liberties while espousing a policy to preserve slavery.[25]

By suspending the writ of habeas corpus, Lincoln knew he had put the safety of the Union above the law. Speaking metaphorically, he said, "A limb must often be amputated to save a life, but a life must never be given to save a limb. I felt measures, however unconstitutional, might become lawful by becoming indispensable to the preservation of the constitution, through the preservation of the nation." The problem with Lincoln's proclamation was its erratic implementation, partly because of the question of constitutionality and partly because Democrats fought it. When in 1862 Bates could not decide whether he agreed with the proclamation, Lincoln handed the implementation of the policy to Seward, who was totally absorbed in foreign affairs. In 1863, when Democratic jurists involved in the Copperhead movement attempted to nullify the proclamation, Bates spoke up. "No *judicial officer*," he insisted, "had the power to take a prisoner or soldier, out of the hands of the President, by Habeas Corpus." In 1866 the Supreme Court overruled the president and the attorney general, but during the war Lincoln succeeded in sacrificing a limb of the Constitution to save the life of the nation. The administration executed nobody, established no police state, and created no reign of terror, and many petty traitors escaped prosecution. The absence of a codified system, however, allowed innocent men to be abused by arbitrary arrests and the swift judgment of military tribunals instead of enjoying their right to be heard in civil courts.[26]

The Copperhead movement evolved after a number of outspoken Democrat editors, judges, and lawyers, landed in Old Capitol Prison because they denounced presidential policies. Stanton fueled the fire by summarily arresting two brokers for interfering with enlistments by recruiting substitutes. The brokers provided a service by enabling a draftee to avoid the army by paying someone else to serve in his place. The case circulated through the courts and finally landed on Secretary Stanton's desk. After the 1862 elections Stanton freed the brokers and all civilian prisoners against whom no evidence existed, providing they came from states having filled their draft quotas. Such arbitrariness on the part of the war secretary brought more criticism from peace Democrats. Stanton was only following the proclamation's guidelines, which included "aiders and abettors" of the rebellion and "all persons discouraging volunteer enlistments, resisting military drafts, or guilty of any disloyal practice."[27]

Horatio Seymour, a powerful New York Democrat, used Stanton's arrests to unify the party in the East and align it with the Copperhead movement in the Midwest. Civil rights issues gained national momentum, rising and falling with the fortunes of war, and thousands of uneasy citizens joined the Democrats. Significant congressional and gubernatorial gains by Democrats in the 1862 elections, during which Seymour became governor of New York, had as much to do with the unpopularity of Lincoln's suspension of civil rights as with the military draft and the administration's inability to snuff out the rebellion.

From political turmoil came forty-two-year-old Clement L. Vallandigham, a handsome Ohio congressman and conservative Democrat who blamed the war on Lincoln and Republicans. He voted against national conscription, refused to support congressional war measures, alienated war Democrats of his own political party, lost his seat in the 1862 election, and failed in the 1863 Ohio primary in his bid for governor. He believed in the preservation of the Union but was indifferent, as Lincoln had once been, to the future of slavery. Like many Westerners, Vallandigham looked into the future and envisioned tens of thousands of freedmen emigrating into the North and taking jobs from whites. Stanton had raised concerns by herding blacks into Cairo, Illinois, and shipping them north to replace laborers drafted into the army. Vallandigham claimed to be a Union man, but as an 1860 congressman declared, "He never would . . . vote one dollar of money whereby one drop of American blood should be shed in a civil war." By 1863 he had become the most vocal agitator in the Midwest against Lincoln's proclamations, which in his view deprived the nation of peace and civil liberties in exchange for abolition.[28]

On April 13, 1863, General Ambrose Burnside, commanding the Department of the Ohio at Cincinnati, issued General Order No. 38 forbidding the expression of sympathy for the enemy. Fresh from the Fredericksburg disaster, Burnside wanted to avoid trouble and became the prime mover against "treason, expressed or implied." His order specified that "all persons found within our lines who commit acts for the benefit of the enemy" would be "tried as spies or traitors," and if convicted, executed.[29]

On May 1, in defiance of this order, Vallandigham delivered a fiery speech against the administration during a mass meeting of Copperheads at Mount Vernon, Ohio. Soldiers broke into Vallandigham's Dayton home, arrested the former congressman while fending off rioters, transported him to Cincinnati, and threw him in jail. Vallandigham went before a military tribunal accused of "declaring disloyal statements." He offered no plea, arguing a military court had no jurisdiction to try him for exercising his constitutional guarantee to freedom of speech. Vallandigham used the trial as a platform "for giving more aid and comfort to the rebellion" by declaring, among other things, that the war was being fought for the liberation of blacks and the enslavement of whites, and "no more volunteers could be had" for "King Lincoln's" ongoing prosecution of the war.[30]

Fellow Ohioan Samuel S. Cox, another critic of the administration, appeared at the trial for the defense, claimed to have been informed by Burnside that Vallandigham "would not be convicted," and conveyed the welcome news to the defendant's distressed wife. Cox testified there had been no threats to Cincinnati since the autumn of 1862; hence, there was no reason for martial law, and if necessary, civil courts could settle the case. The military tribunal, however, declared Vallandigham guilty and sentenced him to prison for the remainder of the war. Burnside found himself trapped by his own general orders. To keep from looking foolish, despite earlier assurances of acquittal to Cox, Burnside approved the sentence.[31]

Several days passed before Vallandigham's case vaulted into the White House. On May 8, when Lincoln first telegraphed Burnside to say he supported the arrest, he did not have all the facts. Two weeks later he became aghast on learning that Burnside had arrested other suspected traitors and in one case planned to hang Thomas M. Campbell of Kentucky for spying. Lincoln stopped the execution. On May 29 Burnside offered to be relieved because his actions had not been "approved by a single member of your Cabinet." Lincoln replied, "When I shall wish to supersede you I will let you know. All the cabinet regretted the necessity of arresting, for instance, Vallandigham—some perhaps doubting there was a real necessity for it— but, being done, all were for seeing you through with it."[32]

The president could, and some said should, have released Vallandigham because his arrest overshot the scope of Lincoln's intentions when he suspended the writ of habeas corpus. Lincoln instructed Stanton to release Vallandigham to Rosecrans with orders to keep the former congressman within enemy lines. A military escort conducted Vallandigham to a rebel outpost, where Southern leaders greeted him with little enthusiasm. The deported agitator discovered while wandering the South that he enjoyed far less freedom of speech and action there than in the North. He returned to Ohio in 1864 in disguise to run for governor, and Lincoln, who had come to view the entire episode with a sense of humor, let the former congressman run loose on the premise that his re-imprisonment would cause more harm than his freedom. Vallandigham lost his bid for governor as well as his cause, which vindicated Lincoln's hands-off decision.[33]

The Vallandigham case became important because Judge Humphrey H. Leavitt of the United States Circuit Court in Cincinnati agreed to hear the defendant's application for a writ of habeas corpus. The question was whether a federal court could review or overrule proceedings of a military commission—a debate we confront in the twenty-first century. The issue in 1863 was whether a military tribunal could arrest, try, and sentence a civilian for expressing seditious opinions, and if so, could a civil court intervene. Leavitt dodged the fundamental question of whether a civil court had greater oversight and constitutional power than a military court and on the matter of whether Vallandigham's arrest was legal, Leavitt refused to rule. His stated purpose in hearing the case was to explore those issues without necessarily ruling on them, and after listening to arguments from both sides, he refused to grant the writ or interfere with the military court.[34]

Bates wrote five thousand words in defense of the president's power "to preserve, protect and defend the Constitution." He concluded that a president "rules in peace and commands in war, and at this moment he is in the full exercise of all the functions belonging to both those characters." On March 3, 1863, the Thirty-seventh Congress passed an act supporting the president's proclamation suspending the writ of habeas corpus, but this did not stop disgruntled political opponents from expressing contrary views.[35]

Some good came out of the Vallandigham episode but not much. Governor Seymour of New York joined Copperheads in assailing the administration by declaring that Vallandigham's arrest violated the nation's most sacred rights. The harshness of the speeches alienated most Republicans and war Democrats, thereby preventing a political restructuring that threatened to fuse moderate Republicans and peace Democrats into a centrist party. It is difficult to estimate what might have happened to the nation, the presidency, and the cabinet had this occurred.

If midterm ballots signaled the temper of voters looking forward to the 1864 presidential election, Lincoln's chances for a second term looked grim. While the Emancipation Proclamation gathered diplomatic capital abroad, it was not as popular at home as Lincoln hoped. Even though the proclamation suspending the writ of habeas corpus was meant to be a warning rather than a threat to civil liberties, in many areas of the country it became one of the most hated instruments of the war. Nothing would validate the abolition of slavery or ameliorate the denial of civil liberties faster than victories on the battlefield. Chancellorsville was over, and as June approached, Lincoln looked to the summer campaigns with fresh hope.

CHAPTER 14

"Grant is my man and I am his for the rest of the war"

The spring of 1863 marked the midpoint of the Civil War, but antiwar sentiment in the North, diplomatic uncertainty abroad, and the Chancellorsville
disaster bred speculation on how the rebellion would end. Overriding every
issue, Union armies needed decisive victories. Northerners became more
outspoken, complaining volubly against incompetence in the administration.
Democrats accused Republicans of prolonging the war to make themselves
rich. The Confederacy merely had to persevere and wear down Northern
resolve until debt and war-weariness opened the way for Southern independence.[1]

General Robert E. Lee understood a decisive defeat during the summer of 1863, especially within Southern borders, would mean the end of
the struggle, but he also believed a defensive strategy would not win the
war. Having demoralized the Army of the Potomac at Chancellorsville and
aware of Hooker's inactivity, Lee looked north. By invading Pennsylvania,
he counted on exhausting Northern patience and encouraging British and
French intervention, but he also understood the risk of endangering his own
communications.

On the threshold of summer the South controlled its interior lines, but
those lines were being forcibly compressed. The Union navy controlled the
sea and most of the rivers, compelling the South to live off the land. Federal
forces had divided Tennessee; cut deeply into Mississippi and Louisiana;
occupied portions of the Carolinas, Georgia, and Virginia; and made lodg-
ments in Texas, Arkansas, and Florida. As the Confederacy shrank, the
Union expanded, but not fast enough for Lincoln. The South could not win a
war of attrition. Cannon could not be replaced, nor could good horses, good
men, or talented generals like Stonewall Jackson, who had suffered a mortal
wound at Chancellorsville. The Union defeat dispirited the Army of the
Potomac, but on May 7 Lincoln and Halleck visited Hooker's headquarters
at Falmouth and reported the troops "none the worse for the campaign."

Despite victories, the Confederacy showed signs of collapsing. Lee shouldered the burden, knowing he must capitalize on his army's momentum
to offset Confederate losses on other battlefields. Lincoln understood Lee
must be defeated, but after Chancellorsville he could not entrust Hooker

with another battle. Fighting Joe offered to resign, claiming to be content with command of his old division, but no one wanted Hooker's job. While Lincoln studied his options, the initiative for aggressive action shifted to Lee, who in early June took it.[2]

Hooker anticipated Lee's movements and proposed an attack on the Confederate rear if the enemy weakened its forces at Fredericksburg. Lincoln deferred the matter to Old Brains, who cautioned against assaulting entrenchments. On June 5 Lincoln replied, "I would not take any risk of being entangled upon the river like an ox jumped half over a fence and liable to be torn by dogs front and rear without a fair chance to gore one way or kick the other." He said the proper course would be to move into position where the army could strike the head of Lee's offensive rather than nipping at its tail. Halleck proposed a flank attack but left the details to Hooker. Hooker hated Halleck, dismissed all his suggestions, and, like McClellan, wasted time considering different courses of action.[3]

On June 8 Hooker sent Major General Alfred Pleasonton's Cavalry Corps on a reconnaissance in force. The following morning three Union cavalry divisions and two infantry brigades crossed the Rappahannock and clashed with Jeb Stuart's cavalry at Brandy Station. In the largest cavalry battle of the war Pleasonton almost wrecked the cavalry screen Lee depended upon for his march north.

Observing the heights overlooking Fredericksburg had been weakened, Hooker submitted a plan to brush away the small rebel force on Marye's Heights and march directly on Richmond. Hooker believed the army was strong enough to capture and hold Richmond and still provide enough force to stop Lee at any threatened point north of the Potomac. The president clearly understood Hooker's fixation on capturing Richmond and believed the general wanted to ignore Lee rather than fight him. To restrain Hooker, Lincoln replied, "If left to me, I would not go south of the Rappahannock upon Lee's moving north of it. If you have Richmond invested today, you would not be able to take it in twenty days. I think Lee's army, and not Richmond, is your sure objective point. If he comes towards the Upper Potomac, follow on his flank and on his inside track, shortening your lines while he lengthens his; fight him, too, when the opportunity offers. If he stays where he is, fret him and fret him."[4]

After sending the message, Lincoln invited comments from Halleck. Having a keen eye for personality quirks, Gideon Welles noticed how Old Brains, a master of procrastination, always found some reason to disagree with the president. Welles also criticized Lincoln for taking Halleck's advice simply because the general was supposed to be a military expert. Instead, Welles observed, the "dull, stolid, inefficient, and incompetent General-in-Chief . . . sits back in his chair doing comparatively nothing" and takes none of the load off the president. Lincoln, however, used Old Brains mostly as a chief clerk than a military advisor, but the general had developed a bad habit of ignoring the president's wishes when he disagreed with them.[5]

On June 12, after Halleck lost track of Hooker's movements, Lincoln boarded a steamer for Aquia to confer with the general. Along the way he received a dispatch from Stanton stating that Hooker had moved headquarters but nobody knew where. Thinking Hooker was actually moving north on a route parallel to Lee's line of march, Lincoln returned to the White House much relieved.[6]

Lee's Second Corps, now commanded by one-legged General Richard S. Ewell, vanished into the Shenandoah Valley undetected. Longstreet's First Corps followed, but Ambrose P. Hill's Third Corps remained near Fredericksburg until Hooker moved north. During the second week of June, Lee's army stretched a hundred miles, with Stuart's cavalry east of the Blue Ridge Mountains screening the army's flank. On June 14 Ewell's force struck the Federals at Winchester and drove them back to Harpers Ferry. A brigade of rebel cavalry stormed through Martinsburg, Virginia, and galloped toward Pennsylvania. Lincoln wanted to retard the enemy's advance and telegraphed Hooker to strike Lee's flanks. Stuart's cavalry blocked the mountain gaps, thwarting attempts by Pleasonton's cavalry to scout Lee's movements. On the evening of June 14 Lincoln condemned Hooker's inability to interpret Lee's intentions. Welles attributed it to Hooker's fondness for whiskey, adding, "If he is intemperate, God help us!"[7]

Hooker's ignorance of the situation astounded Lincoln. Confederate troops were already passing through Martinsburg when Hooker asked, "Has anything further been heard from Winchester?" Annoyed the general had done nothing to impede Lee's progress, Lincoln replied, "If the head of Lee's army is at Martinsburg and the tail of it . . . between Fredericksburg and Chancellorsville, the animal must be very thin somewhere. Could you not break him?" Hooker never replied except to demand reinforcements. If defeated, he threatened to blame the administration for not supporting him. He insisted Halleck tell him what to do and said he would obey the instructions and let the responsibility for the consequences rest with his superiors.[8]

Lincoln read telegrams passing between Hooker and Halleck and decided neither man understood the military situation. To Hooker he wrote, "If you and [Halleck] would use the same frankness to one another, and to me, that I use to both of you, there should be no difficulty. I . . . must have the . . . skill of both, and yet these suspicions deprive me of both." Lincoln knew he annoyed Halleck by contacting Hooker directly. He tried to reason Hooker out of a paranoiac distrust of Halleck, but he also discontinued communicating directly with Fighting Joe, writing, "To remove all misunderstanding, I now place you in the strict military relation to Gen. Halleck. . . . I shall direct him to give you orders, and you to obey them." Lincoln had no intention of turning the war over to Old Brains, who had not originated an order involving military movements since the Second Battle of Bull Run without first obtaining the president's approval. Lincoln continued to suggest Hooker's movements to Halleck, who had become the president's military mouthpiece, responsible for writing orders in terminology understandable to the recipient.

Lee's communications formed a sweeping outer arc from Richmond to Pennsylvania. The Union line formed a shorter inner arc, putting the Army of the Potomac in good position to strike Lee's communications and force an engagement on a field of Hooker's choice. Lincoln reminded Hooker of McClellan's lost opportunity at Antietam and said, "Now, all I ask is that . . . we can get into our action the best cordial judgment of yourself and General Halleck, with my poor mite added, if indeed he and you shall think it entitled to any consideration at all." That Lincoln put his "poor mite" in a position of possibly being not worth "any consideration at all" gave indecisive generals like Halleck and Hooker the option of interpreting those words literally, though they both knew better.[9]

Hooker renounced alcohol when he took command of the Army of the Potomac, and some said a few drinks may have been what he needed at Chancellorsville. On June 23 rumors of the general's intemperance recurred during a quick visit to Washington to confer with Lincoln at the War Department. The president later returned to the White House looking "much dispirited and dejected" because Halleck and Hooker disagreed over the safety of Harpers Ferry. Whether Hooker arrived at the meeting intoxicated is unlikely, but at least one observer said the general was drunk when he left the capital, drunk the next day, and later returned to Washington on June 25 to get drunk again. Lincoln asked Hooker if the rumor was true. Fighting Joe blamed the press, replying, "You need not believe any more than you choose of what is published in the Associated Press," to which the president replied, "It did not come from the newspapers, nor did I believe it, but I wished to be entirely sure it was not a falsehood."[10]

Despite rumors of Hooker's drunkenness, Lincoln remained upbeat. During a June 26 cabinet meeting Welles said, "If Hooker has generalship in him, this is his opportunity. He can scarcely fail." Lincoln replied, "We cannot help beating them, if we have the man. How much depends in military matters on one master mind! Hooker may commit the same fault as McClellan and lose his chance. We shall soon see, but it appears to me he can't help but win." Stanton remained silent. He wanted Hooker dismissed.[11]

On June 27, perhaps with Stanton's influence, the final rupture between Hooker and Halleck occurred over the defense of Harpers Ferry. Hooker wanted the garrison merged into the Army of the Potomac; Halleck insisted the garrison be reinforced. Hooker rejected Halleck's order and asked to be relieved. Halleck replied, "As you were appointed to this command by the President, I have no power to relieve you." Stanton now had what he wanted, but with a major battle pending, he feared the consequences of changing commanders. He admitted knowing nothing of Hooker's plans or the location of the army—nor did Halleck. Stanton brought Lincoln to the War Department and handed him Hooker's resignation, asking, "What shall be done?" Lincoln's face turned ashen. He handed the telegram back to Stanton and said, "Accept his resignation."[12]

Never had the administration been in greater confusion or the Army of the Potomac at a more critical point. Neither Halleck nor Hooker could pinpoint the location of Lee's army, but everyone knew Pennsylvania had been invaded. Confederate shells landed in Harrisburg, shocked Pennsylvania farmers protested the theft of stock, and people bitterly wondered how this could happen. Governor Curtin of Pennsylvania asked for sixty thousand volunteers to protect the state. Governor Augustus W. Bradford of Maryland asked for ten thousand more. With Hooker's resignation in hand, Lincoln and Stanton could not waste time interviewing a successor. On the evening of June 27, without advice from anyone else, they consulted together and selected Major General George G. Meade. Lincoln liked Meade, a senior corps commander who had earned an unblemished reputation as a fighter ever since First Bull Run. Stanton approved because Meade came from Pennsylvania, the likely scene of the next great battle. Lincoln agreed, adding, "And [he] will fight well on his own dunghill." For Lincoln there were always political considerations. If Meade declined, there would be public pressure to restore McClellan, so Lincoln picked a general who "represented the same political opinions in the army and in the country" as Little Mac.[13]

The following day Lincoln and Stanton went through the formality of consulting with the cabinet on Hooker's replacement, although orders were already in transit to Meade. Welles said Hooker should have been dismissed immediately after Chancellorsville and expressed "relief" on learning of Meade's appointment. Chase was disturbed. He had been the general's strongest supporter, and when Hooker attempted to blame his military misfortunes on Stanton and Halleck, Chase wanted to believe him. Instead of stating his objections to Hooker's removal, Chase shared them with his political friends. Stanton angrily denounced Hooker for quitting on the eve of battle and damned him for selfishly choosing the most inopportune time to resign simply to win concessions from the president. Stanton was right. The fight had gone out of Hooker, and Lincoln had waited too long to replace him.[14]

Although Blair agreed with Meade's appointment, he traced Hooker's problem back to Halleck, grumbling that Old Brains was "good for nothing and knows nothing." Welles suggested they go together to the War Department to discuss the matter with Stanton. Blair refused, saying "he would not go to where Stanton could insult him." As a West Pointer, Blair no longer offered advice on military matters because Stanton refused to listen. Had Blair spoken with the war secretary, he might not have been insulted, but Stanton would certainly have reminded him that Halleck was Lincoln's man, not his.[15]

On the evening of June 27 Stanton issued orders transferring the command of the army to Meade and sent Major General James A. Hardie to deliver them. Hardie found Meade half-dressed and asleep in his tent at Frederick, Maryland. Meade did not want command of the army and grumbled that John Reynolds should have the job. Hardie said the orders were effective immediately, to which Meade gruffly replied, "Well, I've been tried and condemned without a hearing, so I suppose I must submit." When Meade informed his officers, Hardie described them as being "less surprised than Meade" and "were better satisfied with his selection than they might have been with some other."[16]

Forty-seven-year-old George Gordon Meade lacked the charisma of McClellan, the sociability of Burnside, and the bluster of Hooker. He stood six feet tall, and his gaunt, bug-eyed facial expression rarely changed. On horseback he wore a slouch hat that shaded his eyes but not his Roman nose. He wore glasses because of near-sightedness, always looked grim and disheveled, and threw fits of temper, most of which descended on those nearest him. Staff officers called him "the old snapping turtle," but not to his face, and they were always on the lookout for his next dyspeptic outburst.[17]

Had Hooker listened to Meade at Chancellorsville, there may never have been a battle at Gettysburg. Meade passed as an above-average tactician, but he had never been tested as a strategist. No one questioned his courage in battle. He handled troops well but, like other regular army generals, never converted from the defensive approach to warfare. Lincoln understood the nature of this chronic fallibility among Union generals but could never get much help from Old Brains. Halleck assured Meade he "would not be hampered by minute instructions" from the War Department but was free to act as he decided so long as the army remained interposed between Lee's forces and Washington. Halleck asked Meade to keep him informed of all movements, including those of the enemy, and promised full support of the administration.[18]

To reposition the army Meade first had to find Hooker. He became agitated when discovering the army had been scattered all over Maryland, and his reaction upset Hooker. General Reynolds's arrival broke the tension. He came immaculately dressed in a new uniform to congratulate Meade, who had dressed hurriedly and "looked like a wagonmaster in marching clothes." Discussions continued into the afternoon, after which Meade formally took command of the army and began concentrating his forces for a fight.[19]

Having strung his army across southern Pennsylvania from Chambersburg to York, Lee was in no better position for battle than Meade. After Lee lost contact with Stuart's cavalry, the Union army crossed into Maryland undetected. Lee issued orders for his three corps to concentrate on a line extending west from Cashtown, near Gettysburg, and Meade issued orders for his army to move north from Frederick, using roads also leading to Gettysburg.[20]

Considering what little Meade understood of the military situation, he made good decisions. By concentrating his army near the Pennsylvania line, he forced Lee to do the same. By looking to strike the Confederate rear, he would stop Lee from roaming through Pennsylvania and force a fight. Meade assumed a defensive position near Pipe Creek in northern Maryland and on June 30 advanced Reynolds's First Corps and Brigadier General John Buford's cavalry division into southern Pennsylvania.

Confederate scouts reconnoitered Gettysburg and reported the presence of Federal cavalry patrols. Lee worried Meade's army might be nearby and reconnoitered the town. Meade's force, however, with the exception of Reynolds's First Corps and Buford's cavalry, had not moved far from Pipe Creek. Reynolds reported that Gettysburg offered better defensive advantages than Pipe Creek, so Meade, because he wanted to fight defensively, put his forces in motion. The two armies, Union and Confederate, converged on Gettysburg on the morning of July 1 and for three days fought the greatest battle waged in North America.[21]

The fighting began by happenstance on July 1 without a plan. Although

Reynolds lost his life slowing the Confederates, he saved Cemetery Hill, the best defensive position on the field. Lee settled on Seminary Ridge, which ran roughly a mile from and parallel to Cemetery Hill. For two more days the Confederates thrashed against Meade's defenses, first by assaulting the Federal flanks and then on July 3 by attempting and failing to crack the Federal center. On July 4 the two armies stared at each other from across a bloodied field. The following day Lee withdrew toward the Potomac.

Early on July 4, after spending four anxious days at the telegraph office, Lincoln issued a press release announcing victory at Gettysburg. As more reports arrived, he sensed Meade might lose the fruits of his hard-fought battle by letting Lee escape across the Potomac. On July 6 he grew exasperated by Meade's inactivity and expressed his dissatisfaction to Halleck, writing, "You know I did not like the phrase in [your] Orders [to] 'Drive the invaders from our soil.' These things all appear to me to be connected with the purpose to . . . get the enemy across the river again without further collision . . . a dreadful reminiscence of McClellan. Will our Generals never get that idea out of their heads? The whole country is our soil."[22]

While pressuring Halleck to coax Meade into fighting, the president received welcome news of General Grant's operations in the West—Vicksburg had capitulated, surrendering -twenty thousand prisoners. On July 8 came more good news—General Banks had captured Port Hudson, thereby opening the Mississippi from Minnesota to the Gulf of Mexico. The president's spirits quickly improved. He prodded Halleck, writing, "Now, if General Meade can complete his work, so gloriously prosecuted thus far, by the . . . destruction of Lee's army, the rebellion will be over." Halleck forwarded Lincoln's message to Meade but neglected to add any instructions.[23]

As each day passed, Lincoln became more annoyed with Meade's inertia and daily requests for reinforcements. On July 12 Meade informed Halleck he intended "to attack the enemy to-morrow, unless something intervenes to prevent it." Lincoln read the deciphered message, paced the telegraph office wringing his hands, and groaned, "[Meade] will be ready to fight a magnificent battle when there is no enemy to fight." Lee crossed the Potomac that night, and Meade let him go. Two days later Lincoln learned the details. Thoroughly annoyed, he said, "We had them in our grasp. We had only to stretch forth our hands & they were ours. And nothing I could say or do could make the Army move." Welles used the failure as an opportunity to ask why Halleck could not have traveled to Meade's headquarters to order it done. Lincoln knew Welles disapproved of Halleck, having overheard him on past occasions referring to the general-in-chief as an "inert" bureaucrat with "little military capacity or intelligence." Lincoln said he needed Halleck because "his views and mine are widely different. It is better that I, who am not a military man, should defer to him, rather than he to me." Welles disagreed and said in his opinion anyone, including the president, could direct military movements better than Halleck.[24]

The president suffered another emotional blow on July 14, when he received a message from Simon Cameron, who had lasted as minister to Russia long enough to present his credentials, take a furlough, and return to Pennsylvania to run for the Senate. After visiting Meade's headquarters, Cameron reported a council of war had been held and only one corps commander spoke in favor of attacking Lee. "[Meade's] army is in fine spirits & eager for battle," wrote Cameron. "They will win if they get a chance."[25]

Lincoln distrusted Cameron's statement and replied, "I would give much to be relieved of the impression that Meade . . . and all . . . have striven only to get Lee over the river without another fight. Please tell me . . . the one corps commander who was for fighting." After dispatching the telegram, Lincoln turned to his son Robert and said, "If I had gone up there, I could have whipped them myself." According to John Hay, the president almost went. "Our army held the war in the hollow of their hand," Lincoln grumbled, "and they would not close it." He always believed if Lee crossed the Potomac and came north, the Confederacy would be destroyed. He wrote a blunt letter to Meade but never sent it. Instead, he had Halleck inform Meade that Lee's escape had "created great dissatisfaction in the mind of the President." Meade read the message and asked to be relieved. Halleck rephrased the statement, assuring Meade the president's comments were "not intended as a censure, but as a stimulus to an active pursuit."[26]

Cameron never answered the president, but Meade later admitted that "five out of six" corps commanders had opposed an attack but omitted the name of the general willing to fight. On July 17 General James Wadsworth, who had taken temporary command of the First Corps after Reynolds fell, came to Washington. When asked why Lee had escaped, Wadsworth blurted, "Because nobody stopped him." General Oliver O. Howard, commanding the Eleventh Corps, completed the riddle by explaining that he, with Meade, Wadsworth, and Pleasonton, were in favor of pressing the attack but Slocum, Sedgwick, Sykes, French, and Hays were against it. Unimpressed by commanding generals who deferred to councils of war, the president nevertheless seemed satisfied that Meade would fight. By then Lee had recrossed the Potomac, and knowing prodding could no longer delay the rebel escape, Lincoln adopted a softer tone. On July 21 he wrote to Howard,

"A few days having passed, I am now profoundly grateful for what was done, without criticism for what was not done. Gen. Meade has my confidence as a brave and skillful officer and a true man." He then proclaimed August 6 a day of thanksgiving.[27] Army of the Potomac soldiers summed up the escape of Lee's army best, grumbling, "Well, here goes for two years more."[28]

Lincoln yearned for a complete victory. Learning Meade had thanked his troops for driving "the invader from our soil," Lincoln gasped, "My God. Is that all?" Then when word came on July 7 from a virtually overshadowed theater that Grant had taken Vicksburg, Lincoln got his complete victory from the one man in the Union army who seemed to understand the importance of doing the job thoroughly.[29]

News of Vicksburg's surrender reached Welles through Admiral Porter, whose gunboats supported Grant during the eight-month campaign. This gave Welles a chance to get his back patted before Grant notified Stanton. Welles entered the White House, found Lincoln discussing Gettysburg with Chase, and proudly announced the capture of Vicksburg. The president grabbed the secretary, gave him a hug, and, with his face beaming with joy, said, "What can we do for the secretary of the navy for this glorious intelligence? He is always bringing us good news. I cannot, in words, tell you my joy over this result. It is great, Mr. Welles, it is great!"[30]

Lincoln said Stanton must be informed and, while walking across the lawn to the War Department with Welles, remarked, "This . . . will inspire me." Welles's announcement, however, did not inspire Stanton, who listened to the firing of guns, ringing of bells, and the cheering of people gladdened by Grant's victory. For the navy to be the first to announce good news was, by Stanton's standards, unforgivable. The War Department operated its own telegraph expressly for the purpose of being the first to receive military news. Stanton spent hours scanning telegrams constantly in search of good news to deliver to the president. Instead of joining the celebration, he informed Grant that in the future all military successes must be reported to the War Department ahead of the navy.[31]

Nobody in the administration understood the obstacles Grant faced during the Vicksburg campaign. Halleck disliked Grant, and in 1862 Stanton and Lincoln were influenced by the general-in-chief's bias. Major General John A. McClernand, an Illinois acquaintance of the president, also disliked Grant and had peppered the White House with false statements of how he had rescued the general at Shiloh. In September 1862 McClernand visited Washington with a plan to capture Vicksburg. Lincoln succumbed to the scheme because it looked militarily and politically feasible, and McClernand began recruiting. Porter sized up McClernand as a "hybrid general" whose presence on the Mississippi would insult Grant. He predicted that any troops McClernand raised would be wasted.[32]

During the autumn of 1862, while McClernand secretly recruited, Grant designed a complicated maneuver to capture Vicksburg. He planned to march into central Mississippi and wheel westward against Vicksburg while General Sherman's corps moved downriver in transports and assaulted the city from the north. Sherman's operations at Chickasaw Bluffs were intended to divert the attention of the enemy so Grant's main force could pounce on Vicksburg's rear. Halleck approved the plan, and Grant put his army in motion.

When Halleck became aware of Lincoln's meddling, he anticipated enormous confusion if McClernand took an independent command into Grant's department, especially if the two armies became entangled and worked at cross-purposes. Halleck went directly to Lincoln to prevent an avoidable military blunder. Grant also got wind of Lincoln's arrangement and attempted to shield Sherman by getting him out of Memphis. Although Halleck still believed Grant had faults, the thought of McClernand leading a military operation horrified him.

On December 17, 1862, McClernand became furious when Sherman pushed off from Memphis on Grant's order. He telegraphed Lincoln and Stanton, irritably asking if he had been superseded. Stanton spoke with Lincoln and replied that any operations in the department would be under Grant. The following day Grant reorganized the department, with McClernand commanding the Thirteenth Corps, Sherman the Fifteenth Corps, Major General Stephen A. Hurlbut the Sixteenth Corps, and Major General James B. McPherson the Seventeenth Corps. Grant now had a command fashioned after the Army of the Potomac. When the president tried to create a face-saving compromise for McClernand, Halleck disagreed and ignored the president's suggestion.[33]

On January 2, 1863, McClernand arrived at Milliken's Bend on the heels of Sherman's unsuccessful attempt to scale Chickasaw Bluffs. McClernand ranked Sherman, and with Grant in central Mississippi, his presence created instant command confusion. He knew Halleck opposed him, and after blaming Old Brains of failing to clarify questions of command, he urged Lincoln to fire the general-in-chief for gross incompetence and offered to take over the office himself. The bizarre request opened the president's eyes to McClernand's motives—the general wanted no one standing in the way of his political agenda.[34]

On January 11, learning McClernand had gone on a "wild-goose chase" on the Arkansas River; Grant went immediately to Milliken's Bend above Vicksburg to stop another useless expedition. He assumed command of all forces in the area with Lincoln's consent and received a letter from Halleck authorizing the dismissal of McClernand. Out of deference to Lincoln, Grant retained McClernand and put him to work. McClernand resented being subordinated to Grant and appealed to Lincoln. The president realized by thrusting McClernand into Grant's bailiwick, he had created the same jealousies and military grudges that nearly destroyed the morale of the Army of the Potomac under Burnside. Having decided to let Grant dispose of McClernand as he wished, Lincoln tried to save the Illinois politician's career by giving him helpful advice: "I have too many *family* controversies, so to speak, already on my hand to . . . take up another. You are now doing well—well for the country, and well for yourself—much better than you could possibly be if you engaged in open war with General Halleck. Allow me to beg that, for my sake, and for the country's sake, you give your whole attention to the better work."[35]

Instead of taking the president's advice, McClernand shifted his attack from Halleck to Grant and demanded to know his status. Grant calmly replied he had taken command of the Mississippi in compliance with orders from Halleck. McClernand protested in an insulting manner and demanded "the right to command the expedition . . . as its author and actual promoter." Grant bothered no one with McClernand's demands and tasked the general with finding ways to hurt the enemy.[36]

Instead of wasting the winter of 1863 in idleness, as William Rosecrans had done, Grant launched two efforts to assault Vicksburg from the rear by mounting amphibious operations through the flooded swamps and bayous of the Yazoo Delta. None succeeded because rebels blocked the delta's narrow passageways and turned back the transports. Grant also put the army to work digging a canal across the base of the peninsula opposite Vicksburg in an effort to get his army below Vicksburg's river fortifications, which also failed. In another scheme he tried to move the navy through flooded bayous in Louisiana in search of a route to the Red River, from which he could by roundabout means return the army back up the Mississippi and strike Vicksburg from the south. Grant later admitted having doubts any of the projects would succeed, but he wanted to keep the army active and the enemy distracted by his activities.

Admiral Porter's gunboats and spring weather opened the way. On April 16 Porter lined up seven river ironclads and three transports, ran Vicksburg's batteries at night, and delivered enough naval power below the city to enable Grant to march down the west shore of the Mississippi and on April 29 land the first Federal troops on the east shore near Bruinsburg. Grant brought enough supplies to begin the march to Jackson, Mississippi, where he expected to find General Johnston's Confederates. Unlike every other Union general—in particular McClellan, Buell, Rosecrans, and Hooker—he told his troops to live off the land. On May 14 Grant defeated Johnston's army at Jackson and two days later drove General John Pemberton's army from Champion's Hill and into Vicksburg's defenses. He put Vicksburg under siege and lost heavily, making foolish assaults against rebel entrenchments but with a tenacity that characterized his operations for the remainder of the war. Vicksburg surrendered unconditionally on the Fourth of July.

Nobody in Washington took more interest in Grant's winter campaigns than Lincoln. Grant's canal fascinated him. He wondered whether the strong current of the river would widen the canal and eventually alter the flow of the river, thereby reshaping the peninsula and landlocking Vicksburg. Grant's energy and determination astonished him. Halleck probably quoted Lincoln when he informed Grant, "The opening of the Mississippi River will be to us more advantage than the capture of forty Richmonds."[37]

Lincoln said Grant would eventually succeed on the Mississippi and rise in stature. He also told Halleck to give Grant anything he wanted. Lincoln later said, "He doesn't worry and bother me. He isn't shrieking for reinforcements all the time. He takes what troops we can safely give him . . . and does the best he can with what he has got." When in late May some Northern critics questioned Grant's siege tactics, Lincoln replied, "Whether Gen. Grant shall or shall not consummate the capture of Vicksburg, his campaign from the beginning of this month up to the twenty second day of it, is one of the most brilliant in the world."[38]

One matter did disturb the president but only mildly. During the Vicksburg campaign he received messages from McClernand warning of Grant's drunkenness. Lincoln viewed McClernand's accusations suspiciously but became concerned when Chase gave him a letter from reporter Murat Halstead containing more rumors. Lincoln had never met Grant, who was too far away for a personal visit. When Stanton suggested sending an observer to make daily reports on Grant's sobriety, Lincoln agreed. So in January 1863 Stanton dispatched Charles A. Dana, an assistant secretary of war and formerly an editor with the *New York Tribune,* to Grant's headquarters as a friendly spy.[39]

Dana arrived in Grant's department with the ostensible task of investigating unsettled claims in the quartermaster department, but his main assignment was to keep Stanton informed. Adjutant General Lorenzo Thomas, who carried orders to remove Grant if chronically drunk, soon joined Dana. Thomas approved of Grant's handling of the army and may have saved his job. Dana not only defended Grant but helped in other ways. McClernand continued to cause trouble, and Dana informed Stanton of the general's insubordination and incompetence and recommended his removal. Stanton replied, "General Grant has full and absolute authority . . . to remove any person who . . . interferes with or delays his operations." Dana, who had become a great admirer of Grant, conveyed Stanton's comments to the general. Grant waited for a clear case of insubordination and on June 18 relieved McClernand and ordered him to Washington. By then Grant had developed a fairly accurate impression of why Dana was there, and instead of sending daily reports of his movements to Halleck, he let Dana do it.[40]

Lincoln watched Grant's tactics with interest because they closely coincided with his own views. At one point, however, he believed Grant made a great mistake by not joining forces with General Banks in Louisiana and, after failing to do so, separated his army from its base of supplies and went slashing cross-country in expectation of living off the land. Halleck, in reaction to Lincoln's concerns, asked Grant why he had not waited for Banks. Grant merely replied, "I could not lose the time." Lincoln was unaccustomed to hearing such comments from his generals. When the tactic worked, Lincoln's esteem for Grant soared.[41]

During the spring when Grant's alleged drunkenness came under scrutiny in Washington, and before Stanton sent Dana to the general's headquarters as a spy, Lincoln resisted pressure from a number of busybodies lobbying to have Grant relieved. "I rather like the man," Lincoln replied. "I think I will try him a little longer," adding that if Grant captured Vicksburg, then "Grant is my man and I am his for the rest of the war."[42] The president now had his man, but during the summer of 1863 he could not quite decide what to do with him.

CHAPTER 15

"Blood can not restore blood"

In mid-July 1863, following dual victories at Gettysburg and Vicksburg, the battle suddenly shifted to the home front because the Thirty-seventh Congress passed the first national conscription act. The legislation empowered the president to call by draft all able-bodied male citizens between the ages of twenty and forty-five, including persons of foreign birth who had declared their intention to become citizens. The act provided for a force under arms of one million men. States again received quotas, this time by congressional district. Able-bodied men could volunteer, but conscription covered quota shortfalls. The legislation took responsibility away from the states and transferred it to district provost marshals, who divided districts into subdistricts and appointed enrolling officers to induct both volunteers and draftees. The act listed exemptions, allowed substitutes, and provided rules of enforcement. Brigadier General James B. Fry, assistant adjutant general and a man of exceptional talent, became provost marshal general assigned to organize the draft and begin enrollment. In May 1863 the board drafted the first inductees. Fry reported that "some of the officers were maltreated, and one or two assassinated," so in mid-July Secretary of War Stanton authorized military patrols to protect enrolling officers, arrest troublemakers, and preserve order.[1]

Without conscription manpower could not have been replaced. After two years of fighting, losses cut deeply into the ranks. Regiments going to war fully manned had been reduced by battle and disease. Soldiers were tired of army life, and thousands were absent without leave. Lincoln's offer of amnesty for those who returned to their units brought modest response. Out of desperation Lincoln turned to the one untapped source of manpower he had vowed never to use, African Americans. Gideon Welles admitted the presence of "an unconquerable prejudice on the part of many whites against black soldiers." Some generals approved the use of blacks, but General McClellan firmly opposed it.[2]

In 1862 New York failed to fill its quota, and when Horatio Seymour became governor in 1863, the state owed the army twenty-eight thousand volunteers, mostly from New York City. On taking office, Seymour pledged "to maintain and defend the sovereignty and jurisdiction" of his state. Before the conscription act passed in March, Seymour assured the president, "For the preservation of this Union I am ready to make any sacrifice of interest, passion, or prejudice." Lincoln needed the governor's help. What Seymour meant by his pledge can be judged by his acts, not his promises.[3]

On July 11 Irish immigrants and other opposition groups protested when officials publicly drew the names of the first draftees. Two days later rallies spurted into full-scale insurrection. Seymour let the situation get out of control, and for three days working-class mobs roamed the streets looting, burning, and skirmishing with police. Rioters lynched several blacks, burned the Colored Orphan Asylum, and took control of a small section of the city.[4]

When on July 13 news of the New York draft riots reached the White House, the president was absorbed with two problems, one domestic and one military. Mary had suffered a carriage accident meant for the president. Someone unscrewed the bolts holding the driver's seat, and when it came loose with the driver in it, the horses ran off, Mary fell out of the carriage, and her head struck a rock. A few days later the injury became infected, and for three weeks she required constant nursing. Mary recovered but suffered severe headaches for the rest of her life. The accident occurred during a time when the president was fully occupied prodding George Meade to collect the fruits of Gettysburg and destroy Lee's army. Welles went to the morning cabinet meeting but found the chief gloomy and distracted.[5]

Seymour let riots spread through the city, hoping it would force a suspension of the draft. He never agreed with the original quota system and liked conscription even less. "It is believed," he said, "by at least one-half of the people of the United States that the conscription act is in itself a violation of . . . constitutional law." After Seymour refused to act, New York mayor George Opdyke telegraphed Washington for troops. Lincoln answered Opdyke's call by authorizing Stanton to detach five New York regiments from Meade's army. Stanton provided a special train to transport the troops and put General John A. Dix in charge of restoring peace to the city. Dix received no help from Seymour, who came to the city and addressed the rioters affectionately as his "friends," intimating the draft justified the riot. He issued two proclamations halfheartedly condemning the disturbance and urging rioters to return peacefully to their homes. Newspapers quoted hundreds killed after the army arrived, but only seventy-four bodies were ever found. Horace Greeley investigated demonstrations in other cities and noted, while some occurred, those that did were incited by foreigners. Rumors circulated that the second draft call, scheduled for August 19, would be postponed and that Lincoln had been coerced into withdrawing the Emancipation Proclamation, but on that date the draft wheels spun again, and no disturbances occurred.[6]

For several weeks Seymour continued to pester the president over conscription's constitutionality. He argued against what he called discriminatorily high draft quotas merely because New York happened to be the most populous state. Lincoln sent the governor the math behind the calculations and said he would make concessions if Seymour proved that conscription discriminated against New York, but he would not hold up the draft while the governor attempted to obtain a Supreme Court ruling. The "enemy," Lincoln replied, "drives every able-bodied man he can reach, into his ranks, very much as a butcher drives bullocks into a slaughter-pen. . . . It produces an army with a rapidity not to be matched on our side [and time must not be wasted] to re-experiment" with a volunteer system that failed. The president's patient and levelheaded rejoinders to Seymour's arguments produced dividends. The governor remained deeply committed to the Union, supported the war effort, and in 1863 and 1864 met the state's quotas.[7]

Lincoln avoided conscription problems, intervening only when problems occurred. Stanton's department established state quotas and then had to pacify governors who protested the activities of overzealous and often corrupt provost marshals. Specific provisions in the act exempted a man from being drafted if he provided a substitute or paid a three-hundred-dollar commutation fee. Substitutes disappeared after collecting bonuses, and commutation fees disappeared into the pockets of provost marshals. Stanton did not have the president's juggling skills or much patience. As historians Benjamin Thomas and Harold Hyman observed, "Sometimes [Stanton] was tactful; sometimes his temper flared. It was a duty scarcely calculated to increase his popularity." Without conscription and all its fallacies, recruitment would have decreased, slowing the pace of the war as enlistments expired.[8]

During early discussions with the cabinet on emancipation, efforts to increase volunteer enrollment were considered. Chase favored forming an army of black troops, arguing it would nurture the tenets of freedom for all and promote the concept of equality among the races. By doing this in August 1862, Chase hoped to postpone conscription. Seward opposed Chase, and although Lincoln was disinclined to do anything until after the official publication of the proclamation, he allowed "that commanders should, at their discretion, arm, purely for defensive purposes, slaves coming within their lines."[9]

The idea was neither new nor original. In April 1862 General David Hunter had asked Stanton for 50,000 muskets to arm blacks and requested "50,000 pairs of scarlet pantaloons. This is all the clothing I shall require for these people." He believed brilliant-colored pants would serve as an irresistible attraction to former slaves. The requisition drew roars of laughter in the House of Representatives, and blacks shunned the recruiting effort. Hunter eventually formed one company, which disbanded three months later.[10]

In August Stanton authorized Brigadier General Rufus Saxton, commanding at Beaufort, South Carolina, to arm, equip, and drill five thousand former slaves to guard local plantations. Saxton encountered no resistance because whites objected to the work. The Confiscation Act of July 17, 1862, empowered Lincoln "to employ as many persons of African descent as he may deem necessary and proper for the suppression of this rebellion," thus creating opportunities for the army to use former slaves. Congress added a second clause defining the employment of blacks as laborers but gave the president latitude to put them in uniform. Although Stanton, following Lincoln's rule, authorized commanders to arm slaves for "defensive purposes," Colonel Thomas Wentworth Higginson raised the First South Carolina Volunteers. After the rolls reached five hundred, he put former slaves through six weeks of combat training. Having drilled the men to fight, he ignored the president's mandate and led the regiment's first raid on the mainland.[11]

While commanding in New Orleans, General Butler took advantage of the Confiscation Act because he had thousands of blacks milling about army camps with nothing to do and hundreds more arriving each week. Brigadier General John W. Phelps, serving under Butler, declared, "Fifty regiments might be raised among them at once." Stanton hesitated, but Phelps plunged ahead and requisitioned arms, clothing, and camp equipment for three regiments. When Butler discovered Phelps had formed five black companies without approval, he said, "I cannot sanction this course of action," but did nothing to stop it. When Phelps resigned, Butler finished the work. Despite the president's conservative policy of recruiting slaves for labor only, Butler formed one heavy artillery regiment and three black infantry regiments. He called them the Louisiana Native Guards and deployed them in combat operations. Butler succeeded because his officers backed the effort and took a leading role in organizing the regiments.[12]

Meanwhile, Brigadier General James H. Lane, commanding in Kansas, telegraphed Stanton, "I am receiving negroes under the late act of Congress. Is there any objection? [Will] soon have an army." Stanton never responded, so in January 1863 Lane's First Kansas Colored Regiment joined the Jayhawkers. Having organized one regiment, Lane ignored cautions from Stanton's office and continued recruiting.[13]

Also in January, Vice President Hamlin appeared at the White House with a group of officers volunteering to raise more African-American units. Lincoln drolly remarked, "I suppose the time has come." In some districts emancipation had retarded recruitment of whites who objected to fighting for abolition, so Lincoln asked General Dix if forts could be garrisoned by colored troops, thereby freeing whites for service in the field. Dix halfheartedly replied that blacks could be used in forts, providing half of the garrison remained white. His remarks nonetheless encouraged the president. Lincoln abandoned his earlier scheme to colonize blacks outside the United States and decided to find ways of usefully employing them as citizens and soldiers.[14]

The president accelerated recruiting efforts in Louisiana after General Banks took command of the department. On March 29, 1963, he sent Brigadier General Daniel Ullmann to New Orleans to raise a full brigade of four regiments. Banks agreed with the proposition and quadrupled the effort. By midsummer he reported twenty-one African-American regiments formed, plus several companies of artillery and cavalry. Banks folded the units, including Butler's Native Guards, into the Corps d'Afrique. The First and Third regiments participated in the capture of Port Hudson but suffered horribly in assaults against their former masters.[15]

Recruiting former slaves from Union-controlled areas of the South bothered no one, but Northern governors resisted the effort. Only Governor Andrew of Massachusetts, whose antislavery zeal motivated him to do something, asked and received permission from the War Department to raise at least one black regiment. Stanton balked when the governor began recruiting blacks from other states. Andrew circumvented Stanton by forming a private recruiting organization to continue the work. Washington's *National Intelligencer* joked that Andrew's agents "will shortly turn up in Egypt, competing with Napoleon for the next cargo of Nubians."[16]

Andrew personally selected officers who believed blacks would make good soldiers to command the Fifty-fourth Massachusetts Volunteer Infantry Regiment. He involved Frederick Douglass, the North's outspoken black leader on racial equality, to assist in raising the regiment. Douglass lived in Rochester, New York, and after two of his sons joined the Fifty-fourth Massachusetts, enough blacks volunteered to form the Fifty-fifth Massachusetts. On May 28 the Fifty-fourth embarked for South Carolina, and on June 21 the Fifty-fifth embarked for North Carolina.[17]

When no Northern states followed Massachusetts's lead, Lincoln decided that black enlistments, like managing the draft, had to be under Federal control. On October 13, 1863, Stanton established recruiting stations for blacks in Delaware, Maryland, Missouri, and Tennessee. The order provided that freemen, slaves with written consent of their owners, and slaves belonging to rebels could be enlisted. If a sufficient number of troops could not be raised in thirty days, slaves could be enlisted without their owner's consent. When Northern states began recruiting slaves from the occupied South, Stanton feared blacks would fill state enlistment quotas and deprive the army of whites. Grant expressed the same concern until Lincoln suggested raising 100,000 blacks on the Mississippi "to relieve white troops for service elsewhere." To Grant the restricted and supervised use of blacks as occupiers rather than frontline fighters made sense.[18]

Nothing justified the employment of blacks in the army faster than their own acts of heroism. On October 28, 1862, at Island Mounds, Missouri, General Lane's First Kansas (later the Seventy-ninth U.S. Colored Infantry) became the first black regiment to serve in combat. On May 27, 1863, Butler's Louisiana Guards became the first colored regiments to engage in a major battle. On June 7 a garrison of blacks at Milliken's Bend, Louisiana, successfully defended the post in hand-to-hand fighting against former masters intent on murdering them.

The most reckless use of black troops occurred in the Department of the South when on July 6 Rear Admiral John A. Dahlgren arrived off Charleston with invasion on his mind. While Major General Quincy A. Gillmore assaulted Morris Island, Dahlgren intended to enter Charleston Harbor. Success depended on the swift capture of Fort Wagner, which occupied the narrowest part of Morris Island and protected the harbor with heavy guns.

At dawn on July 11 Brigadier General George C. Strong's Seventh Connecticut Regiment Infantry moved on Fort Wagner but suffered heavy casualties. Seven days later the Fifty-fourth Massachusetts, commanded by Colonel Robert G. Shaw, spearheaded the attack. As Shaw's African Americans advanced from the first parallel, guns in Forts Gregg and Sumter joined those of Wagner and pummeled the troops as they pressed forward. Those who survived the bombardment waited until dark and attacked the fort again. Colonel Shaw fell at the head of the regiment. Thinking a full brigade was following in support, the remnants of the Fifty-fourth Massachusetts entered the fort, came under murderous fire, and at midnight, after reinforcements failed to arrive, abandoned a hopeless contest. Of the ten regiments participating in the assault, the Fifty-fourth Massachusetts lost 272 men, the most of all.[19]

Lincoln no longer doubted the ability of African-American soldiers. Three days after the Fifty-fourth Massachusetts led the charge at Fort Wagner, he wrote Stanton, "I desire that a renewed and vigorous effort be made to raise colored forces . . . please consult the General-in-Chief, and if . . . any acceleration of the matter can be effected, let it be done."[20]

No one in the administration went through a more complete reversal of attitude toward blacks serving in the armed forces than Lincoln. Although constantly pressed by Chase, Stanton, Welles, and radicals in Congress, Lincoln waited for the promulgation of the Emancipation Proclamation. Stanton pushed the president toward making the decision by conspiring with Congress to pass the confiscation acts, which made emancipated slaves eligible for enlistment. In his December 1863 annual message to Congress, Lincoln reported 50,000 late slaves under arms. After the government took recruiting out of the hands of the states, 123,156 blacks joined the armed services. According to the provost marshal's report, 186,017 African Americans served in the Civil War. Lincoln's secretaries explained the evolution best, writing, "Doubt about employing Negroes as soldiers was happily removed almost imperceptibly by the actual experiment."[21]

African Americans quickly learned that survival meant fighting and never giving up. Southerners wantonly killed blacks in uniform, even if they surrendered, and nothing stained that practice more than the 1864 massacre at Fort Pillow, Tennessee. The retaliatory Confederate response disturbed Lincoln. "Once begun," he told Frederick Douglass, "I do not know where such a measure would stop." Lincoln said he would like to get hold of the people "guilty of killing the colored persons in cold blood . . . but he could not kill the innocent for the guilty."[22]

The issue transcended the question of color and touched directly upon prisoners of war. On July 30, 1863, Lincoln issued a direct order through the War Department defining the government's position on protecting its citizens, "whatever class, color, or condition." He stipulated, "For every soldier of the United States killed in violation of the laws of war a rebel soldier shall be executed; and for every one enslaved by the enemy, or sold into slavery, a rebel soldier will be placed at hard labor . . . and continued at such labor until the other shall be released and receive the treatment due a prisoner of war." The order received praise from Northerners enraged by Southern acts of inhumanity. Lincoln later softened his tone and rejected retaliation as a means to counteract atrocities. He wrote Stanton that "blood can not restore blood, and government should not act for revenge." The enlistment of blacks, coupled with Jefferson Davis's proclamation and followed by Lincoln's response, intensified a problem that had remained unresolved since the beginning of the war—the exchange of prisoners.[23]

Political complications already existed regarding prisoner exchange. Lincoln avoided any agreement with the South, fearing it might be interpreted as recognition. There were also reasons not to return rebel prisoners. Some wanted freedom from Southern oppression and, if released, preferred to live in the North. Nor did Stanton want to ease the South's shortage of manpower by returning prisoners, but inhumane conditions in Southern prisons brought a barrage of demands for the administration to alleviate the plight of captured Northerners. On July 12, 1862, at Lincoln's behest, Stanton authorized General Dix to open negotiations for prisoner exchange but to avoid acts of recognition. The agreement worked well until African-American units appeared on the battlefield.[24]

At Vicksburg, Grant approached the problem differently and paroled twenty thousand Confederates, including General John Pemberton. Some Northerners wanted Grant censured for not forwarding the rebels to Northern prisons, but the general's parole agreement hastened capitulation. Those who complained did not know half the garrison was sick or wounded, the other half was starving, and the North had no facilities for incarcerating so great an infusion of prisoners. Grant later reversed his position on paroles because Jefferson Davis dishonored the rules and unlawfully released parolees from their pledges. A few months later, after Grant arrived in Tennessee, he found the very same men paroled at Vicksburg occupying the heights at Chattanooga.[25]

Parolees were supposed to be governed by mutually understood terms between combatants. Paroled soldiers still belonged to their army. They were to stay in camp, be subject to military discipline, and not be employed in any fighting capacity until the elaborate machinery of formal exchange released them to active status. Soldiers paroled at Vicksburg were legally no different than prisoners of war confined to Federal compounds. When Grant paroled twenty thousand rebels at Vicksburg, he gambled the South would honor the pledge written on the parolee's certificate. Jefferson Davis, fighting for self-preservation, could not waste time with legalities.[26]

Prisoner exchanges continued off and on, and once after being suspended, a boat from Richmond's Belle Island prison pulled into Annapolis under a flag of truce with 32 Union officers and 363 enlisted men, all wounded, hopelessly ill, emaciated from starvation, or mentally deranged. Stanton ordered photos taken of the worst cases and sent them to Congress as examples of Confederate inhumanity. "There appears to have been a deliberate system of savage and barbarous treatment and starvation," he said, predicting none of the prisoners "will ever again be in condition to render any service or even enjoy life." In retaliation Stanton ordered rations at Federal prisons reduced by 20 percent, which was adequate to maintain health, but many prison keepers skimmed supplies, causing hunger and disease.[27]

Confederate General Nathan Bedford Forrest's Fort Pillow massacre triggered another break in exchanges. Lincoln referred the atrocities to the cabinet, writing, "It is now quite certain that a large number of our colored soldiers, with their white officers, were . . . massacred after they had been surrendered," and asked for opinions regarding what action to take. The cabinet's comments varied, but every member agreed not to take retaliatory steps until the Confederate government avowed or disavowed the massacre. Chase, Seward, Stanton, and Welles thought an equal number of rebel prisoners should be set apart for execution if the Confederate government admitted the massacre. Bates, Blair, and Usher advised against retaliation but thought Forrest and those directly involved should be executed. Perhaps Lincoln remembered the words in his own annual message, delivered to Congress on December 3, 1861, when he said, "In developing the policy to be adopted for suppressing the insurrection, I have been anxious and careful that the inevitable conflict . . . shall not degenerate into a violent and remorseless revolutionary struggle."[28]

When parolees were found bearing arms after being captured a second time, Stanton accused the South of bad faith and discontinued paroles. The edict forced both sides to expand prison camps, provide more guards, and feed and clothe more prisoners. Northern camps became filthy and overcrowded, and Southern camps turned into nightmarish hellholes where even the strong withered away and died of starvation. When Stanton ordered Federal compounds be reduced to conditions in Southern camps, General Hitchcock balked. Stanton rescinded the order and forwarded twenty-four thousand rations to Richmond's Libby Prison for the relief of imprisoned Federals. When rumors spread accusing the rebels of devouring the provisions, Stanton became furious, and the South discontinued the arrangement. Once again retaliation led to counter-retaliation, exchanges stopped, and prisoners continued to suffer. Grant supported Stanton's practices on the premise that returning prisoners would merely extend the war and force Federal armies "to fight on until the whole South is exterminated. If we hold those caught," said Grant, "they amount to no more than dead men."[29]

Troubled over prisoner camps, Lincoln said "he wished he could do something about it." British humanitarians, hearing rumors of Federals starving in Confederate prisons, organized bazaars to raise money for food and clothing. After news of Stanton's retaliation policy, they asked permission to send seventy-five thousand dollars to keep rebel prisoners from starvation. "Almighty God! No!" shouted Stanton. Lincoln became involved, and Seward promptly informed London that rebels were well fed and British agents would not be permitted in Federal prisons. James G. Bennett of the *New York Herald* blamed the problem on "Lincoln's vacillations."[30]

The president seldom interceded in prisoner exchange and left policy making to Stanton. On October 4, 1864, after hearing disturbing news about naval officers being in irons for fifteen months, he approached Secretary Welles, who confirmed the rumor. The Union and Confederate navies had agreed to exchanges, but Stanton objected because of the War Department's policy. After learning of the impasse, Lincoln said he had been troubled through the night and would bring Seward and Stanton to the White House for consultation. According to Welles, "Stanton was ill-mannered . . . and a little offensive" when Lincoln suggested one policy for the navy and another for the army. Stanton argued that "the Rebels would not recognize negroes." Welles said, "No question [of] color had ever come up . . . in naval exchange." Because blacks in naval service were not a distinct organization, Welles argued it was his duty "to see that naval men were not entirely neglected." When Stanton refused to relent, Lincoln said, "The Navy arrangement must go forward, and the navy have its men."[31]

The debate over the proper management of prisoner exchange continued to be investigated long after the war, during which the Federal army took 459,664 captives, the Confederates 187,288. More than 52,000 men died in prison camps. The Federal government exchanged or paroled more than 350,000 Confederates and received in exchange 154,000 Federals. About 72,000 Confederates took the oath of allegiance to the Union and were released. The huge losses in prison camps can be traced in part to the recruitment of African Americans. There were other reasons, but condemning blacks to death and subjecting Union officers to execution for commanding black troops created a cycle of retaliation costing thousands of American lives.[32]

In early 1862, shortly after Stanton became secretary of war, Lincoln attempted to minimize another form of imprisonment by defining loyalty versus disloyalty, treasonable acts versus untreasonable acts, and insurrection by citizens living in the North. He ordered all political and state prisoners held in military custody be released upon "subscribing to a parole engaging them to render no aid or comfort to the enemy." Stanton's provost marshals retained responsibility for making arrests, but Lincoln appointed Judge Edwards Pierrepont of New York to examine the cases and determine whether, with the public safety in mind, the prisoners should be discharged, remain in military custody, or be remitted for trial.[33]

Stanton never quite found the formula for balancing national security with civil rights. He enjoyed the power of his office and used it in ways ordinarily barred to the executive branch. While Lincoln looked at the political environment and asked what the country might say, Stanton saw imminent peril everywhere and reacted instead to what he thought the enemy might do. After Lincoln suspended the writ of habeas corpus, Stanton went to Congress for protection. On December 8, 1862, Pennsylvania congressman Thaddeus Stevens introduced a bill indemnifying the administration "for all arrests and imprisonments" and gave Lincoln the power to suspend the writ at his discretion at any time during the rebellion. The Senate passed the bill on March 3, 1863, during the closing minutes of the session. The new law provided that no officer could be compelled, in response to a writ of habeas corpus, to relinquish a detainee. Because arresting officers received protection under the authority of the president, Stanton assumed an equal measure of power in prosecuting his duties as the president's designated protector of national security.[34]

The tentacles of Stanton's dragnet stretched across the North and deep into Union-occupied districts in the South. In addition to army officers he used militia, police, and vigilantes to root out the disloyal. Any loyal citizen who happened to be in dispute with one of Stanton's agents could land in prison and languish there without a civil trial. Such excesses were few, but Stanton received blame for all of them. Most arrests were legitimate, and those tried before military tribunals were usually found guilty. Stanton tried to move the court process along quickly so anyone falsely arrested could obtain their freedom quickly. Most prisoners were freed immediately by swearing allegiance and promising not to consort with the Confederacy or sue for damages. If, however, strong evidence of disloyalty existed, Stanton applied harsh penalties, and he was especially ruthless if a prisoner lied to obtain his freedom and was caught a second time.

Lincoln decided early in the war not to meddle with freedom of the press, and Stanton rarely did. The War Department controlled information sent by telegraph, but postal letters went uncensored. Reporters traveled back and forth between army camps, often picking up and printing military secrets. War correspondents came under military jurisdiction, and Stanton treated journalistic irresponsibility more harshly than one might expect under the First Amendment, but his job was to win battles and not lose them because of reckless reporting. In rare cases a reporter could face death for treason, but offenders were seldom prosecuted. Lincoln kept reign on Stanton. Although provost marshals generally made the arrests without intervention on the part of the president or the secretary, Lincoln wanted no one executed. By mid-1864 arrests subsided, except in extreme cases when guilt was certain.[35]

After Gettysburg and Vicksburg the Union armies took a breather, but Grant disliked idleness. While the administration muddled with issues emanating from confiscation acts, conscription, prisoners of war, recruitment of African Americans, and martial law, Grant looked for employment against other strategic targets. For this he would have to wait.

CHAPTER 16

"This nation, under God, shall have a new birth of freedom"

Ulysses S. Grant proposed marching through Mississippi, destroying General Johnston's thirty thousand–man army, swinging into Alabama, capturing Mobile, and using the port as a base for operations against the Deep South. Lincoln approved Grant's energy but vetoed the plan because of a troubling diplomatic situation. The safety of the Southwest came suddenly into focus on June 10, 1863, when French forces entered Mexico City. President Benito Juárez fled north and moved his capital to San Luis Potosí. General Porfirio Díaz fled south to Oaxaca and surrounded himself with the Mexican army. Louis Napoleon III called the French occupation temporary, but Lincoln did not believe him. Grant understood the political situation with France and fully endorsed a campaign into Texas. His stance surprised Lincoln, who had grown accustomed to wrangling with generals over everything.[1]

Napoleon occupied Mexico after England and Spain settled financial claims with the Juárez government and withdrew their forces. Although France had been there for the same purpose, Napoleon kept forces in Mexico because the financially weakened country was ripe for conquest. Jefferson Davis welcomed the takeover, believing Napoleon would aid the South. Lincoln took a broader view, expecting France to take advantage of Confederate weakness and enter Texas.

Seward believed France intended to interfere with the American rebellion without appearing to do so. Napoleon once hatched a plan for a small power like Belgium to pick a quarrel with the United States so France and England could take the European side of the argument and intervene. After that scheme failed, he considered setting up an empire in Mexico to menace the United States. Union victories at Gettysburg and Vicksburg thwarted the plan, but he nevertheless dispatched envoys to Washington to advise Seward that France intended to establish a puppet government in Mexico and offer an imperial crown to Archduke Ferdinand Maximilian, brother of Franz Josef of Austria. Maximilian accepted with reluctance but refused to move until Mexican resistance ceased.

Aware of Welles's earlier efforts to interest Lincoln in occupying Brownsville, Seward suggested meeting with the president. Welles observed that Seward now believed Napoleon intended to "get Texas." Lincoln sent a message to Stanton, asking, "Can we not renew the effort to organize a force to go to Western Texas?"[2]

Lincoln thought the best strategy would be to retain Grant in Mississippi and send Nathaniel Banks's army in Louisiana to occupy the line of the Rio Grande. To reinforce Banks, he transferred ten thousand troops from Grant's army. Lincoln disliked idling Grant, but he believed Texas took precedence over Mobile. The West had to be protected from foreign intervention, and with many months of good fighting weather ahead, Lincoln believed generals Rosecrans and Burnside had ample time to occupy the rest of Tennessee while Grant contained Johnston in Mississippi.[3]

Blair Sr., however, forwarded a letter to Lincoln from William Alexander, a pro-Union Texan and New York lawyer, who described Banks as an "incapable as well as incurable" officer who "has not the capacity to run an omnibus on Broadway." Alexander suggested Frank Blair command the Texas expedition, which explains why Blair Sr. forwarded the letter to the president. Lincoln ignored the suggestion and on August 5 asked Banks to accelerate the Texas campaign.[4]

Banks wanted to capture Sabine Pass as a steppingstone to the mouth of the Rio Grande, but when that failed, he decided to go directly to Brownsville and work backwards. In early November and aided by the navy, Banks landed McClernand's Eighteenth Corps at Brownsville but failed to capture Galveston. Lincoln expected Banks to ascend the Rio Grande, but the general never tried. Halleck snubbed Banks's demand for more troops and suggested Texas be invaded by way of the Red River. Banks returned to New Orleans to plan the Red River campaign.[5]

Napoleon's designs on Mexico in 1863 malfunctioned when Maximilian and his ambitious wife, Carlotta, delayed their arrival until May 1864, so the Lincoln administration continued to recognize Benito Juárez as the legally elected president. What Banks failed to do militarily Seward succeeded in doing with diplomacy by maneuvering France into disavowing any interest in permanently occupying Mexico. In a dispatch to William Dayton, U.S. minister at Paris, Seward stressed Mexico's preference for a republican government free from European influence. He further said the United States intended to assist the Mexican people in controlling their own affairs. The Confederacy conveniently forgot the Monroe Doctrine, recognized Maximilian as emperor of Mexico, and tried to form an alliance with France. Napoleon soon realized his Mexican venture had failed. Maximilian wanted recognition from the Union, not the South, but he did not get it. In

May 1866 Napoleon deserted Maximilian and withdrew French troops from Mexico. In June 1867 Juárez overthrew and executed Maximilian.[6]

During the summer of 1863, as Banks prepared his Brownsville expedition, Grant remained on the sidelines in Mississippi. As each day passed, Lincoln's restlessness mounted as he waited for George Meade to launch an offensive in Virginia and for William Rosecrans to finish the campaign in Tennessee. When Meade threatened to resign on July 14, Stanton colluded with Old Brains to stop wasting Grant's talents in idleness but have him appointed, instead, commander of the Army of the Potomac. Before proposing the idea to Lincoln, Stanton used intermediaries to broach the matter with Grant. Without explaining why, Grant asked Assistant Secretary Charles A. Dana to use his influence with Stanton to kill the proposal. By then Meade had withdrawn his resignation. A few days later Grant expressed his appreciation to Dana, adding, "Whilst I would disobey no order I should beg very hard to be excused before accepting that command." Grant admitted knowing nothing about the capabilities of Meade's generals, but Meade did.[7]

Lincoln would not have brought Grant east with so much unfinished business in the West. After driving Braxton Bragg's army into Chattanooga, Rosecrans fortified his position and stalled. After Vicksburg surrendered, he lost his excuse for delaying offensive operations. He promised to attack Bragg without saying when. Toward the end of July Lincoln began to wonder whether Rosecrans intended to rest on his fading laurels for the remainder of the summer. Stanton wanted the general dismissed, so Halleck advised Rosecrans, "I have deemed it absolutely necessary, not only for the country but also for your own reputation, that your army shall remain no longer inactive." When Rosecrans failed to reply, Halleck tried again, writing, "You [must] drive Bragg from East Tennessee before he can be re-enforced by Johnston." Rosecrans promised to move promptly, but he objected volubly to the "tone" of messages coming from Washington.[8]

As the first days of August passed without Rosecrans straying from his fortifications, Lincoln asked Halleck for an explanation. Old Brains had none, so he ordered Rosecrans to cross the Tennessee River and capture Chattanooga. Rosecrans replied he was ready to move, but if he had no discretion in directing operations, he wanted to be relieved. Halleck blew off steam and ordered Rosecrans to refrain from burdening the department with such "mere details" and to "carry out the wishes of the Government." Two days later Rosecrans learned that Stanton wanted him removed. He asked for clarification, and Halleck said the secretary felt no personal animosity, although, he explained, "many of your dispatches have been exceedingly annoying" and "conveyed the impression that you were not disposed to carry out the wishes of the Department, at least in the manner and the time desired."[9]

Rosecrans needed coddling and asked Lincoln whether the administration was dissatisfied with his performance and added a litany of reasons for being idle. Part of the letter made no sense, including the general's excuse for doing nothing until Grant captured Vicksburg. Lincoln replied with a letter carefully crafted to calm the general's disturbed state of mind and boost his confidence. Although the president reminded Rosecrans that he should have attacked Bragg during Grant's siege of Vicksburg and mildly rebuked him for stalling, he told the general to forget bygones and capture Chattanooga before the fall rains began. After performing psychological therapy to motivate a clearly inert general, Lincoln closed with a word of caution, "I rather think by great exertion, you can get to East Tennessee. But a very important question is: Can you stay there? I make no order in the case—[leaving that] to General Halleck and yourself."[10]

Instead of accepting the president's good advice, Rosecrans continued to debate the three-month-old Vicksburg question. He desperately tried to defend himself against the president's forgiving criticism. Lincoln refused to get into an argument with Rosecrans over military matters and told him so. He once again expressed his thanks for Rosecrans's past accomplishments, but he privately agonized over the general's lack of focus at a time for action and probably wondered what could be expected from the general in the future.[11]

On August 31, 1863, Rosecrans's Army of the Cumberland consisted of 95,905 officers and enlisted men, Bragg's Army of Tennessee 53,612. To reach Chattanooga Rosecrans had to march over the Cumberland Mountains and shuttle troops across the Tennessee River. When Rosecrans began moving on the morning of August 16, he was still debating with Lincoln and Halleck over trivial differences in military strategy. On September 4, without fighting a major battle, the Army of the Cumberland crossed the river and five days later marched into Chattanooga. To avoid being trapped in the city, Bragg withdrew to Georgia. Meanwhile, Burnside's corps entered East Tennessee and began liberating the pro-Union mountain area Lincoln had wanted secured since the outbreak of war.[12]

The capture of Chattanooga had been too easy. "Chattanooga is ours without a struggle," Rosecrans crowed, "and East Tennessee is free!" Believing Bragg's army had been beaten and demoralized, Rosecrans sought complete victory and plunged into Georgia. Bragg's army, however, had never been defeated on the battlefield and was as strong as ever. Bragg merely retired to a favorable defensive position and assimilated two Virginia divisions from General Longstreet's corps. Bragg turned on Rosecrans, who soon realized he had led his army into a mincing machine. With no time to make tactical adjustments, Rosecrans drew his three corps together to meet the Confederate attack.

On September 19, 1963, the first day of the Battle of Chickamauga, Rosecrans checked Bragg's assault. A day later Confederates breached the Union line because of tactical errors made by Rosecrans. Rebels poured through a gap and routed the two Union corps on the right. Rosecrans became swallowed up in the panic and galloped madly to Chattanooga with both corps commanders. Meanwhile, Major General George Thomas continued fighting on the Union left. Rosecrans could hear the battle but, in his frenzied race to safety, abandoned Thomas and made no effort to support him. Despite being outnumbered and short on ammunition, Thomas held his position and did not withdraw until Rosecrans ordered him back to Chattanooga.[13]

Among the Confederate dead lay Lincoln's brother-in-law, Ben Hardin Helm, the husband of Mary's sister, Emilie. The president once offered Helm a position as paymaster in the Union army with the rank of major, a good safe job for a friend and relative. The Kentuckian turned it down to become a Confederate brigadier general. Lincoln felt great fondness for Helm, and when writing to his wife in New York, he tried to spare her grief by leaving out the details. Three of her four brothers—Samuel, David, and Alexander—had already been killed fighting for the Confederacy. She had suffered enough. Northerners had accused her of disloyalty, and the South condemned her for being Lincoln's wife. As her sister-in-law Katherine Helm observed, "There was no one in the land upon whom the unnatural hatreds and distortions of that day bore more relentlessly than upon her"—and what burdened her also burdened the president.[14]

Lincoln spent hours at the telegraph office with Stanton and Halleck waiting for news from Rosecrans. Tension magnified on September 19, when the general informed the administration he had been attacked, adding, "The defeat of the enemy will be total tomorrow." Lincoln became uneasy because Burnside, who was to have stayed in supporting distance of Rosecrans, could not be found. Lincoln had already gone to bed on the twentieth when a courier arrived. Shaking sleep from his eyes, he read the first lines of a brief telegram from Rosecrans: "We have met with a serious disaster; extent not yet ascertained."[15]

At 12:35 a.m. the president dressed and, hoping to infuse Rosecrans with a little backbone, telegraphed, "Be of good cheer. We have unabated confidence in you." He told Rosecrans to save the army and promised reinforcements from Burnside. Lincoln hoped for the best when he sent a message to Knoxville ordering Burnside to Chattanooga "without a moment's delay." The message reached Burnside at Jonesboro. Having ordered Burnside to stay in supporting distance of Rosecrans but finding him a hundred miles from Knoxville, Lincoln blurted, "Damn Jonesboro!" According to the telegraphers, it was the only time they ever heard the president swear.[16]

Lincoln returned to the White House but could not sleep. He woke John Hay and, while sitting on his bed, said, "Well, Rosecrans has been whipped as I feared. I feared it for several days. I believe I feel trouble in the air before it comes." He returned to the telegraph office, found no more reports from Rosecrans, and asked Halleck to tell the general to hold Chattanooga. Lincoln heard nothing more from Rosecrans. On September 22 he wrote, "We have not a word here as to the whereabouts or condition of your Army. . . . Please relieve my anxiety." Rosecrans had not assessed his losses, which during two days' fighting were proportionately greater than in the three-day Battle of Gettysburg. Nor did he relieve the president's anxiety. Lincoln continued to fret and told Halleck that Rosecrans must hold Chattanooga and, if attacked, defeat Bragg.[17]

Rosecrans exaggerated the situation. He reported having only thirty thousand men when he had twice that number. He told Lincoln the army was "in the hands of God" one day and a day later said his forces "cannot be dislodged except by very superior numbers and after a great battle." Rosecrans wanted to withdraw and tried to prepare the president for that eventuality because Confederates were perched on hills surrounding the city. They had cut off supplies and were merely waiting for Rosecrans to evacuate.[18]

Rosecrans's erratic statements were followed by Burnside's equally puzzling explanation of why, after wandering off to Jonesboro, he had promised to reinforce Rosecrans but never did. "It makes me doubt whether I am awake or dreaming," the president wrote in a letter drafted to Burnside but never sent. By then Lincoln had begun to relax. What Burnside seemed unable to do from Knoxville, Grant did from Memphis by detaching two divisions under General Sherman and started them by steamboat for Chattanooga.[19]

Exhausted by Washington's heat and nerve-racking days, the president rode to the Soldier's Home on the evening of September 23 to rest. Hay went to the War Department with dispatches and found Stanton preparing to leave for the Soldier's Home because of disturbing news from Rosecrans, who was building a case to evacuate the city. "I know the reason well enough," Stanton blurted. "Rosecrans ran away from his fighting men and did not stop for 13 miles." When someone remarked that two other corps commanders deserted the field with him, Stanton testily replied, "But Rosecrans beat them both."[20]

Hay rode to the Soldier's Home, woke the president, and explained the situation. Lincoln became alarmed, dressed rapidly, and rode to the War Department. With Stanton he found Chase, Halleck, and Seward gathered for the grim news when another telegram arrived from Rosecrans announcing he could hold Chattanooga "against double his number." Because Rosecrans's dispatches oscillated from hysteria one hour to sublime confidence the next, no one in Washington could assess the situation in Chattanooga. Because Meade seemed unwilling to use the Army of the Potomac, Stanton suggested sending two corps to Rosecrans. Lincoln and Halleck opposed weakening Meade, but Chase, Seward, and Colonel General Daniel C. McCallum, director of military transportation, backed Stanton.[21]

Lincoln agreed to detach the Eleventh and Twelfth corps, place General Hooker in charge of both, and send twenty thousand men by rail to Chattanooga. When the president asked how long it would take, Halleck said three months. Stanton jumped to his feet and said it could be done in five days. Lincoln replied, "I will bet that if the order is given tonight, the troops could not be got [farther than] Washington in five days." Stanton refused to take the bet, but he turned to Halleck and told him to have the Eleventh and Twelfth corps cook five days' rations and be in Washington in twenty-four hours. To Lincoln's astonishment the plan worked. Nearly twenty thousand men with five thousand horses and mules and seven hundred wagons traveled by special cars from Virginia to Tennessee, covering 1,159 miles in less than two weeks.[22]

Without Dana monitoring Rosecrans's gyrations, neither Lincoln nor Stanton would have obtained a clear picture of the general's actual situation. Welles blamed Halleck for allowing Rosecrans to exist in military limbo. Although Rosecrans was safe from attack, his ammunition and supplies were dwindling. Bragg's army surrounded the city, and Brigadier General Joseph Wheeler's cavalry smashed roads and railways supplying Chattanooga from the north. Rosecrans put the army on reduced rations and sulked. When Dana reported the general unwilling to fight, Stanton suggested replacing Rosecrans with Thomas, who had fought bravely at Chickamauga. He also showed the president a telegram from Dana claiming that Major Generals

Thomas L. Crittenden and Alexander M. McCook, the two corps commanders who had wilted at Chickamauga, disgracefully "returned to Chattanooga
and—went to sleep."[23]

Lincoln admitted having lost confidence in Rosecrans but said "it would
not do to send one of our generals from the East." While mulling over alternatives, he urged Rosecrans to hold Chattanooga, draw supplies from East
Tennessee, live off the land, and make a stronger effort with Burnside to
protect communications. Aside from strengthening his fortifications, Rosecrans did little. Dana probably hastened the decision to replace him when
on October 12 he wrote, "In the midst of [these problems] the commanding
general devotes that part of his time which is not employed in pleasant gos-
sip to the composition of a long report to prove that the Government is to
blame for his failure. I have never seen a . . . man possessing talent with . . .
greater practical incapacity than General Rosecrans."[24]

Armed with Dana's reports, Stanton spent three weeks urging the presi-
dent to recall Rosecrans. Lincoln made an intelligent decision by expanding
Grant's Mississippi department to include the armies of the Cumberland,
Ohio, and Tennessee and then sent the general to Chattanooga to relieve
Rosecrans. Other than Banks's army in Louisiana, Grant became supreme
commander in the West.

Although Lincoln respected Grant, he usually preceded his choice of generals with a personal relationship. He had never met Grant. He only knew the
general as a fighter who had given him the least personal annoyance and some
remarkable victories. The president wrote two sets of orders for Stanton to
deliver personally, giving Grant the option of retaining or superseding Rosecrans with Thomas. Stanton met Grant for the first time in Louisville, and
when asked to make the choice, Grant replied that Rosecrans would never
obey orders and chose Thomas. He then placed Sherman in charge of Mississippi, hoping the administration would not waste the general's talents in idleness. Lincoln endorsed Grant's choices and the speed with which he acted.[25]

At nightfall Stanton received an urgent message from Dana warning that
Rosecrans planned to abandon Chattanooga. Stanton began a frantic search
to find Grant, who was somewhere in Louisville socializing with his wife. The
general returned to the hotel around midnight, went to Stanton's room, and
found the nervous secretary pacing the floor in a bulky nightgown. Stanton
read Dana's dispatch and said Rosecrans must not be allowed to retreat.
Grant immediately wired Thomas to take command and "hold Chattanooga
at all hazards. I will be there as soon as possible." Thomas replied, "I will hold
the town till we starve."[26]

On October 23 Grant reached Chattanooga, conferred with Thomas, and learned the troops were nearly out of ammunition. Lincoln's instructions were to "hold" Chattanooga, revealing the president's ignorance of Grant's aggressive nature. Grant formulated a bold plan to break the siege by attacking the rebels at two points, one on the east bank and one on the west bank of the Tennessee. He coordinated the attack with Hooker's expected arrival and on October 26 initiated the "Cracker Line Operation," which successfully opened the Tennessee to steamboats and ended the siege. With the arrival of Sherman, Grant launched an all-out offensive on Bragg's fortified lines and on November 25 drove the Confederates off Missionary Ridge. On November 26 Bragg's scattered elements abandoned Tennessee and withdrew to Georgia, leaving Grant with a springboard for launching the Atlanta campaign in the spring of 1864. Grant detached Sherman's corps and sent it to Knoxville to rescue Burnside, who was besieged by Longstreet. Longstreet did not wait for Sherman. He withdrew to Virginia, leaving the entire state of Tennessee in Union control.[27]

Grant's rescue of Chattanooga changed the political landscape. Republicans had lost heavily in 1862, and Lincoln's enforcement of the conscription act and martial law in mid-1863 had put the party at risk. Rescuing Chattanooga could not have come at a better time for Republicans. Vallandigham lost the governor's race in Ohio; Republicans carried California, Iowa, Maine, and New York; and Governor Curtin won reelection in Pennsylvania.

Delighted with the outcome of the elections, James K. Moorhead of Pennsylvania urged the president to "now declare for *A Lincoln* in 1864." Elihu B. Washburne, one of Lincoln's best friends, wrote, "You ought to let some of your confidential friends know your [reelection] wishes." On October 26 the president replied, "A second term would be a great honor and a great labor, which together, perhaps I would not decline, if tendered." Lincoln already had his eyes on the 1864 election and no inclination to leave unfinished business to someone else.[28]

With the exception of Chickamauga and Chattanooga, a lull existed in the East. Meade maneuvered around Virginia and seemed content to avoid serious fighting, and Banks blundered trying to establish a foothold in Texas. The reprieve gave the president time to concentrate on the 1863 elections.

One threat to the Republican Party's political welfare occurred on July 4, 1863, when Alexander Stephens, vice president of the Confederacy and one of Lincoln's former friends from the House of Representatives, arrived off Hampton Roads under a flag of truce and requested a meeting with the president for the ostensible purpose of discussing prisoner exchange. Lincoln suspected the meeting's real purpose was to propose peace negotiations. He knew Stephens disagreed with Davis's policies but had no power to change them. Although curious to hear what Stephens wished to discuss, Lincoln could not decide whether to send someone, go himself, or turn Stephens's party away. When he put the matter before the cabinet, Seward said any official communication with the rebel government would only strengthen the enemy. He accused Stephens of being "a dangerous man, who would make mischief anywhere." If Stephens wanted to discuss prisoner exchange, Seward said he should talk to General Dix. Stanton and Chase objected to any contact with Stephens, but Blair thought an unofficial discussion would be acceptable if "something more important was involved." Welles thought Stephens should not be permitted to pass through the blockade. Seward changed his mind three times, finally deciding against a conference. The question remained unresolved until the following day, when Seward proposed and Lincoln accepted a compromise denying Stephens's access to Washington but allowing him to place his questions with the military commander of Fort Monroe.[29]

Lincoln understood there were differences of opinion in the Confederate government. Stephens believed in diplomacy, and Davis trusted nothing but the army. During a picture-taking session at Gardner's studio, Lincoln spoke suddenly, as if struck by an elusive concept. "Davis is right," he declared. "His army is his only hope, not only against us, but against his own people. If that were crushed the people would be ready to swing back to their old bearings." According to Hay, Lincoln cheered right up, saying, "Rebel power is at last beginning to disintegrate . . . they will break to pieces if we only stand firm now."[30]

Meeting with Stephens, who could only have negotiated for Southern independence, would have been politically hazardous for the administration. Any communication would have provided fodder for the opposition press, especially after the *Richmond Enquirer* outlined the actual purpose of Stephens's mission. Lincoln recognized the threat for what it was. His terms for ending the war never strayed from an irrevocable pledge to reunite the nation, a condition Jefferson Davis could never accept.[31]

With the future firmly fixed in his mind and time to think, Lincoln recalled his response to serenaders who had appeared outside the White House following the victories at Gettysburg and Vicksburg. Called upon for an impromptu speech, he spoke, asking, "How long ago is it?" and answered his own question, "Eighty odd years—since on the Fourth of July for the first time in the history of the world a nation by its representatives, assembled and declared as a self-evident truth that 'all men are created equal.' That was the birthday of the United States of America." The word *united* held special significance for Lincoln, and so did the Declaration of Independence's guarantee of equality.[32]

Those simple words, articulated spontaneously to a group of serenaders, became the precursor of the president's historic message delivered four months later. By then the 1863 elections were over, Grant had broken the Chattanooga siege, and signs pointed to the end of the war. The debate had begun regarding the readmission of Southern states to the Union, and Lincoln needed a public platform to announce his views on restoration. The opportunity came with an invitation to speak at the dedication of the Gettysburg National Cemetery on November 19. Thousands of bodies, many poorly identified and buried haphazardly, were to be reinterred in the first national cemetery of the Civil War.

As ceremonial orator, the Gettysburg Cemetery Commission chose Edward Everett, who had been Harvard's president, Millard Fillmore's secretary of state, and a U.S. senator. The commission also wanted Lincoln to speak and asked Washington marshal Ward Lamon, Lincoln's bodyguard, to obtain the president's consent, which he did. As reward, commissioners named Lamon grand marshal of the dedication ceremony. According to Lamon, the president approached him a day or two before the dedication complaining he had been too busy to prepare a speech properly. Lamon recalled watching the president pull from his hat a single sheet of foolscap filled with tightly compressed handwriting and read the words aloud, calling them "not at all satisfactory." He made several changes and rewrote it on November 18, before leaving the White House. Sharpening the intent of the message without expanding its length, Lincoln added a flowing cadence. What amendments he made to the speech afterward, and where he made them, has been a matter of speculation ever since. Lamon traveled with the president and his entourage, which included Blair, Seward, and Usher, and said the words taken from his hat "proved to be in substance, if not in exact words, what was afterward printed as his Gettysburg speech." David C. Mearns and Lloyd A. Dunlap, who looked beyond Lamon's affirmations, found five versions of the Gettysburg Address in Lincoln's handwriting.[33]

Lincoln boarded the train to Gettysburg without knowing the content of Everett's speech. He expected to hear a conservative address but was surprised when Everett spoke for two hours on the three-day Battle of Gettysburg. He also expected Everett to speak of peace and restoration, and the president intended to build on that theme. Lincoln wrote only 272 words to make his point and waited four hours listening to lengthy addresses before being introduced. By then some of the crowd had wandered off to the battlefield. Lincoln's address lasted about two minutes, with six short interruptions of courteous applause. The president held the speech in his hand but never looked at it. There were no hearty cheers of approval, but there were moments of reverent silence when Lincoln uttered a wonderfully moving sentence, so touched with meaning, and said, "The world will little note, nor long remember what we here SAY, but it can never forget what they here DID." When a stalwart captain, standing at attention but wearing a coat with an empty sleeve, heard those words, he broke into tears. With cheeks wet from crying and his body shaking with emotion, he lifted his moist eyes to the president and solemnly exclaimed, "God Almighty, bless Abraham Lincoln!" A thousand voices rose in spontaneous affection, replying, "Amen." The president continued with a few more words and ended by promising "that this nation, under God, shall have a new birth of freedom—and that this government of the people, by the people, for the people, shall not perish from the earth." The crowd was astonished when the president sat down. They thought Lincoln was just warming up with a preamble.[34]

Lincoln observed the crowd's puzzled reaction. He turned to Lamon and said, "That speech won't *scour!* It is a flat failure, and the people are disappointed." Seward asked Everett's opinion, who replied, "It is not what I expected of him. I am disappointed." Everett asked what Seward thought, who replied, "He has made a failure, and I am sorry for it. His speech is not equal to him." Even Lamon was unimpressed. Lincoln asked the same question, and all three men agreed with the president's own unfavorable assessment of the speech's merits.[35]

The early press covered Everett's oration and gave the president's remarks minor mention. Gettysburg eyewitnesses never absorbed the president's message because it passed in a flash. There was no warm-up, no time for the audience to adjust from Everett's two-hour monolog to a two-minute address beginning with an arithmetic problem—"Four score and seven years ago"—and ending before some listeners had finished computing the answer. Editors who later studied the speech were among the first to recognize its poignancy. John Hay summed up the aftereffect best when three weeks later he wrote that the "immediate effect of this paper is something wonderful. I have never seen such an effect produced by a single document. Men acted as if the millennium had come." After the speech Lincoln fell ill with varioloid, a mild form of smallpox. Henry Wilson came to the White House, laid his hands on Hay's shoulders, and said, "Tell the President he has struck another bold blow. Tell him for me, 'God bless him.'" John W. Forney, publisher and editor of the *Philadelphia Press* and *Washington Chronicle*, declared, "We only wanted a leader to speak the bold word. It is done and all can follow." Edward Everett, after reading the scripted version of Lincoln's address, admitted he had been outdone. On November 20 he wrote, "I should be glad if I could flatter myself that I came as near to the central idea of the occasion in two hours as you did in two minutes."[36]

Lincoln recovered from illness and began preparing his annual message to Congress. Whatever the opposition believed, the president had made his point in ways far beyond his own expectations, but the battle was not over. He still had a war to win, a troublesome reelection ahead, and new minefields to navigate.

CHAPTER 17

"What can I do with such generals as we have?"

During September 1863 General George Meade remained curiously inactive in northern Virginia. He seemed to Edwin Stanton to be "on the back track . . . without fight." Meade learned Lee had detached Longstreet to aid Bragg in Tennessee and asked Halleck for advice, adding that he saw no reason for advancing because the Army of the Potomac was too small to "follow [Lee] to Richmond . . . and lay siege to that place." Halleck referred the message to the president, who assumed Meade was thinking of Richmond as the objective instead of Lee's army. Lincoln suggested Meade "move upon Lee at once in the manner of general attack." Halleck endorsed the president's comments and forwarded them to Meade, adding it would be wise to reconnoiter Lee's army and carve off elements of it by sudden raids.[1]

Meade advanced slowly and stopped, saying he felt "uncomfortable" going farther without "positive authority" from the president. At the time Lee had fifty-five thousand men, Meade eighty-nine thousand. Meade said if he attacked, nothing would be accomplished. Lee would fall back to Richmond, and by then the Army of the Potomac would be in no condition to follow. In other words Meade would agree to attack Richmond if he first did not have to fight Lee. Baffled by Meade's logic, Halleck forwarded the dispatch to Lincoln.[2]

On September 19, after reading the dispatch, the president sent Halleck a remarkably accurate assessment of Meade's situation. He estimated the two armies at roughly the correct size, with each "midway between the two Capitals, each defending its own Capital, and menacing the other." Lincoln admitted an army deployed defensively enjoyed natural advantages but asked why half of Meade's eighty-nine thousand–man army could not neutralize Lee's fifty-five thousand–man army, thereby making it possible to transfer half of the Army of the Potomac elsewhere. "Having practically come to the mere defensive," Lincoln wrote, "it seems to be no economy at all to employ twice as many men for that object as are needed." He refused to let Meade attack Lee merely to force the Confederates back to Richmond, calling it "an idea I have been trying to repudiate for quite a year. My last attempt upon Richmond was to get McClellan, when he was nearer there than the enemy was, to run in ahead of him. Since then I have constantly desired the Army of the Potomac to make Lee's army and not Richmond, its objective point. If our army cannot fall upon the enemy and hurt him where he is, it is plain to me it can gain nothing by attempting to follow him over . . . intrenched lines into a fortified city." Nine days later, after Meade failed to engage Lee, Lincoln sent the Eleventh and Twelfth corps to Chattanooga.[3]

Meade and Lee continued to maneuver without fighting. When Meade admitted being unable to ascertain Lee's strength, Old Brains replied with one of Napoleon's aphorisms: "Attack him and you will soon find out." Meade vilified the remark as undignified and told his staff he loathed the burden of command and found working with Halleck so unpleasant he hoped to be relieved. In a state of exasperation, Lincoln lamented, "What can I do with such generals as we have?"[4]

Learning Meade's Eleventh and Twelfth corps had been detached, Lee commenced offensive operations. On October 14 Meade repulsed A. P. Hill's corps at Bristoe Station and Stuart's cavalry at Catlett's Station. Sensing an opportunity, Lincoln wrote, "If General Meade can now attack on a field no worse than equal for us, and will do so with all the skill and courage which he, his officers, and men possess, the honor will be his if he succeeds, and the blame may be mine if he fails." Instead, Stuart routed the Federal cavalry at Buckland Mills on October 19, and Meade, though with numerically superior forces, retreated forty miles and lost the Orange & Alexandria Railroad, which his men had spent a month repairing.[5]

After Buckland Mills, Meade suggested suspending active campaigning and bringing the army closer to the capital. Because Meade had not advanced in good weather, Lincoln doubted the general would advance in poor weather. The weather, however, remained mild, so Lincoln asked Halleck what plans had been developed. When Old Brains said none, Lincoln told him to attack Lee. Halleck sent the president's comments to Meade and suggested cavalry raids behind Lee's lines. Instead, Meade proposed changing his base to Fredericksburg and moving on Richmond. Meade was still focused on the wrong objective. Lincoln emphatically vetoed the plan, which may have been what Meade intended by proposing it.[6]

On November 26 Meade attempted to maneuver Lee's army out of its defensive works on the Rapidan River by crossing Germanna Ford with five corps and striking Orange Court House. Stuart reported the movement, and Lee repositioned his army along Mine Run. Meade withdrew and went into winter quarters. William Swinton referred to the Mine Run probe as "an operation which deserved better success than it met." Thus ended 1863 operations. Meade believed he would have been defeated and expected to be relieved because, according to his own admission, he had failed to accomplish the impossible.[7]

Excepting the stalemate in Virginia, Lincoln looked on 1863 as a year of progress, though less than he had hoped. Republicans gained strength in the fall elections, and the administration scored victories in domestic and foreign affairs. In preparing his annual address to the Thirty-eighth Congress, Lincoln spoke of clearing rebels out of Arkansas and Tennessee, opening the Mississippi, and implementing the Emancipation Proclamation. Stanton praised Grant's victory at Chattanooga as opening the way for a spring campaign into Georgia, and Welles reported the strength of the navy at 588 vessels, of which 75 were either ironclads or armored.[8]

In September, after a lengthy diplomatic battle with Great Britain over the building of Confederate commerce destroyers, Seward and Adams succeeded in compelling the Crown to cease further construction. Through William Dayton, minister to France, Seward eventually reached a similar agreement with Napoleon by merely threatening legal action.

During the same period Lincoln and Seward developed a relationship with Russia when Czar Alexander II sent his navy to the United States, ostensibly to keep it from being blockaded in the Baltic Sea if war ensued with Great Britain. Hay attended a Navy Department reception for Rear Admiral Lisovski, noting Russian officers as having "vast [alcoholic] absorbent powers and are fiendishly ugly" and that "Mme Lisovski is not an exception." Lincoln and Seward used the visit to enter into a secret alliance with Russia.[9]

Although military, diplomatic, and political gains in 1863 set the party on the right track, defeats in 1862 had reduced the Republican majority in Congress. Prior to Congress convening in December, Lincoln learned some of his congressional adversaries were discussing the formation of a centrist National Union Party instead of the Republican Party. He opposed the change and took keen interest in the election of the new speaker of the House. The two leading candidates, Schuyler Colfax of Indiana and Frank Blair of Missouri, were both in different ways connected to the cabinet. Chase and the radicals supported Colfax, whom Lincoln labeled an untrustworthy schemer "aspiring beyond his capacity." Lincoln preferred Blair, whose reelection to Congress as a conservative was more acceptable to war Democrats than Colfax. Blair supported the president but was still on duty with Sherman's Army of the Tennessee and fully employed at Chattanooga. Using Montgomery Blair as an intermediary, Lincoln suggested Frank come to Washington, take his seat in Congress, help reorient the House to support the war, and, "if the result shall be the election of himself as Speaker, let him serve in that position; if not, let him re-take his commission, and return to the Army." The plan failed because the general was still engaged in field operations and did not reach Washington until after the House convened. The president had to settle for Colfax, from whom he tried to coax support, but the evasive Indianan stood squarely with Chase and the radicals.[10]

Debates began immediately on ways to restore the South to the Union. This had been on Lincoln's mind ever since the outbreak of war. Now with major gains in Arkansas, Louisiana, Mississippi, and Tennessee, he began voicing his views on reconstruction. The three factions in Congress—radicals, conservatives, and Democrats—each had different ideas. Chase became extremely active with the radicals, and Montgomery Blair became reckless in his accusations against the secretary. Lincoln did not want Chase damaged by Blair's assaults, nor did he want radicals to set the restoration agenda.[11]

Two manic radicals, Hunter Winter Davis of Maryland and the irascible Thaddeus Stevens of Pennsylvania, led the movement in the House. According to Welles, Davis wanted to make the legislature "the controlling power of government." The dignified and statesmanlike Charles Sumner of Massachusetts, who would normally have little in common with Davis and Stevens, led the radical movement in the Senate with Wade. Sumner often conferred with Lincoln on foreign affairs, but Davis, Stevens, and Wade seldom visited the White House because they vilified anyone opposed to their views. Sumner often disagreed with the violent radicals in the House, but he believed the Southern states, by rebelling, had lost their privileges and should be treated as conquered territories subject to congressional jurisdiction. Radicals believed the Emancipation Proclamation should be expanded, but they could not agree on how far to push civil rights issues. They wanted to punish Southern politicians, military leaders, and plantation owners and floated schemes to transfer Southern property to blacks and worthy Northern patriots and demand reparations.[12]

Like Lincoln, conservatives favored letting the conquered South down easily. In his December 9, 1863, annual message the president introduced his views by issuing a carefully constructed Proclamation of Amnesty and Reconstruction, which had the force of law. He offered full pardon and restoration of property "except as to slaves" to Southerners who swore an oath of allegiance to the Union and its laws. The document provided that once 10 percent of the adult white males voting in the 1860 election took the oath, the state could resume governing itself. The 10 percent factor may have coincided with the number of former Southern Whigs, who were mainly planters intelligent enough to see the war was lost and influential enough to lead their states back into the Union. Lincoln never deserted his original concept of an indissoluble Union in which states could not legally secede. Hence, all eleven Southern states were still in the Union if they met the conditions specified in the amnesty proclamation. Lincoln believed his policy would put Southern Unionists in control of state governments, which in turn would accelerate restoration. Montgomery Blair agreed with the proclamation in principle, but he still favored compulsory deportation and colonization of blacks because the government would not know what to do with them and, if freed, their former owners would mistreat them.[13]

The plan advocated by Democrats differed completely with radicals and partly with conservatives. While Democrats agreed with Lincoln that the South had never legally separated from the Union, they wanted the war stopped, general amnesty for all, new legislators sent to Congress, and the Emancipation Proclamation withdrawn. Lincoln said the plan would merely revive conditions that had led to the rebellion, but he also discovered danger in his own plan. What if Southerners swiftly repudiated secession, asserted their rights as bona fide states, and sent only Democrats to Congress? In an unsent letter, perhaps trying to clarify his own thoughts, Lincoln wrote, "I shall dread, and I think we should all dread, to see 'the disturbing element' so brought back into the government, as to make probable a renewal of the scenes through which we are now passing." So Lincoln added loyalty tests and acceptance of the Emancipation Proclamation as a condition of amnesty and reconciliation. He also viewed the war as a rebellion created by certain Southerners, not Southern states. He did not accept, as radicals proposed, that Southern states be treated as captured territories. Instead, he said a reconstructed state would retain its name, boundaries, subdivisions, constitution, and code of laws (excepting slavery) as before the rebellion. This pleased conservatives and war Democrats but ran contrary to the radicals' vision of occupied Southern territories. Lincoln appeased the radicals, however, by pledging to uphold the Emancipation Proclamation. Hence, the Proclamation of Amnesty and Reconstruction offered something for everyone, made a hit with the public, and provided another demonstration of Lincoln's ability to balance extremes without giving anything away he wanted for himself.[14]

Lincoln tested his premise on loyal Southerners. The first experiment occurred in early 1863, when Benjamin F. Flanders and Michael Hahn appeared as elected representatives from Louisiana to take seats in the House. Flanders, formerly from New Hampshire, and Hahn, born in Bavaria, were both citizens of New Orleans. The two were opposites, Flanders being a radical and Hahn a conservative. On February 9, 1863, a fierce debate ensued on the floor of the House over the admittance of Southerners. On February 17, after spending eight days haggling over Louisiana's two representatives, the House granted Flanders and Hahn their seats. A few days later both men returned to Louisiana in disgust and ran against each other for governor. J.Q.A. Fellows entered the race as a proponent of slavery. Hahn, a conservative, won easily, but Fellows, the proslavery candidate, collected more votes than Flanders. The election convinced Lincoln his plan for unity would not come without a struggle, but the process had begun. On March 13, 1864, the president congratulated Hahn for "having fixed your name in history as the first-free-state Governor of Louisiana."[15]

In mid-1863 Edward W. Gantt, the last representative elected to Congress from Arkansas and a former Confederate general, wrote the president, "My only object is to induce the withdrawal of my State from its allies in rebellion and its reentry into the Federal Union." While imprisoned, Gantt spent time thinking and blamed the South's miseries on Jeff Davis, who he described as a "stupid failure . . . [and] supremely ambitious." Two weeks later former Senator-elect William K. Sebastian of Arkansas asked Federal authorities for permission to reclaim his seat, which Lincoln said would be up to the Senate. Gantt and Sebastian, however, represented the very class of people radicals most wanted to punish.[16]

The main threat to the administration continued to be radical Republicans, not Democrats. In preparing his annual message, Lincoln wanted to bring conservatives, radicals, and war Democrats together on reconstruction. He set the stage in his own words and opened the way for compromise: "Saying that reconstruction will be accepted if presented in a specified way, it is not said it will never be accepted in any other way."[17]

Lincoln conferred with the cabinet on reconstruction and received no help from Chase and Blair, but Bates advocated a system of universal amnesty. He believed the vindictive views of radicals would undermine efforts of reunification and thought Southerners might be more willing to end resistance and speed reconstruction if Congress restored their property. Stanton warned once the fighting stopped, provost marshals would be smothered with a multitude of tasks ranging from keeping order to arranging for food, clothes, seeds, farm implements, passes, and a host of other duties. He did not expect Lincoln to understand the complexities of army life, but he said something legal and tangible must be written to guide the army during reconstruction. Lincoln's annual message surpassed the expectations of his cabinet and mollified some radicals by moving them toward his views on reconstruction by attaching to his annual address the Proclamation of Amnesty and Reconstruction, which contained some of Bates's and Stanton's suggestions. Lincoln massaged the proclamation to attract Southerners, seduce them into repudiating the Confederacy, provide them with tools for solving the race problem, and create a moderate path for Republicans to follow.[18]

The proclamation stirred up a mighty tempest among Thad Stevens's cronies. They wanted to impose radical values and institutions on the South but now found themselves blocked by public opinion and Lincoln's war powers. Peace Democrats thought the amnesty and reconstruction plan was too harsh. Stanton, however, wholeheartedly supported the proclamation because it met the needs of the army.

In early 1864 Lincoln began implementing his 10 percent plan in Union-occupied portions of the South by executive order. Working through the War Department, he recognized the restored state governments of Louisiana, Tennessee, Arkansas, and Union-controlled portions of Virginia. The Thirty-eighth Congress refused to seat elected representatives from those states, and the president could not legally force it. Radicals stood their ground because the proclamation posed an obstacle to their plans. On March 26 Lincoln irked them more by expanding the proclamation to make it easier for people to take the oath of allegiance. Other Republicans, though less vindictive than the radicals, worried Lincoln's readiness to forgive could enable an unrepentant South to form an alliance with Democrats, regain power in Congress, circumvent emancipation by keeping former slaves deprived of suffrage, and undo all the gains won by war. Lincoln's accelerated reconstruction program reunified the radical's effort to keep the process under congressional control. What appeared as a clear victory for Lincoln in December drifted into a power struggle with radicals and once again threatened to split the Republican Party as nomination day approached.[19]

Radicals had been searching for a suitable Republican candidate to unseat Lincoln at the forthcoming convention. During the summer of 1863 they considered Salmon Chase, whose views closely matched their own. Chase craved the presidency, partly because he could dismiss Blair, Seward, and Stanton. Chase, however, agreed with Lincoln's approach to reconstruction more than the radicals realized; his main objection being that the president's program did not go far enough. Chase agreed Louisiana should be restored to the Union, but he disagreed with Lincoln's 10 percent rule entitling the entire state to be restored while some sections remained Confederate. Chase thought Louisiana should be separated like Virginia, with one part Confederate and the other part Union. In December 1862 Chase wrote Lincoln, "In every case of insurrection involving the persons exercising the powers of state government when a large body of people remain faithful, that body, so far as the Union is concerned, must be taken to constitute a state." The letter became the cornerstone of Chase's reconstruction views. Having been applied to Virginia, he saw no reason to apply it differently to Louisiana. This left rebel-controlled districts of Louisiana without recourse other than to become what radicals termed "captured territories." The formation of West Virginia emerged from circumstances much different than Louisiana, and when Lincoln promised to retain the original borders of states in secession, he did so to lure those states back to the Union and bring together the nation exactly as promised in his inaugural address.[20]

Chase showed both sides of his character when he became involved in the reconstruction of Louisiana. He sent his cousin, George Denison, to New Orleans in the dual role of acting collector of customs and personal political organizer. Denison stuffed the customhouse with New Yorkers approved by Chase and put forth radical candidates for public office. Like Lincoln, Chase wanted a better life for blacks, but he also wanted their suffrage and support to unseat Lincoln.[21]

Nothing in Louisiana evolved as Chase hoped because he could not control military and civilian appointments. His Louisiana plans failed when Lincoln recalled Butler for irregularities and replaced him with Banks, who was also a Democrat but more in accord with Lincoln's reconstruction views. Butler had been extremely harsh on influential Louisianans, which pleased Chase. Lincoln made the change for political reasons, informing only Seward and Stanton. The action caught Chase off guard. He blamed Seward for inveigling the president into removing Butler and countered by using his radical friends to demand the general's reinstatement. The massive effort to send Butler back to New Orleans almost succeeded. Lincoln wrote the order but never issued it, thus ending Chase's carefully designed plans to radicalize Louisiana. Lincoln replaced Chase's cousin with Cuthbert Bullitt, editor of the conservative *New Orleans True Delta*. Chase howled, but Denison howled louder because the action prevented him from collecting bribes—a nefarious practice Chase would not have endorsed. Chase still needed a reliable spy, so he traveled to Louisiana and appointed Denison acting surveyor. Bullitt replaced all of Denison's customhouse employees, and Chase realized ousting Lincoln in the 1864 election might be the only way to achieve his personal program for the South. On returning to Washington, he discovered Lincoln had taken patronage into his own hands after being warned the "Treasury rats [were] busy night and day and becoming more and more unscrupulous and malicious." Lincoln's intrusion into Chase's sacred bailiwick worsened the fragile relationship between the president and the secretary. For some time neither man thought clearly when it concerned the business of the other. A frail truce followed, but the real test of political strength lay in the months ahead.[22]

With presidential nominations approaching, radical leaders faced a problem. Having no prominent Republican generals in the field and no prominent radical statesmen who could overcome Lincoln's popularity meant they were left with Chase. In early summer 1863 radicals began rallying support for the Treasury secretary, who enjoyed the attention and shrewdly encouraged the movement. Arrogantly convinced of his own suitability and immensely ambitious to become president, Chase announced he would gladly serve in any role offered. His quest for the presidential nomination surprised no one in the cabinet. In July 1863 Blair told Hay that Chase was scheming for the nomination. Informed by Hay of Chase's machinations, Lincoln remarked that the secretary's behavior was in "very bad taste, but that he had determined to shut his eyes to all these performances, that Chase made a good secretary and that he would keep him where he is." Lincoln paused for a moment, adding, "If he becomes pres[ident] all right. I hope we will never have a worse man," but Lincoln admitted being annoyed by Chase's habit of always taking a position contrary to his own.[23]

In October Bates wrote, "I'm afraid Mr. Chase's head is turned by his eagerness in pursuit of the presidency. For a long time back he has been filling all the offices in his own patronage, with extreme partisans, and contrives also to fill many vacancies, properly belonging to other departments." Welles noticed Chase also avoided cabinet meetings, writing, "No one was more prompt and punctual than himself until about a year ago [but now] makes it a point not to attend." Lincoln watched the Chase movement gather momentum but made no effort to stop it. Stanton overtly endorsed Lincoln's reconstruction plan but tried to maintain a friendly working relationship with Chase, and Seward spent little time with the Treasury secretary beyond the obligations of his office.[24]

Despite yearning for the presidency, Chase in 1864 managed his campaign no better than in 1860. He created a stream of correspondence condemning the administration for "no unity" and "no system" but failed to organize a team to promote his candidacy. Senator Samuel C. Pomeroy of Kansas became the Treasury secretary's self-appointed campaign manager and convinced him to run as the National Union candidate. After Chase told his scattered collection of supporters he was a better man than Lincoln, he began to vacillate because he feared losing. Pomeroy began distributing a "strictly private" and scurrilous circular extolling the qualifications of Chase at the expense of the president, whose reelection, he said, was "practically impossible." The so-called Pomeroy Circular, which compared Lincoln to Jefferson Davis and contained other accusations and lies, fell into the hands of the press, "produced a perfect convulsion" among Republicans, and soon became a huge embarrassment for Chase. He attempted to disown the document, but James A. Winchell, who had written it, said, "Mr. Chase was informed of this proposed action and approved it fully." The secretary's congressional friends, disgusted by the circular, withdrew their support. Even Ben Wade, the outspoken radical leader, decided Chase was not fit to become president and like other annoyed Ohioans threw his support to Lincoln. The incident woke up Lincoln's supporters and invigorated their efforts to ensure Lincoln's nomination when, on June 7, 1864, Republicans met in Baltimore.[25]

The storm over the Pomeroy Circular blew the wind out of Chase's bid and on February 22, 1864, the shaken secretary told the president, "I do not wish to administer the Treasury Department one day without your entire confidence." Knowing Chase brought his troubles on himself, Lincoln absolved the secretary of any blame. Days later Chase wrote, "Ohio folks don't want me enough, if they want me at all," and withdrew his name from presidential consideration.[26]

Frank Blair detested Chase and suspected the secretary of orchestrating a new scheme to win the nomination. General John C. Frémont had entered the race, rallied some report, and Blair accused Chase of striving to win the nomination by staying in the contest as a compromise candidate. Chase erroneously believed Lincoln had inspired Blair's assault and for the third time in less than eighteen months told the president he was ready to resign. Lincoln reassured the secretary his resignation was not wanted, but from that day until his final exit from the cabinet Chase remained "continually in hot water" with the president.[27]

Some felt the Treasury secretary's candidacy never existed except in Chase's imagination and a small number of disillusioned supporters. Radicals disenchanted with the administration never took Chase's candidacy seriously. *Chicago Tribune* editor Joseph Medill had followed Lincoln's career ever since the 1860 Republican convention. He represented perhaps the strongest Republican sentiment in the Northwest, yet in 1863 he understood the temper of the nation and wrote, "I presume it is true that Mr. Chase's friends are working for his nomination, but it is all lost labor; Old Abe has the inside track so completely that he will be nominated by acclamation when the convention meets." David Tod of Ohio spoke for most Republicans when he penned a letter to the president, saying, "The policy inaugurated under your lead must be maintained, and it would be suicidal to change leaders in the midst of the contest." Three months before the Republican convention, most Northern states had already caucused and declared for Lincoln.

Although Chase withdrew from the presidential race in early March, his personal pride suffered. Nicolay and Hay said Chase "indulged in sneers and insinuations against the President which show how deeply he was wounded by his discomfiture." Lincoln eventually salvaged Chase's reputation. He understood and respected the secretary's great intelligence and ability to manage almost any challenge in life but politics.[28]

CHAPTER 18

"I will fight it out on this line if it takes all summer"

During the winter of 1864 Congress wanted the command system changed because it relied too heavily on Lincoln. After the relief of Chattanooga, Ulysses S. Grant emerged as the most qualified general to lead the nation to final victory. Congress agreed, most of the army agreed, and the people agreed. While Grant slashed away at the enemy, Meade's Army of the Potomac rested in winter quarters waiting for spring. The only break in the monotony occurred when Meade mounted a poorly executed cavalry raid against Richmond, which cost the life of Colonel Ulric Dahlgren. Meade's lethargy sharply contrasted to Grant's energy. When Meade allowed James Longstreet's divisions to trickle back into Virginia from Tennessee unopposed, Lincoln grumbled, "If this Army of the Potomac was good for anything—if the officers had anything in them—if the army had any legs, they could move thirty thousand men down to Lynchburg and catch Longstreet. Can anybody doubt if Grant were here in command that he would catch him?" Meade had no second in command, while Grant had Sherman. Lincoln also noted that Grant's success stemmed from the absence of the administration meddling with his movements.[1]

Lincoln hesitated to bring Grant from the West because Republicans and Democrats alike were thinking about courting the general for president. If Rosecrans had not faltered at Chattanooga, radicals might have put him on the Republican ticket. Lincoln wanted to explore Grant's political aspirations and asked Elihu B. Washburne, who came from Grant's congressional district, to make inquiries. Washburne admitted "knowing very little" about the general and transferred the task to J. Russell Jones, "the only man who really knows Grant." To Jones's inquiry, Grant said, "He had as big a job on hand as one man need desire; that his only ambition was to suppress the rebellion." Nor, said Grant, could he accept the nomination "so long as there was a possibility of keeping Mr. Lincoln in the presidential chair." Jones appeared at the White House and presented Grant's letter. Finding he had Grant's full support, Lincoln turned to Jones and said, "My son, you will never know how gratifying that is to me. No man knows, when the presidential grub gets to gnawing on him, just how deep it will get until he has tried it; and I didn't know but what there was one gnawing at Grant."[2]

After the relief of Chattanooga, Grant formulated a broad strategy. He suggested a major winter offensive to clear the rebels out of the Mississippi Valley and in the spring invade Alabama and Georgia. He believed the Army of the Potomac should have a new commander, someone to coordinate its movements with campaigns in the West. Grant suggested replacing Meade with either Sherman or William F. "Baldy" Smith. He discussed the details with Charles Dana, assistant secretary of war, and sent him to Washington to lay the plan before Lincoln, Stanton, and Halleck. Lincoln and Stanton were ready to turn Grant loose, but Halleck warned of losing eastern Tennessee. There were still rebels in the area, and Lincoln decided Halleck might be right. Dana objected to Halleck's cautiousness, remarking, "I had unbounded confidence in Grant's skill and energy to conduct such a campaign . . . cutting loose entirely from his base and subsisting off the enemy's country . . . he had the troops, and could have finished the job in three months." Perhaps Old Brains influenced the decision because Grant's proposal violated the maxim against launching more than one major expedition at a time. Lincoln, Stanton, and Halleck agreed to replace Meade and thought Smith, rather than Sherman, might be the best man for the job. The president, however, did not press the issue, and Grant changed his mind about Smith's fitness for command. In Grant's view the Army of the Potomac already had too many generals like Smith.[3]

Another factor in the decision-making process could have been Jefferson Davis's decision to recall Bragg to Richmond and replace him with General Johnston, a more capable commander. Aware of discussions in Congress, the press, and the public about making him general-in-chief, Grant decided he could not spare Sherman. In the president's estimation Grant was the man, but he also wanted to know whether Grant had the capacity to run the whole war and not just part of it.[4]

Challenged by Lincoln to design a strategy to win the war, Grant believed the Trans-Mississippi theater was no different than Virginia, and neither was as vital as everyone in Washington thought. He said capturing territory in the Trans-Mississippi wasted resources that could be used against Atlanta. Instead of arguing the issue with Halleck, he let two of his generals make the case with Dana. He did believe, however, that capturing Atlanta and Mobile would strategically remove the South's heartland from the war. By achieving this, he said, "the war as a war of battles" would be over. Grant still believed Banks should capture Mobile and disregard the Red River campaign, but Banks still operated an independent command, and Lincoln still believed in the importance of invading Texas to keep the French in Mexico.[5]

Several days passed before Grant presented a strategy for Virginia, and he completely missed the point. He looked for ways to capture Richmond as opposed to defeating Lee. He proposed putting sixty thousand troops into North Carolina, closing Wilmington as a Confederate port, and destroying all the railroads feeding Richmond from the South while using the Army of the Potomac to keep Lee busy on the Rappahannock. Grant said the rebels would have to abandon Richmond to protect their communications but never mentioned a decisive battle with Lee.

Grant partly failed the strategy test, but the president recognized that his number one candidate for general-in-chief had not been exposed to the broader complexities of war in the East. Sixty thousand troops could not be raised without taking them from the Army of the Potomac. If the Western army moved south into Georgia and Alabama, the sixty thousand Federals sent to North Carolina could be isolated and cut off by a concentration of Confederate troops from Virginia and the Carolinas. In Lincoln's view Grant missed the point by not making Lee's army the main target. Lincoln, however, had never met Grant, and the president wondered to what degree the general's strategic concepts had been tainted by Halleck. Nor could there be an understanding until they met.[6]

Some historians have accused Halleck of inveigling Grant into expressing an unpopular strategy, but Halleck did no such thing. By February 1864 Halleck knew he would be retained in a similar capacity under Grant. When he received Grant's plan, he knew why Lincoln would reject it and told Grant. The Army of the Potomac and the Army of Northern Virginia had been fighting on the same ground for three years, and Lincoln wanted no more indecisive battles. He wanted Lee defeated, and he wanted it done between Richmond and Washington. Halleck said the president's wishes must be followed, but all the tactical planning would be up to Grant. Halleck informed Grant he would be called to Washington and attempted to prepare him for meeting the president. Grant spent the next two weeks digesting Halleck's advice and revising his own thoughts on Eastern operations.[7]

No general had been more thoroughly trained in battle than Grant. He had risen the hard way with on-the-job training in the field, having started as a regimental commander of the Twenty-first Illinois before proving he could handle greater responsibility. He came to understand the objective was the Confederacy's army and economic resources. Unlike most generals, Grant discarded much of what he learned at West Point, developed his own tactics, and used what worked.

After Grant's Chattanooga victory, Senator Washburne introduced a bill reviving the grade of lieutenant general. Lincoln probably sought Washburne's help, but not according to Lincoln's secretaries. No person had held the rank on a permanent basis since George Washington, who received it shortly before his death. A half-century passed before General Winfield Scott received the rank but as a brevet. By law a lieutenant general assumed command of all armies. Some feared giving such power to one man could threaten the civil liberties of the republic, but on February 26, following two months of debate, Congress passed the bill. Three days later Lincoln signed the document and sent Grant's name to the Senate for approval. Having neither the temperament nor self-confidence to manage the war, Halleck expected to be superseded. Lincoln clearly understood the general's incapacities and remarked to Hay, "[When] we sent for Halleck to take command he stipulated that it should be with the full power and responsibility of Commander in Chief. He ran it on that basis till Pope's defeat: but ever since that event, he has shrunk from responsibility wherever it was possible." The Senate would not have agreed to any other general but Grant and on March 2 confirmed the nomination.[8]

The next day Grant learned of his promotion from Halleck. Ordered to report to the president, Grant expressed his concerns to Sherman, writing that he would reject the commission if he had to make Washington his headquarters.[9] Five days later the forty-one-year-old general arrived at the capital in late afternoon with his thirteen-year-old son Fred and two staff officers. No one met him at the depot, so Grant made his way to Willard's Hotel and entered the lobby travel-worn and rumpled. He wore an army hat and a long linen duster that almost covered, but not quite, the narrow stripe on an army officer's uniform. Theodore Lyman described Grant as "rather under middle height, of a spare, strong build; light brown hair, and short, light-brown beard. His eyes of a clear blue; forehead high [and] jaw squarely set." Lyman characterized Grant as a man who looked determined to butt his head through a brick wall and was about to do it. Horace Porter, who served under Grant, would have said Grant's eyes were actually dark gray, with the left eye a little lower than the other.[10]

Nothing about Grant's appearance attracted attention. Lucius E. Chittenden of the Treasury Department was sitting in Willard's lobby when Grant arrived and noticed the stripe on the general's trousers. He watched as the clerk at the desk paid no more deference to the general than he would a lieutenant until Grant signed the register: "U.S. Grant and son, Galena, Ill." A sudden flush of recognition swept across the clerk's face, transforming him into a "servile menial" who "bowed, scraped, twisted, wriggled" and "begged a thousand pardons." The administration had made reservations at the hotel, and the flustered clerk immediately transferred Grant from the upper floor to commodious Parlor A on the first floor. By the time Grant reached his rooms, everybody on the main floor knew he had arrived.[11]

The president had arranged a reception at the White House and at 9:30 p.m. heard shouting and knew his most important guest had arrived. The crowd separated as the president came forward, extending his hand, and said, "Why, here is General Grant! Well, this is a great pleasure, I assure you."[12]

Lincoln stood eight inches taller than Grant, and for a moment the two men took the measure of each other. After exchanging greetings, Grant entered the East Room to sudden cheers that made him "hot and blushing with embarrassment." Lincoln told Grant, who was about five feet eight inches tall and weighed about 135 pounds, to stand on a sofa to avoid being trampled as guests approached to shake his hand. Noah Brooks spoke of the crowd as "the only real mob I ever saw in the White House." Grant broke into a sweat because nothing in his psyche prepared him for the swarming politicians. The president let Grant endure the hassle for an hour before taking him into the Blue Room for a private discussion.[13]

Lincoln attempted to prepare the general for the following day's formal commissioning ceremony and give him time to prepare a response. After witnessing the reception, Lincoln grew concerned about Grant's ability to speak in public. He read four sentences he intended to reread when conferring the general's third star and informed Grant it would be acceptable to write an acceptance speech and read it. He cautioned Grant to not say anything that might make other generals jealous and to say something positive to establish "good terms" with the Army of the Potomac. When Grant replied, "I can be ready in thirty minutes," Lincoln said the ceremony must wait until tomorrow's cabinet meeting.[14]

After meeting at the War Department in the morning, Grant entered the White House at 1:00 p.m. with Halleck and Stanton and came face-to-face with the cabinet. Lincoln appointed Grant lieutenant general in four sentences, and Grant, after his voice failed, drew himself up and read three barely legible sentences scrawled on a half-sheet of paper: "Mr. President, I accept this commission with gratitude for the high honor conferred. With the aid of the noble armies that have fought on so many fields for our common country, it will be my earnest endeavor not to disappoint your expectations. I feel the full weight of the responsibilities now devolving on me; and I know that if they are met, it will be due to those armies." Grant never mentioned Lincoln's points, nor did he say anything about the Army of the Potomac.

Nicolay attended the ceremony and thought Grant's response "could hardly have been improved." Looking for reasons to explain why Grant had ignored the president's points, Nicolay decided that everyone from Stanton on down had given him advice, and Grant, "with his deep distrust of Washington politicians . . . thought it wise to disregard all their suggestions," even those of the president.[15]

After the ceremony Grant asked what special service the president expected of him. Lincoln said the country wanted the Confederate army defeated and asked if Grant could do it. The general replied he could if he had the troops. Lincoln promised Grant whatever he needed. Neither man mentioned plans or strategies. When a personal friend asked Lincoln whether he had given Grant too much power, the president replied, "Do you hire a man to do your work and then do it yourself?" After the meeting Halleck asked to be relieved as general-in-chief and recommended the title be "imposed upon" Grant. Lincoln granted the request, relieved Halleck, and by law transferred all military authority to Grant.[16]

Grant departed for Brandy Station, Virginia, to meet Meade, whom he remembered vaguely from the Mexican War. Meade greeted Grant magnanimously, offered to step aside, and suggested he be replaced by Sherman. Grant informed Meade no thought had been given to making changes and said Sherman could not be spared. Satisfied he could work with Meade, Grant returned to Washington.[17]

Grant trusted no general more completely than Sherman, and on reaching Washington he found a letter from him, warning: "Do not stay in Washington. Halleck is better qualified than you to stand the buffets of intrigue and policy." At Corinth, Mississippi, Sherman had once warned Halleck to stay clear of Washington, but Old Brains ignored the advice. Grant's three days in the capital were enough to convince him Sherman was right. By then he had changed his mind on how to conduct the war. He understood the importance of staying near the capital but not in it, and this decision was undoubtedly influenced by Lincoln.[18]

On March 11 Grant returned to Nashville, put Sherman in charge of Western forces, and stated his decision to establish supreme headquarters with the Army of the Potomac. During Grant's return to Washington on March 18, Sherman traveled with him as far as Cincinnati. They discussed how Sherman's and Meade's forces could mesh in bringing the war to and end. Johnston's army and Atlanta became Sherman's objective, while Lee's army and Richmond remained Meade's objective. Grant wanted General Banks's program to include the capture of Mobile, but for the present the Red River expedition was too far advanced to stop.[19]

When Grant made the Army of the Potomac his headquarters, Halleck became chief of staff and remained in Washington to provide communication and coordination between Grant, the administration, and generals in the field. Lincoln wanted Halleck involved, mindful in 1863 that Old Brains had once said, "Gen. Grant is a copious worker, and fighter, but a very meager writer, or telegrapher." Halleck's new job suited him. As historian T. Harry Williams observed, Halleck possessed a unique talent "of being able to communicate civilian ideas to a soldier and military ideas to a civilian and make them both understand what he was [saying]." This worked well because Halleck interpreted Lincoln's strategic concepts to Grant and Grant's military jargon to the president. Hence, Halleck became the official middleman between Grant and Lincoln. Because Grant could be anywhere at any time, he asked for John Rawlins be raised to brigadier general as his chief of staff in the field. The Senate could not fathom why Grant needed two generals as chiefs of staff, but somebody had to do the paperwork in the field, and Grant, after exerting pressure on the Senate, got his way. The chief of staff arrangement, which Stanton helped achieve, created a Union command system far superior to anything devised prior to modern warfare. More than anyone else, Halleck made it work. Grant could keep in direct telegraphic communication with Washington, and the two chiefs of staff, Halleck at the War Department and Rawlins at army headquarters, could keep in communication with seventeen different commands in the field, which in early 1864 contained 533,000 men. Without Halleck and Rawlins, Grant would have been buried under paperwork and unable to run the war, and both men knew Grant well enough to interpret what he wanted.[20]

Grant rarely wrote to Lincoln. Stanton and Halleck had warned Grant not to reveal his plans to the president, but Lincoln had covered that point, writing, "The particulars of your plans I neither know, nor seek to know. You are vigilant and self-reliant; and, pleased with this, I wish not to obtrude any constraints . . . upon you." Lincoln merely asked to be informed on strategy so he could use his considerable influence providing the army with resources. The president had already shaped a broad strategy, which Grant summed up to Meade, writing, "Lee's army will be your objective point. Wherever Lee goes, there you will go also." Two political generals were to play roles on the flanks. General Franz Sigel, a favorite among German-American voters, would press up the Shenandoah Valley and approach Richmond from the west as General Benjamin Butler, a favorite among Democrats, would ascend the James River and cut Lee's supply lines at Petersburg. In the West Sherman would move against Johnston's army protecting Atlanta at the same time Meade struck Lee, and Banks would capture Mobile and join Sherman in Georgia. Grant named May 5 as D-day for launching the combined campaigns. Lincoln had finally found a general who after three years of war thought like himself and believed in a strategy of concerted attack. Hay recalled the president consistently recommending to others the importance of moving all forces "at once upon the enemy's whole line so as to bring into action to our advantage our great superiority in numbers," only to have the suggestion "constantly neglected." After agreeing on the right strategy, Grant now had to make it work.[21]

The Committee on the Conduct of War continued to press for Meade's removal, but Stanton argued that because Congress had entrusted Grant with supreme command, they should not interfere with his decisions. Meade remained the tactical commander, Grant the strategic commander. Although Meade commanded the Army of the Potomac, Grant went with it and made the decisions. His orders went directly to and through Meade and seldom to Meade's subordinates. General Joshua Humphreys, Meade's chief of staff, did not like the arrangement and said, "There were two officers commanding the same army. Such a mixed command was not calculated to produce the best results." When questioned about having Grant looking over his shoulder, Meade told Humphreys, "I am glad of it. The Government will support General Grant. You make a mistake. General Grant is a man of very great ability." Not all generals agreed, but relations between Grant and Meade remained mutually supportive. Grant later named Meade and Sherman as the two most capable commanders of large armies.[22]

Grant established headquarters at Culpeper Court House, began preparing for the spring campaign, and consolidated the cavalry under Major General Philip Sheridan. Stanton objected when Grant began drawing troops from unthreatened areas, such as Washington. Grant went to Washington, took Stanton to the White House, and argued his case before the president. Lincoln listened and sided with Grant: "You and I, Mr. Stanton, have been trying to boss this job, and we have not succeeded very well with it. We have sent across the mountains for Mr. Grant, as Mrs. Grant calls him, to relieve us, and I think we had better leave him alone to do as he pleases."[23]

Unlike other generals, Grant intended to use the entire strength of the army, a measure Lincoln had been advocating since Bull Run. Manpower again became a concern because three-year enlistments were to expire. Those battle-hardened veterans represented the core of the army, and Stanton doubted whether the war could be won without them. After calling on loyal governors to encourage volunteer enlistment for a one million–man army, Stanton attempted to induce reenlistments by offering veterans a four hundred dollar bonus, a thirty-day furlough, a special chevron identifying them as veteran volunteers, and the right to retain the same regimental number for the balance of the war. Some 136,000 men took the bait, and Stanton deserved full credit for finding a way to bring the government through another crisis.[24]

The strategy designed by Lincoln and Grant for the spring campaign made perfect sense but only on paper. Lincoln had previously placed three of the Union's worst performing generals—Banks, Butler, and Sigel—into the plan with predictable results. In the Department of West Virginia, Sigel commanded 36,000 men, most of whom he stationed at Harpers Ferry. Butler had been idle at Fort Monroe but now commanded the Army of the James, which in May numbered 39,000 men. Banks commanded 110,000 men in the Department of the Gulf, which included 36,000 men borrowed from Sherman. The plan called for everyone to begin operations at the beginning of May. Banks demonstrated his ineptitude during the Red River campaign and suffered an embarrassing defeat by a small Confederate force ably led by Major General Richard Taylor, son of President Zachary Taylor. Sigel performed no better, being repulsed on May 15 at New Market by a small force of Confederates partly composed of cadets from the Virginia Military Institute. On May 5 Butler put his troops ashore at Bermuda Hundred and allowed them to become bottled up behind a narrow neck of land by a small Confederate force.[25]

On May 21 Lincoln recalled Sigel with Grant's consent and replaced him with David Hunter. At the time, Grant was too busy fighting to evaluate Hunter's credentials but expected him to be more competent than Sigel. Hunter proved to be no more adept than Sigel at executing orders. Defeated at Lynchburg, Hunter vanished with his army into West Virginia and could not be found.[26]

After Banks bungled the Red River expedition, Grant authorized his removal. Lincoln balked at first because Banks, like Butler, was an important political figure and removing him in an election year might cost votes. Grant agreed to retain Banks in Louisiana if he were put under the command of "some good officer." He even suggested Halleck go to New Orleans and take charge until a suitable officer could be named, but Old Brains refused to leave Washington. Grant would not shelve Banks at the president's displeasure, but Lincoln, unwilling to be an obstructionist, agreed to remove Banks if Grant considered doing so a military necessity and would name a replacement. Grant superseded Banks with Major General Edward R. S. Canby, a forty-six-year-old veteran who had been wasted serving as assistant adjutant general in Washington for the past two years. Grant agreed to leave Banks in Louisiana as Canby's subordinate, and Lincoln approved the arrangement. Banks resigned and returned to a career he understood, politics.[27]

On April 30, as Grant prepared to move across the Rapidan, the president dispatched a friendly letter emphasizing his "entire satisfaction with what you have done up to this time" and promised anything "within my power to give." Lincoln knew nothing about Grant's plans, but he now had a general whose word he could trust. Grant's replies were so unlike those issued by former commanders. Instead of complaining about having too few men or sore-tongued horses, Grant thanked the president for his support and said, "Should my success be less than I desire, and expect, the least I can say is, the fault is not with you."[28]

On May 4 elements from the 122,000-man Army of the Potomac moved into the Wilderness—the old Chancellorsville battlefield—and probed the flanks of Lee's 62,000-man army. Grant avoided complicated maneuvers and relied on hard, head-to-head fighting. For Lincoln the Army of the Potomac disappeared from sight. He heard nothing from Grant, only conflicting rumors from unknown sources. Stanton nervously paced, waiting for the War Department's telegraph to break silence. The secretary's uneasiness became infectious. Worry spread that Grant's report, when it came, would be like McClellan's or Hooker's, signaling failure. The only firsthand information came from Henry Wing, a young *New York Tribune* reporter who witnessed the first day's battle in the Wilderness. Stanton brought him to Washington on a special train and learned there had been terrible slaughter but nothing more. Wing gave Lincoln a short verbal message from Grant: "He told me to tell you, Mr. President, that there would be no turning back." According to historian Ida Tarbell, "Lincoln threw his arms about the boy and kissed him." Welles recalled that on May 7 Lincoln had been so troubled over rumors he could not sleep but relaxed after speaking with Wing. When serenaders appeared on the White House lawn, Lincoln came to the portico and said, "I will volunteer to say that I am very glad at what has happened, but there is a great deal still to be done." The president, however, had still not heard from Grant.[29]

On May 9 Stanton received Grant's first dispatch: "More desperate fighting has not been witnessed on this continent than that of the 5th and 6th of May." The slaughter in the Wilderness ended with heavy losses on both sides, and the campaign had just begun. Lincoln winced at the army's fourteen thousand casualties. Grant tried to force Lee into the open by marching around his flank but on May 8 found Confederates waiting at Spotsylvania.

He might have bypassed Lee, but Grant came to fight. Lincoln read the report and said, "How near we have been to this thing before and failed. I believe if any other general had been at the head of that army it would now have been on this side of the Rapidan. It is the dogged pertinacity of Grant that wins." Spotsylvania became a ten-day slugfest not altogether favorable to the Army of the Potomac, but Grant said, "I will fight it out on this line if it takes all summer." Such messages made marvelous publicity, and Stanton lost no time handing Grant's reports to the press. Losses piled up. Grant reported another sixteen thousand casualties. In two weeks Grant lost more than thirty thousand men, 25 percent of his force. If this was the only way to whip Lee, Grant resolved to do it. As Lincoln remarked later, "The great thing about Grant . . . is his perfect coolness and persistency of purpose. I judge he is not easily excited, which is a great element in an officer, and he has the *grit* of a bulldog! Once let him get his 'teeth' *in,* and nothing can shake him off."[30]

Lincoln remained optimistic, but the casualties staggered him. When Schuyler Colfax stopped at the White House, he found the president deeply depressed, with "his long arms behind his back, his dark features contracted still more with gloom; and as he looked up, I thought his face the saddest one I had ever seen." Lincoln peered grimly at Colfax and said, "Could we have avoided this terrible bloody war! Was it not forced upon us! Is it ever to end!" Reflecting on past reverses, Lincoln cheered up and said, "Grant will not fail us now; he says he will fight it out on that line, and this is now the hope of the country." To relieve his mind, Lincoln went to the opera. "People may think strange of it," he told Colfax, "but I must have some relief from this terrible anxiety, or it will kill me."[31]

As summer approached, Lee countered every attempt made by Grant to flank the Confederate army. In a succession of bloody battles lasting more than a month and costing the Army of the Potomac fifty-five thousand casualties, Grant bent Lee's lines but never broke them. Butler's Army of the James, which was to have drawn troops from Lee's army, utterly failed. Because Lee would not fight a decisive battle, as Grant had hoped, and because Butler did nothing, Grant tried once more to force Lee into the open by driving south of Richmond, seizing Petersburg, and assimilating Butler's force. Grant informed Lincoln of his intention to cross the James and change his base, and the president approved the movement, replying, "I begin to see it; you will succeed. God bless you all."[32]

One evening when riding to the Soldier's Home, Lincoln observed long lines of ambulances flowing into Arlington. He encountered Isaac Arnold, a longtime friend, and, pointing across the river, said, "Look yonder at those poor fellows. I cannot bear it. This suffering, this loss of life is dreadful." Arnold replied, "This too will pass away. Never fear. Victory will come." "Yes," Lincoln replied, "victory will come, but it comes too slowly."[33]

In June victory eluded Grant again when his generals disappointed him with a sloppily executed assault, giving Lee just enough time to rush troops to Petersburg. The stalled assault worried Lincoln. Instead of a successful summer campaign, he anticipated a protracted siege. On June 20 he traveled to City Point, Grant's new headquarters on the James, and found the general mildly disappointed by the performance of the army but completely confident Lee would be whipped that summer. The president reviewed the troops and returned to Washington in better spirits. Bates reported the president pleased with Grant's "persistent confidence" and convinced the general would press forward until the job was finished.[34]

Having merged Butler's army into Meade's, Grant inherited a new problem. Because no one in the Army of the Potomac other than himself outranked Butler, Grant worried if he became disabled Butler would assume command. Grant felt uncomfortable relieving Butler, a popular Democrat, because of political ramifications for Lincoln. Expecting Halleck, who despised Butler, to bring the problem to the president's attention, he suggested Butler be reassigned to a military department not engaged in military operations. Halleck said nothing to Lincoln but agreed Butler should be relieved. "As General B[utler] claims to rank me," said Halleck, "I shall give him no orders . . . without the special direction of yourself or the Secretary of War." Halleck did suggest downgrading the Army of the James to a corps and sending Butler to Fort Monroe. Butler would still be under Grant's command but no longer part of the Army of the Potomac.[35]

Grant took Halleck's advice and asked him to get an order from Lincoln authorizing the change. Halleck drafted the order and presented it to Lincoln, who approved it, but, after reconsidering the political fallout from having the order go out in his name, told Grant to sign it. Butler learned of the scheme from friends in Washington and moved to stop it. He confronted Grant at City Point and threatened to turn the Republican convention against the president. Not wanting to damage Lincoln's prospects, Grant never issued the order.[36]

In two months Grant severely damaged Lee's army and drove it into entrenchments protecting Richmond and Petersburg. For nine months Lee's army withered away on the Petersburg line. General Humphreys assessed the situation correctly, writing, "Move as we might, long-continued, hard fighting under great difficulties was before us."[37]

Sherman had also been busy. He launched the Atlanta campaign at the same time Grant moved into the Wilderness. Sherman's campaign became one of relentless pounding against Johnston's defensive wizardry. Sherman reached the outskirts of Atlanta a few days after Grant reached the outskirts of Petersburg. Meade's forces had nowhere to go but through or around Lee's entrenchments and stalled. When Sherman reached Atlanta, he experienced a similar situation and spent the summer flanking the city's defenses. Both generals understood their tasks. The purpose, said Grant, was "to hammer continuously against the armed force of the enemy and his resources until by mere attrition . . . there should be nothing left of him."[38]

CHAPTER 19

"It was best to not swap horses when crossing streams"

Lincoln believed his odds of winning the presidential nomination for a second term would be determined by the spring campaign of 1864, followed by rapid progress ending the war. He became concerned on June 19, when Grant laid siege to Petersburg. Democrat Congressman Samuel "Sunset" Cox of Ohio said "Grant's failure or seeming failure" to subdue the South increased peace sentiment among a war-weary public and thought McClellan could bring peace. Little Mac, however, could not decide whether to be a peace Democrat or a war Democrat, and his comments confounded both wings of the party. He lost support of peace Democrats on June 15, when in a speech he said the rebellion "cannot be justified upon ethical grounds, and the only alternatives for our choice are its suppression or the destruction of our nationality." Democrats had chosen July 4 and Chicago for the convention, but when the Petersburg stalemate began, they saw an opportunity to improve McClellan's popularity by delaying the convention until August 29. McClellan opposed the postponement, warning Grant or Sherman might yet strike a fatal blow, but the committee went ahead and extended the convention date.[1]

Chase's political aspirations were dashed by his own unseemly involvement with the "Pomeroy Circular." This did not stop radical Republicans from searching for a candidate to unseat the president. Despite heavy fighting in Virginia and Georgia, the presidential election began taking center stage. Polish count Adam Gurowski remarked, "The re-election overawes and submerges everything, even sound and common sense."[2]

From the extremists came a splinter group of ultra abolitionists called the "Radical Democracy," which unified around a common hatred of Lincoln. On May 31 the party convened in Cleveland and nominated General John C. Frémont president and General John Cochrane of New York vice president. That Frémont should be found among the Lincoln haters surprised no one. According to James Gordon Bennett of the *New York Herald,* the object of the Radical Democracy Party "is not the election of Frémont, but the defeat of Lincoln." Frémont gave a short acceptance speech, adding, "*If Mr. Lincoln should be nominated* . . . there will remain no other alternative but to organize against him every element of conscientious opposition with the view to prevent the misfortune of his re-election." He found support in New York and St. Louis and among Germans, but even the most outspoken abolitionists did not believe Frémont could beat Lincoln.[3]

Meanwhile, a small group of influential New Yorkers attempted to put Grant before the country as the next president. They set June 4 aside as the day to hold a mass meeting "without distinction of party" on Union Square to express their gratitude to the general "for his signal services in conducting the National armies to victory." Congressman Frederick A. Conkling invited Lincoln to attend the rally, without revealing the underlying purpose. Lincoln sidestepped the trap, although he probably never expected one. He sent his regrets along with a carefully prepared letter praising Grant's progress. The general had earlier expressed no interest in arraying himself in political opposition to the administration, and the president's sagacious recognition of the general's deeds turned the meeting into a mass movement in support of Lincoln.[4]

Lincoln took no perceptible measures to promote his own candidacy. Once, when referring to the general as a possible presidential candidate, he said, "If Grant could be more useful than I in putting down the rebellion, I would be quite content. He is fully committed to the policy of emancipation and employing Negro soldiers; and with this policy faithfully carried out, it will not make much difference who is president." Lincoln often quipped, "If [Grant] takes Richmond, let him have it," meaning the presidential nomination, while Grant assured reporters, "Lincoln is just the man of all others whom the country needs, and his defeat would be a great national calamity." On the eve of the Republican convention both men suffered criticism when the press revealed that in twenty minutes the Army of the Potomac had lost seven thousand men in killed and wounded at Cold Harbor.[5]

Efforts to prevent Lincoln's renomination continued until June 7, the date scheduled for the Republican National Convention. As the day approached, visitors besieged the president. "The Radicals are here in great force," wrote Edward Bates, accusing some of being "in an awkward quandary" or going "'a whoring after' Frémont." Lincoln also had many supporters, including McClure, Raymond, Swett, Weed, and even Cameron, whose political enemies all happened to be radicals.[6]

Friends offered to represent the president's wishes at the convention, but Lincoln casually told them to do what was best for the country. When asked about his choice of a running mate, he dodged the question. He did ask Senator Edwin D. Morgan of New York, chairman of the national committee, to include in the keynote speech and the platform an "amendment of the Constitution abolishing and prohibiting slavery forever." The request appeased many radical delegates who opposed him.[7]

Horace Greeley fought Lincoln's nomination and thought the convention should be delayed two months. When nothing happened, Lincoln haters of the Grand Council of the Union League arrived in Baltimore two days early to undermine Lincoln's nomination. The membership included congressmen, senators, war Democrats, and radicals wanting to draft Grant by persuading delegates to put his name before the convention. They worried when Jim Lane, the notorious Jayhawker and senator from Kansas, showed up unexpectedly and insisted on speaking. The audience gave a shudder because Lane, always an unpredictable and fiery orator, had lately been seen at the White House. He warmed up quickly, soon had his audience on the edge of their seats, and said any nomination other than Lincoln's would be tantamount to nominating McClellan, and to nominate anyone other than Lincoln would destroy the Republican Party and the Union, reinstate the Confederacy, repudiate emancipation, and dishonor the men who had given their lives for freedom. Lane kicked the traces from under the Union League and killed the movement to draft Grant.[8]

On June 7, when the convention opened in Baltimore's Front Street Theatre, most issues had been settled. Every delegate voted for Lincoln on the first ballot but twenty-two anti-Blair radicals from Missouri, who cast theirs for Grant. Finding themselves without support, they changed their votes and nominated Lincoln unanimously. Referring to the Missourians' behavior, Bates wrote, "They were all instructed to vote for Mr. Lincoln, but many of them hated to do it. . . . I shall tell the Prest . . . that his best nomination is not at Baltimore, but his nomination spontaneously, by the People, by which the convention was constrained to name him."[9]

Selecting a running mate became the delegates' most hectic task. Hamlin sought renomination, but he differed politically with the president's policies and won the radical's endorsement. Despite Lincoln's public declaration to the Baltimore delegation of his "wish not to interfere about V.P.," he did encourage a few Pennsylvanians to consider Andrew Johnson of Tennessee, a war Democrat and the military governor of that state. Earlier he had once mentioned Butler.[10]

Lincoln expected a close election and believed a war Democrat, as a matter of practical politics, would bolster the ticket. McClure knew Lincoln wanted Johnson, and if he knew, then others must have known. McClure later claimed he went to the convention with Lamon, who carried a confidential letter from Lincoln endorsing Johnson's nomination with instructions never to show the letter unless it became necessary. According to Edward S. Bradley, Cameron's biographer, the Pennsylvania powerbroker set the stage for Johnson's nomination. Bradley called it a "model for political strategists" to emulate. Cameron created the impression of endorsing Hannibal Hamlin while actually piloting the proceedings toward Johnson. In a secret caucus with Pennsylvania delegates he arranged for a complimentary vote to be cast for Hamlin followed by a quick switch to Johnson. Only Thad Stevens dissented. When Chairman William Dennison called the first ballot for vice president, Cameron presented Hamlin's name on "instruction" from the state and cast a unit vote. Before the tally Cameron took control of the floor, rescinded the vote for Hamlin, and cast all fifty-two votes for Johnson. Cameron's action threw the convention into an uproar. Stevens turned to McClure and said, "Can't you find a candidate for Vice-President in the United States, without going down to one of those damned rebel provinces to pick one?" When Jim Lane made Kansas unanimous for Johnson, other states followed. Hamlin never realized Cameron had tricked him. A few days later he sent the hoodwinker a letter thanking Pennsylvania for supporting him.[11]

Lincoln and fifty-five-year-old Andrew Johnson made strange teammates but had much in common. Both men were born a few weeks apart in log cabins to poor parents. Lincoln received a year of formal education, Johnson none. Both men lost a parent while still in their youth. Johnson apprenticed to a tailor; Lincoln clerked in a store. Johnson went into local politics; Lincoln began studying law. Both men were gifted with intelligence and found constructive ways of applying it. Johnson rose swiftly in politics, becoming a congressman from Tennessee in 1843, governor in 1853, and senator in 1856. Lincoln became active in politics but never matched Johnson's political accomplishments until elected president. In politics, however, Lincoln had less in common with Johnson, who had been a staunch Jacksonian Democrat his entire life. But in 1847, while serving in Congress, they both voted for the Wilmot Proviso, a bill to forbid the extension of slavery in the territories. Lincoln was no longer in the House when in 1850 Johnson took the floor and shouted, "The preservation of the Union is paramount to all other considerations." In 1861 rebellion brought the two men together on the same great issue. When Tennessee seceded, Johnson remained loyal and became the only senator from the South to retain his seat in the Senate until his term expired. When Lincoln made Johnson military governor of Tennessee, he could not have picked a more determined fighter to drag the state back into the Union. Johnson exemplified the meaning of war Democrat. He would not back down to anyone and would, if required, roll up his sleeves and whack a few noses.[12]

The other issue addressed by delegates involved the party platform, which endorsed the president's course in conducting the war, called for the suppression of the rebellion by force of arms, and approved Lincoln's call for a Thirteenth Amendment to the Constitution extirpating slavery "from the soil of the United States." The radicals added a plank calling for harmony in the cabinet, which was their way of saying Chase and Stanton were meaningfully motivated but Bates, Blair, and Seward were obstructionists and should be replaced. Lincoln had not ruled out changes in the cabinet but not to gratify the radicals.

On June 9 the president received a visit from the National Union League and, in thanking the group for support, told a story: "I have not permitted myself, gentlemen, to conclude that I am the best man in the country; but I am reminded, in this connection, of a story of an old Dutch farmer, who once remarked that 'it was best to not swap horses when crossing streams.'" Lincoln, however, was about to swap a few horses.[13]

When Senator Samuel C. Pomeroy issued his "strictly private" circular in late February 1864, extolling the virtues of Chase and sharply criticizing Lincoln, he put wheels in motion for the first major change in the cabinet since the exit of Cameron. The circular thrust Chase in the perceived position of double-dealing against the president. Chase disclaimed all prior knowledge of the circular and submitted his resignation. During a cabinet meeting Welles observed Stanton and Seward chatting in a corner, reveling over Chase's self-induced humiliation. Rather than encourage a storm of criticism for ousting the finance minister over the incident, Lincoln retained Chase despite the strained relationship.[14]

Lincoln's nomination made Chase vulnerable. The cost of paying for the war, combined with Congress's reluctance to boost revenues, frustrated Chase. Because he needed someone to blame, he directed his hostility toward Lincoln by avoiding cabinet meetings. When criticized by Frank Blair in Congress, Chase erroneously blamed the president. To nurse his wounded pride he began writing nonsensical letters to friends, among them: "It seems as if there were no limit to expense. The spigot in Uncle Abe's barrel is made twice as big as a bung-hole." Chase still believed the president conspired against him. He wanted revenge by defeating Lincoln at the polls but had no way of doing it. Stuffing patronage with supporters who might aid his election backfired. Whitelaw Reid, a *Cincinnati Gazette* correspondent who did not like Lincoln, nonetheless summed up Chase's greatest weakness as being "profoundly ignorant of men" and easy prey for "charlatans" and "deceivers."[15]

Lincoln no longer needed Chase in the cabinet and tried to let him down easily. He never lost confidence in his Treasury secretary's capabilities, but he lost faith in Chase's appointments. Before the situation worsened, Lincoln told Massachusetts representative Samuel Hooper he still held Chase in high esteem and intended to appoint him chief justice of the Supreme Court. Hooper neglected to inform Chase until several days later, and Chase continued making patronage appointments to annoy the president.[16]

A crisis occurred in late May, when John J. Cisco, the veteran assistant treasurer in New York City, resigned effective June 30, which corresponded with the close of the fiscal year. Cisco's position ranked next to Chase's in importance, and the president expected the secretary to appoint a financial expert and not a radical supporter. Instead, Chase named Maunsell B. Field, a friend and previous patronage appointee who had no experience raising money. When New Yorkers protested the appointment, Chase planted his feet. He had four weeks to change his mind but on June 27 stubbornly forwarded Field's nomination to the president.[17]

Perplexed by Chase's inflexibility, Lincoln sent a note, writing, "I can not without much embarrassment make this appointment." He explained the reasons why, asked Chase to reconsider, and suggested the names of three qualified New Yorkers provided by Senator Edwin D. Morgan. Chase refused and demanded a meeting. Lincoln replied that a verbal conversation would not likely change his mind and reminded Chase of two previous appointments that brought New Yorkers to the "verge of open revolt." Lincoln said accepting Field as assistant treasurer would only lead to "greater strain" and vetoed it.[18]

Rather than bend to the president's request, Chase implored Cisco to remain in office another three months. According to John Hay, "This was most welcome news to the president." Chase, however, believed "the President had behaved badly and must be subjected to some discipline." His patent formula for punishing the president was to resign. Lincoln found the resignation stuffed with some papers in his pocket. "[My] position here is not altogether agreeable to you," wrote Chase, "and it is certainly too full of embarrassment and difficulty . . . to allow me in the least desire to retain it." Tired of Chase's antics, Lincoln replied on the morning of June 30, "Your resignation . . . is accepted. Of all I have said in commendation of your ability and fidelity, I have nothing to unsay; and yet you and I have reached a point of mutual embarrassment in our official relation which it seems can not be overcome, or longer sustained."[19]

A messenger looking for Senator William Pitt Fessenden found him in a conference with Chase at the Capitol and asked to speak with him privately. Fessenden returned and said, "Have you resigned? I am called to the Senate and told that the President has sent in the nomination of your successor." Chase was flabbergasted. He admitted tendering his resignation but had not yet heard from the president. Chase departed for the Treasury Department and found Lincoln's acceptance letter among the papers on his desk. He seemed unable to comprehend that Lincoln's renomination for the presidency had reshaped the political arena and old tactics no longer worked. After digesting the bad news, Chase received a belated visit from Hooper, who explained the president intended to name him chief justice. The secretary may have forgotten, but Lincoln remembered an earlier conversation when Chase said he would rather be "Chief Justice of the United States than hold any other position that could be given me." For all his wisdom and ability, the one person Chase never understood was the president.[20]

Lincoln waited until the morning of June 30 to notify the secretary. Meanwhile, on the way to the War Department, he encountered Ohio governor John Brough. Lincoln mentioned Chase's resignation and said he had made up his mind to accept it. Brough urged Lincoln to wait, offering to mediate the matter and "get the Ohio men" together in the morning. Lincoln replied, "But this is the third time he has thrown this at me, and I do not think I am called on to continue to beg him to take it back, especially when the country would not go to destruction in consequence. . . . On the whole, Brough, I reckon you had better let it alone this time."[21]

Lincoln acted swiftly. Without consulting anyone, he sent the name of former Ohio governor David Tod to the Senate Committee on Finance, which Fessenden headed. Asked by Hay why he picked Tod, Lincoln replied, "He is my friend, with a big head full of brains." Washburne beat the finance committee to the White House to protest Tod's nomination, saying, "It is a great disaster," without explaining why. Soon Fessenden arrived with the entire finance committee. They began by objecting to making any change and then pointed to the real problem—Tod's inexperience and his opposition to the paper money financing the war. In July 1864 the public debt stood at $1.7 billion, more than $600 million greenbacks were in circulation, the cost of war topped $3 million a day, and Chase had recalled a loan of $32 million in June because of low bids. Tod solved the problem by removing his name, stating poor health.[22]

On July 1 Lincoln prepared a note nominating fifty-seven-year-old Senator Fessenden, a radical from Portland, Maine, to the Treasury but had not told him. Fessenden happened to be waiting in the anteroom to recommend Hugh McCulloch for the post. Lincoln told Hay to "send him [Fessenden] in & go at once to the Senate." Ushered into the office, Fessenden began explaining the virtues of McCulloch as secretary. Lincoln listened with amusement and during a lull in the conversation told Fessenden what he had done. Fessenden sprang to his feet, "You must withdraw it. I cannot accept." The president replied, "If you decline, you must do it in open day, for I shall not recall the nomination." Fessenden returned to the Senate intent on quashing his nomination, only to discover it had already unanimously passed. Lincoln was equally surprised at the swiftness of Fessenden's confirmation, commenting, "It is very singular, considering that this appointment of F[essenden]'s is so popular when made, that no one ever mentioned his name to me for that place."[23]

Fessenden went directly to his room to write a letter of declination. While inking his pen, delegations from the House and Senate arrived urging him to accept. Fessenden clearly did not want the job. He finished the letter and took it to the White House. Learning the president had gone to bed, he waited until morning. When meeting on July 2, Lincoln spied a note in Fessenden's hand and said, "If it was a letter declining to accept the Treasury, he would not receive it," adding, "The crisis was such as demanded any sacrifice, even life itself." He asked Fessenden to wait until Congress adjourned, and the senator agreed.[24]

Fessenden suffered permanent physical disabilities from an 1857 illness, which left him with a disagreeable disposition. Like Tod, he opposed the issuance of greenbacks but by mid-1864 agreed the measure was necessary. He also had two sons serving in the army, which gave him a stake in the outcome of the war. One son, Colonel Francis Fessenden of the Thirtieth Maine Infantry Regiment, had lost a leg during the Red River campaign, which did nothing to improve the senator's disposition. Caught in a dilemma not of his choosing, he asked advice of Stanton, who said, "You can no more refuse than your son could have refused to attack Monett's Bluff, and you cannot look him in the face if you do." Fessenden choked, certain the job would kill him. "Very well," Stanton replied, "you cannot die better than in trying to save your country." Correspondence flowed from across the country urging Fessenden to stop stalling. "For your country's sake, I beg you to accept the charge," wrote the head of the New York Clearing House. Fessenden noticed that immediately after the Senate approved his nomination, government bonds advanced, commodities dropped in price, and gold, having opened early at $250, closed at $220.[25]

On July 4 Fessenden sat with the president and reached agreement. He held a letter from Senator James W. Grimes of Iowa with a piece of advice: "Get rid of Mr. Chase's agents as soon as possible. I believe many of them are corrupt, and whether they be so or not they are thought to be, and that is a sufficient reason for supplanting them with new men." With that in mind, Fessenden asked for complete control of the Treasury. Lincoln agreed not to retain people in the department whom Fessenden did not want, and the new Treasury secretary agreed not to fill vacancies with individuals against whom the president would likely disapprove.[26]

Chase agreed to help in the transfer of responsibility, and when Fessenden mentioned Lincoln's request not to "remove any friends of Governor Chase unless there should be a real necessity for it," Chase "persuaded himself" into believing he would not have resigned had he known this. When Chase resigned, Lucius Chittenden, registrar of the Treasury, wailed, "Who can fill his place? There is not a man in the Union who can do it. I repeat it— Secretary Chase is to-day a national necessity." Later, as the months passed, Chittenden noted that Fessenden's appointment "was entirely satisfactory, and the affairs of the Treasury went on so smoothly that no change in the financial policy . . . was attempted; and from this time until the resignation of Mr. Fessenden [in March 1865] there was no further friction between the Treasury Department and the Executive."[27]

The Fourth of July marked the beginning of Fessenden's service as secretary of the Treasury, but it also marked the end of the first session of the Thirty-eighth Congress. The session accomplished little constructive legislation and ended in a conspiracy against the president having absolutely nothing to do with the resignation of Chase.

The radical movement gathering so much steam before the convention traced back to the president's December 8, 1863, annual message to Congress. His ideas on reconstruction, appended by a proclamation guaranteeing amnesty to almost everyone involved in the rebellion, and his 10 percent plan for reestablishing loyal state governments, met with instant condemnation. Nothing in the document exceeded Lincoln's constitutional powers or violated the act of July 17, 1862, authorizing the president to "at any time by proclamation, extend pardon and amnesty to persons participating in the Rebellion . . . as he may deem expedient for the public welfare.'" Two years later Winter Davis, an outspoken radical antagonistic toward Lincoln, demanded the act be revised.[28]

Davis never forgave Lincoln for denying him a cabinet post and paid him back by being as contrary and vindictive as possible. Marylanders voted Davis out of the House in 1860 but sent him back in 1863. He became chairman of the House Committee on Foreign Affairs and a radical protégé of seventy-two-year-old Thaddeus Stevens, an old curmudgeon filled with hate. Stevens used young, handsome, and energetic Davis to horsepower the radical program in the House by lumping into foreign affairs the South as a hostile territory to be punished for its crimes against the Union. Fiery and persuasive, Davis often got his way. Noah Brooks called him a "singularly alert and singularly violent politician." The House formed a select committee and put Davis in charge of drafting a counterproposal to Lincoln's Proclamation of Amnesty and Reconstruction.[29]

Not every member of the House agreed with Davis. The controversial bill did not reach the floor for discussion until March 22. It repudiated Lincoln's reconstruction plan, shocked many members of the House, and led to a six-week debate. With reconstruction under way in Arkansas, Louisiana, and Tennessee, Davis intended to stop it. The preamble to his bill demanded the South be punished for "waging an unjust war" and denied citizens from states in rebellion the right to "take any part in the political government of the Union." According to Davis, only Congress had the power to determine reconstruction policy: "Until Congress recognizes a State government organized under its auspices there is no government in the rebel States." The Davis bill took executive powers from the president and transferred them back to Congress. By May 4 the wheels of radicalism, promoted behind the scenes by the nefarious efforts of Stevens and his band, succeeded in passing the bill by an unimpressive margin of seventy-four to fifty-nine.[30]

The Davis bill would never see daylight unless radicals in the Senate agreed, and Ben Wade chaired the Senate committee on territories. With Congress to adjourn on July 4, Davis worried whether Wade would have time to push the measure through the Senate. Davis, however, underestimated Wade's dogged ability to move matters that counted. Wade could not discuss issues regarding the South without emphatically swearing. He cursed the president for usurping congressional authority, and when he encountered opposition bringing the bill to the floor, he waited. In the waning days of June, senators could barely stand the sweltering heat of the chamber and yearned to leave Washington and go home. On June 29, five days before adjournment, Wade obtained his hearing. Two days later he pushed the bill to the floor. During the next twenty-four hours he jammed it through a lightning-quick Senate-House compromise and on July 2 presented it to the gallery as the Wade-Davis Bill. The Senate passed the measure by a vote of eighteen to fourteen, causing Welles to complain, "[Seventeen] members have gone home already" and "do wrong in abandoning their post . . . no one who does it should be trusted."[31]

On July 4 those waiting in the House and Senate for the president's signature heard the clock strike noon, signaling adjournment. They extended the session thirty minutes waiting for word from Chandler, who had gone to the president's room at the Capitol to have the bill signed. Minutes ticked away. Senator George S. Boutwell worried the bill might be pocketed, an unusual tactic seldom employed to prevent undesirable legislation. Mere mention of a pocket veto caused great consternation among waiting radicals. When Chandler entered the president's office to ask if the bill had been signed, Lincoln replied, "Mr. Chandler, this bill was placed before me a few minutes before Congress adjourns. It is a matter of too much importance to be swallowed in that way." Chandler disagreed, arguing that failure to sign the bill would damage Republican support in the Northwest. Lincoln saw through the smokescreen and said he believed the bill overstepped congressional legislative authority. Chandler snapped back, "It is no more than you have done yourself." Turning to leave the room, and convinced the bill would not be signed, he added, "I can only say I deeply regret it." As Chandler departed, Lincoln turned to others in the room and said, "I do not see how any of us now can deny and contradict all we have always said, that Congress has no constitutional power over slavery in the States."[32]

By pocketing the Wade-Davis Bill, Lincoln understood he had drawn battle lines around which branch of the government would control reconstruction. With his legal mind at work, he pointed to a flaw and said, "This bill . . . seems to me to make the fatal admission that States whenever they please may of their own motion dissolve their connection with the Union. If that be true, I am not President, and these gentlemen are not Congress." Failing to understand why an amendment to the Constitution abolishing slavery passed the Senate but failed in the House, Lincoln lamented, "I thought it much better, if it were possible, to restore the Union without the necessity of a violent quarrel among its friends, as to whether certain States have been in or out of the Union during the war: a merely metaphysical question and one unnecessary to be forced into discussion." On returning to the White House with the president, Hay said he doubted whether radicals "would bolt their ticket on a question of metaphysics." Lincoln replied, "If they choose to make a point upon this I do not doubt they can do some harm. They have never been friendly to me & I don't know this will make any special difference. . . . At all events, I must keep some consciousness of being somewhere near right: I must keep some standard of principle fixed within myself."[33]

"To day, at 12:30," Bates noted, "Congress adjourned—God be thanked." After accusing the legislative branch of being leaderless, he added, "They are doing their worst, by practical facts, to put all the revolted States *out of the Union* . . . so that they may govern them, as England governs India."[34]

When Chandler reported Lincoln's comments, bitter hatred crossed Davis's face. As members adjourned, Davis could not leave his desk. He stood defiantly, sweat pouring down his flushed face, his thinning hair tousled and his arms waving, shouting invectives into an emptying chamber. James Blaine of Maine had heard it all before: the "authority of Congress is paramount and must be respected," and the president had no authority to meddle in legislative matters. When Lincoln learned of Davis's outburst, he said, "I have heard that there was insanity in his family; perhaps we might allow the plea in this case."[35]

Although the pocket veto infuriated members of his own party, Lincoln did not want progress in the Southern states undone by a congressional bill stipulating 50 percent voter participation versus the 10 percent margin stated in his proclamation. Nor did he want to alienate the fragile coalition of Republicans and war Democrats upon whom he depended for reelection. Because the president still had several days left to sign the bill, radicals attempted to get his signature by working through Chase. Lincoln waited until July 8 to explain his action in a carefully composed proclamation aimed at calming angry radicals. Rather than criticize Wade or Davis, he admitted being "fully satisfied with the system for restoration contained in the Bill" but did not want to be "inflexibly committed to any single plan of restoration." He agreed, however, to support the bill in any state wishing to adopt it, knowing none would.[36]

Radicals found nothing appeasing about Lincoln's veto explanation. Having called the president's earlier proclamations a usurpation of congressional powers, along came another one justifying the others. "What an infamous proclamation!" Stevens growled. "The idea of pocketing a bill then issuing a proclamation as to how far we will conform to it is matched only by signing a bill and then sending in the veto. . . . But what are we to do?" It made no difference to Stevens that the public accepted the proclamation, as they had the one issued in December, calling it "the wisest and most practical solution for handling the [reconstruction] problem." James Blaine, however, noted that Lincoln's action met with "violent opposition from the more radical members of both Houses," and "a very rancorous hostility would have developed against the President" had Congress been in session.[37]

Davis and Wade sought ways to unseat Lincoln as the Republican candidate and found Horace Greeley amenable to providing the soapbox. On August 5 the *New York Tribune* published in two inflammatory columns the so-called Wade-Davis Manifesto, which Lincoln's secretaries called "the most vigorous . . . attack that was ever directed against the President from his own party." With vicious ferocity the manifesto declared, "A more studied outrage on the legislative authority of the people has never been perpetrated," and charged Lincoln with "grave Executive usurpation. The whole body of Union men of Congress will not submit to be impeached by him of rash and unconstitutional legislation; and if he wishes our support he must confine himself to his executive duties—to obey and execute, not make the laws—to suppress by arms the rebellion, and leave political reorganization to Congress." There was the rub. With election three months away the threat would have made any presidential nominee squirm and Democrats celebrate. The manifesto intended to drive Lincoln from the presidential canvass. The declaration stunned the public and befuddled the president, who reacted with a quizzical comment to Seward, "I would like to know whether these men intend openly to oppose my election—the document looks that way."[38]

Welles recognized the manifesto as an insidious effort to "pull down the President." He observed that "Davis's conduct is not surprising, but I should not have expected that Wade, who has a good deal of patriotic feeling, common sense, though coarse and vulgar mind, would have lent himself to such a despicable assault on the President." Stanton, however, remained on close terms with Davis and Wade, giving rise to speculation he agreed with them, or at least with their legal argument. Stanton had been trying to coax the president toward the center of the party. While the manifesto accurately summarized the position of Congress on reconstruction in 1864, Stanton disagreed with its effort to dethrone Lincoln. He continued to support the president's reconstruction plan, but a year after Lincoln's assassination he told the Senate Judiciary Committee that while his and Lincoln's efforts to create loyal state governments in the South were legal and necessary, he believed reconstruction did belong "to the controlling power of Congress."[39]

Lincoln never read the manifesto, though Seward read it to him, and he felt no obligation to respond. The rancor distressed him, and he expressed his feelings to Noah Brooks: "To be wounded in the house of one's friends is perhaps the most grievous affliction that can befall a man." But, he added, "It is not worth fretting about." But fretting could not be avoided. The president now had two wars to fight in his quest for reelection: one against the Confederacy and the other against the radical leaders of his own party.[40]

CHAPTER 20

"I begin to see it"

War in 1864 did not wait for politics, and in the early weeks of summer Lincoln found himself beleaguered by his own party on one side and horrendous casualties on the other. By July the five-prong grand strategy hatched by Ulysses S. Grant resembled a grand fiasco. The Virginia campaign left the bloodiest trail of all. When on May 5 Grant sent the Army of the Potomac into the Wilderness, he had 120,000 men. The butcher's bill from the Wilderness to the James tallied 54,929 in killed, wounded, captured, and missing—nearly half of the number available at the beginning of the campaign. When Grant complained about the army's heavy casualties, George Meade replied, "Well, General, we can't do these little tricks without losses." Making matters worse, Grant asked Lincoln and Stanton to replace his losses.[1]

Because the War Department censored reports from the field, the public received the bright side of the news. They expected great things from Grant and believed major victories had been won—and why not? The Army of the Potomac was marching to Richmond, pushing Lee back. Headlines reported Grant's accomplishments, and the general could do no wrong until the public saw the butcher's bill. Casualties staggered the imagination, as did gruesome reports from the field of dead soldiers heaped one upon another, of amputated legs and arms piled outside the surgeon's tent, and of the screams and groans of the maimed and dying. In May the first bloodstained cars of wounded rumbled into Washington. National grief and anger intensified. Soldiers' letters home arrived, and some found their way to the press. When news of the slaughter at Cold Harbor reached the public, people began questioning Grant's fitness to command.[2]

In mid-June Grant tried new tactics. He ably executed a swift change of base to the south side of the James River, liberated Butler's army, and picked up thirty thousand effectives. Having maneuvered around Richmond to a base where the army could be supplied by sea, Grant ordered Butler to assault Petersburg, through which three railroads supplied Lee's army and Richmond. "Baldy" Smith's Eighteenth Corps from the Army of the James mishandled the attack, and the blunder extended the war eight months. By the morning of June 16 all of Petersburg's railroads and fortifications should have been in Federal possession. Lee, after being completely deceived by

Grant, rushed forces to Petersburg and repulsed Smith's slipshod assault. Several years later General P. G. T. Beauregard summed up Smith's missed opportunity, writing, "Petersburg at that hour was clearly at the mercy of the Federal commander, who had all but captured it."[3]

With Lee's army occupying Petersburg's trenches, Grant faced the task of strengthening his own defenses and settled into months of siege. Pickets from both sides met after dark between the trenches and established friendships. When Meade learned of the gatherings, he wrote his wife, "I believe these two armies would fraternize and make peace in an hour, if the matter rested with them."[4]

Peace again became a national issue. On July 7 Horace Greeley, after volunteering space in the *New York Tribune* to publish the Wade-Davis Manifesto, informed the president, "I venture to remind you that our bleeding, bankrupt, almost dying country . . . longs for peace." He warned Lincoln to begin peace talks with the Confederacy now or suffer the consequences in the national election. Greeley said he had been contacted by Confederate agents and urged the president to meet with them.

Lincoln offered to study "any proposition of Jefferson Davis in writing" and told Greeley to come immediately with the officials, their credentials, and the document, and he would guarantee safe conduct for all. Greeley had no credible documents, only a letter from two Confederate politicians, Clement C. Clay of Alabama and Jacob Thompson of Mississippi, who lived as expatriates in Canada and were suspected of being rebel spies. After Greeley failed to appear in Washington with the self-appointed emissaries, Lincoln expressed exasperation, writing, "I am disappointed that you have not already reached here with those commissioners." He suspected the publisher had been duped and dispatched John Hay to New York to provide safe conduct to Washington for the Southerners claiming to represent the Confederate government.

Hay arrived in New York, met with Greeley, and advised the president that four Confederate commissioners would be waiting at Niagara, New York. Lincoln replied, "If there is, or is not, anything in the affair, I wish to know it, without unnecessary delay." On the president's authority Hay prepared a document guaranteeing safe conduct for Clay, Thompson, George N. Sanders, and James B. Holcombe and with Greeley boarded a train for Niagara.[5]

During the trip Hay discovered Greeley had few facts pertaining to the meeting and was "a good deal cut up at what he called the president's great mistake in refusing to enter into negotiations without conditions." At the suspension bridge spanning the Niagara River, Greeley met "William Cornell

Jewett of Colorado," who claimed to be the commissioners' intermediary. Greeley handed him Hay's letter guaranteeing safe passage to Washington and containing a provision requiring the commissioners to be "duly accredited from Richmond" to discuss peace.

Jewett never expected the scheme to go this far; neither did Greeley. "As it turned out," wrote Hay, "[Greeley] had been misinformed as . . . none of them had any authority to act in the capacity attributed to them." Realizing he had been deceived, Greeley hurried to New York to publish a handful of documents received from Jewett, leaving Hay behind to negotiate. Later, after Hay returned to the White House, Lincoln invited Greeley to Washington in an effort to prevent the publication of the phony "peace mission" papers. Greeley considered the matter, decided Lincoln was right, and put the documents away until after the president's death. He declined the invitation to come to Washington but agreed to make the trip if Lincoln dismissed Seward.[6]

While Greeley lobbied for peace and radicals schemed against the president, the war took an unexpected detour. On June 12 Lee detached General Jubal A. Early and ten thousand men, half of them barefoot, to curb General David Hunter's depredations in the Shenandoah Valley. After driving Hunter into West Virginia, Early's divisions marched down the Valley Pike, entered Maryland, and levied tribute of $20,000 at Hagerstown and $200,000 at Frederick. When Early crossed the Potomac on July 5, Stanton became concerned, and four days later when the rebels defeated Major General Lew Wallace's Eighth Corps at Monocacy, Halleck began looking for reinforcements to safeguard Washington. Old Brains contacted Grant, who believed a consolidation of Hunter's corps and Wallace's corps could converge on Early's hecklers and put the raiders out of business. Halleck informed Grant of Hunter's disappearance and said the general's army could not be located.[7]

General Hitchcock considered the situation serious enough to inform Stanton, who said that Grant had the problem under control. Hitchcock doubted whether Grant understood the threat and alerted Lincoln. The president, who was suffering from exhaustion, repeated Stanton's assurances. Hitchcock concluded that neither man wanted to ask Grant for troops and nothing would be done. Hitchcock was right. Stanton asked the governors for 100,000 militia to serve one hundred days and requested 12,000 Pennsylvanians be sent to Washington. Governor Curtin, quarrelsome as usual, insisted he control the troops but Stanton pay them. Stanton replied that unless the men came under army control, they would be useless. Curtin realized Stanton was correct and reluctantly conceded.[8]

On July 9 Grant became aware of the situation through Halleck and began detaching divisions from the Army of the Potomac to defend the capital. He offered to put Meade's forces strictly on the defensive and come to Washington in person. Lincoln received the telegram on the afternoon of the tenth and calmly replied that Washington had enough men to withstand attack but Baltimore could not. Lincoln wanted Early put out of business and suggested Grant come to Washington with enough troops to destroy the raiders, adding, "This is what I think upon your suggestion, and is not an order." Lincoln did not believe Early could do more than demonstrate against the capital, but he saw a clear opportunity to put an end to rebel operations in the Shenandoah Valley.

After digesting Lincoln's proposal, Grant detached Major General Horatio G. Wright's Sixth Corps to protect Washington and elements from Major General Quincy A. Gillmore's Nineteenth Corps to protect Baltimore. "I think, on reflection," wrote Grant, "it would have a bad effect for me to leave here." Lincoln called the general's plan "very satisfactory." His only concern was the enemy would retire across the Potomac before reinforcements arrived or Hunter's wandering corps returned from West Virginia to block the rebels' escape.[9]

When Early marched on Washington, thousands of panic-stricken Marylanders streamed into the capital. Rebels cut telegraph lines and disabled railroads, severing communications with the North. No trains arrived or departed. Soldiers from convalescent camps shouldered rifles and limped out to the forts. Brooks described the scene, writing, "Washington was in ferment; men were marching to and fro, able-bodied citizens were swept up and put into the district militia; and squads of department clerks were set to drilling in the parks." Halleck lived at Georgetown Heights with his own bugler and bodyguards. According to Brooks, some locals hoped Early would swoop through the heights and seize the "bitterly unpopular" general.[10]

The Lincolns had been staying at the Soldier's Home in Georgetown, which lay halfway between the capital and the outer defenses. Toward midnight on July 10 Stanton sent a carriage to move the family back to the city. Lincoln trusted Stanton's judgment and returned to the White House, where he found Assistant Secretary of the Navy Fox waiting with another carriage to usher the family to a fast steamer waiting at the navy yard. The president made it clear he had no intention of leaving Washington. He later learned that Admiral Samuel P. Lee, not Stanton or Welles, had arranged for the vessel. Welles could not understand why Lee had made an unauthorized trip from Hampton Roads to Washington with four steamers and an ironclad and rebuked him for abandoning his station and contributing to the general panic.[11]

Unable to control his nerves, Stanton also overreacted to the crisis. He took five thousand dollars in government bonds and four hundred dollars in gold belonging to his wife from the office safe, carried the valuables home, and hid them in a mattress.[12]

Early reached the outskirts of Washington around noon July 11 and observed reinforcements filing into Washington's defenses. He spent the day reconnoitering and exchanging artillery fire. Lincoln rode to Fort Stevens to witness the fighting, paying little attention to the whine of bullets whizzing by his ears. According to Hay, a soldier "roughly ordered" the president "to get down or he would have his head knocked off." Lincoln returned to the White House in good spirits and without concerns for the safety of the capital. In the morning he stopped again at Fort Stevens and came under fire a second time. After a bullet struck a soldier standing beside him, Lincoln returned to the city, predicting Early would retire and said he hoped Wright and Hunter would move rapidly enough to "bag" the rebels.[13]

On the evening of July 12, after torching Montgomery Blair's mansion at Silver Springs, the Confederates withdrew. The Blairs were away: Montgomery went to Pennsylvania on a fishing trip, and the family went to Cape May to escape the heat. As Lincoln feared, the rebels escaped loaded with plunder and crossed the Potomac at Leesburg. Eight hours later Wright arrived on the far side of the river with two divisions and bivouacked, waiting for Hunter. Assistant Secretary of War Dana attempted to locate Hunter, who could not be found. Two days later Early reentered the Shenandoah Valley. After Lincoln digested the reports, he commented that Wright feared "he might come across the rebels & catch some of them." Brigadier General George Crook's command arrived several days later but without Hunter. Dana explained Wright's poor performance, writing Grant of too many elements chasing Early with no one in overall command. "Halleck will not give orders except as he receives them," Dana said, "There is no head to the whole and it seems indispensable that you at once appoint one." Had Hunter been nearby, he would have been the ranking officer. No one had confidence in Hunter, and Stanton wanted him relieved. "Until you direct positively and explicitly what is to be done," Dana warned Grant, operations in the Shenandoah would continue in the same "deplorable and fatal way."[14]

After Early escaped, Grant became annoyed at Old Brains for doing nothing to coordinate Federal forces in Maryland. Bates complained to Lincoln about "the ignorant imbecility of the late military operations, and my contempt for Genl. Halleck." The problem cut deeper. Feeling powerless to make decisions without Grant's instructions, Halleck also felt bitter about being reduced from general-in-chief to Grant's clerk. After Early withdrew,

Grant expected the rebels to return to Petersburg and sent a staff officer to Washington to get the Sixth and Nineteenth corps. Halleck refused without written orders and abused the staff officer by asking him to explain why Grant had not taken Petersburg. After receiving an unsatisfactory explanation, he openly criticized Grant for taking the army to the James and leaving Washington defenseless. If that was not enough insubordination for one day, Halleck then complained about his situation to General Sherman, perhaps not realizing anything said would get back to Grant.[15]

When Blair returned from Pennsylvania and found his Silver Springs mansion torched, he lashed out at Stanton's "useless generals" luxuriating in Washington and cited Halleck as among the incompetent "poltroons." Halleck resented the insult and told Stanton that Blair should be dismissed from the cabinet. Stanton forwarded Halleck's comments to Lincoln, who said he could not condone such remarks, nor would he dismiss a member of his cabinet for making them "in a moment of vexation at so severe a loss." Stanton agreed with Blair and urged Halleck's removal, but Lincoln refused, leaving such matters to Grant.[16]

Grant expected more from Halleck. He agreed to put a general in command of the four military districts closest to Washington, but not Halleck. If Early could make random thrusts at the capital and each time escape because of disunity in the Federal command system, Grant would always be detaching reinforcements to safeguard the capital, instead of concentrating on Lee.[17]

Grant acted swiftly. On July 18 he wrote Halleck proposing the four departments be merged under the command of General William B. Franklin, a former corps commander who had been replaced after disagreements with Ambrose Burnside at Fredericksburg. Halleck disliked Franklin and told Grant the president would not approve because of the Burnside incident. Grant took advantage of Halleck's warning. In addition to suggesting Franklin for the post, Grant grasped an opportunity to shed Meade as an alternative to Franklin. If Lincoln preferred Meade for the Washington command, Grant recommended General Winfield S. Hancock as Meade's replacement. Knowing his suggestion might trouble the president, Grant offered to send John A. Rawlins to Washington to explain the proposal.[18]

While waiting for Rawlins, Lincoln asked Hunter, "Are you able to take care of the enemy when he turns back upon you, as he probably will, on finding that Wright has left?" Hunter expressed doubts but promised to be watchful and keep Halleck informed of enemy movements. Shortly after Rawlins arrived in Washington, John McCausland's Confederate cavalry slipped by Hunter undetected; raided Chambersburg, Pennsylvania; demanded $500,000 in currency or $100,000 in gold; and, when the terms could not be met, set fire to the town.[19]

Three weeks before Rawlins arrived in Washington to confer with the president, Dana warned Stanton of Meade's problems with the Army of the Potomac. The general's vicious temper undercut his effectiveness. "I do not think he has a friend in the whole army," Dana declared, adding that Meade had recently lost ten thousand men in a badly delivered assault because of poor cooperation from his generals. Wright confirmed Dana's allegations, accusing Meade of attacking "without brains and without generalship." Rawlins merely informed the president what Stanton already knew: the situation between Meade and his generals had become so volatile that Grant faced the prospect of having to relieve him.[20]

Grant wanted Meade eased out of the Army of the Potomac and given lighter duty without demotion, but on August 1 he made a decision without asking anyone. He detached Major General Philip H. Sheridan from the Army of the Potomac and wrote Halleck, "I want Sheridan put in command of all the troops in the field, with instructions to put himself south of the enemy and follow him to the death. Wherever the enemy goes let our troops go also."[21]

Stanton and Halleck knew little about Sheridan, who lately had been Grant's top cavalry commander. The five-foot-five-inch, 115-pound, thirty-three-year-old bandy-legged Irishman looked younger than his age and too inexperienced for major field command. The president thought about Grant's proposal for twenty-four hours before responding with the best advice a president could give any general. He approved Grant's decision to put a fighting man into the Valley but added a caveat, "This, I think, is exactly right as to how our forces should move, but please look over the dispatches you may have received . . . ever since you made that order, and discover, if you can, that there is any idea in the head of anyone here of 'putting our army south of the enemy,' or of following him to the 'death' in any direction. I repeat to you, it will neither be done nor attempted, unless you watch it every day and hour, and force it."[22]

Grant also wondered whether Halleck could be trusted to issue correct and timely instructions to Sheridan and departed for Washington to assess the situation for himself. Grant disliked being in the capital, so he went directly to General Hunter's headquarters at Monocacy. "I asked the general where the enemy was," said Grant, and "he replied he did not know." When questioned why, Hunter complained of Halleck's confusing orders. Pressed further, Hunter asked to be relieved. Grant said "very well" and summoned Sheridan to Monocacy to take command of the Middle Military Division.

Before leaving Washington, Sheridan walked to the White House with Stanton and spoke briefly with Lincoln. According to Sheridan, Stanton wanted an older person to replace Hunter, but Lincoln accepted Grant's decision and "hoped for the best." Sheridan entrained for Monocacy understanding "the necessity for success from the political as well as from the military point of view." He reported being unenthused by his Washington reception.[23]

On reaching Monocacy, Sheridan discovered Grant had dispatched thirty thousand troops and eight thousand cavalry to find Early. Grant told Sheridan to clean the rebels out of the Shenandoah Valley, to make his headquarters in the field, and to stay away from Washington. On August 7 Grant returned to the capital and, before departing for City Point, rescinded Halleck's control of the four departments reporting to Washington and transferred them to the Middle Military Division "temporarily" commanded by Sheridan.[24]

The president's decision to make Sheridan's promotion temporary stemmed from concerns over the general's youth and fitness for independent command. Grant suspected Halleck's meddling. After returning to City Point, he decided Old Brains had become his enemy and tried to have him replaced. Although Stanton agreed with Grant, he knew the president relied on Halleck and vetoed the request. Grant returned to the task of hammering away at Petersburg's fortifications until Lee decided to fight or surrender.[25]

Although Union armies sometimes stumbled and at other times made remarkable progress, Welles's navy never paused in its efforts to close Southern ports. Unlike the War Department, Welles set the course for the navy and caused comparatively little wake in the executive office by doing it. No naval expedition early in the war contributed more to the Union cause than Admiral Farragut's closing of the lower Mississippi and the capture of New Orleans on April 25, 1862. Although General Butler had twelve thousand men to assist in the operation, Farragut did it without them.

Farragut spent as much time in the Mississippi as he did in the Gulf of Mexico, but he never underestimated the importance of Mobile. Unlike Grant, Farragut put strategic emphasis on occupying Mobile Bay. He believed the city of Mobile would lose its importance the moment it could no longer serve as a port. After Banks failed to mount an expedition against Mobile, Grant suspended his plans for operations in Alabama. Welles, however, took the initiative and began shuttling four ironclads to Farragut's blockading squadron off Mobile Bay. Three Confederate forts and a network of submerged mines guarded the entrance to the bay, along with a squadron of gunboats and the CSS *Tennessee,* the strongest and most dangerous ironclad built by the Confederacy.

In Washington the president had become immersed in a mountain of military and political problems. Wade and Davis had issued their manifesto, radicals were splitting the Republican Party, inflation continued to spiral upward, Grant wanted another half-million men, and the national election crept ominously closer. From the president's perspective the future looked grim indeed.

Out of the gloom came news of the Civil War's greatest naval battle. The fight involved eighteen Union warships against a small Confederate squadron led by the impregnable CSS *Tennessee.* Early on the morning of August 5, 1864, sixty-three-year-old David Farragut damned the torpedoes, swept through the minefield at the mouth of Mobile Bay, ran the gantlet of Fort Morgan's heavy guns, and by 10:00 a.m. destroyed the Confederate fleet and captured the *Tennessee.* Fort Powell and Fort Gaines hoisted the white flag, and on August 23 Fort Morgan surrendered. A few days later Farragut told General Canby he was not "in favor of taking Mobile, except for the moral effect," because it would require twenty to thirty thousand men to capture and hold for no purpose other than political effect.[26]

On August 8 news of the capture of Mobile Bay filtered into Washington through General Butler, who, while lounging in his tent at Bermuda Hundred, spied the account in the *Richmond Sentinel.* At that time Lincoln was discussing with Grant, Stanton, and Halleck the appointment of Sheridan to the Middle Military District. Welles returned later but became drawn into a discussion of the Wade-Davis Manifesto. The following day he tried again but found Lincoln occupied with the Niagara peace conference fiasco. Later, when news of Farragut's victory reached the White House, Lincoln merely borrowed a line from Halleck's comments and spoke of Farragut's feat as useful "because it would tend to relieve Sherman." Welles returned to his office annoyed by Halleck's narrow view, muttering Old Brains "has done nothing new and only speaks of the naval achievement as a step for the army." Lincoln's preoccupation with other problems prevented him from recognizing the importance of Farragut's victory. The public seized upon it as the first good news in months. As if by magic, the capture of Mobile Bay broke the dam. The entire landscape of the war began to change, first in Georgia and then in Virginia.[27]

Few Civil War movements were driven as relentlessly as the Atlanta campaign. Had Grant not recognized Sherman's ability early in the war, the forty-four-year-old general with the unkempt red hair may never have risen to command military operations in the West. In 1861, when Sherman

sharply criticized Cameron's unrealistic strategy, he risked ejection for insubordination. His fiery feud with the press, which labeled him insane and
unstable, almost ended his useful service. Sherman was all business and left
little room for diplomacy. He suffered a severe wound while commanding a
division at Shiloh and attracted Grant's attention when he refused to leave
the field. Sherman became devoted to Grant, and it was during the Corinth
campaign that he convinced Grant to tolerate Halleck's abuse and not resign.
Sherman never lost his loathing for Halleck and Washington politics, even
though his brother, John, served as a powerful radical senator from Ohio.
Long after the war, Sherman still served Grant.

Dana first crossed paths with Sherman on the Mississippi and characterized the general "as a man of genius and of the wildest intellectual
acquisitions." Theodore Lyman saw Sherman as a "tall, spare, and sinewy
[Yankee] with a very long neck, and a big head . . . all his features express
determination, particularly the mouth. . . . He is a very homely man, with a
regular nest of wrinkles on his face." After Chattanooga, when Grant became
general-in-chief, he turned the Military Division of the Mississippi over to
Sherman and fit him into the grand strategy for ending the war in 1864.[28]

Sherman advanced into Georgia at the same time Meade stumbled
into the Wilderness. Grant's orders to Sherman were simply stated: "You
I propose to move against Johnston's army, to break it up and get into the
interior of the enemy's country as far as you can, inflicting all the damage
you can against their war resources." Grant never mentioned Atlanta, but
Sherman understood the goal without asking. Nor did Grant offer any plan
for the campaign, leaving it for Sherman to design and execute as conditions
permitted. Sherman merely replied, "Georgia has a million inhabitants; if
we can live we should not starve." Grant expressed one concern. While the
Army of the Potomac kept Lee occupied, he wanted Sherman to press Johnston's army so neither rebel force could concentrate to support the other.[29]

On May 7 Sherman found Johnston's position at Dalton too strong to
attack frontally. Using McPherson's Army of the Tennessee and Hugh Judson
Kilpatrick's cavalry, Sherman turned the Confederates out of their entrenchments and drove them south to Resaca. On May 15 Sherman tried to sur-
round the rebels, but Johnston steadily backpedaled in an effort to save his
army by avoiding battle. Lincoln watched Sherman's progress interestedly,
noting with "admiration" that Johnston's army had been driven with "vigor"
more than fifty miles in eleven days, while in Virginia Meade's army had
been stopped at Spotsylvania.[30]

On June 27 Sherman's advance faltered at Kennesaw Mountain. Frustrated by Johnston's unwillingness to stand and fight, Sherman ordered a savage frontal assault instead of a turning movement and suffered a bloody setback. He never admitted the mistake. "I had to do it," he wrote Halleck. "The enemy and our own army had settled down into the conviction that the assault of lines formed no part of my game." To Grant he wrote, "Had the assault succeeded I could have broken Johnston's center and pushed his army back in confusion, with great loss." Johnston never intended to hold Kennesaw Mountain. His men were already digging stronger defenses for the defense of Atlanta.[31]

After burying the dead, Sherman drove Johnston into new works on the north bank of the Chattahoochee River. Jeff Davis disapproved of Johnston's defensive maneuvers and on July 17 replaced him with Lieutenant General John Bell Hood, a fanatical admirer of Stonewall Jackson and an aggressive fighter who had been severely crippled in battle. Sherman crossed the river and on July 25 invested Atlanta. He made adjustments to his siege lines, turned Hood's position by a swift movement to the south, broke the Confederate line of communications by a raid on Jonesboro, and on September 1 forced Hood to give up Atlanta. Two days later Sherman wrote Halleck, "Atlanta is ours and fairly won." He brought the army into the captured city, writing, "Since May 5 we have been in one constant battle or skirmish and need rest."[32]

Sherman understood the political importance of capturing Atlanta and never took his eye off the objective. In August John Nicolay observed, "The want of any decided military successes thus far, and the necessity of the new draft . . . has materially discouraged many of our friends . . . and croakers are talking everywhere about the impossibility of re-electing Mr. Lincoln 'unless something is done.'"[33]

Lincoln now had cause to celebrate. On September 3 he tendered the thanks of the nation to the two men who had virtually ensured his reelection, Farragut and Sherman, and acknowledged the victories by ordering hundred-gun salutes and issuing a Proclamation of Thanksgiving and Prayer. The sudden announcement of Atlanta's surrender induced one hack to suggest Sherman for the Democratic ticket. The general cleared the air quickly. "Some fool seems to have used my name," he declared. "If forced to choose between the penitentiary and White House for four years . . . I would say the penitentiary."[34]

Joseph Medill, sitting in his office at the *Chicago Tribune*, had been instrumental in putting Lincoln into office in 1860 and wanted him there for four more years. He fired his own salute in newsprint, writing, "Union men! The dark days are over. We see our way out. . . . Thanks be to God!" Then he declared, "The Republic is safe!" In June, when Grant reached Petersburg and Sherman approached Atlanta, Lincoln had said, "I begin to see it. You will succeed. God bless you all." Now the nation saw it, too.[35]

Two weeks later, as if on cue, Sheridan took the field with thirty-seven thousand men and struck Early. Grant arrived with a plan of operations but discovered Sheridan had his own. After listening to Sheridan's plan, Grant merely said, "Go in."[36]

On September 19 Sheridan whipped Early at Winchester and drove him into a strong natural defensive position on Fishers Hill, two miles south of Strasburg. Sheridan telegraphed Grant, "We have just sent them whirling through Winchester, and we are after them to-morrow." Nicolay and Hay said the announcement "became a household word a few hours after it was written." Lincoln expressed astonishment because he believed Sheridan's orders had been to hold Early in the Valley and not go on the offensive. Grant celebrated by telling Sheridan to "push his success," and the president rewarded the diminutive cavalryman by advancing him to brigadier general in the regular army and placed him in permanent command of the Middle Military Division. Mindful of the positive political effect on the upcoming election, Lincoln wrote Sheridan, "Have just heard of your great victory. God bless you all. Strongly inclined to come up and see you."[37]

Three days later Sheridan routed the Confederates at Fishers Hill. Lincoln decided Sheridan had done enough and warned Grant that Lee might detach forces from Petersburg to bolster Early's army and make an effort to recover the Valley. With the election a month away, Lincoln wanted no military setbacks. Sheridan agreed to go on the defensive, though at first Grant did not. On October 6 Sheridan began destroying all the subsistence in the Valley and retired to Cedar Creek. Early observed the withdrawal and moved troops back to Fishers Hill. On October 15 Sheridan received an invitation from Stanton to come to Washington for a conference and left Wright in command.[38]

Sheridan spent October 17 in Washington and the following day returned by special train to Winchester. At 9:00 a.m. he heard the rumble of distant artillery and encountered long lines of blue-clad fugitives straggling in great disorder. Whipping his horse to a gallop, Sheridan rode rapidly toward the sound of fighting. Approaching Cedar Creek, he located Wright and Crook, took a bearing on the enemy, reformed the army, and counterattacked. Stunned by the impact of the unexpected counterattack, Early retreated to Fishers Hill with heavy losses. The action at Cedar Creek brought an end to heavy fighting in the Shenandoah Valley. Early retired up the Valley, his force in shambles.[39]

Sheridan's Cedar Creek success came as an unexpected bonus for the president. The general had completely exceeded Lincoln's expectations and delighted Stanton. "With great pleasure," wrote the president, "I tender you and your brave army, the thanks of the Nation, and my own personal admiration and gratitude, for the month's operations in the Shenandoah Valley."[40]

Weeks later, after permanently promoting Sheridan to major general in the regular army, Lincoln went to City Point and noticed a small man wearing a dirty brown slouch hat and a mud-stained uniform with no insignia or epaulets. He strode over to the cavalryman, grasped his hand, and said, "General Sheridan, when this peculiar war began I thought a cavalryman should be at least six feet four high; but," he added, looking down on Little Phil, "I have changed my mind—five feet four will do in a pinch."[41]

On October 9 Sarah Josepha Hale wrote Seward, urging him to remind the president of the approach of Thanksgiving. On four previous occasions the president had proclaimed a day of thanksgiving, but only twice did the day fall on the last Thursday of November. Miss Hale hoped the president would perpetuate the custom because she had written an article about "National Thanksgiving" for the November issue of *Godey's Lady's Book*. Lincoln read a copy of her proof, decided that Miss Hale was right, and on October 20, the day after Sheridan's victory at Cedar Creek, he created what all Americans celebrate today as Thanksgiving Day.[42] By then the only stumbling block giving life to the Confederacy was a line of Confederate entrenchments stretching from Richmond to Petersburg.

CHAPTER 21

"What is the Presidency worth to me if I have no country?"

In early August 1864, when the war appeared to have lapsed into a dismal stalemate, Dana summed up politics, writing, "The country is deeply discouraged and the party for peace at any price very active. Still more active, if possible, is the anti-Lincoln party among the Republicans, composed of all the elements of discontent that a four-year administration could produce." Democrats intending to capitalize on Republican discord were hard-pressed to find a presidential candidate who agreed with them. The resignation of Chase on the last day of June hinted at dissension within the administration, and the veto of the Wade-Davis Bill signaled a breakup within the party. To allow more time for Republicans to self-destruct and to give themselves time to declare a candidate, Democrats rescheduled their July 4 national presidential nominating convention for August 29.[1]

In the first political test at the polls, the administration took another step in the direction of self-destruction. On August 1 Kentucky became the first state to hold elections since Lincoln's renomination. The closely watched polls provided an important indicator of how border states would vote in September. Stanton became involved in efforts to make Kentucky swing the president's way. Lincoln declared martial law, and Stanton quelled disturbances by using the army to arrest a few prominent Democrats. Governor Thomas Bramlette, elected in 1863, complained of outrages: "We are dealt with as though Kentucky was a rebellious and conquered province." The public agreed, and Democrats swept the polls. After the election Kentucky war Democrats who had supported Lincoln at Baltimore sent delegates to Chicago with instructions to back George B. McClellan for president and Bramlette for vice president.[2]

In late August the Blairs predicted McClellan would win the Democrat nomination and defeat Lincoln. Blair Sr. hatched a scheme to keep this from happening and went to New York to talk with the general. On no authority other than his own, he offered to restore McClellan to command of the army if he would disavow interest in the presidency. McClellan remained noncommittal, and when Blair mentioned the proposal to the president, Lincoln also remained silent. The scheme had merit because Stanton wanted to dispose of Halleck, and Lincoln believed McClellan might be a better man for the job. According to Cameron, Lincoln said if McClellan did not receive the Democrat nomination, he would "appoint him to his 'old place.'" Cameron never made it clear whether Lincoln meant Grant's place or Halleck's.[3]

Democrat strategy appeared to be working. On August 22 Thurlow Weed told Henry Raymond, the Republican national chairman, that Lincoln's "re-election was an impossibility" and urged him to tell the president before "all is lost." Raymond warned Lincoln, writing, "Nothing but the most resolute and decided action on the part of the Government can save the country from falling into hostile hands."[4]

On August 25 Raymond arrived at the White House and implored Lincoln to send a peace commission to Richmond. Horace Greeley's effort at Niagara, though a farcical venture, had had the effect of energizing the nation's yearning for peace. Greeley and Weed agreed peace could be negotiated if Lincoln scuttled his demand for emancipation. Raymond told the president to act quickly and silence his critics because nothing short of an ostensible effort to bring peace would salvage his reelection.[5]

Lincoln shielded concerns about his electability from Raymond and brought Seward, Stanton, and Fessenden into the meeting. He said suing for peace would be worse than losing the presidential election, and he certainly would not surrender it in advance because the public still had faith in him. The cabinet stood solidly behind the president, and when Raymond departed, he admitted feeling more "encouraged" than when he first arrived.[6]

As the Chicago convention approached, it became settled that McClellan, though a war candidate, would become the Democrat's presidential nominee. Delegates began to wonder how they were going to sell the public a war candidate on a peace platform. Noah Brooks asked Lincoln, who replied, "They must nominate a Peace Democrat on a war platform, or a War Democrat on a peace platform; and I personally can't say that I care much what they do."[7]

Lincoln did care, and more than a little. Six days before the Chicago convention he noted his thoughts in a memorandum: "This morning, as for some days past, it seems exceedingly probable that this administration will not be reëlected. Then it will be my duty to so coöperate with the President-elect as to save the Union between the election and the inauguration; as we will have secured his election on such ground that he cannot possibly save it afterwards." Lincoln folded the note, unread by others, and asked each member of the cabinet to sign his name to the back. He pasted the paper to ensure it could only be opened with scissors and tucked it away without telling anyone why.[8]

The convention promised to be hectic. In the opening remarks New York financier August Belmont attempted to harmonize the convention's platform conundrum by saying, "We are here, not as war Democrats or peace Democrats, but as citizens of the great Republic." Belmont's rhetoric failed to set the tone. War Democrats wanted McClellan as the nominee and no one else. With the war going nowhere, and with radicals threatening to defect from Lincoln, Democrats had only McClellan to rally behind. The general had voiced his political position at Harrison's Landing, and war Democrats stitched those remarks together and made copies for everyone. McClellan would assuredly win the army vote, and if he gained the presidency, which on August 29 seemed almost a certainty, Democrats would regain lost power.[9]

Delegates spent a day condemning the administration and Lincoln in particular. The debate finally shifted to designing a platform that satisfied both peace and war Democrats. Work progressed smoothly until discussions butted against the plank defining the party's position on the war. Clement Vallandigham, back from exile and as voluble as ever, called the war a failure, but he also articulated the grievances differentiating Democrats from Republicans. Vallandigham's resolution became known as the "war failure" plank. He referred to the war as an "experiment" sculpted "under the pretense of military necessity, or war power higher than the Constitution." He appealed to peace and war Democrats alike and said "the public welfare demand that immediate efforts be made for a cessation of hostilities, with a view to . . . at the earliest practicable moment peace may be restored on the basis of the Federal Union of the States."

The remarkable resolution both condemned the war but also sustained it and created the open-ended peace platform Lincoln expected. Jefferson Davis would not discuss peace without the assurance of Southern independence, and Vallandigham's resolution called for restoration "of the Federal Union of the States." War Democrats might have fought the peace plank were it not for the ending phrase. Knowing McClellan stood for the reunification of the nation, they adopted the resolutions without debate. Despite opposition from peace Democrats, Little Mac won the nomination on the first ballot.[10]

On the day Democrats named their nominees, "the stars in their courses seemed to fight against them." As the streets of Chicago blazed with torches carried by happy peace men and bands played "Dixie," General John Hood evacuated Atlanta. The press could not decide how to fashion morning headlines. The convention declared the war a failure, but Sherman's army occupied the great manufacturing metropolis of Georgia. Democrats had their ticket, but they also had Vallandigham's war failure plank. Disillusioned delegates returned home, few of them cheering.[11]

McClellan read the war news. His acceptance address puzzled the peace Democrats. "The reestablishment of the Union in all its integrity," wrote the general, "is, and must continue to be, the indispensable condition in any settlement." McClellan implied if the South refused to accept peace "upon the basis of the Union," the war would continue. The general also agreed to receive any Southern state back into the Union with full constitutional rights, but "the Union must be preserved at all hazards." There is no question where McClellan stood. After Democrats worked so diligently to differentiate themselves from Republicans, McClellan's acceptance address read like something scripted by Lincoln. After repudiating the Democrat platform on which he was nominated, McClellan closed by adding, "Believing that the views here expressed are those of the Convention . . . I accept the nomination." Shocked delegates abhorred McClellan's comments but could not stop them from being published.[12]

When reports of the Chicago convention reached Washington, Welles studied the resolutions and decided the Democrats had deceived themselves, writing, "It is whether a war shall be made against Lincoln to get peace with Jeff Davis." The outcome of the convention, that Democrats would nominate a general committed to war on a peace platform, seemed ironic to Welles. "I think the president will be reelected," Welles wrote, "and I shall be surprised if he does not have a large majority."[13]

On August 30, while Democrats convened in Chicago, a group of disaffected Republicans supported by Weed met at David Dudley Field's mansion in Gramercy Park, New York, because they believed Lincoln could not defeat McClellan. Chase avoided the meeting, and though he held grievances against the president, he thought the group should not meddle with the ticket. Weed had become critical of the president for making peace negotiations impossible by insisting the South accept emancipation. Writing Seward on August 26, he said, "As things now stand Mr. Lincoln's re-election is an impossibility. The people are wild for peace. They are told that the President will only listen to terms of Peace on condition slavery be abolished." Weed thought the country should revert to the Crittenden Resolution of 1861, which stipulated the sole purpose of war was for the preservation of the Union.[14]

The New Yorkers called for a new Republican convention to meet in Cincinnati on September 28 to nominate a candidate who could unite the country. Greeley, Parke Godwin, and other publishers decided to distribute circulars ahead of the meeting asking governors whether they could carry their respective states for Lincoln or whether another candidate should be chosen. Greeley felt no personal animosity toward Lincoln. He only wanted to back a winner. "I shall fight like a savage in this campaign," he told Nicolay. "I hate McClellan." Although malcontents believed Lincoln should be replaced, they thought he should graciously withdraw from the nomination and open the way for another candidate.[15]

As Greeley's circulars reached the governors, Atlanta surrendered. "The fall of Atlanta puts an entirely new aspect upon the face of affairs," one conspirator observed. Not one governor thought Lincoln should be dumped. One week after proposing the Cincinnati convention, the New York instigators abandoned the project. Having been deeply involved in the scheme, Weed tried to disassociate himself by notifying Seward, "The conspiracy against Mr. Lincoln collapsed on Monday, last." Greeley admitted the whole enterprise had been a mistake. He concentrated efforts on supporting the Republican Party but seldom mentioned Lincoln by name.[16]

Notwithstanding the Wade-Davis Manifesto and revolt within the party, the president sought ways to enlist Republican support. The sixth plank of the Baltimore platform, now two months old, included a call for harmony in the cabinet. Lincoln understood the meaning. Radicals wanted the cabinet homogenized by removing conservatives. Blair knew he was a target. After the convention he offered to resign, but Lincoln refused, so he promised to resign whenever the president wished. Lincoln made matters worse by accepting the resignation of Chase, whom the radicals regarded as their special watchdog inside the administration. Lincoln clearly understood radicals would gain more from his reelection than from the election of a Democrat, and their illogical behavior bewildered him.

On August 13 Thad Stevens made a rare, imperious visit to the White House to demand Blair's removal. Lincoln became unusually bristled by the petulance of Stevens's demands. "Am I to be the mere puppet of power," Lincoln rebutted, "to have my constitutional advisers selected for me beforehand, and to be told I must do this or leave that undone? It would be degrading to my manhood to consent to any such bargain—I was about to say it is equally degrading to your manhood to ask it." Stevens never learned the art of diplomacy, nor did he care. Hate and discord suited him better. "I confess that I desire to be re-elected," Lincoln added. "God knows I do not want the labor and responsibility of the office for another four years. . . . I honestly believe that I can better serve the nation in its need and peril than any new man could possibly do. I want to finish the job of putting down the rebellion, and restoring peace and prosperity to the country. But I would . . .

refuse the office rather than accept it on such disgraceful terms, as not really to be the President after I am elected." Stevens departed from the White House accompanied by his usual cloud of loathing.[17]

Toward the end of August, Chandler picked up where Stevens had failed. Like Greeley, he hated McClellan and began seeking ways to reconcile the radicals with the president. Homogenizing the cabinet meant removing Seward and Blair but to sacrifice one if it meant saving the other; Blair won the prize for being the most obnoxious.

Chandler shouldered the task of unifying the party because it had to be done. He visited Wade, who agreed Lincoln might salve some wounds if he dismissed Blair. Wade already knew his manifesto, coauthored by Davis, had not won the approbation of the public. He agreed to support Lincoln if Davis did. After laying the groundwork, Chandler called on Davis, perhaps the greatest Blair hater of all. Davis agreed one of his greatest objections to the administration would be eased if Blair left the cabinet. Chandler returned to the White House to say he had spoken with Wade and Davis and that removing Blair would conciliate the most hostile radicals and bring the entire party back into the canvass. Senator Henry Wilson, whose opinion the president respected, added his two cents, writing, "Blair everyone hates. Tens of thousands of men will be lost to you or will give a reluctant vote on account of the Blairs."[18]

Chandler then went to New York to speak with third party candidate John Frémont, who had no hope of winning the election but could pull votes from Lincoln, whom he hated. Frémont appeared to be on the verge of abandoning the race when Chandler arrived. On September 21 Frémont fired a parting salvo and withdrew, "not to aid in the triumph of Mr. Lincoln, but to do my part towards preventing the election of a Democratic candidate." Frémont spit out more sour grapes, accusing the administration of being "politically, militarily, and financially a failure, and that its necessary continuance is a cause of regret for the country." Lincoln expected nothing less from Frémont and refused to distinguish the general's remarks by commenting.[19]

Two days later Lincoln rewarded Chandler's efforts by asking Blair to keep his promise: "You have generously said to me more than once, that whenever your resignation could be of relief to me, it was at my disposal. The time has come. You very well know that this proceeds from no dissatisfaction of mine with you personally or officially. Your uniform kindness has been unsurpassed by that of any friend." Lincoln regretted losing the warm friendship of the postmaster general. He informed Blair Sr. that his son "made the best Post master Genl that ever administered the department." Lincoln meant what he said. During Blair's tenure, war and all, there had been no complaints of corruption.[20]

Blair believed radical opposition toward him had diminished. Although surprised and somewhat offended by the president's request, he kept his word and resigned, writing, "I can not take leave of you without renewing the expressions of my gratitude for the uniform kindness which has marked your course towards [me]."[21]

Welles and Bates were talking outside the White House when Blair suddenly came through the doorway and said, "I suppose that you are both aware that my head is decapitated—I am no longer a member of the Cabinet." Having heard nothing, Welles asked Blair why he resigned. Blair shrugged and said "he was a peace-offering to Frémont and his friends," unaware Lincoln's action was meant to appease the radicals and not Frémont. Welles replied, "The President would never have yielded to that." Blair decided Welles might be right. After giving the matter more thought, he blamed his dismissal on Seward, remarking that it must have "been instigated and stimulated by Weed." Blair overlooked his own quarrelsome habits. He fought constantly with Chase, hated Halleck, and barely tolerated Stanton. Internal squabbles upset Lincoln. When Wade and Davis demanded Blair's dismissal, perhaps they understood the underlying problems in the cabinet better than the president.[22]

Lincoln lost no time acquiring a new postmaster general. Nor did he want to lose the support of the Blairs. He immediately telegraphed forty-nine-year-old former Ohio governor William Dennison, "Mr. Blair has resigned, and I appoint you Post-Master General. Come on immediately." Dennison, though once a Chase supporter, had aligned himself with the Blairs. Lincoln's telegram arrived at an opportune time, Dennison having lost the nomination for Ohio governor to David Tod, a war Democrat. Dennison's pomposity exceeded his administrative skill, but Blair had done the hard work of filling postal appointments with competent people. Three days later Dennison departed for Washington and on October 4, 1864, became the president's new postmaster general.[23]

On the day the Democrats nominated McClellan, the presidential campaign of 1864 began. Neither nominee actively participated in the campaign. "I cannot run the political machine," Lincoln said when pestered to do something on his own behalf. "I have enough on my hands without *that*. It is the *people's* business." The statement made good rhetoric, but during September and October barely an hour passed without Lincoln becoming immersed in the "people's business."[24]

The people's business did not exclude cabinet members from wielding their considerable influence. On September 3 Seward unofficially kicked off the president's campaign in Auburn, New York, and expressed exactly what Lincoln had been saying and might have said had campaign protocol permitted him to make political speeches: "While the rebels continue to wage war against the Government of the United States, the military measures affecting slavery, which have been adopted from necessity to bring the war to a speedy and successful end, will be continued . . . with a view to the same end. When insurgents shall have disbanded their armies and laid down their arms the war will instantly cease; and all the war measures then existing . . . whether they arose before the civil war began, or whether they grew out of it, will, by force of the Constitution, pass over to the arbitrament of courts of law and to the councils of legislation."[25]

Ten days later Seward returned to Washington and received a serenade, which meant the public wanted to hear more. His comments set the tone for the president's entire campaign. "The Democracy of Chicago," Seward declared, "after waiting six weeks to see whether this war for the Union is to succeed or fail, finally concluded that it would fail, and therefore went in for a nomination and platform to make it a sure thing by a cessation of hostilities and an abandonment of the contest. At Baltimore . . . we determined there should be no such thing as failure, and therefore we went in to save the Union by battle to the last. Sherman and Farragut have knocked the bottom out of the Chicago nominations. . . . The issue is squarely made up—McClellan and disunion, or Lincoln and Union."[26]

Detractors picked apart Seward's Auburn speech and spread rumors that Lincoln intended to overthrow the government if his reelection failed. Meanwhile, a countermove occurred among Democrats to reconvene and nominate someone who would at once seize control of the government. Because the president felt barred from making public statements, he said nothing, so the rumor gathered momentum. Lincoln could not find an acceptable platform for putting the matter to rest until October 19, when a note arrived from Henry Willis indicating that Marylanders intended to be at the White House at 8:00 p.m. to deliver a serenade. The president grasped the opportunity to comment and, referring to Seward's remarks, said, "I am struggling to maintain government, not overthrow it. I am struggling especially to prevent others from overthrowing it. I therefore say, that if I shall live, I shall remain President until the fourth of next March; and whoever shall be constitutionally elected . . . shall be duly installed as President . . . and that in the interval I shall do my utmost that whoever is to hold the helm for the next voyage, shall start with the best possible chance to save the ship."[27]

During September and October Republicans across the country descended on the White House to urge the president to suspend the draft until after the election. A new draft of a half-million men, scheduled to begin September 5, caused great consternation for every Republican incumbent from Maine to Oregon. Cameron wanted the draft delayed in Philadelphia. Chase telegraphed from Ohio to say that Republicans carried the state elections but implored Lincoln to suspend the draft until after the national election. General Sherman telegraphed from the field, "If the President modifies it [the draft] to the extent of one man, or wavers in its execution, he is gone forever; the army will vote against him." When Judge William Johnson and his committee stopped at the White House to request temporary suspension of the draft, Lincoln replied, "What is the Presidency worth to me if I have no country?"[28]

Complaining politicians also descended on the War Department to harangue Stanton, whose frayed nerves could not absorb much more pressure. Grant provided good advice, writing, "A draft is soon over, and ceases to hurt after it is made. The agony of suspense is worse upon the public than the measure itself," and urged it be done "in the shortest possible time." Stanton went forward with the draft, and Lincoln refused to interfere.[29]

During September Stanton learned that New York Democrats had connived to capture the soldiers' vote for McClellan. Since midsummer political tracts promoting Lincoln's reelection had been circulated through army camps. Because of the lateness of McClellan's nomination, Democrats had nothing prepared. A few of McClellan's former officers were observed destroying boxes of Republican leaflets. Stanton dismissed twenty quartermaster clerks working on McClellan's behalf. When one complained, Stanton replied, "When a young man receives his pay from an administration and spends his evenings denouncing it in offensive terms, he cannot be surprised if the administration prefers a friend on the job." Stanton's action rippled through the army, and the pilfering stopped.[30]

Despite pressure from political friends to find ways of capturing the military vote, Lincoln played it straight. When some generals in the field faithful to McClellan tried to obstruct the soldiers' vote, Lincoln declared, "Whenever the law allows soldiers to vote, their officers must also allow it." He said no more. The rest he left to Stanton, who sent generals home to make speeches and emptied hospitals of sick and wounded soldiers who were well enough to travel home and vote. He set rules for voting in the field where states allowed it. After learning Confederates in Canada were sending men into New York, New England, and Michigan to vote for McClellan, he sealed the border. Stanton also planted agents to spy on political gatherings. A number of colonels supporting McClellan felt the brunt of Stanton's power when the secretary sent them to the front to spend the balance of war serving as captains.[31]

When New York governor Seymour planned to order out the National Guard to supervise the polls on Election Day, Stanton called the attempt an effort to bully Republican voters. He asked Grant to send Butler to New York to neuter the effort. Butler arrived with forty-three hundred infantry, smothered the city's polls with veteran soldiers, and on November 8 advised Stanton that during the election New York became "the quietest city ever seen." According to Hay, "The President had nothing to do with it."[32]

Lincoln did not need a campaign manager. He had Stanton. "All the power and influence of the War Department was employed to secure the re-election of Mr. Lincoln," Dana recalled. The government provided no funds for political campaigns, but Dana observed Stanton making "vast expenditures" from the War Department without the president's knowledge. With Chase no longer in office "to clamor against the inefficiency" of the War Department, Stanton spent and used whatever resources he needed to reelect Lincoln. Halleck remarked that if the army were to respond to every request to protect the polls, "we would not have a single soldier to meet the rebels in the field!"[33]

State returns foreshadowed the national election, and Lincoln and Stanton monitored the results. In October's polling in Ohio and Indiana, Republicans scored victories in the gubernatorial races and gained seats in Congress. "I am deeply thankful for the result in Indiana," wrote Hay. "I believe it saves Illinois in November."[34]

Pennsylvania remained in limbo because the two most powerful Republicans, Governor Curtin and Senate hopeful Simon Cameron, disliked each other. Lincoln did not want the feud to spill over into the presidential election. He tabulated the expected electoral vote from all states and, by adding the new state of Nevada, predicted he would win by three votes. The slim margin provided no comfort. He needed Pennsylvania's twenty-six electoral votes, which on October 13 he had given to McClellan.[35]

As chairman of the Pennsylvania State Committee, Cameron was partly responsible for the unimpressive election results in October. Concerned by the state election, Lincoln invited Alexander McClure, a Curtin man, to the

White House. McClure had been state committee chairman when Lincoln won Pennsylvania in 1860, and the president asked for his help. McClure said he could not work with Cameron. "Of course, I understand that," Lincoln replied, "but if Cameron shall invite you can you give your time fully to the contest?" McClure agreed but said Cameron would never contact him. Lincoln immediately wrote Cameron, and two days later McClure received an invitation to join the chairman at campaign headquarters in Philadelphia. To avoid accusations of infidelity from the Curtin faction, McClure stayed at another hotel, met with Cameron privately, and issued a nightly report to keep the president informed.[36]

Lincoln could have expedited the admission of Colorado and Nebraska, netting six electoral votes, and the partially reconstructed Southern states, but he refused to become involved in a scheme certain to infuriate Congress. When Andrew Johnson issued a proclamation to enfranchise Tennessee, McClellan supporters shouted "unfair" and sent reporters to the White House to question the president's involvement. Lincoln told the press to see the New York politicians who had "concoct[ed] that paper." After stating his position, Lincoln added, "I expect to let the friends of George B. McClellan manage their side of this contest in their own way; and I will manage my side of it in MY way." Lincoln refused to put his answer in writing and bid the press good-bye.[37]

Lincoln had explained his position months ago, writing, "I don't think it is personal vanity, or ambition," with reference to wanting a second term, but "the weal or woe of this great nation will be decided in the approaching canvas." If the people chose dismemberment in the next election, it would be their choice, not his. "You cannot conciliate the South," he said, "you have to fight them." The war was a conflict no longer merely for salvation of the Union but for the American form of government. When Lincoln told the press he would manage his side of the campaign "MY way," it was because, in his perspective, no other way offered an acceptable alternative.[38]

No prior campaign in the United States ever underwent the vote-gathering effort to secure a second term for a president. Although restrained from campaigning, behind the scenes Lincoln pressed Stanton and Welles to make certain every soldier and sailor voted. Hospitals and camps emptied, and men came home. Steamers passed through the blockade on the Atlantic to collect the sailors' vote. Federal offices closed so employees could go to the polls. Stanton's agents made arrests when a military commission investigating possible fraud found several boxes of Lincoln ballots replaced by McClellan ballots. Once charges of fraud broke the news, Democrats counterattacked with their own charges. They found several sick soldiers who voted in the field, went home, and voted again. Most of the hullabaloo involved the military vote, which in some states proved the decisive factor and in other states increased Republican majorities. Balloting in the field gave Lincoln 119,754 votes and McClellan 34,291. Soldiers voting at home merely added to the count.[39]

The soldiers' vote gave Lincoln Connecticut and New York. In the Empire State, Lincoln polled 368,000 to McClellan's 362,000, a mere difference of 6,000 votes. In Connecticut, where soldiers cast 2,898 votes for Lincoln, the president won by the slim margin of 2,406 votes. Stanton's efforts to corral the soldiers' vote had mattered, and so did the president's personal involvement.[40]

Lincoln took special interest in the outcome of Maryland's vote, where citizens were called upon to adopt or reject a new state constitution abolishing slavery forever and disenfranchising any resident who abetted the rebellion. He wanted the Maryland constitution adopted to serve as a model for border states, and when he heard Henry Winter Davis had become involved in the campaign, Lincoln remarked, "If he and the rest can succeed in carrying the state for emancipation I shall be willing to lose the electoral vote." Lincoln, of course, wanted the electoral vote and the new constitution. In the final tabulation—30,174 for and 29,699 against—the constitution would not have passed, nor would Lincoln have received Maryland's popular vote, without the soldiers' vote.[41]

On the evening of November 7, the day before the national election, fog settled over Washington. In the far reaches of the divided nation war came to a standstill. Northerners waited for polling centers to open. Southerners waited also, but they had abdicated their right to vote. The destiny of the United States waited for the people's business to begin. Lincoln went to bed. There was nothing more for him to do.

CHAPTER 22

"It shows . . . how *sound,* and how *strong* we still are"

On Election Day, November 8, 1864, morning rain fell from thick dark clouds and soaked the streets of Washington. The same weather front dampened the cities and fields from New England to Petersburg, Virginia. War took a day off, and from all appearances so did the nation. The only people on Washington's streets were those under umbrellas walking to polling centers. "The house has been still and almost deserted today," John Hay observed. "Everybody in Washington, not at home voting, seems ashamed of it and stays away from the President." John Nicolay returned to Springfield to vote; Hay remained behind to assist the president. Lincoln sat quietly reflecting until Hay entered the room. "It is a little singular that I, who am not a vindictive man, should have always been before the people for election in canvasses marked for their bitterness." Hay remembered the occasion as "one of the most solemn days" of Lincoln's life.[1]

Noah Brooks called at noon and found the president alone and pensive. Only two members attended the morning cabinet meeting. Stanton stayed home, ill with fever. Dennison, Seward, and Usher had returned to their home states to vote. Fessenden was in New York placing new loans. Welles and Bates attended the meeting and, having nothing to discuss, returned to their offices to "run the machine." Brooks remained at the White House to keep the president company. Lincoln could not relax. "I am just enough of a politician to know that there was not much doubt about the result of the Baltimore convention," he said, "but about this thing I am very far from being certain. I wish I were certain."[2]

At 7:00 p.m. Brooks, Hay, and Lincoln gathered under umbrellas and slopped through dark wet streets to the telegraph office. As Lincoln entered, a clerk handed him a dispatch from John W. Forney, secretary of the U.S. Senate, claiming a 10,000 majority in Philadelphia. Lincoln doubted the report. Perhaps forgetting that Cameron and McClure had joined forces to snatch the election from McClellan, Lincoln said, "Forney is a little excitable." Minutes later Charles C. Fulton, editor of the *Baltimore American,* reported "15,000 in the city, 5,000 in the States. All hail, free Maryland!" On hearing Boston had gone Republican by 4,000 votes, the president said it must be a clerical error. Minutes later Charles Sumner reported from Boston that Lincoln had taken the city by 5,000 votes. Sherman wrote from Atlanta, "The vote in this army today is almost unanimous for Lincoln. Give Uncle Abe my compliments and congratulations." Alexander H. Rice, chairman of the naval committee, said with no irreverent intention, "The Almighty must have stuffed the ballot-boxes."[3]

Lincoln remained circumspect because Pennsylvania and New York remained close. In 1864 there were no exit polls, but observers noticed the immigrant vote, composed mainly of Catholics living in large cities, went to McClellan. Immigrants were workingmen. They opposed war and took no interest in emancipation. Lincoln believed he had a better chance of winning Pennsylvania than New York and said, "As goes Pennsylvania, so goes the Union."[4]

Nicolay telegraphed from Springfield, describing how voters went to the polls in the afternoon and stood waiting under rain-drenched umbrellas. "The line stretched from the Courthouse door out on and along the sidewalk past the banks," he reported. "There was scarcely any of the usual electioneering about the polls." The people, not to be deterred by weather, came to vote for their fellow townsman. Nicolay did not have the final count for Illinois but predicted the outcome, "Thank God, night brought the right results for the nation, and as it now appears to us for this State."[5]

Welles and Fox joined the gathering at the telegraph office with news of their own. "There are two fellows that have been especially malignant to us," said Fox, "and retribution has come to both of them." Henry Winter Davis of Maryland lost his seat in the House, and John P. Hale of New Hampshire, a perpetual irritant to the Navy Department, lost his seat in the Senate. Lincoln replied, "You have more of that feeling of personal resentment than I. Perhaps I may have too little of it, but I never thought it paid. A man has not time to spend half of his life in quarrels. It has seemed to me recently that Winter Davis was growing more sensible to his own true interests and has ceased wasting his time attacking me. He has been very malicious against me but has only injured himself by it." To anyone suggesting political revenge, Lincoln patently replied, "I am in favor of short statutes of limitations in politics." He gathered up the early election results and sent them to his wife at the White House. "She is more anxious than I," he said, but not everyone believed him.[6]

By midnight Lincoln had tabulated enough returns to know, with reasonable certainty, he had captured New England, Maryland, Ohio, Indiana, Michigan, and Wisconsin. At 1:00 a.m. Nicolay reported Lincoln ahead by twenty thousand votes. His lead in Pennsylvania continued to improve, and though New York remained in doubt, Lincoln still held a slim lead. An hour later his friends began to leave the telegraph office. One by one they congratulated the president, who said "he was glad to be relieved of all the suspense, and . . . grateful that the verdict of the people was likely to be so full, clear, and unmistakable that there could be no dispute." When the door opened, a brass band blared a hifalute. He went to the window to say a few words but found a White House messenger waiting to tell him Pennsylvania serenaders had gathered on the lawn outside his empty chamber and were singing their lungs out. Lincoln made haste to the Executive Mansion and delivered a second speech, saying, "It is no pleasure to me to triumph over anyone, but I give thanks to the Almighty for this evidence of the people's resolution to stand by free government and the rights of humanity."[7]

Commotion at the White House continued into the early hours of the morning. Ward Lamon came into Hay's bedroom, poured himself a glass of whiskey, but refused Hay's offer of a bed. He borrowed a few blankets and rolled himself up outside the president's door. "In that attitude of touching and dumb fidelity," said Hay, "[Lamon passed the night] with a small arsenal of pistols & bowie knives around him." Hours later, after ensuring the president's safety, Lamon quietly left. In the morning Hay found the blankets rolled up on the floor outside his door.[8]

Congratulatory messages arrived in bundles. The president tried to accept the good news with modesty and, in a private conversation with Brooks, said, "Being only mortal, after all, I should have been a little mortified if I had been beaten in this campaign before the people." A day later a note arrived from McClellan: "I have the honor to resign my commission as a Major General in the Army of the U.S.A." The defeated candidate sent no words of concession or congratulation, but to his friend Samuel Barlow he wrote, "For my country's sake I deplore the result—but . . . feel that a great weight is removed from my mind. I can imagine no combination of circumstances that can ever induce me to enter [public life] again." On November 13 the president accepted McClellan's resignation without comment.[9]

With every ballot tallied, Lincoln polled 2,213,665 votes to McClellan's 1,802,237. He won every state but Delaware, Kentucky, and New Jersey, giving him an electoral majority of 212 to 21. Yet Carl Schurz later wrote, "The size of the majority did not come up to the expectation of Lincoln's friends." The statement may have been true in some quarters, but Senator John Sherman, writing in December to his brother, said, "The election of Lincoln scarcely raised a ripple on the surface. It was anticipated."[10]

General Grant, writing Stanton from City Point, said, "Congratulate the

President for me. . . . The election having passed off quietly, no bloodshed or riot throughout the land, is a victory worth more to the country than a battle won. Rebeldom and Europe will soon construe it." Stanton appreciated the message but remained in bed. For several days he had been close to death.[11]

While relaxing, Lincoln told Brooks about a peculiar incident following his election in 1860. Returning home exhausted, he settled on a lounge and saw his full-length body reflected from a swinging glass on his bureau. His face, however, formed two separate and distinct images, one sharp and the other pale, with the tips of his nose about three inches apart. He got up, looked in the mirror, and the illusion vanished, but when he returned to the lounge it reappeared. Bothered by this peculiar aberration, he experimented the following day, and "Sure enough!" he told Brooks, "the thing came again," but never afterward, no matter how many times he tried. He finally mentioned the incident to his wife, who became instantly alarmed. "She thought it was a 'sign,'" said the president, "that I was to be elected to a second term of office, and that the paleness of one of the faces was an omen that I should not see life through the last term." Other business soon occupied the president's time, and the foreboding shared with Brooks soon vanished.[12]

At nightfall a procession gay with banners and resplendent with lanterns marched to the White House. The vast crowd flooded the main entrance, blocked the semicircular drive, and filled the grounds as far as the eye could see. Martial music blared, people cheered, and cannon parked in the driveway boomed, rattling windows. Lincoln appeared at the portico window above the doorway to read a text hastily but thoughtfully written: "It has long been a grave question whether any government, not *too* strong for the liberties of the people, can be strong *enough* to maintain its own existence, in great emergencies." Affirming the importance of elections, he said, "We can not have free government without elections; and if the rebellion could force us to forgo, or postpone a national election, it might fairly claim to have already conquered and ruined us. . . . It has demonstrated that a people's government can sustain a national election, in the midst of a great civil war. Until now it has not been known to the world that this was a possibility. It shows also how *sound*, and how *strong* we still are." Having praised the people for being strong, he asked them to remain strong a little longer because "the rebellion continues, and now that the election is over, may not all, having a common interest, re-unite in a common effort, to save our common country? For my own part I have striven, and shall continue to strive to avoid placing any obstacle in the way. . . . May I ask those who have not differed with me, to join me, in this same spirit towards those who have?" After finishing, he gave Hay a glance and said, "Not very graceful, but I am growing old enough not to care much for the manner of doing things."[13]

On November 11 Lincoln removed a glued folded note from his desk and asked the cabinet if they remembered signing their names to it without knowing the words inside. "This is it," Lincoln said. "Now, Mr. Hay, see if you can get this open without tearing it." Dated August 23 (six days before the Chicago convention), the note said, "This morning, as for some days past, it seems exceedingly probable that this administration will not be reëlected. Then it will be my duty to so coöperate with the President-elect as to save the Union between the election and the inauguration; as we will have secured his election on such ground that he cannot possibly save it afterwards." Everything had changed since then. Lincoln explained how he would have approached President-elect McClellan, saying, "General, the election has demonstrated that you are stronger, have more influence with the American people than I. Now let us get together, you with your influence and I with all the executive power of the Government, try to save the country. You raise as many troops as you possibly can for this final trial, and I will devote all my energies to assisting and finishing the war." Seward commented, "And the General would answer you '*Yes, Yes,*' and the next day when you saw him again & pressed these views upon him, he would say, 'Yes, Yes' & so on forever and would have done nothing at all." "At least," Lincoln replied, "I should have done my duty and have stood clear before my own *conscience.*"[14]

When the day ended, so did the reflections. As the first president since Andrew Jackson elected to a second term, Lincoln still had a war to fight.

In September, as fall elections heated up, Chase still felt wounded by the circumstances leading to his resignation. Since June 30 he had rarely seen the president, nor had he spoken with him privately. There had been no further mention of a Supreme Court appointment, and Chase wondered why. He had put his bitterness aside and on September 17 noted in his diary, "It is my conviction that the cause I love and the general interests of the country will be best promoted by [Lincoln's] reelection, and I have resolved to join my efforts to those of almost the whole body of my friends in securing it."[15]

On October 12 eighty-six-year-old Chief Justice Roger B. Taney died. Chase wanted the judicial post, believed it had been promised him, and was prepared to do most anything to get it. Among rivals were two of his antagonists, Edwin Stanton and Montgomery Blair, both with excellent judicial credentials. Blair needed a job, having been removed from the cabinet, and he wanted the appointment. His natural abilities, legal experience, former judicial training, and familiarity with matters coming before the Court more than qualified him for the post. Many years had passed since Chase, though a lawyer and a constitutional scholar, had last put his legal skills before a court. Those who opposed him argued that his practical knowledge of the law was limited because his life had been devoted almost exclusively to politics. To this and other unsolicited advice, Lincoln made no reply.[16]

Chase did some fence mending when he decided to stump for Lincoln's reelection, and he also decided not to place the president under any obligation. Between September 24 and November 5 he spoke to large crowds at least twenty times in support of the Republican ticket. He appeared in Kentucky, Michigan, and Missouri but spent most of his time speaking in Ohio and Pennsylvania. The press followed wherever he went. His remarks were well received by the public and certain to catch the president's attention.[17]

After Taney died, Chase's friends began calling on Lincoln, who merely replied he would make no nominations until after the elections. He still intended to nominate Chase, knowing the appointment would please the radicals. Although Chase had his own views on reconstruction, Lincoln knew the former secretary did not agree with the extreme measures proposed by the radicals.

Lincoln's one reservation involved Chase's ambition to become president and how it might affect his decisions on the bench. Blair voiced the same concern to Senator Henry Wilson, adding, "Chase would certainly not be nominated." Wilson went directly to the president for comment. "Oh! As to that, I care nothing," Lincoln replied. "Of Mr. Chase's ability and of his soundness on the general issues of the war there is, of course, no question. I have only one doubt about his appointment. He is a man of unbounded ambition, and has been working all his life to become President. That he can never be; and I fear that if I make him chief-justice he will simply become more restless and uneasy and neglect the place in his strife and intrigue to make himself President. If I were sure he would go on the bench and give up his aspirations and do nothing but make himself a great judge, I would not hesitate a moment."[18] After the election Chase waited in Ohio hoping to hear from the president. When no invitation came, Chase began to fret.

On November 24 Attorney General Bates resigned, effective the end of the month. A friend, Isaac Newton, informed Bates he had good news. After speaking with the president, Lincoln had mentioned Bates as a possible choice for chief justice but said "Chase was turning every stone to get it." Bates was not interested, having his mind "made up to private life."

Lincoln offered a vacant judgeship to Bates, but he declined, complaining of the "uselessness of a legal system in a State dominated by the revolutionary spirit which then ruled in Missouri."[19]

On November 30 Judge Advocate General Joseph Holt rejected the offer to replace Bates but recommended fellow Kentuckian, fifty-two-year-old James Speed, as being loyal, professionally qualified, and of spotless personal character. Lincoln immediately contacted Speed, writing, "I appoint you . . . Attorney General. Please come on at once." James Speed was the brother of Joshua Speed, one of Lincoln's closest friends during the early Springfield years. For political reasons Lincoln wanted Bates replaced by someone from a border state. He believed Speed balanced the conservative side of the cabinet, but in this calculation he erred. Six months later, writing from retirement, Bates referred to Speed as a man "with not much reputation as a lawyer, and no strong confidence in his own opinions, [but] was caressed and courted by Stanton and Seward, and sank, under the weight of their blandishments, into a mere tool. . . . I cannot help pitying my poor successor!"[20]

Chase heard nothing from the president, but the sudden resignation of Bates and the hurried appointment of Speed caught his attention. As the second session of the Thirty-eighth Congress approached, Chase could no longer constrain his impatience and started for Washington. Lincoln enjoyed catching Chase off guard. The practice began in 1860 and seemed never to stop. On December 6, on arriving in Washington, Chase learned to his amazement that Lincoln had nominated him earlier that day, and the Senate unanimously confirmed the appointment. The president knew Chase's mind and ignored the formality of asking him if he still wanted the appointment. Nor did he sit with Chase beforehand to air his concerns over the former secretary's presidential aspirations.

Chase went home and received a salute at the door from his pregnant daughter, Kate Chase Sprague, who for years had pressed her father to become president. He at once sent a note to Lincoln, whom he had not seen since returning to Washington: "I cannot sleep before I must thank [you] for this mark of your confidence, and especially for the manner in which the nomination was made. I will never forget either, and trust you will never regret either."[21] Lincoln made no comment. Nicolay probably spoke for others when he wrote, "Probably no other man than Lincoln would have had, in this age of the world, the degree of magnanimity to thus forgive and exalt a rival who had so deeply and so unjustifiably intrigued against him."[22]

Noah Brooks, who enjoyed many private conversations with the president, said Lincoln never intended to appoint anyone but Chase to the chief justiceship. Brooks called it a "peculiar trait" of the president to preclude any doubt in his own mind by constantly inviting opinions from others to confirm his own decisions. "It was this mental habit," said Brooks, "that induced him to argue with his visitors as though his mind was not already made up," when actually it was. Nine days after his nomination Chase said, "So help me God," and in a simple ceremony became chief justice of the Supreme Court.[23]

On November 15, a week after the national election, General Sherman destroyed the military resources of Atlanta and with sixty-two thousand men marched toward Savannah, Georgia. Having laid before the rebels his own maxim for war, he left behind nothing but destruction, declaring, "If the people raise a howl against my barbarity and cruelty, I will answer that war is war. . . . If they want peace, they and their relatives must stop the war." Responding on behalf of Grant, Halleck replied, "Not only are you justified by the laws and usages of war . . . I am fully of the opinion that the nature of your position, the character of the war, the conduct of the enemy . . . will justify you in gathering up all the forage and provisions which your army may require for . . . your march farther into the enemy's country." The "March to the Sea" had begun.[24]

Weeks before Sherman set out for Savannah, General Hood abandoned Georgia and moved into Alabama. He hoped to draw Sherman out of Atlanta by breaking up Union communications. Sherman ignored Hood. On October 18 he detached the Fourth and Twenty-third corps, all the cavalry but Kilpatrick's division, and sent them to Nashville to reinforce General Thomas. As Hood headed for Tennessee, Sherman divided the remainder of his force into two wings and prepared to march in a manner designed to confuse the enemy. "I can make this march," Sherman telegraphed Grant, "and make Georgia howl."[25]

Grant disliked the notion of Hood roaming free through Alabama and Tennessee and suggested Sherman first destroy the Confederates, after which the army could go wherever it pleased with impunity. Sherman replied, "If I turn back the whole effect of my campaign will be lost." Sherman believed that Thomas, if attacked, could defeat Hood. At first Grant disagreed, but Sherman insisted. Grant could not see the field from City Point, Virginia, and finally replied, "I say, then, go as you propose."[26]

Lincoln and Stanton monitored Sherman's activity but never interfered. On November 6, two days before Election Day, Sherman made a political point: "If we can march a well-appointed army right through [the enemy's] territory it is a demonstration to the world, foreign and domestic, that we have a power which [Jefferson] Davis cannot resist." No one argued the point. On November 12, moments before Sherman cut communications at Atlanta and began marching to Savannah, Thomas sent a final message to say that if he were attacked, "I believe I shall have men enough to ruin [Hood], and if he attempts to follow you I will follow him." Weeks passed before Sherman and Thomas communicated again.[27]

Sherman had more in mind than Savannah. "I was strongly inspired," he wrote, "with a feeling that the movement on our part was a direct attack upon the rebel army and the rebel capital at Richmond, though a full thousand miles of hostile territory intervened; and that for better or worse it would end the war." If Grant could not crack the rebel lines, the Army of the West would do it.[28]

Sherman's marching orders were clear, concise, and a model of completeness. He omitted mentioning the destination but laid out exactly how the two wings would operate, each taking separate roads running roughly parallel to each other and converging from time to time to communicate. Foraging parties were to collect provender along routes of travel, enough to keep the army supplied for ten days, but no homes were to be entered. Horses, mules, and wagons, however, were fair confiscations. As long as the army passed unmolested, Sherman ordered no private property destroyed other than mills, cotton gins, and factories capable of supporting the Confederates. Any effort to impede the army would result in the total devastation of the area. Sherman anticipated that thousands of blacks might try to follow the army and made it clear only a small number of able-bodied young men, if needed, would be allowed to join the march.[29]

At 7:00 a.m. November 16 Sherman's sixty-two thousand–man army moved out of Atlanta with the band playing "John Brown's Body," which later became "The Battle Hymn of the Republic." When Senator John Sherman stopped at the White House to inquire about his brother, Lincoln replied, "I know what hole he went in at, but I can't tell what hole he will come out at."

For a winter campaign the weather remained unseasonably delightful. Sixty thousand men remembered the march for the balance of their lives. There were skirmishes and cavalry clashes but no battles. Jeff Davis implored Georgians to hide their "negroes, horses, cattle, and provisions . . . and burn what you cannot carry. . . . Assail the invader in front, flank, and rear, by night and by day. Let him have no rest." Most Georgians had enough sense to let Sherman's bummers pass without agitating the long blue line. The army cut a fifty- to sixty-mile-wide swath through central Georgia and on December 10 invested Savannah.[30]

Sherman encountered resistance at Savannah, but he captured Fort McAllister and notified the South Atlantic Blockading Squadron stationed offshore. A boat took him to the flagship, where he met with Admiral John A. Dahlgren, opened communications with Washington, and made arrangements to receive supplies. Dahlgren handed Sherman two dumbfounding letters written by Grant several days earlier. One read, "I have concluded that the most important operation toward closing out the rebellion will be to close out Lee and his army." Sherman did not dispute the statement, but he disagreed with the method. Grant asked Sherman to leave artillery and cavalry at Fort McAllister and transport the army to Virginia by sea. Sherman wanted to capture Savannah first and questioned the wisdom of moving the army to Virginia. On December 21 Lieutenant General William J. Hardee solved one of Sherman's problems by abandoning Savannah.[31]

Sherman recovered quickly from any disappointment he may have felt over Hardee's escape. Occupying Savannah left the Confederacy with only two ports, Charleston and Wilmington. Savannah also provided Sherman with a port for keeping his army supplied. In a high state of elation he telegraphed the president, "I beg to present you as a Christmas gift, the city of Savannah, with 150 heavy guns and plenty of ammunition, also about 25,000 bales of cotton." Sherman sent the telegraph on December 22, but it first went by boat to Fort Monroe and eventually reached the White House on Christmas Day. Noah Brooks recalled how "the sleeping works of Washington was aroused at an early hour . . . by the thunders of one hundred guns, fired by order of the War Department."[32]

The following day Lincoln sent thanks to Sherman, admitting he had never been in favor of the operation, yet on December 6 in his annual message to Congress he referred to Sherman's "march of three hundred miles directly through the insurgent region" as the "most remarkable feature in the military operations of the year." To Sherman he wrote, "Now, the undertaking being a success, the honor is all yours for I believe none of us went farther than to acquiesce." Lincoln had become enough of a military strategist to recognize what Sherman had accomplished. "In showing to the world that your army could be divided, putting the stronger part to an important new service, and yet leaving enough to vanquish the old opposing force of the whole . . . brings those who sat in the darkness, to see a great light. But what next?" asked the president then, answering his own question, said, "I suppose it will be safer if I leave Gen. Grant and yourself to decide."[33]

Grant changed his mind about shipping Sherman's army to Virginia. Two months would be lost with water transportation, and Sherman said he could do more damage to impede Lee's supplies by marching through the Carolinas. Savannah's capture convinced Grant that Lee would have to weaken his army and send reinforcements to the Carolinas or give up the South, which Jeff Davis could not afford to do. Sherman prepared an excellent plan—a right-wheel movement compelling Lee's army either to come out and fight or to starve. "General Grant's wishes," Halleck advised Sherman, "are that this whole matter of your future actions should be left entirely to your own discretion." Sherman could not have asked for more.[34]

Halleck never approved Sherman's March to the Sea because it violated a military tenet of operating deep in hostile territory with no line of communications. With less than twenty-two hundred casualties, Sherman destroyed Georgia's ability to support the Confederacy and put his army in position to cooperate with Grant. Now free to plan his next campaign, Sherman began reorganizing his force to end the war.

When on November 16 Sherman marched from Atlanta, Lincoln felt uneasy about leaving General Thomas in Nashville to deal with Hood. Nor did Grant share Sherman's trust in Thomas. Hood's best chance of victory was to move into Tennessee quickly and smash Thomas's small army before reinforcements arrived. Hood moved slowly and on November 30 suffered a demoralizing defeat by Major General John M. Schofield's Twenty-third Corps at Franklin. After Schofield withdrew to Nashville, Hood advanced, took position in the hills south of the city, and waited.

Thomas reorganized his force, which with Schofield's corps increased to thirty thousand effectives. Thomas never rushed but made extensive preparations, but when ready to attack, he struck hard. Lincoln and Stanton waited and, after nothing happened, concluded that Thomas intended to winter behind his fortifications. Lincoln did not know Hood's army was badly damaged, but as each day passed he feared Hood would skirt Nashville and invade Kentucky. The president mentioned his fears to Stanton, who notified Grant that Thomas was manifesting McClellan-like symptoms. Stanton said Thomas wanted more cavalry to stop rebels raiding the countryside. "If he waits for [cavalry] to get ready," Stanton warned Grant, "Gabriel will be blowing his last horn." Aware of Thomas's tendency to be slow and methodical, Grant sent several dispatches urging the general to attack at once. Thomas replied that he would attack when ready.[35]

Grant had not witnessed Thomas's dogged fight at Chickamauga. Having observed the general mainly in defensive actions, he warned Stanton that Thomas would probably never attack and suggested replacing him with Schofield. Halleck replied the order must come from Grant, although no one in the administration "so far as I am informed" favored Thomas's removal. Grant continued to pressure Thomas and, after waiting twenty-four hours for the general's answer, telegraphed orders to Halleck to relieve Thomas and put Schofield in command.[36]

Before Halleck sent the order, Thomas informed Grant he had advanced but a sleet storm halted the operation. Halleck immediately telegraphed Grant asking if he still wanted Thomas relieved. Grant agreed to suspend the order, subject to seeing what Thomas did when the weather improved.[37]

Several days passed and Thomas remained idle. Grant departed for Washington to confer with Lincoln before going to Nashville to relieve Thomas. On December 15 he met with Halleck, Stanton, and Lincoln, who cautioned against changing commanders on the eve of battle and argued that Thomas was in the field and better able to assess the situation. Grant, however, remained adamant, and Lincoln reluctantly agreed to let the general-in-chief have his way. Grant wrote the order removing Thomas, gave it to Major Eckert for transmission, and returned to Willard's Hotel to leave for Tennessee in the morning. Lines at Nashville had been down, so Eckert tried once more before retiring for the night. At 10:00 p.m. the line opened. As Eckert prepared to send Grant's order, a message arrived by way of Louisville stating that on the fifteenth Thomas had attacked Hood, routed the enemy, and planned to finish off the Confederates in the morning. Eckert recalled Lincoln's reluctance to remove Thomas, held Grant's order, and turned the matter over to Stanton, who had gone to bed. Stanton shouted "Hurrah," dressed, and hurried with Eckert to the White House. Lincoln had also gone to bed, but Stanton woke him up. The president appeared on the second story landing in his nightshirt holding a candle. When Stanton announced Thomas's victory, Lincoln held the candle over his head, his face gleaming with satisfaction, thanked the secretary for bringing such great news, and went back to bed.[38]

During the midnight excitement Eckert took Stanton aside to explain why he had held Grant's order. "Mr. Secretary," said Eckert, "I fear I have violated a military rule and have placed myself liable to be court-martialed." Stanton put his arm around Eckert and replied, "Major, if they court-martial you, they will have to court-martial me . . . you did right."[39]

Meanwhile, a messenger delivered a copy of Thomas's telegram to Grant at Willard's Hotel. The general read it, turned to the officer beside him, and said, "I guess we will not go to Nashville." Uncertain of whether the order relieving Thomas had been sent, Grant telegraphed the general, "I was just on my way to Nashville, but receiving a dispatch . . . detailing your splendid success . . . I shall go no farther." "Push the enemy now," he added, "and give him no rest until he is entirely destroyed." Caught in an error, Grant was not effusive with praise, though he should have been. Stanton, however, tendered genuine thanks, promising Thomas a hundred-gun salute.[40]

Without knowing Grant's reaction to Thomas's victory or the particulars of the battle, Lincoln telegraphed his personal congratulations. Having become a true strategist, Lincoln added, "You made a magnificent beginning; a grand consummation is within your easy reach. Do not let it slip." Thomas had not painstakingly made his preparations to let anything slip. As promised, he shattered Hood's army, forced the rebels back into Mississippi, and followed the enemy retreat with one of the most relentless cavalry pursuits of the war. Only a small ineffective remnant of Hood's force survived. Historian T. Harry Williams wrote, "The victory at Nashville was the only one in the war so complete that the defeated army practically lost its existence. It was also a complete vindication of Lincoln's faith in Thomas. Again the President had been more right than Grant."[41]

As 1864 came to a close, the Confederacy had retracted on every front, but Lee's long line of trenches still stretched unbroken from Richmond to Petersburg. There were still enemy troops in the Deep South and the Trans-Mississippi, but the large armies were gone, except in Virginia. Gone, too, was the Confederate navy. Hugh McCulloch, soon to become the next secretary of the Treasury, summed up the month of December best when he said, "Our joy was irrepressible . . . it was an assurance that the days of the Confederacy were numbered. Every member of the cabinet knew, at last, that the war was won and the Union safe."[42]

CHAPTER 23

"It made my heart jump"

During the winter of 1864–65 little changed along the fortified trenches that stretched through forty miles of mud between Richmond and Petersburg, Virginia. In early December, after approving William T. Sherman's Carolina campaign, Grant became concerned about logistics. Capturing Wilmington would achieve two goals. Sherman would have a base for drawing supplies, and the last gateway between the Confederate States and the outside world would be closed. The administration agreed with this perfectly logical plan.[1]

Wilmington rested on the Cape Fear River about twenty-eight miles upriver from Fort Fisher, a heavily fortified earthwork located at the river's mouth. The river defense system provided effective protection for blockade-runners, which waited below the horizon for nightfall before dashing into the river. Wilmington could not be assaulted from the sea without first eliminating Fort Fisher, which required a massive joint army-navy amphibious operation, so Gideon Welles brought Admiral David D. Porter from the Mississippi River and put him in charge of the North Atlantic Blockading Squadron. Porter worked well with Grant during the Vicksburg campaign, and the general wanted him to organize and lead the amphibious phase of the operation.[2]

Grant named Major General Godfrey Weitzel, commanding the Eighteenth Corps, to lead the assault phase of the operation. He oversimplified the task, telling the general, "Weitzel, this is to be another Mobile affair," meaning that the troops were to go ashore and wait until Porter's navy blew the fort to pieces.

Wilmington lay within the military district commanded by General Butler, who immediately sidetracked the plan and imposed changes. Several weeks passed while he packed five thousand tons of gunpowder into a hulk he planned to detonate close to shore on the theory the explosion would bury the fort in its own dirt. According to Butler, Welles endorsed the plan. Butler fibbed. "I have no faith in General Butler's scheme of knocking down Fort Fisher by blowing up a vessel filled with powder," said Welles, "though the powder-boat may fail, I hope the expedition will not." Lincoln remained circumspect and left the decision to the experts.[3]

Nobody wanted Butler involved in the expedition, but he resented being bypassed by Grant, who went directly to Weitzel. Butler slowed the expedition to prepare his powder boat, and several weeks passed, during which

Grant became increasingly impatient. With Sherman about to move, Grant could wait no longer. He ordered Weitzel to move immediately, but this time he sent the orders through Butler. Butler intercepted them, took personal command of the army phase of the expedition, and never mentioned Grant's orders to Weitzel.

The fleet sailed from Hampton Roads, Virginia, on December 13 with Weitzel's sixty-five hundred troops following on transports. Ten days later the navy towed the hulk *Wilderness* within four hundred yards of Fort Fisher and lit fuses to the ship's powder-packed compartments. At 1:30 a.m. on December 24 the *Wilderness* exploded without injuring the fort. Porter moved his ships off Fort Fisher and wasted ammunition waiting for Butler's arrival. The following morning, Christmas Day, Weitzel put twenty-five hundred men ashore. After several boats capsized, he stopped. When Weitzel's men on the beach came under heavy fire, Butler deserted the expedition, leaving Porter to rescue the troops on shore. Butler hurried back to Fort Monroe, informed Grant the expedition had miscarried, and blamed Porter. When Grant learned the details of Butler's mismanagement, he told Porter to "hold on where you are for a few days and I will endeavor to be back again with an increased force and without the former commander."[4]

On learning the Wilmington expedition had failed, Lincoln asked Grant for an explanation. The general replied the assault had been "a gross and culpable failure" and the person to blame "will be known." The president expressed no surprise when he learned from Stanton and Grant that Butler was to blame. On January 4, 1865, Grant asked Stanton for permission to remove Butler from command. With the 1864 elections over, Lincoln no longer needed Butler's influence at the polls and authorized Stanton to do it.[5]

On January 8 Butler bid the army farewell but never took blame for his expulsion. Some expected Butler's dismissal to cause political repercussions, but it passed with barely a ripple. "He [Butler] does not conceal his chagrin but has hardly discovered whom to strike," Welles remarked to his diary. "It will soon be known," he added, "that General Grant desired to get rid of him." Lincoln had at last removed the one political general who had given him nothing but trouble and military disasters.[6]

On January 2 Grant placed Major General Alfred H. Terry in command of a second Fort Fisher expedition with instructions to cooperate with Admiral Porter each step of the way. At 8:00 a.m. on January 15 Porter opened a massive naval bombardment on Fort Fisher. Terry's infantry landed on the beach and took possession of the fort. General Lee, whose army had become largely dependent upon Wilmington for supplies, rushed troops to the area. While

Porter took his ships up the river, the army followed in transports. On February 23 Wilmington surrendered to General Terry, thereby closing, with the exception of Charleston, the Confederacy's last lifeline to the outside world.[7]

During the Fort Fisher expedition Congress finally passed a joint resolution calling for a Thirteenth Amendment to abolish slavery wherever it existed. The first step began on July 17, 1862, when the Thirty-seventh Congress passed a sweeping radical-inspired bill abolishing slavery in the District of Columbia and the territories. The bill virtually repealed the Fugitive Slave Law and provided for the confiscation of slaves. The president supplemented the legislation on September 22 by issuing the Emancipation Proclamation, which became operational on January 1, 1863. Lincoln understood that without constitutional amendments courts could nullify legislation and proclamations, so in his annual message of December 8, 1863, he asked Congress to "omit no fair opportunity of aiding these important steps to a great consummation" by authorizing an amendment. Later, when speaking to Governor Edwin D. Morgan of New York, he said, "We are like whalers who have been long on a chase: we have at last got the harpoon into the monster, but we must now look how we steer, or with one *flop* of his tail he will send us all into eternity."[8]

Six days after Lincoln delivered his annual address, James M. Ashley of Ohio introduced a bill, and James F. Wilson of Iowa introduced a resolution to the House proposing an amendment banishing slavery throughout the United States. On January 11, 1864, John B. Henderson of Missouri proposed a similar resolution to the Senate. The resolution went to Lyman Trumbull's Judiciary Committee, where it sat for a month. When Charles Sumner warned he would take the resolution into a select committee, Trumbull proposed rephrasing it:

> Article XIII
> SECTION 1. Neither slavery nor involuntary servitude, except as a punishment for crime, whereof the party shall have been duly convicted, shall exist within the United States, or any place subject to their jurisdiction.
> SECTION 2. Congress shall have power to enforce this article by appropriate legislation.

On April 11, 1864, the Senate passed the resolution, but on May 31 it failed to muster the required two-thirds vote in the House. Knowing on June 7

Governor Morgan would be making the opening speech at the Baltimore convention, Lincoln asked him to put the resolution before the delegates. Morgan worked the resolution into the Republican platform, and two days later, after being renominated for president, Lincoln reminded the party that "such amendment of the Constitution as now proposed" was indeed "a fitting, and necessary conclusion to the final success of the Union cause."[9]

When the lame-duck Congress reconvened in December, Lincoln argued that because the adoption of the amendment was merely a "question of time . . . may we not agree that the sooner the better." Having gained a second term and with impressive military gains, he expected more cooperation from the Republican majority in Congress. Of matters on abolition he expected radicals to twist arms until the House served up the required two-thirds vote. Lincoln no longer took a back seat in the effort. He brought Democrats and border state congressmen to the White House and did some arm-twisting himself.[10]

The issue drifted until January 31, 1865, when the galleries in the House filled once more to vote. "Up to noon," a reporter wrote, "the pro-slavery party are said to [be] confident of defeating the amendment." One supporter admitted, "'Tis a toss of a copper." Debate ended at 4:00 p.m., and voting began. Using the exact words composed by Trumbull's Judiciary Committee in January 1864, the measure passed 119 to 56. According to Indiana congressman George Julian, "Members joined in the shouting and kept it up for some minutes, many embracing each other, and others completely surrendering themselves to tears of joy. It seemed to me I had been born into a new life." One would think a major battle had been won. A salute of one hundred guns thundered as congratulations spread through the city.[11]

To serenaders Lincoln referred to the amendment as "a very fitting if not an indispensable adjunct of winding up a great difficulty." He said the amendment was necessary because "a question might be raised whether the [Emancipation] proclamation was legally valid." Congratulating everyone "upon the great moral victory," Lincoln said, "This amendment is a king's cure-all for all evils. It winds up the whole thing." Had Lincoln been mindful of his Gettysburg Address, he might have added his promise to the nation for a "new birth of freedom."[12]

When Lincoln delivered his annual message to Congress on December 6, 1864, he faced a fourth year of war, but indications pointed to a swift collapse of the Confederacy. He also spoke of the Confederate president, whose name he avoided using, as a man who "would accept nothing short of severance of the Union—precisely what we will not and cannot give." Believing Southerners desired peace, Lincoln said, "No attempt at negotiation with the insurgent leader could result in any good. What is true . . . of him who heads the insurgent cause, is not necessarily true of those who follow. Although he cannot reaccept the Union, they can." He directed his message to the Southern people, not their president: "They can at any moment, have peace simply by laying down their arms and submitting to the national authority under the Constitution." His year-old proclamation of amnesty remained unchanged. Thousands of Southerners had subscribed to it; many more would. "But," Lincoln warned, "the time will come—probably will come—when . . . more rigorous measures than heretofore shall be adopted."[13]

Lincoln's address revived peace efforts. Blair Sr., being long acquainted with the people of the South, asked Lincoln to empower him as mediator. "Come to me after Savannah falls," the president replied. Three days after Christmas Blair received a simple card from Lincoln allowing him to "go South and return." Blair said nothing to the president of his intentions, nor did he ask advice. Blair and Davis were old colleagues, and the Confederate president was curious about what a man with Blair's credentials might offer.[14]

On January 12 Blair spoke at length with Davis, whose haggard appearance showed the marks of a long and devastating war. The discussion represented the most thorough and direct conversation held between Davis and a Lincoln confidant since the formation of the Confederacy. Because Blair acted without presidential guidance, the conversation rambled over a wide range of topics, some which Lincoln would have placed off limits. Blair knew Lincoln's three inviolable tenets were emancipation, reunification, and the cessation of hostilities. Yet he told Davis, "Slavery no longer remains an insurmountable obstruction to pacification." The Confederate Congress had recently authorized the induction of blacks into the army, and Blair believed this move would lead to the institution's eventual death. Without using the exact words, Blair so much as said, so why fight over it.[15]

Blair's most bizarre suggestion involved Texas and France's puppet ruler, Maximilian, whose presence in Mexico had destabilized the border. He suggested Davis agree to an armistice, the terms of which would allow him to move his army into Texas, establish a dictatorship, and drive the French invaders out of Mexico. Blair extended the so-called dictatorship to possibly include control of Central America to the Isthmus of Panama. If Davis agreed to the proposal, Blair predicted many Northerners would join the enterprise, including his son, Frank Blair Jr.

Davis liked the proposal, but he questioned Seward's reaction, whom he personally despised. Blair admitted Seward "would betray any man [who] stood in the way of his selfish and ambitious schemes," but he assured Davis that Lincoln would make any sacrifice "necessary for the good of the country; and you may rely on it." Davis admitted having no confidence in Seward but was satisfied Lincoln would keep his word.

The wild scheme of expanding the South's dominion to the isthmus appealed to Davis because it might absolve him from a ruinous personal defeat and perhaps a hangman's noose. Blair spent three or four days in Richmond talking to other prominent Confederates and found everyone "eager to seize upon any contrivance to help them out of their direful prospects." After scrutinizing Blair's proposal, Davis replied that he would be willing "to enter into negotiations for the restoration of peace" and would send a commission if Lincoln would appoint one also. Lincoln knew nothing about the proposed political crusade in Mexico until he read Blair's report.[16]

Lincoln quashed the proposal. Nor would he agree to negotiate with Davis, whom he had consistently labeled as the leader of an insurgency, not a government. He did, however, send a message to Blair allowing him to go back to Richmond to express a willingness to receive informally a Confederate commission "with a view of securing peace to the people of our *one common country.*" Lincoln's position should have discouraged further discussions, but Blair, seeing his work rejected, suggested Lincoln and Davis step away from negotiations and let Grant and Lee enter into peace discussions. Lincoln quickly vetoed that proposal.[17]

With Blair circulating through Richmond and every influential person in the capital aware of his peace mission, Davis felt compelled to do something, although his only two alternatives were independence or reunion. With the fall of Fort Fisher coupled with rumors of Richmond's abandonment, Davis tried to buy time. He assigned Vice President Alexander Stephens, Senator Robert M. T. Hunter, and Assistant Secretary of War John A. Campbell as Confederate commissioners to Blair's proposed peace conference.[18]

Davis created an impasse by instructing his commissioners to discuss "the issues involved in the existing war, and for the purpose of securing peace to the *two countries.*" Lincoln refused to receive commissioners unable to discuss reunification but disliked wasting an opportunity for peace. He sent Major Thomas T. Eckert to the Richmond lines to detain the commissioners unless their instructions were changed to exclude any reference to the Confederacy as a separate nation.[19]

Being eager to end the war, Grant intervened, met the commissioners, and persuaded them to remove from their instructions the odious reference to two separate countries. The commissioners complied, and on February 2, 1965, Stanton received from Grant a message stating the offensive wordage had been removed. Lincoln replied, "Say to the gentlemen I will meet them personally at Fortress Monroe as soon as I can get there." According to historians Benjamin P. Thomas and Harold M. Hyman, Stanton became concerned, fearing "the kindhearted President might yield too much if he sat down with the commissioners."

Lincoln originally planned for only Seward to attend the February 1 conference and had instructed him to listen without authority to "consummate anything." He also informed Grant to "Let nothing . . . change, hinder, or delay your Military movements, or plans." The receipt of Grant's message on February 2 changed Lincoln's mind. When the general mentioned the commissioners would be compelled to go back to Richmond "without any expression from any one in authority," Lincoln decided he had better hear for himself what they had to say.[20]

On the morning of February 3, Stephens, Hunter, and Campbell joined Lincoln and Seward aboard a steamer at Fort Monroe for a four-hour conference. The president had not seen Stephens for sixteen years, when as Whigs they held seats in the House of Representatives. Lincoln stood a full foot taller and weighed twice as much as Stephens, and when the latter came into the ship's saloon, he wore a huge shaggy gray woolen overcoat. As he loosened the shawls to step out of it, Lincoln came forward, shook his hand, and remarked, "Never have I seen so small a nubbin come out of so much husk." The comment broke the ice. The participants agreed the meeting would be informal, and Seward made it clear no official record would be kept.[21]

Stephens opened the business phase of the meeting, asking, "Mr. President, is there no way of putting an end to the present trouble?" Lincoln replied, "There was but one way . . . and that was for those who were resisting the laws of the Union to cease that resistance." Stephens said his commission "had been induced to believe that both parties might for a while leave their present strife in abeyance and occupy themselves with some continental question" until their anger cooled. "I suppose you refer to something Mr. Blair has said," the president replied. Stephens confirmed the remark, admitting that Davis wanted a truce to join forces and pursue Blair's Mexican project. The president explained that whatever Blair said was of his own accord. "I was always willing to hear propositions for peace on the conditions of this letter," Lincoln said, pointing to the one Seward held, "and on no other. The restoration of the Union is a *sine qua non* with me, and hence my instructions that no conference was to be held except upon this basis."

The Confederate vice president attempted to argue that the Mexican project would, over time, bring about reunion and probably without any agreement beforehand. Lincoln said he would make no concessions of any kind with a confederation of states in rebellion without first disposing of the question of unification. Seward happened to have a copy of the president's annual message to Congress and read several passages, including one in particular: "In stating a single condition of peace, I mean simply to say that the war will cease on the part of the Government whenever it shall have ceased on the part of those who began it."[22]

Stephens tried to change the president's mind because Blair's Mexican project gave Jefferson Davis a face-saving solution. Davis certainly needed a graceful way to ease away from defeat, but Lincoln needed nothing but a little more time to end the war victoriously. Discussions reached an impasse, and Lincoln closed the session, saying, "Well, Stephens, I will reconsider it [the Mexican plan]; but I do not think my mind will change." Thus ended the Hampton Roads Peace Conference.

During the meeting Seward informed the commissioners of the passage of the Thirteenth Amendment, which, when ratified by three-fourths of the states would abolish slavery throughout the Union. According to Stephens, Seward said if the South agreed to immediate reunification, the restored states might have the vote to defeat the amendment. It is doubtful Seward made such a statement, but it is also possible he offered the bait to induce a reaction.[23]

Lincoln would not have altered his principles, but he would have been willing to give Southern states quick representation in Congress. The Senate had already denied Arkansas, Louisiana, and Tennessee the right to send representatives to the Electoral College, so rather than debate reconstruction issues with a war still in progress, Lincoln decided to wait. He might also have allowed gradual emancipation, provided some form of restitution to slaveholders, restored property and civic rights, and granted immediate amnesty. Radicals would never agree to a program so liberal, and the president knew it. In the end Lincoln returned to Washington to finish the war, and Davis's commissioners returned to Richmond knowing war would continue. Davis used the conference as a reason to appeal to his armies to fight harder, even though the South could no longer provide the resources with which to fight. On returning to Washington, Lincoln met with Stanton, who promptly telegraphed Grant that "nothing . . . transpiring with the three gentlemen from Richmond, is to cause any change, hindrance or delay, of your military plans or operations."[24]

Meeting the Confederate commissioners gave Lincoln insight into the deplorable condition of the South. He sincerely wanted to find a way to stop the wreckage and bloodshed. On returning from Fort Monroe, he drafted a joint resolution proposing to Congress an appropriation of $400 million for the abolishment of slavery on a pro rata basis of the slave population in all border states and states in rebellion. When it was presented to the cabinet, Welles warned "in the present temper of Congress" the proposal would only cause suspicion and distrust because the enemy was helpless and on the verge of collapse. Others agreed, arguing that Thaddeus Stevens, Benjamin Wade, and others still demanded retaliation, confiscation, death, desolation, and bloody revenge and would not only fight the resolution but would stir up both houses of Congress.[25]

Surprised by the cabinet's opposition, Lincoln asked, "How long will the war last?" When no one answered, he said, "A hundred days. We are spending now in carrying on the war three millions a day, which will amount to all this money, besides all the lives." He gave a deep sigh and said, "But you are all opposed to me, and I will not send the message." He picked up a pen, and perhaps having reached the same conclusion himself, noted on the document, "To-day these papers . . . were drawn up and submitted to the Cabinet and unanimously disapproved by them."[26]

On February 8, 1865, the Electoral College met and voted 212 for Abraham Lincoln and Andrew Johnson and 21 for George B. McClellan and George Hunt Pendleton. Since the 1860 election three states had been added to the Union—Kansas, West Virginia, and Nevada—and three states denied representation—Arkansas, Louisiana, and Tennessee. When Trumbull and his judicial committee arrived at the White House to notify the president of his reelection, Lincoln replied, "Having served four years in the depths of a great, and yet unended national peril, I can view this call to a second term, in nowise more flatteringly to myself, than as an expression of the public judgment, that I may better finish a difficult work, in which I have labored from the first, than could any one less severely schooled to the task."[27]

At noon on March 4, 1865, the president entered the Senate chamber to be sworn in for a second four-year term. African-American organizations with a military escort of black troops participated for the first time in an inaugural ceremony. Snow and rain fell overnight, and drizzle continued to ooze from a thick, murky overcast, yet people swarmed the Capitol to watch the ceremony. "The mud in the city," Noah Brooks recalled, "certainly excelled all other varieties I have ever seen before or since, and the greatest test of feminine heroism—the spoiling of their clothes—redounded amply to the credit of the women who were so bedraggled and drenched on that memorable day." When doors opened, women charged into the Senate chamber and, showing no deference to the proceedings, "chattered and clattered . . . just as though there was no Senate in session." Welles, who disliked turmoil, wrote, "All was confusion and without order,—a jumble."[28]

The presiding officer pounded an ivory mallet to bring the Senate to order and seat as many diplomats, dignitaries, and guests as possible. Cabinet members took front seats to the left of the chairman, with Seward at the head, followed by Stanton, Welles, James Speed, and William Dennison. William Pitt Fessenden occupied his old seat in the Senate, and John Palmer Usher missed the ceremony because of illness. Lincoln sat in the middle of the front row. Stanton looked particularly drawn and pale from the strain of ensuring Lincoln's protection. Hundreds of rebel deserters and Northern rowdies now lived in the city, but not a single disturbance occurred.

When the chamber quieted, members of the Supreme Court entered in flowing robes. Chief Justice Salmon Chase looked "very young and also very queer carrying a stove-pipe hat and wearing his long black silk gown." People craned their necks to see the former secretary of the Treasury, and the hubbub began all over again.[29]

At the stroke of twelve the main entrance swung open, and Vice President–elect Andrew Johnson entered arm in arm with Hannibal Hamlin and took seats on the dais of the presiding officer. Hamlin made a brief speech and presented Johnson, who rose flushed and unsteady. Having just arrived from Tennessee, Johnson was still recovering from a serious illness. Earlier Hamlin had taken Johnson, a temperate man unaccustomed to alcohol, to his room and reinforced him with liberal doses of whiskey. When Johnson stood to acknowledge members of the cabinet, he could not remember Welles's name. Obviously intoxicated—some blamed Hamlin for making him purposely so—Johnson stumbled through his speech and delivered an attack on secessionists and personal enemies. Speed whispered, "All this is in wretched bad taste. . . . The man is certainly deranged." Welles nudged Stanton, muttering, "Johnson is either drunk or crazy." Stanton replied, "There is evidently something wrong." Noah Brooks watched "Andy's" behavior from the gallery, writing, "Once in a while . . . I could observe Hamlin nudging Johnson from behind," trying to get him to sit down. Johnson continued to rant, while Lincoln somberly watched, "patiently waiting," said Welles, "for his extraordinary harangue to be over." In the end Johnson took the oath, though inaudibly, but as a final encore, he snatched the Bible, faced the audience, and, in "a loud, theatrical voice," gestured and said, "I kiss this Book in the face of my nation of the United States." Then he sat.

John Forney, secretary of the Senate, took the floor, read the president's request convoking an extra session, and swore in the newly elected senators. The procession then moved to the inauguration platform, which had been built outside on the east front of the Capitol. As the president passed through the door, he turned to a marshal and said, "Do not let Johnson speak outside!" Two days later, in a passing remark to Hugh McCulloch, he said, "I have known Andy Johnson for many years; he made a bad slip the other day, but you need not be scared; Andy ain't a drunkard."[30]

From the portico one could look across the great plaza in front of the Capitol at a "sea of heads" stretching "as far as the eye could reach." John Nicolay, soon to become consul to Paris, believed there were at least twice as many people standing outside as four years ago. When Lincoln came to the platform to read his inaugural address, "a tremendous shout, prolonged and loud, arose from the surging ocean of humanity." After several minutes of bedlam the Senate sergeant-at-arms motioned the crowd to be still.[31]

As Lincoln rose to speak, Brooks noticed at that exact moment "the sun, which had been obscured all day, burst forth in its unclouded meridian splendor, and flooded the spectacle with glory and with light." "Every heart beat quicker," he said, "at the unexpected omen." Even the president reacted, confiding later to Brooks, "Did you notice that sunburst? It made my heart jump."[32] As Lincoln came forward, foreign diplomats noticed how much he had aged since taking the oath four years earlier. When he began to speak, one diplomat gasped as "a shaft of light pierced the low clouds and rested like a benediction on his weary shoulders."[33]

Lincoln's voice carried clear and distinct across a multitude of upturned faces. The crowd erupted in applause when the president, speaking of the rebellion, said, "Both parties deprecated war; but one of them would *make* war rather than let the nation survive; and the other would *accept* war rather than let it perish. And the war came." The inaugural address, the shortest ever, made a great hit, and the president, whose eyes welled with tears, closed by reciting the same noble words struck forever into history at Gettysburg: "With malice toward none; with charity for all; with firmness in the right; as God gives us to see right; let us strive on to finish the work we are in; [and] to bind up the nation's wounds."[34]

Silence being restored, Lincoln turned to Chief Justice Chase, laid his hand on the Bible, and repeated the oath of office. Saying, "So help me God," he leaned forward and kissed the Bible. When he stood up, "a salvo of artillery echoed across the plaza, cheer upon cheer rang out . . . and after bowing to the assembled hosts," the president returned through the Senate to a waiting carriage, which returned him to the White House for a reception.[35]

Chase observed where Lincoln's lips touched the Book and circled the verses in pencil. He later presented the Bible with a note to Mary Lincoln, mentioning how "the beautiful sunshine dispersed the clouds that had previously darkened the sky may prove an auspicious omen of the dispersion of the clouds of war."[36]

Noah Brooks watched it all—the inauguration, the handsome reception at the White House, and the inaugural ball—and wrote, "But chiefly memorable in the mind of those who saw that second inauguration must still remain the tall, pathetic, melancholy figure of the man who, then inducted into office in the midst of the glad acclaim of thousands of people, and illuminated by the deceptive brilliance of a March sunburst, was already standing in the shadow of death."[37]

CHAPTER 24

"Now he belongs to the ages"

As spring approached, the president expected the Confederacy to collapse quickly when operations commenced in Virginia. He continued to monitor Ulysses S. Grant's actions by making regular visits to the War Department's telegraph office. When curious, he contacted Grant directly, and if satisfied, he always said so. Lincoln also watched William Tecumseh Sherman's activities, whose operations in the Carolinas had been impeded by foul weather.[1]

On February 1 Sherman crossed with sixty-two thousand veterans into South Carolina and encountered his old adversary, General Joseph E. Johnston, who commanded a small army to prevent Sherman from combining forces with Grant. As Federal troops resumed their path of destruction toward Columbia, Grant prepared to apply pressure in Virginia. Although Sherman forbade the destruction of civilian property, his soldiers felt a particular malice toward South Carolinians for having started the war.[2]

Grant's strategy remained unchanged. Robert E. Lee could not be allowed to prolong the war by joining forces with Johnston, but if Sherman defeated Johnston and combined with Grant, Lee would be isolated from the rest of the Confederacy and forced to surrender.

The ordinary Confederate soldier could see what the Richmond administration refused to admit. Desertion became widespread, and the army lost heart when Jefferson Davis authorized the execution of thousands of men who had been arrested after returning to their homes. Lee remitted executions, only to be criticized and stopped by Davis for doing so. With each passing day people of the South steadily lost confidence in the Confederate government.[3]

On February 9, 1865, Davis belatedly transferred the command of all Confederate forces to Lee. As general-in-chief, Lee understood what was happening. Had he wished, he could have taken over the discredited rebel government and, with the blessings of the people, brought peace. But Lee would not do this. Honor bound, he fought on.

During prisoner exchange negotiations on March 2, General Edward Ord received word from James Longstreet that Lee wanted to meet with Grant to end hostilities. There is no evidence Lee suggested a meeting, and Longstreet may have hatched the scheme to stop the killing. A month earlier

Lincoln had informed the rebel commissioners that Lee could surrender his army, but he could not negotiate with Grant for the surrender of the Confederate government. Grant never learned the details of the conference because the participants issued no reports. Longstreet evidently told Lee that Grant wanted to meet, and Ord told Grant that Lee wanted to meet. Lee had no reason to reject the meeting. He invited Grant to a "military convention" and said he had "authority to act." Grant questioned his own authority to become a peace negotiator and quite properly asked Secretary of War Stanton for instructions.[4]

Stanton received the telegram during a cabinet meeting at the White House on the eve of Inauguration Day. He read Grant's message and handed it to the president. Lincoln misread the message and, believing the war was coming to an end, said he would be "favorably disposed towards granting the most lenient and generous terms to a defeated foe." According to Ward Lamon, Stanton flew into a "towering rage" and said, "If any other authority than your own be for a moment recognized; or if terms of peace do not emanate from yourself, and do not imply that you are the supreme head of the nation,—you are not needed." Lincoln thought a moment and finally said, "Stanton, you are right; this dispatch did not, at first sight, strike me as I now consider it." He picked up a pen and scratched a message for Stanton to send, ordering Grant not to meet unless "for the capitulation of General Lee's army or on some minor or purely military matter. [Political] questions the President holds in his own hands, and will submit them to no military conferences or conventions." "Meantime," Stanton added, "you are to press to the utmost your military advantages." Grant gave Lee his reasons for canceling the meeting, and he also assured Stanton that he understood his role as purely military and would only meet with Lee to accept his surrender.[5]

Stanton suspected General Ord of having more to do with arranging the meeting than Grant realized. He informed Grant that "General Ord's conduct in holding intercourse with General Longstreet upon political questions not committed to his charge is not approved," adding, "Please in the future instruct officers appointed to meet rebel officers to confine themselves to the matters specially committed to them." The episode clearly defined the wall existing between civilian political authority and military authority.[6]

On March 20 Grant finalized plans for a turning movement against the Confederate right flank and invited the president to City Point, Virginia, for a visit. "I would like very much to see you," Grant wrote, "and I think the rest would do you good." Lincoln understood the purpose of the invitation and accepted. He needed time away from Washington, and he hoped to witness an end to the long struggle. He also wanted to see his son Robert, who served as a captain on Grant's staff. Three days later he departed by steamer for City Point with his wife, Tad, a bodyguard, and a friend from the War Department. Stanton had fallen ill and been ordered to bed, but the secretary ignored the surgeon and returned to his office to run the war in Lincoln's absence.[7]

On March 24 the *River Queen* reached City Point and for thirteen days served as Lincoln's home and headquarters. Having come there to see Grant defeat Lee, the president spent most of his time waiting for it to happen. During the day he wandered through camps, visited the wounded, and occasionally made trips to the entrenchments, where on March 25 he witnessed an engagement at close range. He spent part of every day in Grant's hut reading dispatches, and when he had nothing else to do, he relaxed and shared stories with those around him.[8]

On March 23 Sherman reported the capture of Goldsboro, North Carolina, and suggested he sail to City Point to discuss final operations with the president. Three days later Philip Sheridan arrived, after destroying the remnants of Jubal Early's army and raiding communications west of Richmond. On March 27 generals Grant, Sheridan, and George Meade met with Sherman in the cabin of the *Ocean Queen*. "The President was also there," wrote John Nicolay and John Hay, "and an interesting conversation took place between these famous brothers-in-arms." Lincoln enjoyed the get-together but excused himself during the session on military planning. Sherman departed the following day, predicting either he or Grant "would have to fight one more bloody battle, and that it would be the *last*."[9]

At 10:15 p.m. on the rainy and moonless night of March 29, Lincoln believed the final battle had begun. For two hours he listened to a furious cannonade followed by intense firing along the lines. In the morning he wrote Stanton, "It seemed to me a great battle, but the other hands here scarcely noticed it, and sure enough, this morning it was found that very little had been done." To the contrary, much had happened, but Lincoln remained sheltered from the opening of Grant's spring campaign. While admitting he should return to Washington, Lincoln told Stanton he wanted to see "nearer to the end." Stanton encouraged him to "see it out" at City Point. He believed the troops would respond better if they knew the president had come to witness Lee's defeat, and he assured Lincoln there was nothing to do in Washington but "petty" tasks. Lincoln stayed but sent his wife back to Washington.[10]

On March 29 Lincoln suspected the battle had begun and became restless and overly anxious to hear from Grant. Early in the morning two actions marked the beginning of the final campaign. A Confederate corps led by Major General John B. Gordon attacked Fort Stedman, suffered heavy losses, and withdrew. Farther to the south Sheridan led Wesley Merritt's three cavalry divisions and stormed around Lee's extended right flank. The maneuver, timed with simultaneous advances by the Second and Fifth corps, threatened to destroy the Southside Railroad, sever Lee's lifeline, and turn the Confederates out of Petersburg's trenches. As Grant anticipated, Lee weakened the Petersburg line by sending nineteen thousand men under General George Pickett to defend the railroad and important crossroads at Five Forks, Virginia. Sheridan broke through the extended line and struck Lee's rear. "I now feel like ending the matter," Grant informed Sheridan. "We will act all together as one army here until it is seen what can be done with the enemy."[11]

With the campaign under way, Lincoln tracked Grant's movements around Lee's right flank with great interest and on April 1 learned Sheridan had captured Five Forks. As news from the front poured into Grant's hut, farmland roads west of Richmond turned into a virtual racetrack. The president used the telegraph like a radio station to keep Seward, Stanton, and Mary Lincoln posted on progress. "All is going finely," he reported when Grant broke through Petersburg's fortifications. In another telegram he described the destruction of the Southside Railroad and hours later reported that Sheridan's cavalry was leading the pursuit of Lee's retreating army, while the Army of the James, taking a parallel route west, had joined the race to beat the Confederates to the rail junction at Danville. Early on the morning of April 3 Lincoln wired Stanton, "Gen. Grant reports Petersburg evacuated; and is confidant Richmond also is. He is pushing forward to cut off, if possible, the retreating army. I start to him in a few minutes."[12]

Lincoln met Grant at a deserted house in Petersburg. The streets were empty, without a person or a dog in sight. He shook Grant's hand and said, "Do you know, General, that I have had a sort of sneaking idea for some days that you intended to do something like this." Lincoln expected Sherman to be involved in the final assault, which had been the plan until the recent meeting at City Point, but Grant wanted the Eastern armies to "vanquish their old enemy." He did not want Sherman's force brought into the theater because politicians would give all the credit to the Army of the West. Lincoln admitted "he saw that now, but had never thought of it before because his anxiety was so great he did not care where the aid came from so the work was done."[13]

Lincoln's trip to Petersburg startled Stanton. On returning to City Point, he found a telegram from the war minister with a prudent warning: "You ought [not] to expose the nation to the consequence of any disaster to yourself in the pursuit of a treacherous and dangerous enemy like the rebel army." Lincoln replied, "Thanks for your caution; but I have already been to Petersburg, staid with Gen. Grant an hour & a half and returned here. It is now certain that Richmond is in our hands, and I think I will go there tomorrow. I will take care of myself."[14]

Stanton left no record of his reaction to Lincoln's plans to visit the Confederate capital, and before he could respond, somebody shouted "Richmond has surrendered!" The news did not come until after a telegraph operator turned down the armature spring on the receiving instrument and deciphered a message from General Godfrey Weitzel: "We took Richmond at 8:15 this morning. . . . The city is on fire in two places."[15]

Fifteen-year-old William E. Kettles of Vermont, the youngest operator in the telegraph office, copied the message, opened the windows, and shouted, "Richmond had fallen!" The news echoed across Washington. People flooded the streets and flocked to the War Department. Cannon thundered, whistles howled, horns blew, and traffic came to a standstill. Stanton sauntered into the telegraph office and, learning Kettles had received the message, picked up the boy, lifted him to the windowsill, and shouted to the crowd below, "My friends, here is the young man who received the telegram that tells us of the fall of Richmond." Someone demanded a speech from Kettles, but this proved too much of a strain for the teenager. He bowed but could not remember anything he had said. Later he admitted, "The Republic was saved, and I felt that I had saved it."[16]

Early on April 4 the *River Queen* steamed into the James River and, escorted by Admiral David Dixon Porter in the gunboat *Malvern* and three other ships, headed upriver for Richmond. A few miles from the city the steamers struck shoal water and stopped. At the president's request Porter transferred Lincoln and Tad to a barge and with a small escort of twelve marines towed the presidential party the rest of the way by tug. As Lincoln approached Richmond, he saw smoke curling from the ashes of dozens of warehouses. Buildings still blazed throughout the city, the work of Jeff Davis's firebrands. As the party bumped against Rockett's wharf, Porter remarked, "Here we were in a solitary boat . . . hoping to enter the conquered capital in a manner befitting the rank of the President with a further intention of firing a national salute in honor of the happy result." Amused by his grand entrance being reduced to a barge, Lincoln said, "But it is well to be humble."[17]

The streets of Richmond were empty except for wandering former slaves, who soon recognized the tall president in his long black coat and high silk hat. They fell at his feet, shouting, "Bless the Lord" and "Hallelujah! Here is the great Messiah!" Lincoln told them to stand, but Porter observed the president's face "lit up with a divine look," and for a moment "he really seemed of another world."

"Don't kneel to me," Lincoln gently said, "that is not right. You must kneel to God only and thank him for the liberty you will hereafter enjoy."

The presidential entourage walked up Main Street in search of General Weitzel's headquarters. Liberated slaves followed, making it difficult for Porter's marines to control the burgeoning crowd. Spotted by a small patrol of Union cavalry, Lincoln obtained an escort and soon reached Weitzel's headquarters, where he seated himself in Davis's chair and enjoyed a drink of water. Together with Porter and Weitzel, the president and his son spent the day visiting vacated public offices formerly occupied by Confederate leaders. He spoke with the only member of the government who had not fled, Judge John A. Campbell, one of the three commissioners attending the Hampton Roads Peace Conference. When Campbell asked how Virginia could be restored to the Union, Lincoln wrote a document outlining his three inviolable requirements and urged the judge to act quickly. He traveled about the city in a carriage, reviewed troops, and examined buildings destroyed by fire. "It was a gala day," Porter wrote, "and no man was ever accorded a warmer welcome." Late in the afternoon Lincoln departed for City Point, anxious to learn if Grant had succeeded in corralling Lee's army.[18]

As celebrations over the capture of Richmond subsided, Stanton recalled with trepidation Lincoln's plans to visit the Confederate capital. He summoned Charles Dana and told him to go down to City Point and keep a close eye on the president. On April 5 Dana arrived and found Lincoln relaxing from his Richmond excursion and pouring over dispatches from the field. A message from Sheridan described how the cavalry and infantry had just routed the rebels at Burkeville and captured several thousand prisoners. Lincoln did not need Dana monitoring his movements and sent him to Richmond to help Weitzel and Campbell restore legislative authority in Virginia.[19]

In a message to Grant on April 6, Sheridan said, "If the thing is pressed, I think Lee will surrender." Lincoln read the statement and the following day wrote Grant, "Let the *thing* be pressed." He wanted to be in Virginia when Lee surrendered and urged his wife, Seward, and other officials to come to City Point to join the victory celebration. On April 7 Lincoln hurriedly changed his plans on learning Seward had been thrown from his carriage.

A day later Stanton telegraphed, "Seward although severely injured is not in danger," but with the secretary ailing and Grant still chasing Lee, Lincoln sailed for Washington.[20]

At sunset April 9 the *River Queen* docked at the capital, where people were still building bonfires to celebrate the capture of Richmond. Lincoln went directly to Seward's home and found him in pain, having both arms and his jaw broken. Seward tried to turn his head, but Lincoln solved the problem by climbing onto the bed and, leaning on his elbow, spoke directly into Seward's ear. He discussed Grant's progress and said, "I think we are near the end at last." Seward could not speak without pain and, after a half-hour of listening to the president's comments, lapsed into a feverish slumber. Lincoln departed, and according to Frederick Seward, the meeting would be their last.[21]

During the afternoon Grant accepted Lee's surrender at Appomattox Courthouse, a small hamlet ninety miles west of Richmond. Before going to bed, Lincoln heard the news, and the night passed quietly until dawn. At daylight a five hundred–gun salute thundered across the rain-drenched capital, shaking the earth and shattering windows in Lafayette Square. Noah Brooks called the noise "Stanton's way of telling the people that the Army of Northern Virginia had at last laid down its arms." In the chill morning air people sprinted out of their homes and raced about in the mud looking for someone to explain the commotion. Others remained in bed, knowing only one military event could cause such turmoil. Newsmen had worked all night setting their presses for a morning edition. As skies brightened, Welles heard "bells ringing . . . men laughing, children cheering," and wrote, "All are jubilant." Nobody, however, took particular notice when John Wilkes Booth, a popular actor, checked into Washington's National Hotel.[22]

After indulging uproariously over the capture of Richmond, the people descended on the White House. While Lincoln ate breakfast, Treasury employees appeared on the lawn and serenaded him with "The Star-Spangled Banner." He tried to conduct a cabinet meeting in the morning because none had been held for two weeks. The shouting outside, augmented by the quartermaster's band and six howitzers dragged up the street from the navy yard, drowned out the discussions. When Tad appeared at a second-story window waving a Confederate flag, the public howled for the president to speak. Lincoln yielded to the pandemonium and joined his son. Noah Brooks, peering from the upper windows, said "the surface of the crowd looked like an agitated sea of hats, faces, and arms." Lincoln quipped with the crowd and promised to speak later, adding, "I shall have nothing to say if you dribble it all out of me before." He cut the session short by asking the band to play "Dixie," which he claimed to have been fairly captured, and after offering "three good hearty cheers for General Grant," he disappeared from the window with strains of "Yankee Doodle" still ringing in his ears. Despite distractions, Lincoln spent most of his time composing a speech for the following evening.[23]

On Tuesday, April 11, the entire city swarmed the streets to celebrate. The weather remained misty, but nobody cared. Lights shined from government buildings, including General Lee's former home in Arlington, where thousands of former slaves gathered to sing "The Year of Jubilee." Light reflecting from the illuminated dome of the Capitol brightened the moist air hanging from overhead clouds, while thousands of people carrying lanterns and umbrellas made their way to the White House.

At six o'clock Lincoln appeared at a second-story window under the portico to read his speech. It would be his longest and his last. Discovering he could not hold a candle in one hand and several pages of foolscap in the other, Lincoln looked for help. Brooks, who had followed the president upstairs, stood behind the curtain and, with only the shadow of his arm showing, held a light. Tad hid on the floor beneath the windowsill to retrieve the pages his father dropped.[24]

People accustomed to the president's brief, plain-spoken impromptu messages were surprised by the tone of the address. He opened by giving everyone what they expected: "We meet this evening, not in sorrow, but in gladness of heart." After giving thanks to General Grant's brave men and to the gallant navy, he shifted to the problems of reconstruction. Although mostly incomprehensible to his listeners, Lincoln wanted public and press support for his reconstruction policies, which were more generous and humane than those of Congress. The reunification of the country "is fraught with great difficulty," he said, because no precedents existed to settle a war. "We simply must begin with, and mould from, disorganized and discordant elements." The most serious problem is "we, the loyal people, differ among ourselves as to the mode, manner, and means of reconstruction." After reiterating his often expressed views on reconstruction, the president spoke of peace and policy-making problems and soon lost the crowd's attention.[25]

Lincoln's speech wandered, as if he were hesitating to take a stand apt to agitate dissonant factions in Congress. He anticipated opposition from both radicals and conservatives and at times appeared to be unclear about his own convictions. Although he admitted "the Executive claimed no right to say when, or whether members should be admitted seats in Congress" from states recently in rebellion, he endorsed it as a necessary step toward reunification and the suffrage of former slaves. He felt uneasy stating his deepest feelings on policy or what he had once told Sherman, when on March 28 the general asked how captured "political leaders, such as Jeff. Davis, etc.," should be treated. Lincoln said all he wanted "was to defeat the opposing armies, and to get the men . . . back to their homes, at work on their farms and in their shops." He thought Davis and his cohorts should "clear out [and] escape the country, only it would not do for him to say so openly." Sherman implied from the conversation that "Mr. Lincoln wanted Davis to escape 'unbeknown' to him."[26]

Lincoln mentioned nothing in his address about the Confederate leaders, who had escaped from Richmond and were making their way south. Nor did he mention Johnston's army, which Sherman surrounded but did not attack. There were still Confederate elements ranging farther south and west that had not laid down their arms, but from Lincoln's perspective the war was over. He issued a proclamation terminating the blockade of Southern ports, and he prepared a memorandum reducing the regular army to a ratio of one soldier per thousand citizens. On April 14 he also opened the door to the South by discontinuing passes to Richmond and Petersburg, thereby enabling people to "go and return just as they did before the war." And perhaps to officially signal an end to rebellion, he authorized Stanton to send Major General Robert Anderson back to Fort Sumter to raise the American flag on April 14 in a solemn ceremony marking the beginning and end of exactly four years of war.[27]

The surrender of Lee's army gave Stanton great personal satisfaction, and on the night of April 9 the word GRANT blazed from the upper windows of the War Department. Stanton had once told Chase if Richmond fell and Lee surrendered, his job would be finished and he would resign. The following day he tried to keep his word and handed the president his resignation. Lincoln, who stood a full foot taller than the secretary of war, looked down, placed his hands on Stanton's shoulders, and said, "Stanton, you have been a good friend and a faithful public officer and it is not for you to say when you will be no longer needed here." Unable to say no, Stanton agreed to stay on.[28]

Stanton's decision to remain in the cabinet probably saved Lincoln from compounding a blunder made during his visit to Richmond. Stanton's views corresponded closely to those of Congress, and he gasped when Dana reported from Richmond that Lincoln had authorized Judge Campbell to convene Virginia's legislature and begin the process of normalization with the Union. Lincoln had also instructed General Weitzel to allow the meeting and provide protection.[29]

Stanton fumed, arguing that such instructions were inadvisable and asked the president to retract the order because Campbell could take Virginia's legislature beyond acceptable limits. On April 7 Campbell suggested an armistice, which would have stopped war in Virginia on the eve of Lee's surrender. It became apparent to Stanton that if Campbell convened the defunct legislature, the same program might be extended throughout the South. Stanton suspected Campbell of edging toward peace negotiations and that the well-meaning president was about to wallow in a quagmire of his own creation. Still, Lincoln did nothing, and Lee's surrender on April 9 partially spared him from further embarrassment.[30]

Lincoln's generosity created a situation that was threatening to get out of control. On April 9 Dana reported Campbell's crowd meddling in matters detrimental to the president's wishes. Stanton did not want Virginia's legislators to convene and ordered Weitzel to "hold no further conferences with Mr. Campbell on any subject without specific authority." Weitzel replied that his authority came from the president. While the problem continued to be debated between Stanton, Attorney General Speed, and the president, Campbell convened thirty-three influential Virginians and, with Weitzel's approval, issued a request for the governor and the state legislature to assemble on April 25 in Richmond. Whether Stanton's resignation had anything to do with this disagreement is not clear, but for several days he implored Lincoln to revoke Weitzel's instructions. Even Welles, who routinely agreed with the president, said the legislature should not be permitted to meet, although he understood Lincoln's desire for pursuing reconciliation. According to Welles, the president believed Virginians were "too badly beaten, too much exhausted," to continue the war, and "the members of the legislature, comprising the prominent and influential men of their respective counties, had better come together and undo their own work." Not one member of the cabinet agreed with him.[31]

On April 12 Lincoln attempted to placate Stanton by preparing a message modifying Weitzel's instructions. Stanton read it and said it was not good enough. Speed read the draft and agreed with Stanton. Although irritated, Lincoln wrote another message rescinding any effort by Virginia's legislature to assemble, and Stanton relaxed. If Lincoln had not retracted his instructions, it is difficult to predict what might have happened during the coming weeks. In a later report to members of the "insurgent" legislature, Campbell quoted the president as saying, "If the government of Virginia will administer the laws in connection with the authority of the United States, *no attempt* will be made to establish or sustain any other authority." This move clearly exceeded his executive authority and was one of those kind-hearted gestures Stanton feared the president might make when in Richmond. Lincoln later said if he knew the surrender would come so soon, he would not have suggested the idea to Campbell.[32]

On April 14 General Ord contacted Campbell and showed him Lincoln's message. Campbell asked Ord for permission to visit Washington with Robert Hunter, a colleague at the Hampton Roads Peace Conference, to discuss the matter further. At 9:00 p.m. the telegram arrived at the War Department. Lincoln was not at the White House. He had gone with his wife to Ford's Theatre.[33]

Congress eventually investigated the Lincoln-Campbell arrangement, which included Stanton's testimony. Although the secretary added a few embellishments to his statement, he was correct in blocking Lincoln's reconstruction policy to insurgent legislators who were no longer elected representatives of the people. Referring to the April 12 meeting, Stanton lamented, "It was the last time he [Lincoln] was in the war department." Major Albert E. H. Johnson, Stanton's clerk, witnessed the discussion and remembered it as "a solemn occasion, and upon that interview hung the destiny of reconstruction, of peace, and orderly government for the Southern people, and Mr. Stanton prevailed." Whoever would have prevailed in the months to come remains moot. Lincoln would not be at the nation's helm.[34]

For two years an active conspiracy existed to kidnap Lincoln and his cabinet. On one occasion the conspirators almost nabbed Stanton and were twice foiled attempting to capture Lincoln. The grand plan was to kidnap everyone at the same time. In March 1865, after another plot failed, twenty-six-year-old John Wilkes Booth, a handsome actor from a family of renowned thespians, turned to murder.

Lincoln ignored concerns about his safety. In December 1864 Ward Lamon, who considered himself among the most ardent of the president's protectors, threatened to resign as marshal of the District of Colombia when Lincoln, on several occasions, dismissed a bodyguard while at the theater. *"You are in danger,"* Lamon wrote, adding, "You know, or ought to know, that your life is sought after, and will be taken unless you and your friends are cautious; for you have many enemies within our lines." The only other person to penetrate the president's indifference to safety had been Count Adam Gurowski, who warned repeatedly to take the threat of violent assault seriously, but in mid-April, as war reached its end, the president became less concerned about personal protection. Even on the afternoon of April 14, a few hours before leaving for the theater, he told former congressman Cornelius Cole of California, "The people know I come among them without fear." Booth also observed the president's lapses of caution.[35]

On April 13, when Grant arrived in Washington, Lincoln invited the general, Secretary Stanton, and their wives to accompany him and Mrs. Lincoln to Ford's Theater the following evening to enjoy a performance of "Our American Cousin," featuring popular actress Laura Keene. Stanton declined, but Grant accepted. Mrs. Grant, who disliked Mary Lincoln, changed the general's mind, and he, too, declined, after being advised by Stanton it would be unwise for the president and the general-in-chief to be together at a public function. Grant's cancellation annoyed Lincoln, so he searched about the War Department for someone to share the presidential box. After Major Thomas Eckert, whose company he thoroughly enjoyed, declined, Lincoln recruited Major Henry R. Rathbone and his fiancée, Clara Harris. After supper the president, his wife, and their two guests went to the theater, while Stanton called on the bedridden secretary of state, who lived nearby on Franklin Square. Stanton returned home around 10:00 p.m., about the same time John Wilkes Booth began creeping though the upstairs corridors leading to the president's box at Ford's Theatre.[36]

After the *Washington Evening Star* reported that Grant would be attending the performance with Lincoln, people rushed to obtain tickets in the hope of seeing the general. Nor did the announcement escape Booth's notice, so he planned to perform his diabolical act before a packed house.[37]

Booth had united a band of malevolent secessionists at the boarding-house of Mary E. Surratt and for several days plotted to assassinate Lincoln, Johnson, Seward, Stanton, and other members of the cabinet to foment "a reign of anarchy." Booth grasped the opportunity to murder Grant along with the others, but the general escaped by leaving the city for New Jersey a few hours before the time fixed for the assassination. Booth's group consisted of Lewis Powell, alias Payne, a deserter from Alabama; George Atzerodt, a Confederate spy and former blockade-runner; David E. Herold, a druggist's clerk from Maryland; Samuel Arnold and Michael O'Laughlin, Confederate deserters from Maryland; and John H. Surratt, a Confederate spy whose mother ran the boardinghouse. What Booth expected to accomplish for the Confederacy by murdering Lincoln and the cabinet is puzzling because Jefferson Davis and most of his cabinet were then skulking through the South in an attempt to flee the country.

Not all of Booth's cronies agreed to murder, but on April 14 the deranged actor set the scheme in motion. At approximately 10:00 p.m. he planned to assassinate the president while Payne murdered Seward, Atzerodt killed Johnson, and Herold prepared the escape through Maryland. A witness later claimed a stranger approached Stanton's door at that time, and if true, a broken doorbell may have saved the secretary's life.[38]

Between 10:15 and 10:30 p.m. Booth, who had been drinking heavily, found the guard unaccountably absent from outside Lincoln's box. He opened the door, stepped behind the president, and shot him in the head with a .44-caliber single-shot derringer. After slashing Rathbone with a hunting knife, Booth leaped to the stage. His spur caught on a flag draped in front of the president's box and turned him slightly, causing his left leg to break when he struck the stage. Standing unsteadily before the crowd, Booth shouted, "Sic semper tyrannus," limped backstage to a carriage waiting behind the theater, and fled the city. The following morning at 7:22 a.m. the president died, and one of the greatest manhunts in the history of the country commenced.

As Booth entered the president's box, Payne forced his way into Seward's home and attacked the bedridden secretary with a knife. The wrappings around Seward's jaw and neck probably saved him from having his throat slit. Payne then slashed Fred Seward and escaped, accompanied by Herold. Vice President Johnson did not know he had been targeted in the assassination plot until later because George Atzerodt had lost courage and fled.[39]

Three days later Welles recalled a remark Lincoln had made during the April 14 cabinet meeting. "I had this strange dream again last night," he said, "and we shall, judging from the past, have great news very soon. I think it must be from Sherman. My thoughts are in that direction, as are most of yours." It was not unusual for the president to discuss his dreams, and he liked to speculate on their meaning. Being something of a fatalist, Lincoln never joined a church. "He seemed to be in some singular, indescribable vessel," Welles recalled, "and that he was moving with great rapidity towards an indefinite shore; that he had this dream preceding Sumter, Bull Run, Antietam, Gettysburg, Stones River, Vicksburg, Wilmington, etc." During the discussion Grant said Stones River was not a victory, implying the dream must be meaningless. The president nodded, as if to say, "We must wait and see." "Great events did indeed follow," lamented Welles, "for within a few hours the good and gentle, as well as truly great, man who narrated his dream closed forever his earthly career."[40]

Shortly after Lincoln died, Stanton sent a delegation with an armed guard to Andrew Johnson's hotel to prepare the vice president for the oath taking.

Other cabinet members arrived at the hotel with Chase. In the lobby at 1:00 p.m. Chase administered the oath, and Johnson became the seventeenth president of the United States. "May God guide, support, and bless you in your arduous labors," said Chase. No one could possibly have anticipated President Johnson's ordeal during the next four years. One historian called it the "Age of Hate." [41]

Immense political turbulence followed the death of Lincoln, but on the morning he passed away an "unspeakable peace came upon his worn features." At 7:22 a.m., when Dr. Phineas Gurley pronounced the president dead, those clustered in the small room became silent. Stanton, who had been with the president through the night, cleared his voice and softly said, "Now he belongs to the ages." [42]

And to the ages he still belongs.

NOTES

Abbreviations

B&L   Johnson, Robert U., and Clarence C. Buell, *Battles and Leaders of the Civil War,* 4 vols. (New York: Century Co., 1886–90).

BU   Brown University, Providence, R.I.

DCHS   Dauphin County Historical Society, Harrisburg, Pa.

HL   Huntington Library, San Marino, Calif.

ISHL   Illinois State Historical Library, Springfield

JCCW   *Report of the Joint Committee on the Conduct of the War*

LC   Library of Congress, Washington, D.C.

LC-RTL   Robert Todd Lincoln Collection   in Library of Congress

NYPL   New York Public Library

ORA   *War of the Rebellion: A Compilation of the Official Records of the Union and Confederate Armies*

ORN   *Official Records of the Union and Confederate Navies in the War of the Rebellion*

PHS   Pennsylvania Historical Society, Philadelphia

UR   University of Rochester, Rochester, N.Y.

Preface

1. Noah Brooks, *Washington in Lincoln's Time* (New York, 1896), 192–93.

2. Roy P. Basler, ed., *The Collected Works of Abraham Lincoln,* 9 vols. (New Brunswick, N.J., 1953–55), 192, 193. Hereafter cited as Basler, *Works.*

Chapter 1. "Make no contracts . . ."

1. Frederic Bancroft, *Life of William Seward,* 2 vols. (New York, 1900), 1:459.

2. Basler, *Works,* 2:461.

3. Bancroft, *Life of William Seward,* 2:458–59.

4. John George Nicolay and John Hay, *Abraham Lincoln: A History,* 10 vols. (New York, 1891), 2:261, 1:393. Hereafter cited as Nicolay and Hay, *Lincoln.*

5. F. B. Sanborn, ed., *The Life and Letters of John Brown* (Boston, 1891), 364; Albert Bushnell Hart, *Salmon Portland Chase* (Boston, 1899), 177, 183.

6. Basler, *Works,* 3:512; Henry Villard, *Memoirs of Henry Villard,* 2 vols. (Boston, 1904), 1:96.

7. Howard K. Beale, ed., *Diary of Edward Bates, 1859–1866* (Washington, D.C., 1933), 11, 30, 106.

8. Patricia Faust, ed., *Historical Times Illustrated, Encyclopedia of the Civil War* (New York, 1986), 105; Erwin Stanley Bradley, *Simon Cameron, Lincoln's Secretary of War: A Political Biography* (Philadelphia, 1966), 36–39.

9. Basler, *Works,* 3:491.

10. Alexander K. McClure, *Abraham Lincoln and the Men of War-Times* (New York, 1892), 33–35.

11. Lee F. Crippen, *Simon Cameron: Ante Bellum Years* (New York, 1942), 209.

12. Nicolay and Hay, *Lincoln*, 2:255, 273.

13. Basler, *Works*, 3:509.

14. Judd to Lincoln, November 18, 1858, and April 21, 1861, Lincoln Mss., LC-RTL.

15. Basler, *Works*, 3:517.

16. George Haven Putnam, "The Speech That Won the East for Lincoln," *Outlook* 130, February 8, 1922, 220.

17. Basler, *Works*, 3:522ff.

18. Hiram Barney to Lincoln, February 28, 1860, Lincoln Mss., LC-RTL.

19. Basler, *Works*, 3:550–55; 4:2, 13.

20. Basler, *Works*, 4:45.

21. Henry C. Whitney, *Life on the Circuit with Lincoln* (Boston, 1892), 62; Basler, *Works*, 10:48.

22. Gilbert A. Tracy, ed., *Uncollected Letters of Abraham Lincoln* (Boston, 1971), 138–39; Basler, *Works*, 4:36.

23. John G. Nicolay and John Hay, eds., *Complete Works of Abraham Lincoln*, 12 vols. (New York, 1905), 6:7. Hereafter cited as Nicolay and Hay, *Works*.

24. J. G. Randall, *Lincoln the President*, 4 vols. (New York, 1945–55), 1:139–43.

25. Helen Nicolay, "A Candidate in His Home Town," *Abraham Lincoln Quarterly* 1 (September 1940): 130–32.

26. William E. Baringer, *Lincoln's Rise to Power* (Boston, 1937), 186.

27. Basler, *Works*, 4:50; William H. Herndon and Jesse W. Weik, *Abraham Lincoln: The True Story of a Great Life*, 3 vols. (Chicago, 1890), 3:462.

28. David Herbert Donald, *Lincoln* (New York, 1995), 247–48.

29. Basler, *Works*, 4:50.

30. Bancroft, *Life of William Seward*, 1:535 n. 1.

31. Harriet A. Weed, ed., *The Life of Thurlow Weed, Including His Autobiography and a Memoir*, 2 vols. (Boston, 1883–84), 2:291. Hereafter cited as Weed, *Autobiography*, or Weed, *Memoir*.

32. Carl Sandburg, *Abraham Lincoln: The Prairie Years*, 2 vols. (New York, 1925–26), 2:341, 342.

33. William H. Herndon and Jesse W. Weik, *Herndon's Life of Lincoln* (New York 1983), 381.

34. Nicolay and Hay, *Works*, 6:21.

35. Joseph Casey to Cameron, May 24, 1860, and Purviance to Cameron, May 23, 1860, Cameron Mss., DCHS.

36. Quoted in Donald, *Lincoln*, 250.

37. Murat Halstead, *Caucuses of 1860: A History of the National Conventions of the Current Presidential Campaigns* (Columbus, Ohio, 1860), 144–48.

38. Benjamin P. Thomas, *Abraham Lincoln* (New York, 1952), 225.

39. Thomas, *Abraham Lincoln*, 225.

40. Halstead, *Caucuses of 1860*, 149.

41. Halstead, *Caucuses of 1860*, 151.

42. Sandburg, *Abraham Lincoln: The Prairie Years*, 2:346.

43. Weed, *Autobiography*, 2:271.

44. Ward Hill Lamon, *The Life of Abraham Lincoln: From His Birth to His Inauguration as President* (Boston, 1872), 450–53.

45. Basler, *Works*, 4:84.

Chapter 2. "Your troubles are over . . ."

1. Davis to Lincoln, May 18, 1860, Lincoln Mss., LC-RTL.

2. Allen Thorndike Rice, ed., *Reminiscences of Abraham Lincoln by Distinguished Men of His Time* (New York, 1888), 168–71; Basler, *Works*, 4:51.

3. Carl Schurz, *The Reminiscences of Carl Schurz*, 3 vols. (New York, 1907–8), 2:188–89.

4. Weed, *Autobiography*, 1:602; McClure, *Abraham Lincoln*, 41.

5. Weed, *Memoirs*, 2:271.

6. Weed, *Autobiography*, 1:603.

7. Basler, *Works*, 4:68.

8. Basler, *Works*, 4:60–67.

9. Quoted in Donald, *Lincoln*, 254; Basler, *Works*, 4:91.

10. Charles Francis Adams, *Autobiography* (Boston, 1916), 64; Burton J. Hendrick, *Lincoln's War Cabinet* (Boston, 1946), 26.

11. Hendrick, *Lincoln's War Cabinet*, 30.

12. Frederick W. Seward, ed., *Seward at Washington, as Senator and Secretary of State*, vols. 2–3 (New York, 1891), 2:459.

13. Quoted in Randall, *Lincoln*, 1:248.

14. Basler, *Works*, 4:126–27.

15. Purviance to Cameron, May 23, 1860, Cameron Mss., DCHS.

16. Willard L. King, *Lincoln's Manager: David Davis* (Cambridge, 1960), 153, 155–56.

17. Helen Nicolay, *Lincoln's Secretary: A Biography of John G. Nicolay* (New York, 1949), 26, 33; Charles M. Segal, ed., *Conversations with Lincoln* (New York, 1939), 40.

18. Basler, *Works*, 4:126.

19. McClure, *Abraham Lincoln*, 42, 43.

20. Quotes from Sandburg, *Abraham Lincoln: The Prairie Years*, 2:372, 373.

21. Herndon and Weik, *Herndon's Life of Lincoln*, 378; William E. Baringer, *A House Dividing: Lincoln as President Elect* (Springfield, Ill., 1945), 3–4.

22. Cameron to Lincoln, November 6, 1860, Lincoln Mss., LC-RTL.

23. *New York Times*, February 14, 1932.

24. Gideon Welles, *Diary of Gideon Welles: Secretary of the Navy under Lincoln and Johnson*, 3 vols. (Boston, 1911), 1:82.

25. Edward Stanwood, *A History of the Presidency from 1788 to 1897* (Boston, 1916), 297.

26. *New York Times*, February 14, 1932.

Chapter 3. "They have gambled me . . ."

1. Basler, *Works*, 4:136, 138, 139–40.

2. Basler, *Works*, 4:141; Baringer, *House Dividing*, 85.

3. Henry Villard, *Lincoln on the Eve of '61* (New York, 1941), 13–15, 17.

4. Ward Hill Lamon, *Recollections of Abraham Lincoln, 1847–1865* (Lincoln, Nebr., 1994), 214.

5. Basler, *Works*, 4:130, 129.

6. Personal note, [November 6, 1860], Lincoln Mss., LC-RTL.

7. Harry J. Carman and Reinhard H. Luthin, *Lincoln and the Patronage* (New York, 1943), 11–12; Charles E. Hamlin, *The Life and Times of Hannibal Hamlin* (Cambridge, 1899), 367–70; Nicolay and Hay, *Works*, 6:86–87.

8. Welles, *Diary,* 2:389; Hamlin, *Life and Times,* 372.

9. Basler, *Works,* 4:148; Hamlin, *Life and Times,* 372.

10. Trumbull to Lincoln, December 2, 1860, Lincoln Mss., LC-RTL; Horace White, *The Life of Lyman Trumbull* (Boston, 1913), 139–40; Basler, *Works,* 4:148

11. Carman and Luthin, *Lincoln and the Patronage,* 15; Seward to Lincoln, December 13, 1860, Lincoln Mss., LC-RTL.

12. Weed, *Memoir,* 2:293, 301; Seward to Weed, December 13, 1860, Weed Mss., LC; Gideon Welles to Mary Welles, May 20, 1860, Welles Mss., LC.

13. Basler, *Works,* 4:170; Weed, *Autobiography,* 1:603–11, 614.

14. Basler, *Works,* 4:156–57, 158; Bancroft, *Life of William Seward,* 2:9–10.

15. Bancroft, *Life of William Seward,* 2:10; David M. Potter, *Lincoln and His Party in the Secession Crisis* (Baton Rouge, La., 1995), 169–70.

16. Seward to Lincoln, December 25, 1860, Lincoln Mss., LC-RTL.

17. Quoted in Baringer, *House Dividing,* 207–8.

18. Basler, *Works,* 4:159; Lincoln to Winfield Scott, November 9, 1860, Lincoln Mss., LC-RTL.

19. Mark M. Boatner III, *The Civil War Dictionary* (New York, 1959), 67.

20. Preston King to Trumbull, Trumbull Papers, LC.

21. Faust, *Historical Times Illustrated,* 65.

22. Frank Blair Jr. to Frank Blair Sr., December 23, 1860, Gist-Blair Mss., LC; Basler, *Works,* 4:162.

23. Beale, *Diary of Edward Bates,* 164.

24. Beale, *Diary of Edward Bates,* 164–65.

25. Basler, *Works,* 4:154.

26. Charles Francis Adams Jr., *Charles Francis Adams* (New York, 1980) 143; Nicolay and Hay, *Works,* 6:87.

27. Hamlin, *Life and Times,* 370; Hamlin to Lincoln, December 29, 1860, Lincoln Mss., LC-RTL.

28. Carman and Luthin, *Lincoln and the Patronage,* 16.

29. Joseph Casey to Leonard Swett, November 27, 1860, Lincoln Mss., LC-RTL; Bradley, *Simon Cameron,* 165.

30. Casey to Swett, November 27, 1860, and Swett to Lincoln, November 30, 1860, Lincoln Mss., LC-RTL.

31. Weed, *Autobiography,* 1:607–8.

32. Bradley, *Simon Cameron,* 166.

33. Basler, *Works,* 4:165–67, 168; Carman and Luthin, *Lincoln and the Patronage,* 26nn.

34. Seward to Lincoln, December 28, 1860, Lincoln Mss., LC-RTL; Basler, *Works,* 4:168.

35. Schurz, *Reminiscences,* 2:34.

36. Quoted in Carman and Luthin, *Lincoln and the Patronage,* 33; John Niven, *Salmon P. Chase: A Biography* (New York, 1995), 224.

37. Basler, *Works,* 4:169–70, 174.

38. Niven, *Salmon P. Chase,* 225–26.

39. Basler, *Works,* 4:171.

40. Basler, *Works,* 4:174.

41. Hiram Barney to William Cullen Bryant, January 17, 1861, Bryant-Godwin Papers, NYPL.

42. Davis to Lincoln, November 19, 1860, Lincoln Mss., LC-RTL; Carman and Luthin, *Lincoln and the Patronage*, 37; O. J. Hollister, *Life of Schuyler Colfax* (New York, 1886), 147n.

43. Salmon P. Chase, "Diary and Correspondence of Salmon P. Chase," *Annual Report of the American Historical Association*, 2 vols. (Washington, D.C., 1903), 2:491, 493; Chase to James T. Worthington, January 14, 1861, Lincoln Collection, John Hay Mss., BU.

44. Parke Godwin, *A Biography of William Cullen Bryant*, 2 vols. (New York, 1883), 2:152.

45. Herndon to Trumbull, January 27, 1861, Trumbull Mss., LC.

46. Davis to Cameron, Cameron Mss., LC.

47. Basler, *Works*, 4:171.

Chapter 4. "I can't afford to let Seward . . ."

1. James D. Richardson, *A Compilation of the Messages and Papers of the Presidents, 1789–1905*, 11 vols. (Washington, D.C., 1896–99), 5:626–53; Nicolay and Hay, *Lincoln*, 3:286.

2. Basler, *Works*, 4:162–63.

3. Nicolay Memorandum, Nicolay Mss., LC; Basler, *Works*, 4:153, 149–50.

4. Basler, *Works*, 4:190.

5. Seward, *Seward at Washington*, 2:493; Faust, *Historical Times Illustrated*, 238.

6. John Purviance to Cameron, February 15, 1861, Cameron Mss., LC.

7. Baringer, *House Dividing*, 280.

8. Villard, *Lincoln on the Eve*, 88.

9. Judd to Trumbull, February 17, 1861, Trumbull Papers, LC.

10. Lamon, *Recollections*, 34; Carman and Luthin, *Lincoln and the Patronage*, 47; *The Diary of a Public Man: Unpublished Passages of the Secret History of the American Civil War* (Chicago, 1945), 41–42.

11. Harry E. Pratt, "Simon Cameron's Fight for a Place in Lincoln's Cabinet," *Bulletin of the Abraham Lincoln Association*, no. 49 (September 1937): 10–11; Purviance to Cameron, February 23, 1861, Cameron Mss., LC.

12. Seward to Lincoln and Stone to Lincoln, February 21, 1861, Lincoln Mss., LC-RTL; Frederick W. Seward, *Reminiscences of a War-Time Statesman and Diplomat, 1830–1915* (New York, 1916), 134–38.

13. Seward, *Reminiscences*, 138.

14. Nicolay and Hay, *Lincoln*, 3:310; Lamon, *Recollections*, 38–40; Seward, *Reminiscences*, 138–39.

15. Lamon, *Recollections*, 41–43; Nicolay and Hay, *Lincoln*, 3:314–15.

16. James D. Horan, *The Pinkertons: The Detective Dynasty That Made History* (New York, 1967), 57.

17. Lamon, *Recollections*, 46; Rice, *Reminiscences*, 38–39.

18. Whitney, *Life on the Circuit*, 15; William E. Smith, *The Francis Preston Blair Family in Politics*, 2 vols. (New York, 1933), 1:514–15.

19. *Diary of a Public Man*, 61–63.

20. Nicolay and Hay, *Lincoln*, 3:370; Lincoln to Seward, March 4, 1861, Seward Papers, LC; Seward, *Seward at Washington*, 2:518.

21. Jacob W. Schuckers, *Life and Public Services of Salmon Portland Chase* (New York, 1874), 207 (hereafter cited as Schuckers, *Life of Chase*); Chase to Lincoln, March 6, 1861, Lincoln Mss., LC-RTL; Chase, "Diary and Correspondence," 2:295.

22. Harry E. Pratt, ed., *Concerning Mr. Lincoln: In Which Abraham Lincoln Is Pictured as He Appeared to Letter Writer's of His Time* (Springfield, Ill., 1944), 42.

23. Nicolay and Hay, *Lincoln*, 3:374.

24. George W. Julian, *Political Recollections, 1840 to 1872* (Chicago, 1884), 194; Villard, *Lincoln on the Eve*, 102.

25. *New York Evening Post*, November 14, 1860, in Baringer, *House Dividing*, 12.

26. Seward, *Reminiscences*, 189; Seward, *Seward at Washington*, 2:519.

27. Carman and Luthin, *Lincoln and the Patronage*, 55, 57–59.

28. Carman and Luthin, *Lincoln and the Patronage*, 61.

29. Carman and Luthin, *Lincoln and the Patronage*, 55–56.

30. Faust, *Historical Times Illustrated*, 713–14.

31. Quoted in Clarence Edward Macartney, *Lincoln and His Cabinet* (New York, 1931), 20.

Chapter 5. "If this must be done . . ."

1. Lincoln to Cameron, March 15, 1861, *ORA*, ser. 1, 1:197 (all subsequent citations refer to ser. 1 unless otherwise specified); Nicolay and Hay, *Lincoln*, 3:377–78; Beale, *Diary of Edward Bates*, 177.

2. Scott to Cameron, March 12, 1861, *ORA*, 1:197.

3. Welles, *Diary*, 1:6; Joseph Totten to Lincoln, March 15, 1861, *ORA*, 1:198–200; Basler, *Works*, 4:284–85.

4. Basler, *Works*, 4:285; Chase to Alphonso Taft, April 28, 1861, Chase Papers, PHS; Blair to Lincoln, March 15, 1861, Lincoln Mss., LC-RTL.

5. Cameron to Lincoln, March 16, 1861, *ORA*, 1:197–98; Robert Means Thompson and Richard Wainwright, *Confidential Correspondence of Gustavus Vasa Fox, Assistant Secretary of the Navy 1861–1865*, 2 vols. (Freeport, N.Y., 1972), 1:8–9.

6. Basler, *Works*, 4:424; Nicolay and Hay, *Lincoln*, 3:382.

7. Cameron to Lincoln, March 17, 1861, *ORA*, 1:197; Fox to Montgomery Blair, February 23, 1861, *ORA*, 1:204.

8. Cameron to Scott and Scott to Fox, March 19, 1861, *ORN*, 4:227; Fox Report, February 24, 1865, *ORN*, 4:247.

9. Anderson to Lorenzo Thomas, March 22, 1861, *ORA*, 1:211.

10. Seward to Lincoln, March 15, 1861, Lincoln Mss., LC-RTL.

11. Nicolay and Hay, *Lincoln*, 3:390–91; Lamon, *Recollections*, 70–72, 74; Hurlbut to Lincoln, March 27, 1861, Lincoln Mss., LC-RTL.

12. Beauregard to Anderson and Anderson to Beauregard, March 26, 1861, *ORA*, 1:222.

13. Beale, *Diary of Edward Bates*, 178–80; Montgomery Meigs Diary, March 12, 1861, LC; Welles to Andrew H. Foote, March 12, 1861, *ORN*, 4:90–91.

14. Scott Memorandum to Cameron, n.d., *ORA*, 1:200–201; Gideon Welles, *Lincoln and Seward* (Freeport, N.Y., 1969), 65–66.

15. David C. Mearns, ed., *The Lincoln Papers*, 2 vols. (Garden City, N.Y., 1948), 2:483–84; James Ford Rhodes, *History of the United States from the Compromise of 1850 to the Final Restoration in 1877*, 7 vols. (New York: 1896–1919), 3:333; Potter, *Lincoln and His Party*, 360.

16. Meigs Diary, March 29, 1861, LC.

17. Walker to Pickens, March 1, 1861, and Beauregard to Walker, March 6, 1861, *ORA*, 1:259, 26.

18. Potter, *Lincoln and His Party*, 343.

19. Commissioners to Toombs, March 14, 1861, and Toombs to Commissioners, March 9, 11, 12, and 20, 1861, Robert A. Toombs Mss., LC; Frank A. Moore, comp., *The Rebellion Record*, 12 vols. (New York, 1861–68), 1:43–44, 427.

20. Beale, *Diary of Edward Bates*, 180; Chase Memorandum, Welles Memorandum, Blair Memorandum, March 29, 1861, Lincoln Mss., LC-RTL.

21. Seward Memorandum and Smith Memorandum, March 29, 1861, Lincoln Mss., LC-RTL.

22. Fox to Lincoln, March 28, 1861, Lincoln Mss., LC-RTL; Lincoln to Welles, March 29, 1861, *ORN*, 4:227; Lincoln to Cameron, March 29, 1861, *ORA*, 1:226.

23. Isaac Toucy to Samuel Barron, January 21, 1861; Edward D. Townsend to Israel Vodges, March 12, 1861; Foote to Welles, March 16, 1861, and Craven to Welles, March 29, 1861, *ORN*, 4:66, 90, 96, 102.

24. Fox Report, February 4, 1865, *ORN*, 4:248; Basler, *Works*, 4:321–22, 323–24.

25. Seward Memorandum, March 29, 1861, Lincoln Mss., LC-RTL; Meigs Diary, March 29, 1861, LC.

26. Meigs Diary, March 30–31, 1861, LC.

27. David Dixon Porter, *Incidents and Anecdotes of the Civil War* (New York, 1885), 13–15.

28. Porter, *Incidents and Anecdotes*, 16; Lincoln to Seward, Porter, Mercer, and Breese, April 1, 1861, *ORN*, 4:108–9; Chester G. Hearn, *Admiral David Dixon Porter: The Civil War Years* (Annapolis, Md., 1996), 36–52.

29. Welles to Foote and Welles to Breese, April 1, 1861; Foote to Welles, April 4, 1861; and Welles to Foote, April 5, 1861, *ORN*, 4:229, 234; Porter, *Incidents*, 18.

30. Foote to Welles and Welles to Foote, and Porter to Foote, April 5, 1861, *ORN*, 4:236, 237, 111.

31. Welles, *Diary*, 1:23–25.

32. Seward to Porter and Porter to Seward, April 6, 1861, *ORN*, 4:112.

33. Welles, *Diary*, 1:38, 39; Seward to Lincoln, April 1, 1861, Lincoln Mss., LC-RTL.

34. Schurz to Lincoln, April 5, 1861, Lincoln Mss., LC-RTL; Bancroft, *Life of William Seward*, 2:98.

35. Bancroft, *Life of William Seward*, 2:134

36. Lincoln to Seward, April 1, 1861, Lincoln Mss., LC-RTL.

37. Nicolay and Hay, *Lincoln*, 4:44.

38. Basler, *Works*, 4:321–22; Walker to Beauregard, April 6, 1861, and Beauregard to Walker, April 9, 1861, *ORA*, 1:288, 291; Anderson to Thomas, April 5, 1861, *ORA*, 1:241.

39. Walker to Beauregard and Hartstene to Beauregard, April 10, 1861, Beauregard Report, April 27, 1861, *ORA*, 1:297, 299, 26.

40. Samuel W. Crawford, *The Genesis of the Civil War: The Story of Sumter, 1860–1861* (New York, 1887), 422–24; Beauregard to Walker, April 11, 1861, *ORA*, 1:301.

41. Beauregard to Anderson, Anderson to Beauregard, James Chesnut and Stephen D. Lee to Anderson, April 12, 1861, *ORA*, 1:13–14.

42. John Foster Report, October 1, 1861, *ORA*, 1:18–23.

43. Cameron to Fox, April 4, 1861, *ORN*, 4:232; Welles to Mercer, April 5, 1861, *ORN*, 4:235.

44. Fox Report, February 24, 1865, *ORN*, 4:249–50; Anderson to Cameron, April 18, 1861, *ORA*, 1:12.

45. Basler, *Works*, 4:271.

46. Theodore C. Pease and James G. Randall, eds., *The Diary of Orville Hickman Browning*, 2 vols. (Springfield, Ill., 1925–33), 1:476.

47. Nicolay and Hay, *Lincoln*, 4:76; Basler, *Works*, 4:264–71.

Chapter 6. "The president is the best . . ."

1. Basler, *Works*, 4:331–32.

2. Thomas, *Abraham Lincoln*, 272–74, 281; *Congressional Globe*, March 15, 1861, 1459–62.

3. Bradley, *Simon Cameron*, 183–84; Margaret Leech, *Reveille in Washington* (New York, 1941), 56.

4. Bradley, *Simon Cameron*, 184.

5. Boatner, *Civil War Dictionary*, 169.

6. James R. Gilmore, *Personal Recollections of Abraham Lincoln and the Civil War* (Boston, 1898), 25–27; Beale, *Diary of Edward Bates*, 182–83.

7. Nicolay and Hay, *Lincoln*, 4:79.

8. Schuckers, *Life of Chase*, 419–20, 429.

9. Cameron to governors, April 15, 1861, *ORA*, ser. 3, 1:68–69.

10. Letcher to Cameron, April 16, 1861, *ORA*, ser. 3, 1:76.

11. Isham Harris to Cameron, April 17, 1861, *ORA*, ser. 3, 1:81.

12. Magoffin to Cameron, April 15, 1861; Cameron to Hicks, April 17, 1861, *ORA*, ser. 3, 1:79–80; and Jackson to Cameron, April 17, 1861, *ORA*, ser. 3, 1:70, 79–80, 82–83.

13. Andrew to Cameron, April 17, 1861, *ORA*, ser. 3, 1:79.

14. John W. Hanson, *Historical Sketch of the Old Sixth Regiment of Massachusetts Volunteers during Its Three Campaigns* (Boston, 1866), 24–41; George W. Brown Report, May 9, 1861, *ORA*, 2:12–13.

15. John P. Usher, *President Lincoln's Cabinet* (Omaha, Nebr., 1925), 19; William B. Hesseltine, *Lincoln and the War Governors* (New York, 1948), 154–56; Hicks to Lincoln, April 22, 1861, *ORA*, 2:588.

16. William Roscoe Thayer, *John Hay*, 2 vols. (Boston, 1915), 1:106.

17. Beale, *Diary of Edward Bates*, 185; Chase to Lincoln, April 25, 1861, Lincoln Mss., LC-RTL.

18. General Orders No. 12, April 27, 1861, *ORA*, 2:607.

19. Basler, *Works*, 4:347.

20. J. G. Randall, *Constitutional Problems under Lincoln* (New York, 1926), 120–21; Beale, *Diary of Edward Bates*, 306; Basler, *Works*, 4:430–31.

21. Nicolay and Hay, *Lincoln*, 4:171–72.

22. Butler to Scott, May 6, 1861, *ORA*, 2:623–24; Basler, *Works*, 4:370; Scott to Butler, May 18, 1861, *ORA*, 2:640–41.

23. Beale, *Diary of Edward Bates*, 183; Scott to Lincoln, April 16 and 17, 1861, Lincoln Mss., LC-RTL; Welles to Etting, March 31, 1861, *ORN*, 4:274.

24. Welles Orders to McCauley, April 10, 16, and 17, 1861, and McCauley to Welles, April 25, 1861, *ORN*, 4:270, 274, 277–79, 288–89.

25. Scott to Lincoln, April 17, 1861, Lincoln Mss., LC-RTL; Jones to Scott, April 18, 19, and 20, 1861, *ORA*, 2:3–5.

26. Beale, *Diary of Edward Bates,* 178, 180; Davis Proclamation, April 17, 1861, *ORN,* 5:796–97.

27. Basler, *Works,* 4:338–39; James R. Soley, *The Blockade and the Cruisers* (New York, 1883), app. A, 241–43; Davis to Congress, April 29, 1861, *ORA,* ser. 4, 1:264.

28. "The Interdiction of Commerce and the Insurgent States," Gideon Welles Mss., LC; Welles to Lincoln, August 5, 1861, *ORN,* 5:53–56.

29. Bancroft, *Life of William Seward,* 2:153n; Clarence E. Macartney, *Lincoln and His Cabinet* (New York, 1931), 154.

30. Bancroft, *Life of William Seward,* 2:170–72.

31. Randall, *Lincoln,* 2:36; Basler, *Works,* 4:376–80.

32. Bancroft, *Life of William Seward,* 2:168, 176.

33. Basler, *Works,* 4:531–32.

34. Magoffin to Cameron, April 15, 1861, *ORA,* ser. 3, 1:98; Nicolay and Hay, *Lincoln,* 4:230.

35. Morton to Cameron, April 28, 1861, *ORA,* ser. 3, 1:126; Moore, *Rebellion Record,* Documents, 1:75–76.

36. Nicolay and Hay, *Lincoln,* 4:232; Segal, *Conversations with Lincoln,* 116.

37. Nicolay and Hay, *Lincoln,* 4:234.

38. Nicolay and Hay, *Lincoln,* 4:206–7.

39. Blair to Cameron, March 11, 1861; Special Orders No. 74, March 13, 1861; Thomas to Harney, April 21, 1861; and Thomas to Lyon, April 20 and 21, 1861, *ORA,* 1:656, 658, 669, 670.

40. Davis to Jackson, April 23, 1861; Thomas to Lyon, April 30, 1861; Lyon to Thomas, May 10, 1861; and Blair to Cameron, April 19, 1861, *ORA,* 1:688, 669.

41. Basler, *Works,* 4:353–54.

42. Niven, *Salmon P. Chase,* 251; Welles to Breese, April 27 and May 13, 1861, *ORN,* 4:342–43.

43. Welles to Lincoln, May 8, 1861, Lincoln Mss., LC-RTL.

44. Thompson, *Fox Correspondence,* 1:44–46; Basler, *Works,* 4:363.

45. John Niven, *Gideon Welles: Lincoln's Secretary of the Navy* (New York, 1973), 352–53.

46. Seward, *Seward at Washington,* 2:590.

Chapter 7. "The fat is all in the fire . . ."

1. Scott to Cameron, May 17, 1861, *ORA,* ser. 3, 1:209.

2. General Orders No. 12, April 27, 1861, and Mansfield to Scott, May 3, 1861, *ORA,* 2:607, 618–19.

3. Heintzelman Report, July 20, 1863, and Farnam Report, May 24, 1861, *ORA,* 2:40–41; Nicolay and Hay, *Lincoln,* 4:313–14.

4. Segal, *Conversations with Lincoln,* 122–23.

5. Scott to Patterson, May 24, 1861; Patterson to Cameron, June 10, 1861; and Patterson to Townsend, June 16, 1861, *ORA,* 2:652, 672, 692.

6. Scott to Patterson, June 16, 1861, *ORA,* 2:694–95.

7. Scott to Butler and Butler to Cameron, May 18, 1861; and Butler to Scott, May 24, 1861, *ORA,* 2:640–41, 641–42, 649–50; Benjamin F. Butler, *Autobiography and Personal Reminiscences of Major General Benjamin F. Butler: Butler's Book* (Boston, 1892), 256–58: Deane to Butler, March 14, 1891, Butler Mss., LC.

8. Cameron to Butler, May 30, 1861, and John Dix to Cameron, August 8, 1861, *ORA*, ser. 3, 1:243, 404.

9. Jessie Ames Marshall, comp., *Private and Official Correspondence of Gen. Benjamin F. Butler*, 5 vols. (Norwood, Mass., 1917), 1:116–17, 119, 121–22; Moore, *Rebellion Record*, Documents, 2:437; Edward McPherson, *The Political History of the United States during the Great Rebellion* (Washington, D.C., 1865), 195.

10. Butler to Scott, June 10, 1861, *ORA*, 2:77–80.

11. Randall, *Constitutional Problems*, 120–21.

12. Basler, *Works*, 4:431–32; Rhodes, *History of the United States*, 3:441; Pease and Randall, *Diary of Orville Hickman Browning*, 1:475–76.

13. *Congressional Globe*, July 22, 1861, 222.

14. Basler, *Works*, 4:370; Faust, *Historical Times Illustrated*, 561–62.

15. General Orders No. 26, May 27, 1861, *ORA*, 2:653.

16. Weed, *Memoir*, 2:333.

17. McDowell to Chase, May 16, 1861, Chase Papers, PHS; Niven, *Salmon P. Chase*, 254.

18. T. Harry Williams, *Lincoln and His Generals* (New York, 1952), 19–20.

19. McDowell to Townsend, June 24, 1861, and Scott to Patterson, July 13, 1861, *ORA* 2:718–21, 106.

20. Colin R. Ballard, *The Military Genius of Abraham Lincoln* (London, 1926), 49–50.

21. McDowell Testimony, *JCCW*, 1863, 2:35–38; Patterson to Townsend, July 18, 1861, *ORA*, 2:168–69.

22. General Orders No. 17, July 16, 1861, and McDowell to Townsend, July 17, 19, 21, and 22, 1861, *ORA*, 2:303–5, 307, 316–17.

23. Mendell to Thomas, July 21, 1861, *ORA*, 2:747; Helen Nicolay, *Lincoln's Secretary*, 109.

24. Alexander to War Department, July 21, 1861, *ORA*, 4:747; Katherine Helm, *The True Story of Mary, Wife of Lincoln* (New York, 1928), 179.

25. Quotes from Nicolay, *Lincoln's Secretary*, 111.

26. William H. Russell, *My Diary North and South* (Boston, 1863), 507; William T. Sherman, *Memoirs of General W.T. Sherman*, 2 vols. (New York, 1875), 1:190–91.

27. Marshall, *Private and Official Correspondence*, 1:155; Kerrigan to Cameron, July 22, 1861, *ORA*, 2:753.

28. Thomas to McClellan, July 22, 1861, *ORA*, 2:753.

29. General Orders, July 25 and 26, 1861, *ORA*, 2:762, 763; Niven, *Salmon P. Chase*, 260–61.

30. George B. McClellan, *McClellan's Own Story: The War for the Union* (New York, 1887), 66–67, 82–83.

31. Faust, *Historical Times Illustrated*, 456; Basler, *Works*, 4:457–58.

32. General Orders No. 40, July 3, 1861, *ORA*, 3:390; Marvin R. Cain, *Lincoln's Attorney General: Edward Bates of Missouri* (Columbia, Mo., 1965), 162.

33. Edward C. Smith, *The Borderland in the Civil War* (New York, 1927), 245–46; Bates to Chase, September 11, 1861, Chase Papers, PHS.

34. Frémont Proclamations, August 14 and 30, 1861, *ORA*, 3:442, 466–67.

35. T. Harry Williams, *Lincoln and the Radicals* (Madison, Wis., 1941), 33.

36. Basler, *Works*, 4:506–7; Frémont to Lincoln, September 8, 1861, Lincoln Mss., LC-RTL.

37. Basler, *Works*, 4:515; Allan Nevins, *Frémont, Pathmarker of the West* (New York, 1939), 516–19; Macartney, *Lincoln and His Cabinet*, 279, 286.

38. Lincoln to Frémont, September 11, 1861, Lincoln Mss., LC-RTL.

39. Bates to Chase, September 11, 1861, Chase Papers, PHS; Cameron to Frémont, August 27, 1861, Cameron Mss., LC; Smith, *Francis Preston Blair Family,* 2:83–84; Beale, *Diary of Edward Bates,* 198.

40. Basler, *Works,* 4:562–63; Faust, *Historical Times Illustrated,* 376; Nicolay and Hay, *Lincoln,* 4:415.

41. Faust, *Historical Times Illustrated,* 332.

Chapter 8. "The bottom is out of the tub"

1. McClellan, *McClellan's Own Story,* 82; McClellan Report, August 4 and October 27, 1861, and General Orders No. 1, August 20, 1861, *ORA,* 5:6, 10, 575.

2. McClellan, *McClellan's Own Story,* 85; Russell, *My Diary North and South,* 535.

3. Zachariah Chandler to Letitia Chandler, October 27, 1861, Chandler Mss., LC; McClellan, *McClellan's Own Story,* 84, 85, 86.

4. McClellan, *McClellan's Own Story,* 87, 88, 168, 169.

5. Tyler Dennett, ed., *Lincoln and the Civil War in the Diaries and Letters of John Hay* (New York, 1939), 31; hereafter cited as *Hay Diary.*

6. General Orders No. 94, November 1, 1861, *ORA,* 5:639; Hay Diary, n.d., covering November 1, 1861, BU; Stephen W. Sears, ed., *The Civil War Papers of George B. McClellan* (New York, 1989), 85, 106.

7. Beale, *Diary of Edward Bates,* 200; Sears, *Civil War Papers of George B. McClellan,* 114.

8. Scott to Cameron, August 12, 1861, *ORA,* 11, pt. 3, 5; Sears, *Civil War Papers of George B. McClellan,* 106; Chase quoted in Niven, *Salmon P. Chase,* 270.

9. Sears, *Civil War Papers of George B. McClellan,* 106–7.

10. Nicolay and Hay, *Lincoln,* 4:469n; *Hay Diary,* 34–35.

11. Norman B. Ferris, *The Trent Affair: A Diplomatic Crisis* (Knoxville, Tenn., 1977), 43–53; Worthington Chauncey Ford, *A Cycle of Adams Letters, 1861–1865,* 2 vols. (Boston, 1920) 1:88.

12. Beale, *Diary of Edward Bates,* 202, 213–17.

13. Donald, *Lincoln,* 321–22.

14. Robert B. Warden, *Account of the Private Life and Public Services of Salmon Portland Chase* (Cincinnati, 1874), 394. Hereafter cited as Warden, *Life of Chase.*

15. Ford, *Cycle of Adams Letters,* 1:99; Richardson, *Messages and Papers,* 6:44–58.

16. Nicolay, *Lincoln's Secretary,* 124–25; Commissioners to Stanton, July 1, 1862, *ORA,* ser. 3, 2:190–95; White, *Life of Lyman Trumbull,* 179–80, 182–83; Alexander H. Meneely, *The War Department,* 1861 (New York, 1928), 264–65; George M. Davis to Lincoln, August 24, 1861, Lincoln Mss., LC-RTL.

17. Cameron Report, altered by Lincoln, December 1, 1861, *ORA,* ser. 3, 1:708; Nicolay and Hay, *Lincoln,* 5:125–26; Niven, *Salmon P. Chase,* 284.

18. Frank A. Flower, *Edwin McMasters Stanton, the Autocrat of Rebellion, Emancipation, and Reconstruction* (New York, 1905), 116; Welles, *Diary,* 1:127.

19. Chase Diary, LC, January 11 and 12, 1862, Chase Mss., LC; Welles, *Diary,* 1:59.

20. Basler, *Works,* 5:96–97; Cameron to Lincoln, January 11, 1862, Lincoln Mss., LC-RTL; McClure, *Abraham Lincoln,* 164–65.

21. Herndon and Weik, *Abraham Lincoln,* 2:355–56.

22. Quoted in Macartney, *Lincoln and His Cabinet,* 315–16.

23. Welles, *Diary,* 1:128–29.

24. Flower, *Edwin McMasters Stanton,* 125; McClellan, *McClellan's Own Story,* 153; Stanton to Dana, January 24, 1862, Charles A. Dana Mss., LC.

25. Julian, *Political Recollections,* 204.

26. Benjamin P. Thomas and Harold M. Hyman, *Stanton: The Life and Times of Lincoln's Secretary of War* (New York, 1962), 151.

27. Julian, *Recollections,* 203; Basler, *Works,* 5:94; Montgomery C. Meigs Diary, January 10 and 12, 1862, LC.

28. McClellan, *McClellan's Own Story,* 447, 450–51, 477; McClellan to S.L.M. Barlow, July 15, 1862, Samuel L. M. Barlow Papers, HL.

Chapter 9. "I can't spare this man . . ."

1. Basler, *Works,* 5:34–35; McClellan to Lincoln, December 10, 1861, *ORA,* 11, pt. 3, 6; Johnston Report, December 27, 1861, *ORA,* 5:1015.

2. Beale, *Diary of Edward Bates,* 220.

3. Henry J. Raymond, *The Life and Public Services of Abraham Lincoln* (New York, 1865), 773.

4. William Swinton, *Campaigns of the Army of the Potomac* (Secaucus, N.J., 1988), 79–85; McClellan, *McClellan's Own Story,* 158.

5. General War Order No. 1, January 27, 1862, *ORA,* 5:41.

6. Buell to McClellan, February 1, 1862, *ORA* 7:931–31; Halleck to McClellan, January 20 and February 6, 1862, *ORA,* 8:508–11, 574; Buell to McClellan, November 27, 1861, *ORA,* 7:451; Buell to Halleck, January 31 and February 26, 1862, *ORA,* 7:574, 425.

7. Halleck to McClellan, February 6, 1862, and Foote to Welles, March 4, 1862, *ORA,* 7:574, 436.

8. Special Orders No. 1, January 31, 1862; Lincoln to McClellan, February 3, 1862; and McClellan to Lincoln, February 3, 1862, *ORA,* 5:41, 41–42, 42–45; Joseph E. Johnston, *Narrative of Military Operations Directed during the Late War between the States* (New York, 1874), 96–97.

9. Swinton, *Campaigns,* 73; Basler, *Works,* 5:124.

10. *Hay Diary,* 36; Nicolay to Bates, February 11, 1862, Nicolay Mss., LC; Williams, *Lincoln and His Generals,* 67.

11. John G. Nicolay Diary, February 27, 1862, Nicolay Mss., LC; Nicolay, *Lincoln's Secretary,* 143.

12. McClellan, *McClellan's Own Story,* 195–96.

13. General Orders No. 151, March 13, 1862, *ORA,* 5:18; *Hay Diary,* 36.

14. Welles, *Diary,* 1:61–67.

15. Welles, *Diary,* 1:66–67; Dahlgren to Ulrich Dahlgren, March 11, 1862, Dahlgren Papers, LC.

16. *Annals of the War, Written by Leading Participants North and South* (Edison, N.J., 1996), 28–29.

17. McClellan Report, August 4, 1863, *ORA,* 5:51; Johnston, *Narrative,* 78, 102; Johnston to Whiting, March 15, 1862, *ORA,* 5:1101.

18. McClellan Report, August 4, 1862, *ORA,* 5:51–52.

19. Basler, *Works*, 5:155; *Hay Diary*, 38; Stanton to Dana, February 1, 1862, Dana Papers, LC.

20. Sears, *Civil War Papers of George B. McClellan*, 207; Beale, *Diary of Edward Bates*, 224, 240.

21. Pease and Randall, *Diary of Orville Hickman Browning*, 1:537–38.

22. McClellan Memorandum and Stanton to McClellan, March 13, 1862, McClellan Report, August 4, 1862, *ORA*, 5:55–56, 46.

23. McClellan to Mary Ellen McClellan, April 1, 1862, McClellan Mss., LC; Lincoln to Stanton, April 3, 1862, Stanton Papers, LC.

24. *Hay Diary*, 39.

25. Grant to Halleck, February 6, 1862; Grant to Buckner, February 16, 1862; and Grant to Halleck, February 16, 1862, *ORA*, 7:124, 161, 625.

26. Nicolay Memorandum, February 27, 1862, Nicolay Mss., LC.

27. Halleck to McClellan, February 17, 1862, *ORA*, 7:628; War Order No. 3, March 11, 1862, *ORA*, 8:605.

28. Halleck to Grant, March 1, 1862, and McClellan to Halleck, March 3, 1862, *ORA*, 7:674, 680; Halleck to Grant, March 13, 1862, *ORA*, 10, pt. 2, 32.

29. Halleck to Buell, March 16, 1862, and Grant to Buell, March 19, 1862, *ORA*, 10, pt. 2, 42, 47; Jacob Ammen's Diary, *ORA*, 10, pt. 1, 329–31.

30. Johnston to Davis, April 3, 1862, and Grant to Halleck April 5, 1862, *ORA*, 10, pt. 2, 387, 94.

31. Grant to Buell, April 6, 1862, *ORA*, 10, pt. 2, 95.

32. Boatner, *Civil War Dictionary*, 754–57.

33. Grant to Halleck, April 9, 1862; Stanton to Halleck, April 9, 1862; and Field Orders No. 31, April 28, 1862, *ORA*, 10, pt. 2, 99, 100, 138.

34. Stanton to Halleck, April 23, 1862, and Halleck to Stanton, April 24, 1862, *ORA*, 10, pt. 1, 98–99; Halleck to Ethan Allen Hitchcock, April 18, 1862, Hitchcock Mss., LC.

35. McClure, *Abraham Lincoln*, 195–96.

36. Sherman, *Memoirs*, 1:251–52.

37. Thomas and Hyman, *Stanton*, 191.

38. Welles, *Diary*, 1:69.

39. Chester G. Hearn, *Ellet's Brigade: The Strangest Outfit of All* (Baton Rouge, La., 2000), 6–8; Stanton to Ellet, March 27, 1862, *ORN*, 22:680, 681.

40. Hearn, *Ellet's Brigade*, 13–15, 27–42.

Chapter 10. "If I could save the Union . . ."

1. McClellan, *McClellan's Own Story*, 307, 308, 312; McClellan Report, August 4, 1863, *ORA*, 11, pt. 1, 10; Lincoln to McClellan, April 9, 1862, Lincoln Mss., LC.

2. Testimony, *JCCW* (1863), pt. 1, 630–31.

3. Magruder Report, May 3, 1862, *ORA*, 11, pt. 1, 406; Testimony, *JCCW* (1863), pt. 1, 346–47; Alexander S. Webb, *The Peninsula* (New York, 1881), 59, 63, 64; Beale, *Diary of Edward Bates*, 253.

4. Stanton to McClellan, May 6, 1862, *ORA*, 11, pt. 3, 145; Niven, *Salmon P. Chase*, 287–88.

5. Chase to Janette "Nettie" Chase, May 8 and 11, 1862, Chase Mss., LC; Goldsborough to Lincoln, May 9, 1862, *ORA*, 11, pt. 3, 155–56; Donald, *Inside Lincoln's Cabinet*, 85; Stanton to Watson, May 10 and 11, 1862; *ORA*, 11, pt. 3, 162–63, 163–64.

6. Johnston, *Narrative*, 117; McClellan to Lincoln, May 14, 1862, *ORA*, 11, pt. 1, 26.

7. Stanton to McClellan, May 17, 1862, and Stanton to McDowell, May 17, 1862, *ORA*, 11, pt. 1, 27, 28; Sears, *Civil War Papers of George B. McClellan*, 269.

8. Beale, *Diary of Edward Bates*, 249; McClellan to Lincoln, May 21, 1862, *ORA*, 11, pt. 1, 29.

9. McClellan to Stanton, May 9, 1862, Stanton Papers, LC; Lincoln to McClellan, May 9, 1862, Lincoln Mss., LC-RTL.

10. Lincoln to McClellan, May 24, 1862, *ORA*, 11, pt. 1, 30; Matthew F. Steele, *American Campaigns* (Washington, D.C., 1935), 229.

11. McClellan to Lincoln, May 26, 1862, *ORA*, 11, pt. 1, 33; McClellan, *McClellan's Own Story*, 398; Stanton to McClellan, June 2, 1862, *ORA*, 11, pt. 1, 44.

12. Stanton to McClellan, June 5, 1862, and McClellan to Stanton, June 7, 1862, *ORA*, 11, pt. 1, 46; Dix to Stanton, June 9, 1862, *ORA*, 11, pt. 3, 221.

13. McClellan to Lincoln, June 18, 1862; McClellan's Returns, June 20, 1862; and McClellan to John Rodgers, June 24, 1862, *ORA*, 11, pt. 3, 233, 238, 250; Basler, *Works*, 5:276.

14. Sears, *Civil War Papers of George B. McClellan*, 244–45; Webb, *Peninsula*, 119–20; McClellan to Stanton, June 25, 1862, *ORA*, 11, pt. 3, 254.

15. General Orders No. 75, *ORA*, 11, pt. 2, 498–99; McClellan Report, August 4, 1863, *ORA*, pt. 1, 51; Testimony, *JCCW* (1863), 1:436, 592.

16. McClellan to Stanton, June 28, 1862, *ORA*, pt. 1, 61; David Homer Bates, *Lincoln in the Telegraph Office* (New York, 1939), 109–10; Basler, *Works*, 5:289, 291 n. 2; McClellan to Stanton, July 3, 1862, *ORA*, 11, pt. 3, 291–92; John Bigelow, *Retrospections of an Active Life*, 5 vols. (New York, 1909–13), 1:563.

17. McClellan, *McClellan's Own Story*, 465; McClellan to Lincoln, June 20, 1862, *ORA*, 11, pt. 1, 48.

18. McClellan, *McClellan's Own Story*, 487–89, 446; Basler, *Works*, 5:309–12; McClellan to Mary Ellen McClellan, July 9, 1862, George B. McClellan Mss., LC.

19. Lincoln to McClellan, July 13, 1862, and McClellan to Lincoln, July 15, 1862, *ORA*, 11, pt. 3, 319, 321–22; Sears, *Civil War Papers of George B. McClellan*, 345.

20. Basler, *Works*, 5:312–13n; Halleck to Stanton, July 27, 1862, and Halleck to McClellan, August 5, 1862, *ORA*, 11, pt. 3, 337–38, 359; McClellan, *McClellan's Own Story*, 465.

21. Horan, *Pinkertons*, 117.

22. Niven, *Salmon P. Chase*, 292, 294, 299, 300; Donald, *Inside Lincoln's Cabinet*, 105–7; Chase, *Diary and Correspondence*, 2:48.

23. Frémont's Proclamation, August 30, 1861, *ORA*, 3:466–67; William E. Barton, *The Life of Abraham Lincoln*, 2 vols. (Indianapolis, 1925), 2:82.

24. Basler, *Works*, 5:29–30, 48, 144–45, 192; Nicolay and Hay, *Lincoln*, 5:208, 216.

25. Francis P. Blair Sr. to Lincoln, November 16, 1861; Montgomery Blair to Lincoln, November 21, 1861; and Chase to Lincoln, November 12, 1861, Lincoln Mss., LC-RTL.

26. Gideon Welles, "Administration of Abraham Lincoln," *Galaxy* 23 (February 1877): 156; Basler, *Works*, 5:219, 222–23, 328–31; Thomas and Hyman, *Stanton*, 232–33; Francis Fessenden, *Life and Public Services of William Pitt Fessenden*, 2 vols. (Boston, 1907), 1:273–74.

27. Welles, *Diary*, 1:70–71.

28. Bates, *Lincoln in the Telegraph Office*, 138–42; Basler, *Works*, 5:336–37.

29. Salmon P. Chase, "Diary and Correspondence of Salmon P. Chase," *Annual Report of the American Historical Association for the Year 1902*, 2 vols. (Washington, D.C.: 1903), 2:48–49; Welles, "Administration of Lincoln," 156.

30. Carpenter, *Six Months at the White House*, 21–22; Stanton Memorandum, July 22, 1862, Stanton Papers, LC.

31. Stanton Memorandum, July 22, 1862, Stanton Papers, LC; Chase, "Diary and Correspondence," 2:311; Thomas and Hyman, *Stanton*, 233–34; James G. Hollandsworth, *The Louisiana Native Guards: The Black Military Experience during the Civil War* (Baton Rouge, La., 1995), chap. 2.

32. *New York Tribune*, August 20, 1862, in Basler, *Works*, 5:388–89, 389n.

33. Weed to Seward, August 23, 1862, Lincoln Mss., LC-RTL; Basler, *Works*, 420; Welles, *Diary*, 1:143.

Chapter 11. "In my position . . ."

1. Order Constituting the Army of Virginia, June 26, 1862, Stanton Papers, LC; Welles, *Diary*, 1:108.

2. Quoted in Faust, *Historical Times Illustrated*, 593.

3. Pope's Address, July 14, 1862, *ORA*, 12, pt. 3, 473–74; Porter to Hon. J.C.G. Kennedy, July 17, 1862, McClellan Mss., LC; Sears, *Civil War Papers of George B. McClellan*, 382–83, 388.

4. Douglas Southall Freeman, *R. E. Lee: A Biography*, 4 vols. (New York, 1934–35), 2:263–64.

5. McClellan, *McClellan's Own Story*, 520, 528; Board of Army Officers to Stanton, March 19, 1878, *ORA*, 12, pt. 2, 515; Thomas and Hyman, *Stanton*, 216, 217.

6. Pope to Halleck, August 13, 1862, *ORA*, 12, pt. 2, 133–35; Jackson Report, April 4, 1863, *ORA*, 12, pt. 2, 184–85; Halleck to Pope, August 14, 1862, *ORA*, 12, pt. 2, 135.

7. McClellan, *McClellan's Own Story*, 474–75, 500–504; Halleck to Pope, August 12, 1862, *ORA*, 12, pt. 3, 564; Halleck to Stanton, August 30, 1862, Stanton Mss., LC.

8. McClellan, *McClellan's Own Story*, 508–9; Halleck to McClellan, August 27, 1862, *ORA*, 16, pt. 2, 691.

9. Halleck to Stanton, November 25, 1862, *ORA*, 12, pt. 2, 7–8; Pope to Halleck, August 30, 1862, *ORA*, 12, pt. 3, 741; *Hay Diary*, 46.

10. McClellan, *McClellan's Own Story*, 512–15; Halleck to McClellan, August 27, 1862, *ORA*, 12, pt. 3, 691.

11. Townsend's Order, August 30, 1862, McClellan Papers, LC; McClellan, *McClellan's Own Story*, 525–26, 534.

12. *Hay Diary*, 45, 46.

13. McClellan, *McClellan's Own Story*, 534–36; General Orders No. 122, *ORA*, 12, pt. 2, 807.

14. Chase, Diary, September 2, 1862, LC, 456; Welles, *Diary*, 1:102–5; Flower, *Edwin McMasters Stanton*, 177.

15. Welles, *Diary*, 1:110, 111; Halleck to Pope, September 5, 1862, *ORA*, 12, pt. 3, 812–13.

16. Welles, *Diary*, 1:113; McClellan, *McClellan's Own Story*, 567–68.

17. *Hay Diary*, 46; Welles, *Diary*, 1:105–6.

18. William Marvel, *Burnside* (Chapel Hill, N.C., 1991), 110–11; Stanton to Curtin, September 8, 1862, *ORA*, 19, pt. 2, 217.

19. John Gibbon, *Personal Recollections of the Civil War* (New York, 1928), 73; McClellan to Lincoln, September 13, 1862, *ORA*, 19, pt. 2, 281; Welles, *Diary*, 1:129–30.

20. McClellan to Halleck, September 15, 1862, *ORA*, 19, pt. 2, 294; Basler, *Works*, 5:426.

21. McClellan, *McClellan's Own Story*, 618–20; Williams, *Lincoln Finds a General*, 2:458–60; Welles, *Diary*, 1:142.

22. Chase, "Diary and Correspondence," 2:87–88; Warden, *Life of Chase*, 162; Welles, Gideon, "History of Emancipation," *Galaxy* 14 (December 1872): 846–47; Basler, *Works*, 5:434.

23. Basler, *Works*, 5:438; *Hay Diary*, 50.

24. Basler, *Works*, 5:444; Hamlin to Lincoln, September 25, 1862, Nicolay Mss., LC.

25. Randall, *Lincoln*, 2:173.

26. Basler, *Works*, 5:436–37.

27. McClellan, *McClellan's Own Story*, 615; McClellan to Lincoln, October 7, 1862, *ORA*, 19, pt. 2, 395–96.

28. Horan, *Pinkertons*, 129–34.

29. Basler, *Works*, 5:442–43, 508; Montgomery Blair to McClellan, September 27, 1862, McClellan Mss., LC.

30. *Hay Diary*, 218; Halleck to McClellan, October 6, 1862, and McClellan to Halleck, October 7, 1862, *ORA* 19, pt. 1, 10–12.

31. Halleck to McClellan, October 6, 1862, *ORA*, 19, pt. 1, 10–11; McClellan, *McClellan's Own Story*, 613–14; Welles, *Diary*, 1:160; Garrett Davis to Lincoln, September 7, 1862, Lincoln Mss., LC-RTL.

32. Nicolay, *Lincoln's Secretary*, 157; Basler, *Works*, 5:460–61, 474.

33. Sears, *Civil War Papers of George B. McClellan*, 516.

34. Carl Schurz to Lincoln, May 19, 1862, Lincoln Mss., LC-RTL.

35. Welles, *Diary*, 1:179; Lincoln to Halleck, November 5, 1862, Lincoln Mss., ISHL; Halleck to McClellan, November 5, 1862, *ORA*, 19, pt. 2, 545; Thomas and Hyman, *Stanton*, 225, 226.

36. Smith, *Francis Preston Blair Family*, 2:144–45.

37. Basler, *Works*, 5:460–61; Halleck to Buell, October 13, 1862, *ORA*, 16, pt. 2, 638.

38. Halleck to Buell, October 24, 1862, *ORA*, 16, pt. 2, 642; Basler, *Works*, 5:478.

39. Donn Piatt, *Memories of the Men Who Saved the Union* (New York, 1887), 81; Thomas and Hyman, *Stanton*, 227–28.

40. Halleck to Banks, November 9, 1862, *ORA*, 15:590–91; Lincoln to Banks, November 22, 1862, Lincoln Mss., LC-RTL.

41. McClernand to Lincoln, September 28, 1862, *ORA*, 17, pt. 2, 849–53; Thomas and Hyman, *Stanton*, 265; Stanton to McClernand, October 21, 1862, *ORA*, 17, pt. 2, 282.

42. Welles, *Diary*, 1:217; Stanton to McClernand, December 17, 1862, *ORA*, 17, pt. 2, 420.

Chapter 12. "If there is a worse place . . ."

1. Nicolay and Hay, *Lincoln*, 6:192.

2. *B&L*, 3:104; McClellan, *McClellan's Own Story*, 660.

3. Charles A. Dana, *Recollections of the Civil War* (Lincoln, Nebr., 1996), 138; George Gordon Meade, *The Life and Letters of George Gordon Meade, Major-General United States Army*, 2 vols. (New York, 1913), 1:304; Daniel Larned to Henry Larned, November 22, 1862, Larned, Mss., LC; quotes in Marvel, *Burnside*, 162.

4. *B&L*, 3:106; Oliver O. Howard, *Autobiography of Oliver Otis Howard*, 2 vols. (New York, 1908), 1:314.

5. Burnside to Cullum, November 7, 1862, *ORA*, 19, pt. 2, 552–54; Burnside Report, January 20, 1863, *ORA*, 21:83–84; Herman Haupt, *Reminiscences of General Herman Haupt* (Milwaukee, 1901), 160.

6. Halleck Report, November 15, 1862, *ORA*, 21:46–47; Burnside Report, January 20, 1863, *ORA*, 21:84.

7. Burnside Report, January 20, 1863, *ORA*, 21:84, 148–49; Testimony, *JCCW*, 1, 1863, 665, 671, 675; Halleck Report, November 15, 1863, *ORA*, 21:47.

8. Lincoln to Halleck, November 27, 1862, Lincoln Mss., LC-RTL; Larned to Amelia Larned, November 27, 1862, Larned Mss., LC; Nicolay and Hay, *Works*, 8:88.

9. Boatner, *Civil War Dictionary*, 310–13.

10. Howard, *Autobiography*, 1:321; Testimony, *JCCW*, 1:653, 668; *B&L*, 3:82, 138; Larned Notes, December 15, 1862, Larned Mss., LC; Moore, *Rebellion Record*, 10:163.

11. Wadsworth to Barlow, December 18, 1862, Barlow Papers, HL.

12. Burnside to Halleck, December 17, 1862, and Lincoln to Burnside, December 19, 1862, *ORA*, 21:66, 866; Larned to Amelia Larned, December 23, 1862, Larned Mss., LC; Henry W. Raymond, "Excerpts from the Journal of Henry J. Raymond," *Scribner's Monthly* 19 (November 1879): 424.

13. Lincoln to the Army of the Potomac, December 22, 1862; Lincoln to Burnside, December 30, 1862; Halleck to Burnside, December 30, 1862; and Burnside to Lincoln, January 1, 1863, *ORA*, 21:67–68, 900, 941.

14. Raymond, "Excerpts from the Journal," 422.

15. Basler, *Works*, 6:31; Halleck to Stanton, January 1, 1863, *ORA*, 21:940–41.

16. Burnside to Halleck, January 6, 1863; Halleck to Burnside, January 8, 1863; and Lincoln to Halleck, January 8, 1863, *ORA*, 21:945, 953–54.

17. Marvel, *Burnside*, 212–23; General Orders No. 8, January 23, 1863, *ORA*, 21:998–99; Testimony, *JCCW* (1863), 1:721.

18. *B&L*, 3:239–40; General Orders No. 20, January 25, 1863, and Halleck to Franklin, May 29, 1863, *ORA*, 21:1004–5, 1009; Basler, *Works*, 6:78–79.

19. Nicolay and Hay, *Lincoln*, 6:254–55, 261, 262; Schuckers, *Life of Chase*, 379–80, 443; Warden, *Life of Chase*, 487, 500, 505; Chase to Butler, July 31, 1862, in Marshall, *Private and Official Correspondence*, 2:132.

20. Fessenden, *Life and Public Services*, 1:232, 234, 237; Pease and Randall, *Diary of Orville Hickman Browning*, 1:596–99, 601; Welles, *Diary*, 1:194; Seward, *Seward at Washington*, 3:146; Seward to Lincoln, December 18, 1862, Seward Mss., UR.

21. Beale, *Diary of Edward Bates*, 270; Pease and Randall, *Diary of Orville Hickman Browning*, 1:600.

22. Nicolay and Hay, *Lincoln*, 6:266; Chase to Chandler, September 20, 1862, Chandler Mss., LC.

23. Pease and Randall, *Diary of Orville Hickman Browning*, 1:601; Fessenden, *Life and Public Services*, 1:242–46; Welles, *Diary*, 1:194–98.

24. Nicolay and Hay, *Lincoln*, 6:266; Beale, *Diary of Edward Bates*, 270; Welles, *Diary*, 1:197–98.

25. Welles, *Diary*, 1:201–2, 204.

26. Basler, *Works*, 6:12–13; Pease and Randall, *Diary of Orville Hickman Browning*, 1:603.

27. Seward, *Seward at Washington*, 3:148.

28. Nicolay and Hay, *Lincoln*, 6:226–29, 241; Schuckers, *Life of Chase*, 245.

29. Nicolay and Hay, *Lincoln,* 6:230–37; Schuckers, *Life of Chase,* 358; Niven, *Salmon P. Chase,* 298.

30. Nicolay and Hay, *Lincoln,* 6:242–43; Basler, *Works,* 5:522–23: Niven, *Salmon P. Chase,* 330–31; Beale, *Diary of Edward Bates,* 292.

31. Basler, *Works,* 7:347; Nicolay and Hay, *Lincoln,* 9:395.

32. Nicolay to Therena Bates, December 23, 1862, Nicolay Mss., LC; Welles, *Diary,* 1:204.

33. Nicolay and Hay, *Lincoln,* 6:300–311; Beale, *Diary of Edward Bates,* 271; Basler, *Works,* 6:26–28.

34. Basler, *Works,* 6:28–31; Seward, *Seward at Washington,* 151.

35. Warden, *Life of Chase,* 468; *Hay Diary,* 112.

36. Beale, *Diary of Edward Bates,* 272.

Chapter 13. "My God, my God, what will . . ."

1. Halleck to Rosecrans, December 4 and 5, 1862, and Rosecrans to Halleck, December 4, 1862, *ORA,* 20, pt. 2, 117, 118, 123.

2. Rosecrans to Halleck, January 3–5, 1863, *ORA,* 20, pt. 1, 184–86; Lincoln to Rosecrans, January 5, 1863, Rosecrans Papers, BU.

3. Lincoln to Rosecrans, February 17, 1863, Stanton Papers, LC.

4. Halleck to Rosecrans, March 1, 13, 1862, *ORA,* 23, pt. 2, 138; Rosecrans to Halleck, March 6, 1863, *ORA,* 23, pt. 2, 111.

5. Rosecrans to Lincoln, March 16, 1863, *ORA,* 23, pt. 2, 146–47; Basler, *Works,* 6:138–39; Halleck to Rosecrans, April 20, 1863, *ORA,* 23, pt. 2, 255–56.

6. Villard, *Memoirs,* 2:66–68; Williams, *Lincoln and His Generals,* 250.

7. Lincoln to Rosecrans and Rosecrans to Lincoln, May 28, 1863, *ORA,* 23, pt. 2, 369.

8. Halleck to Rosecrans and Rosecrans to Halleck, June 2, 1863, *ORA,* 24, pt. 3, 376–73.

9. Halleck to Rosecrans, June 11 and 12, Rosecrans to Halleck, June 11, 1863, *ORA,* 23, pt. 1, 10, 8.

10. Halleck to Rosecrans, June 16, 1863, and Rosecrans to Halleck, June 16 and 24, 1863, *ORA,* 23, pt. 1, 10.

11. Halleck to Hooker, January 31, 1863, *ORA,* 25, pt. 1, 12; John Bigelow Jr., *Chancellorsville* (New York, 1995), 108.

12. Lincoln to Joseph Hooker, April 3, 1863, Lincoln Papers, ISHL; Beale, *Diary of Edward Bates,* 287–88; Brooks, *Washington in Lincoln's Time,* 49–51.

13. Basler, *Works,* 6:164–65, 169; Hooker to Lincoln, April 11, 1863, *ORA,* 25, pt. 2, 199; Bigelow, *Chancellorsville,* 140–41.

14. Lincoln to Hooker, April 14 and 15, 1863, and Stanton to Hooker, April 18, 1863, *ORA,* 25, pt. 2, 209, 214, 227.

15. Hooker to Lincoln, April 27, 1863, Lincoln Mss., LC-RTL; Heintzelman Journal, May 1, 1863, LC.

16. Swinton, *Campaigns,* 275; *B&L,* 3:169–71.

17. Butterfield to Lincoln, May 3, 1863; Lincoln to Butterfield, May 3, 1863; and Hooker to Lincoln May 3, 1863, *ORA,* 25, pt. 2, 377, 378, 379.

18. Lincoln to Hooker, May 4, 1863, and Hooker to Lincoln, May 4, 6, 1863, *ORA,* 25, pt. 2, 401, 421–22; Welles, *Diary,* 1:291–92; Butterfield to Lincoln, May 5 and 6, 1863, *ORA,* 25, pt. 2, 434, 435; Brooks, *Washington in Lincoln's Time,* 57–58.

19. Stanton to Hooker, May 6, 1863, *ORA*, pt. 2, 435; Meade, *Life and Letters*, 1:373, 379; Heintzelman Journal, May 5, 1863, LC.

20. Basler, *Works*, 6:201; Reports, *JCCW* (1865), 1:151.

21. Wilkes to Welles, February 26 and March 15, 1863, *ORN*, 2:97–98, 99–100; Randall, *Lincoln*, 3:334–35.

22. Welles, *Diary*, 1:269, 270–72, 286–89, 304; Beale, *Diary of Edward Bates*, 293; Niven, *Gideon Welles*, 456–57.

23. Welles, *Diary*, 1:287, 302–4, 310, 489–90.

24. Donald, *Lincoln*, 414; Basler, *Works*, 6:63–65.

25. Basler, *Works*, 5:436–37; Welles, *Diary*, 1:150.

26. Nicolay and Hay, *Works*, 7:281–82; Beale, *Diary of Edward Bates*, 306.

27. Allan Nevins, *The War for the Union*, 4 vols. (New York, 1959–71), 2:316–17; Thomas and Hyman, *Stanton*, 249; Basler, *Works*, 5:437.

25. Randall, *Lincoln*, 3:212–13; James L. Vallandigham, *A Life of Clement L. Vallandigham* (Baltimore, 1872), 141; Chase to Hiram Barney, October 26, 1862, Chase Mss., LC.

29. General Orders No. 38, April 13, 1863, *ORA*, 23, pt. 2, 237.

30. Vallandigham, *Life of Clement L. Vallandigham*, 277–80; Vallandigham Trial, *ORA*, ser. 2, 5:633–45; Rhodes, *History of the United States*, 4:247.

31. Samuel S. Cox, *Three Decades of Federal Legislation, 1855 to 1885* (Providence, R.I., 1885), 83; Vallandigham Trial, *ORA*, ser. 2, 5:646.

32. Burnside to Lincoln, May 8, 1863, Lincoln Mss., LC-RTL; Basler, *Works*, 225, 237.

33. Rhodes, *History of the United States*, 4:250–55; Stanton to Burnside, May 19, 1863, *ORA*, ser. 2, 5:657; Vallandigham, *Life of Clement L. Vallandigham*, 300ff.

34. Habeas Corpus Proceedings, *ORA*, ser. 2, 5:573–84.

35. Bates to Lincoln, July 5, 1861, *ORA*, ser. 2, 20–30; Beale, *Diary of Edward Bates*, 307.

Chapter 14. "Grant is my man . . ."

1. Stanton to L. C. Turner, September 19, 1863, Stanton Mss., LC.

2. Boatner, *Civil War Dictionary*, 140; Miers, *Lincoln Day by Day*, 3:183; *B&L*, 3:241.

3. Hooker to Lincoln, June 5, 1863; Lincoln to Hooker, June 5, 1863; and Halleck to Hooker, June 5, 1863, *ORA*, 27, pt. 1, 30, 31.

4. Hooker to Lincoln and Lincoln to Hooker, June 10, 1863, *ORA*, 27, pt. 1, 34, 35.

5. Welles, *Diary*, 1:320.

6. Basler, *Works*, 6:270, 271; Stanton to Colin B. Ferguson and Stanton to Lincoln, June 13, 1863, Lincoln Mss., LC-RTL.

7. Halleck Report, November 15, 1863, *ORA*, 27, pt. 1, 15; Welles, *Diary*, 1:328, 329.

8. Hooker to Lincoln, June 14, 1863, *ORA*, 27, pt. 1, 39–40; Basler, *Works*, 6:273, 276; Haupt, *Reminiscences*, 205–6.

9. Hooker to Lincoln, June 16, 1863, Lincoln Mss., LC-RTL; Basler, *Works*, 6:281, 282.

10. Welles, *Diary*, 1:340; Heintzelman Journal, June 27, 1863, LC; Lincoln to Hooker, June 27, 1863, *ORA*, 27, pt. 1, 27, 58.

11. Welles, *Diary*, 1:344.

12. Hooker to Halleck and Halleck to Hooker, June 27, 1863, *ORA*, 27, pt. 1, 60; Rice, *Reminiscences*, 128.

13. Rhodes, *History of the United States*, 4:279; Bradford's Proclamation, June 16, 1863, and

Curtin's Proclamation, June 26, 1863, *ORA*, 27, pt. 3, 169–70, 347–48; Heintzelman Journal, June 27–28, 1863, LC; Rice, *Reminiscences*, 128–29.

14. Welles, *Diary*, 1:348–49; Chase to David Dudley, June 30, 1863, Chase Mss., LC; John Bigelow Diary, April 2, 1867, NYPL.

15. Welles, *Diary*, 1:352.

16. General Orders, No. 194, June 27, 1863, *ORA*, 27, pt. 3, 369; Seward, *Reminiscences*, 239–41.

17. Isaac R. Pennypacker, *General Meade* (New York, 1901), 3; George R. Agassiz, ed., *Meade's Headquarters, 1863–1865: Letters of Col. Theodore Lyman from the Wilderness to Appomattox* (Boston, 1922), 73.

18. Halleck to Meade, June 27, 1863, *ORA*, 27, pt. 1, 61.

19. *B&L*, 3:243.

20. General Orders No. 67, June 28, 1863, *ORA*, 27, pt. 3, 374.

21. Reports, *JCCW* (1865), 1:439; Meade to Halleck, July 2, 1863, *ORA*, 27, pt. 1, 72.

22. Bates, *Lincoln in the Telegraph Office*, 155, 156; Nicolay and Hay, *Works*, 6:314; Lincoln to Halleck, July 6, 1863, *ORA*, 27, pt. 3, 567; General Orders No. 68, July 4, 1863, *ORA*, 27, pt. 3, 559; *Hay Diary*, 67.

23. Lincoln to Halleck and Halleck to Meade, July 7, 1863, *ORA*, 27, pt. 1, 83.

24. Meade to Halleck, July 12 and 13, 1863, *ORA*, 27, pt. 1, 91; Bates, *Lincoln in the Telegraph Office*, 157; *Hay Diary*, 67; Welles, *Diary*, 1:331, 370–71.

25. Bradley, *Simon Cameron*, 221, 223; Cameron to Lincoln, July 14, 1863, Lincoln Mss., LC-RTL.

26. Basler, *Works*, 6:329–30; *Hay Diary*, 67; Nicolay and Hay, *Lincoln*, 7:278–79, 280–81; Halleck to Meade, Meade to Halleck, and Halleck to Meade, July 14, 1863, *ORA*, 27, pt. 1, 93–94.

27. *Hay Diary*, 67–68; Howard to Lincoln, July 18, 1863, Lincoln Mss., LC-RTL; Basler, *Works*, 6:340, 332.

28. Brooks, *Washington in Lincoln's Time*, 94.

29. Rice, *Reminiscences*, 402.

30. Welles, *Diary*, 1:364.

31. Welles, *Diary*, 1:364–65.

32. McClernand to Lincoln, June 20, 1862, Lincoln Mss., LC-RTL; McClernand to Lincoln, February 27, 1862, Nicolay Mss., LC; McClernand to Lincoln, September 28, 1863, *ORA*, 17, pt. 2, 849–53; Hearn, *Admiral David Dixon Porter*, 142–43.

33. McClernand to Lincoln and Stanton, and Stanton to McClernand, December 17, 1862, Grant to McClernand, December 18, 1862, all in *ORA*, 17, pt. 2, 420, 425; General Orders No. 210, December 18, 1862, *ORA*, 17, pt. 2, 432; Halleck to Grant, December 18, 1862, *ORA*, 17, pt. 1, 476.

34. McClernand to Lincoln, January 7 and 16, 1863, Lincoln Mss., LC-RTL.

35. Grant to Halleck, January 11, 1863, *ORN*, 24:106; Halleck to Grant, January 12, 1863, *ORA*, 17, pt. 2, 555; Lincoln to McClernand, January 22, 1863, Lincoln Papers, ISHL.

36. McClernand to Grant, January 30 and February 1, 1863, and Grant to McClernand, January 31, 1863, *ORA*, 24, pt. 1, 12–14.

37. Halleck to Grant, January 25 and March 20, 1863, *ORA*, 24, pt. 1, 10, 22.

38. James F. Rusling, *Men and Things I Saw in Civil War Days* (New York, 1899), 16–17; Basler, *Works*, 6:230.

39. McClernand to Lincoln, March 15, 1863; Halstead to Chase, April 1, 1863; and Chase to Lincoln, April 4, 1863, Lincoln Mss., LC-RTL; Dana, *Recollections*, 16–17.

40. Dana, *Recollections*, 14–15; Porter, *Incidents and Anecdotes*, 181–83; Washburne to Lincoln, April 30 and May 1, 1863, Lincoln Mss., LC-RTL; Stanton to Dana, May 5, 1863, and Dana to Stanton, with Grant's messages to McClernand embedded in it, June 22, 1863, *ORA*, 24, pt. 1, 84, 102–3.

41. Halleck to Banks, May 11, 1863, and Grant to Halleck, May 15, 1863, *ORA*, 24, pt. 1, 36.

42. Rusling, *Men and Things I Saw*, 17.

Chapter 15. "Blood can not restore blood"

1. Nicolay and Hay, *Lincoln*, 7:5–7.

2. Welles, *Diary*, 1:218, 324.

3. Nicolay and Hay, *Lincoln*, 7:10, 12; Seymour to Lincoln, April 14, 1863, Lincoln Mss., LC-RTL.

4. Faust, *Historical Times Illustrated*, 225.

5. Welles, *Diary*, 1:370.

6. Seymour to Lincoln, August 3, 1863, *ORA*, ser. 3, 3:612–19; Opdyke to Stanton, Stanton to Opdyke, July 14, 1863, *ORA*, 27, pt. 3, 916; Irving Werstein, *July, 1863: The Incredible Story of the Bloody New York City Draft Riots* (New York, 1957), 223–24.

7. *Hay Diary*, 78; Basler, *Works*, 6:369–70.

8. Thomas and Hyman, *Stanton*, 283.

9. Warden, *Life of Chase*, 441.

10. Hunter to Stanton, April 3, 1862, *ORA*, 6:264; Thomas W. Higginson, *Army Life in a Black Regiment* (Boston, 1870), 272–74.

11. Stanton to Saxton, August 25, 1863, *ORA* 14:377; Warden, *Life of Chase*, 441.

12. Phelps to R. S. Davis, June 16, 1862, *and* Butler to Phelps, August 2, 1862, *ORA*, 15:489, 536; Hollandsworth, *Louisiana Native Guards*, 16–22, 23.

13. James Lane to Stanton, August 6, 1862, Stanton Mss., LC; Higginson, *Army Life*, 277.

14. Hamlin, *Life and Times*, 431; Lincoln to John A. Dix, January 14, 1863, and Dix to Lincoln, January 15, 1863, Lincoln Mss., LC-RTL.

15. Lincoln to Banks, March 29, 1863, and Banks to Lincoln, August 17, 1863, Lincoln Mss., LC-RTL; Hollandsworth, *Louisiana Native Guards*, 53–58.

16. Quotes from Dudley Cornish, *The Sable Arm: Black Troops in the Union Army, 1861–1865* (New York, 1966), 108.

17. William Schouler, *History of Massachusetts in the Civil War*, 2 vols. (Boston, 1868–71), 1:361, 408.

18. Hesseltine, *Lincoln and the War Governors*, 287–90; Moore, *Rebellion Record*, Documents, 8:145; Basler, *Works*, 6:374: Grant to Lincoln, August 23, 1863, Lincoln Mss., LC-RTL.

19. Gillmore Report, November 15, 1863, *ORA*, 28, pt. 1, 3–4, 15–16, 41, 210.

20. Lincoln to Stanton, July 21, 1863, Stanton Mss., LC.

21. Stanton Report, April 2, 1864, Lincoln Mss., LC-RTL; Nicolay and Hay, *Lincoln*, 6:468, 469.

22. Moore, *Rebellion Record*, Documents, 8:73–74, 10:724; Nicolay and Hay, *Lincoln*, 6:474.

23. Basler, *Works*, 6:357; Donald, *Lincoln*, 489.

24. William B. Hesseltine, ed., *Civil War Prisons* (Kent, Ohio, 1962), 7–30; Stanton to Dix, July 12, 1862, *ORA*, ser. 2, 4:174.

25. Nicolay and Hay, *Lincoln*, 7:307–8.

26. Bruce Catton, *Grant Moves South* (Boston, 1960), 473–74.

27. Hoffman to Stanton, May 3, 1864; Stanton to Wade, May 4, 1864; and Hoffman to Stanton, May 19, 1864, *ORA*, ser. 2, 7:110–11, 150–51.

28. Basler, *Works*, 7:328–29; Nicolay and Hay, *Lincoln*, 6:481–84.

29. Halleck to Stanton, November 15, 1863, and Ould to Meredith, December 11, 1863, *ORA*, ser. 2, 6:523–24, 686; Hitchcock to Stanton, November 22, 1865, *ORA*, ser. 2, 8:800–801; Grant to Stanton, August 18, 1864, *ORA*, ser. 2, 7:606–7.

30. Welles, *Diary*, 2:169; Flower, *Edwin McMasters Stanton*, 236–37; Nevins, *War for the Union*, 4:61.

31. Welles, *Diary*, 2:170–71.

32. Flower, *Edwin McMasters Stanton*, 236–38.

33. Raymond, *Life and Public Services*, 379–81; General Orders No. 193, November 22, 1862, *ORA*, ser. 2, 4:746–47; Morgan Dix, ed., *Memoirs of John Adams Dix*, 2 vols. (New York, 1883), 2:43.

34. Nicolay and Hay, *Lincoln*, 8:34–35; *Congressional Globe*, December 8, 1862, 20–22.

35. Thomas and Hyman, *Stanton*, 375–76; Randall, *Constitutional Problems*, 155; Nicolay and Hay, *Lincoln*, 8:40–41.

Chapter 16. "This nation, under God . . ."

1. Basler, *Works*, 6:374; Jay Monaghan, *Diplomat in Carpet Slippers: Abraham Lincoln Deals with Foreign Affairs* (Indianapolis, 1945), 313; Grant to Lincoln, August 23, 1863, Lincoln Mss., LC-RTL; Ulysses S. Grant, *Personal Memoirs of U. S. Grant*, 2 vols. (New York, 1886), 1:578.

2. Seward, *Reminiscences*, 216–17; Welles, *Diary*, 1:387, 390; Basler, *Works*, 6:354.

3. Halleck to Banks, July 24 and 31, 1863, and Halleck to Grant, July 30, 1863, *ORA*, 26, pt. 1, 652–53, 664.

4. Francis P. Blair Sr. to Lincoln, July 30, 1863, and Lincoln to Banks, August 5, 1863, Lincoln Mss., LC-RTL.

5. Banks Report, April 6, 1865, *ORA*, 26, pt. 1, 18–20; James W. Daddysman, *The Matamoros Trade: Confederate Commerce, Diplomacy, and Intrigue* (Newark, Del., 1984), 91–95; Banks to Halleck, November 4, 1863, *ORA*, 26, pt. 1, 397–98.

6. Seward to Dayton, September 26, 1863, and April 7, 1864, Seward Mss., UR; Frank L. Owsley, *King Cotton Diplomacy: Foreign Relations of the Confederate States of America*, 2nd ed. (Chicago, 1931), 520, 522–23, 526–27; Monaghan, *Diplomat in Carpet Slippers*, 355–59.

7. Meade to Halleck, July 14, 1863, *ORA*, 27, pt. 1, 93; Grant to Dana, August 5, 1863, Dana Mss., LC; Kenneth P. Williams, *Lincoln Finds a General*, 5 vols. (New York, 1949–59), 5:319 n. 33.

8. Halleck to Rosecrans and Rosecrans to Halleck, July 24 and 25, 1863, *ORA*, 23, pt. 2, 552, 554–55, 556.

9. Halleck to Rosecrans, August 4, 7, and 9, 1863, and Rosecrans to Halleck, August 4, 6, and 7, 1863, *ORA*, 23, pt. 2, 592, 597, 601, 602, 592, 594, 597.

10. Rosecrans to Lincoln, August 1, 1863, Lincoln Mss., LC-RTL; Basler, *Works*, 6:377–78.

11. Rosecrans to Lincoln, August 22, 1863, and Lincoln to Rosecrans, August 31, 1863, *ORA*, 52, pt. 1, 439, 442.

12. Department of the Cumberland Returns, August 31, 1863, *ORA*, 30, pt. 3, 276; Department of Tennessee Returns, August 20, 1863, *ORA*, 30, pt. 4, 519; Rosecrans Report, October [?], 1863, *ORA*, 30, pt. 1, 47–53; Halleck Report, November 15, 1863, *ORA*, 30, pt. 2, 545–46.

13. Rosecrans to Halleck, September 9, 1863, Lincoln Mss., LC-RTL; *B&L*, 3:669–71.

14. Lincoln to Cameron, April 16, 1861, Cameron Mss., LC; Lincoln to Mrs. Lincoln, September 24, 1863, Lincoln Papers, ISHL; quotes from Randall, *Lincoln*, 3:370.

15. Rosecrans to Halleck, September 19 and 20, 1863, *ORA*, 30, pt. 1, 136, 142; Bates, *Lincoln in the Telegraph Office*, 158, 161.

16. Lincoln to Rosecrans and Lincoln to Burnside, September 21, 1863, *ORA*, 30, pt. 1, 146; Bates, *Lincoln in the Telegraph Office*, 202.

17. *Hay Diary*, 92; Basler, *Works*, 6:470–71, 474; Lincoln to Halleck, September 21, 1863, *ORA*, 30, pt. 1, 148.

18. Rosecrans to Lincoln, September 22 and 23, 1863, *ORA*, 30, pt. 1, 161, 168.

19. Burnside to Lincoln, September 23, 1863, *ORA*, 30, pt. 3, 808–9; Basler, *Works*, 6:480–88; Grant to Halleck, September 22, 1863, *ORA*, 30, pt. 1, 163.

20. *Hay Diary*, 93; Dana to Stanton, September 22, 1863, *ORA*, 30, pt. 1, 197.

21. *Hay Diary*, 93–94; Rosecrans to Lincoln, September 23, 1863, *ORA*, 30, pt. 1, 168; Dana to Stanton, September 22, 1863, 9:30 p.m., *ORA*, 30, pt. 1, 197; Donald, *Inside Lincoln's Cabinet*, 201–3.

22. Halleck to Meade, September 24, 1863, *ORA*, 29, pt. 1, 147; Walter H. Hebert, *Fighting Joe Hooker* (Indianapolis, 1944), 250–51.

23. Welles, *Diary*, 1:444, 446–47; see Dana to Stanton, September 27–October 17, 1863, *ORA*, 30, pt. 1, esp. 189–220; Stanton to Dana, September 30, 1863, *ORA*, 30, pt. 3, 946.

24. Welles, *Diary*, 1:447; Basler, *Works*, 6:498, 510–11; Dana to Stanton, October 9 and 12, 1863, Dana Mss., LC.

25. Halleck to Grant, October 16, 1863, and General Orders Nos. 404 and 80, October 16, 1863, *ORA*, 30, pt. 4, 404, 410; Grant, *Memoirs*, 1:669.

26. Grant, *Memoirs*, 2:20–27; Dana, *Recollections*, 129; Grant to Thomas and Thomas to Grant, October 19, 1863, *ORA*, 30, pt. 4, 479; Stanton to Halleck, October 20, 1863, *ORA*, 31, pt. 1, 666.

27. See Dana Correspondence, October 21–30, 1863, *ORA*, 31, pt. 1, esp. 68–74, and October 30–November 26, 1863, *ORA*, 31, pt. 2, esp. 52–70.

28. Moorhead to Lincoln, October 15, 1863, Lincoln Mss., LC-RTL: Basler, *Works*, 6:540n.

29. Alexander H. Stephens, *A Constitutional View of the Late War between the States*, 2 vols. (Philadelphia, 1868–70), 2:560; Welles, *Diary*, 1:359–63.

30. *Hay Diary*, 77.

31. Moore, *Rebellion Record*, Diary, 7:26–27.

32. Basler, *Works*, 6:319–20.

33. Frank L. Clement, "Ward H. Lamon and the Dedication of the Soldiers' Cemetery at Gettysburg," *Civil War History* 31 (December 1985): 293–308; Lamon, *Recollections*, 172–73; Basler, *Works*, 7:17–23.

34. Basler, *Works*, 7:22–23; Nicolay, *Lincoln's Secretary*, 177–79; Segal, *Conversations with Lincoln*, 291.

35. Lamon, *Recollections*, 173, 174.

36. *Hay Diary,* 131–32; Edward Everett to Lincoln, November 20, 1863, Lincoln Mss., LC-RTL.

Chapter 17. "What can I do . . ."

1. Cyrus Ballou Comstock Diary, March 11, 1864, LC; Meade to Halleck, September 14, 1863, *ORA,* 29, pt. 2. 179–80: Basler, *Works,* 6:450; Halleck to Meade, September 15, 1863, *ORA,* 29, pt. 2, 186.

2. Meade to Halleck, September 18, 1863, Returns of the Army of the Potomac and Returns of the Army of Northern Virginia, September 30, 1863, *ORA,* 29, pt. 2, 201–2, 239, 764.

3. Basler, *Works,* 6:466–67, 486.

4. Halleck to Meade, October 10, 1863, and Meade to Halleck, October 18, 1863, *ORA,* 29, pt. 2, 278, 346; Agassiz, *Meade's Headquarters,* 36–39.

5. Basler, *Works,* 6:518; Halleck to Meade and Meade to Halleck, October 16, 1863, *ORA,* 29, pt. 2, 332–33.

6. See Meade and Halleck's correspondence on October 21 and 24 and November 2, 1863, *ORA,* 29, pt. 2, 361, 362, 375, 409–10, 412; Meade, *Life and Letters,* 2:154; Basler, *Works,* 6:534.

7. Swinton, *Campaigns,* 390; Agassiz, *Meade's Headquarters,* 60–61; Meade, *Life and Letters,* 2:163–64.

8. Basler, *Works,* 7:43–44, 49.

9. Albert A. Woldman, *Lincoln and the Russians* (Cleveland, 1952), 141, 153; *Hay Diary,* 134.

10. Welles, *Diary,* 1:481; Lincoln to Montgomery Blair, November 2, 1863, Blair Papers, PHS.

11. Niven, *Salmon P. Chase,* 347–48.

12. Welles, *Diary,* 2:202; McClure, *Abraham Lincoln,* 282.

13. Basler, *Works,* 7:51, 53–56; Smith, *Francis Preston Blair Family,* 2:237.

14. Basler, *Works,* 6:411, 7:54–56; *Hay Diary,* 131–32.

15. Randall, *Lincoln,* 4:13–14, 17; Basler, *Works,* 7:243.

16. Edward W. Gantt to Lincoln, July 15, 1863, Lincoln Mss., LC-RTL; Randall, *Lincoln,* 4:30.

17. Basler, *Works,* 7:52.

18. Cain, *Lincoln's Attorney General,* 286, 290; Thomas and Hyman, *Stanton,* 306–7.

19. Basler, *Works,* 7:269–70.

20. Chase to Lincoln, December 29, 1862, Lincoln Mss., LC-RTL; Basler, *Works,* 7:269-70.

21. Niven, *Salmon P. Chase,* 316–18.

22. Chase to Bullitt, April 14, 1863, Chase Papers, PHS; Basler, *Works,* 6:73–74, 76–77n, 100n, 428–29; Chase to Butler, April 10, 1863, Butler Mss., LC; Chase, "Diary and Correspondence," 2: 346, 357, 365–66, 376–79, 382–87; Chase to Lincoln, February 27 and March 2, 1863, Lincoln Mss., LC-RTL; Mark Howard to Chase, December 19, 1862, Chase Mss., LC.

23. Smith, *Francis Preston Blair Family,* 2:252; *Hay Diary,* 70, 100.

24. Beale, *Diary of Edward Bates,* 310, 343; Welles, *Diary,* 1:536, 2:58.

25. Nicolay and Hay, *Lincoln,* 8:312–14, 319–20; James A. Winchell, "The Pomeroy Circular," *New York Times,* September 15, 1874; Richard Parsons to Chase, March 2, 1864, Chase Mss., LC; Nicolay, *Lincoln's Secretary,* 188.

26. Chase to Lincoln, February 22, 1864, and Lincoln to Chase, February 29, 1864, Lincoln Mss., LC-RTL.

27. Segal, *Conversations with Lincoln*, 310–16; Brooks, *Washington in Lincoln's Time*, 125.

28. Nicolay and Hay, *Lincoln*, 7:323; David Tod to Lincoln, February 24, 1864, Lincoln Mss., LC-RTL.

Chapter 18. "I will fight it out . . ."

1. Swinton, *Campaigns*, 398–400; Nicolay Diary, December 7, 1863, Nicolay Mss., LC.

2. Tarbell, *Life of Lincoln*, 3:187–89.

3. Dana, *Recollections*, 156–57; Dana to Stanton, November 29 and December 12, 1863, *ORA*, 31, pt. 2, 71–72, 73; Grant to Halleck, December 7, 1863, and Halleck to Grant and Dana to Grant, December 21, 1863, *ORA*, 31, pt. 3, 349–50, 457–58; Grant to Halleck, February 20, 1865, *ORA*, 48, pt. 1, 917.

4. Johnston, *Narrative*, 263–64; *New York Herald*, December 9, 1863; Bruce Catton, *Grant Takes Command* (Boston, 1969), 99; Grant to Halleck, January 15, 1864, *ORA*, 32, pt. 2, 99–101.

5. Catton, *Grant Takes Command*, 101–2.

6. Grant to Halleck, January 19, 1864, *ORA*, 33:394–95.

7. Halleck to Grant, February 17, 1864, *ORA*, 32, pt. 2, 411–13; Grant Report, July 22, 1865, *ORA*, 34, pt. 1, 19.

8. Nicolay and Hay, *Lincoln* 8:334–36; *Hay Diary*, 167; Grant, *Memoirs*, 2:114.

9. Halleck to Grant, March 3, 1863, *ORA*, 32, pt. 3, 13; Grant, *Memoirs*, 2:114; Grant to Sherman, March 4, 1864, *ORA*, 32, pt. 3, 18.

10. Agassiz, *Meade's Headquarters*, 80–81; Horace Porter, *Campaigning with Grant* (New York, 1897), 14–15.

11. L. E. Chittenden, *Recollections of President Lincoln and His Administration* (New York, 1891), 317–18.

12. Quoted from Porter, *Campaigning with Grant*, 19

13. Brooks, *Washington in Lincoln's Time*, 135; Dana, *Recollections*, 15, 61.

14. Nicolay Memorandum, March 8, 1864, Nicolay Mss., LC.

15. Nicolay Memorandum, March 8, 1864, Nicolay Mss., LC; Grant, *Memoirs*, 115–16; Basler, *Works*, 7:234–35, with notes; Nicolay and Hay, *Lincoln*, 8:341–42.

16. Gilmore, *Personal Recollections*, 228; Halleck to Stanton, March 9, 1864, Lincoln Mss., LC-RTL; Stanton's Orders of March 10, 1864, *ORA*, 33:663.

17. Grant, *Memoirs*, 2:117.

18. Sherman, *Memoirs*, 1:399–400; Grant, *Memoirs*, 2:116–19.

19. Grant, *Memoirs*, 2:118–20; Adam Badeau, *Military History of Ulysses S. Grant, from April, 1861 to April, 1865*, 3 vols. (New York, 1868–81), 2:12–14.

20. Williams, *Lincoln and His Generals*, 301, 302; Catton, *Grant Takes Command*, 135–36; Basler, *Works*, 6:350.

21. Basler, *Works*, 7:324; Grant to Meade, April 9, 1864, *ORA*, 33:827–28; *Hay Diary*, 178.

22. Andrew Atkinson Humphreys, *The Virginia Campaign of '64 and '65: Army of the Potomac and the Army of the James* (New York, 1963), 83; Grant *Memoirs*, 2:117–18.

23. Quoted in Catton, *Grant Takes Command*, 139.

24. Thomas and Hyman, *Stanton*, 298.

25. General Orders No. 80, February 29, 1864, and General Orders No. 8, March 10, 1864, *ORA*, 33:618, 664; Babcock to Smith, April 29, 1864, *ORA*, 33:1019.

26. Grant to Halleck, May 19, 1864, and General Orders No. 28, May 21, 1864, *ORA*, 37, pt. 1, 492, 508; Halleck to Hunter, May 21, 1864, *ORA*, 37, pt. 1, 507.

27. Grant to Halleck, April 22, 29, 1864; Halleck to Grant, April 26 and 29 and May 3, 1864; and Special Orders No. 171, May 7, 1862, *ORA*, 34, pt. 3, 252–53, 331, 293, 331–32, 409–10, 490.

28. Basler, *Works*, 7:324, 325n; Grant to Lincoln, May 1, 1864, Lincoln Mss., LC-RTL.

29. Ida M. Tarbell, *A Reporter for the Union: Story of Henry E. Wing, Soldier and Newspaperman* (New York, 1927), 1–13; Welles, *Diary*, 2:25; Basler, *Works*, 7:334.

30. Grant, *Memoirs*, 2:204; Humphreys, *Virginia Campaign*, 66–67; *Hay Diary*, 180–81; Tarbell, *Reporter for the Union*, 41; Carpenter, *Six Months*, 283.

31. Rice, *Reminiscences*, 338; Schuyler Colfax, *Life and Principles of Abraham Lincoln* (Philadelphia, 1865), 11–12.

32. Grant to Halleck, June 5, 1864, *ORA*, 40, pt. 1, 12; Basler, *Works*, 7:393.

33. Isaac N. Arnold, *The Life of Abraham Lincoln* (Lincoln, Nebr., 1994), 375.

34. Welles, *Diary*, 2:55, 58; Beale, *Diary of Edward Bates*, 378.

35. Grant to Halleck, July 1, 1864, and Halleck to Grant, July 3, 1864, *ORA*, 40, pt. 2, 558–59, 598.

36. Grant to Halleck, July 6, 1864, *and* General Orders No. 225, July 7, 1864, *ORA*, 40, pt. 3, 31, 59, 69; Williams, *Lincoln and His Generals*, 321–23; Special Orders No. 62, *ORA*, 40, pt. 3, 334.

37. Humphreys, *Virginia Campaign*, 9.

38. Grant, *Memoirs*, 2:556.

Chapter 19. "It was best to not swap . . ."

1. Samuel S. Cox to Manton Marble, June 20, 1864, Manton Marble Mss., LC; Randall, *Lincoln*, 4:190; John C. Waugh, *Reelecting Lincoln: The Battle for the 1864 Presidency* (New York, 1997), 205–8.

2. Pomeroy Circular in Nicolay and Hay, *Lincoln*, 8:319–20; Basler, *Works*, 201n; Adam Gurowski, *Diary of Adam Gurowski*, 3 vols. (Boston, 1862–66), 3:159.

3. Segal, *Conversations with Lincoln*, 321–22; McPherson, *Political History*, 413–14.

4. Frederick Conkling to Lincoln, May 31, 1864, Lincoln Mss., LC-RTL; Basler, *Works*, 7:374.

5. Albert D. Richardson, *A Personal History of Ulysses S. Grant* (Hartford, Conn., 1868), 407, 434; Nicolay and Hay, *Lincoln*, 9:59.

6. Beale, *Diary of Edward Bates*, 373.

7. Arnold, *Life of Abraham Lincoln*, 358.

8. McClure, *Abraham Lincoln*, 321–22; Waugh, *Reelecting Lincoln*, 184–87.

9. Beale, *Diary of Edward Bates*, 374–75.

10. McClure, *Abraham Lincoln*, 115; James F. Glonek, "Lincoln, Johnson, and the Baltimore Ticket," *Abraham Lincoln Quarterly* 6 (March 1951): 255–71.

11. Randall, *Lincoln*, 4:133–34; McClure, *Abraham Lincoln*, 457–59, 461–63, 466–68, 281–82; Hamlin to Cameron, June 18, 1864, Cameron Mss., LC.

12. Chester G. Hearn, *The Impeachment of Andrew Johnson* (Jefferson, N.C., 2000), 3–4; John Savage, *Life and Public Services of Andrew Johnson* (New York, 1866), 123.

13. Basler, *Works*, 8:381–82, 383–84.

14. Welles, *Diary*, 1:536.

15. Warden, *Life of Chase*, 586, 591; Whitelaw Reid, *Ohio in the War: Her Statesmen, Her Generals, and Soldiers*, 2 vols. (Cincinnati, 1868), 1:18.

16. Donald, *Inside Lincoln's Cabinet*, 224.

17. Nicolay and Hay, *Lincoln*, 9:91–92.

18. Basler, *Works*, 7:412–13, 413–14.

19. *Hay Diary*, 199; Nicolay and Hay, *Lincoln*, 9:94–95; Basler, *Works*, 7:414n, 419.

20. Donald, *Inside Lincoln's Cabinet*, 223–24.

21. Segal, *Conversations with Lincoln*, 330–31.

22. *Hay Diary*, 198–99; Nicolay and Hay, *Lincoln*, 9:96–99; Fessenden, *Life and Public Services*, 1:313.

23. *Hay Diary*, 201, 202, 203; Fessenden, *Life and Public Services*, 1:315–17.

24. Fessenden, *Life and Public Services*, 1:317.

25. Fessenden, *Life and Public Services*, 320–21.

26. Fessenden, *Life and Public Services*, 323–25.

27. Donald, *Inside Lincoln's Cabinet*, 231; Chittenden, *Recollections*, 377, 383.

28. Basler, *Works*, 7:36–56; Nicolay and Hay, *Lincoln*, 9:112.

29. Nicolay and Hay, *Lincoln*, 9:113; Brooks, *Washington in Lincoln's Time*, 164–65.

30. *Congressional Globe*, May 4, 1864, 2107; Nicolay and Hay, *Lincoln*, 9:115–17, 119.

31. Brooks, *Washington in Lincoln's Time*, 25–26; Welles, *Diary*, 2:65.

32. *Hay Diary*, 204–5.

33. *Hay Diary*, 205–6.

34. Beale, *Diary of Edward Bates*, 382–83.

35. Brooks, *Washington in Lincoln's Time*, 168, 170; James G. Blaine, *Twenty Years of Congress from Lincoln to Garfield*, 2 vols. (Norwich, Conn., 1884–86), 2:44.

36. Donald, *Inside Lincoln's Cabinet*, 232–33; Basler, *Works*, 7:433–34.

37. Thaddeus Stevens to Edward McPherson, July 10, 1864, Thaddeus Stevens Papers, LC; Nicolay and Hay, *Lincoln*, 9:124; Blaine, *Twenty Years of Congress*, 2:43.

38. Wade to Horace Greeley, August 1, 1864, Greeley Papers, LC; Henry Winter Davis to Wade, August 3, 1864, Benjamin F. Wade Papers, LC; Nicolay and Hay, *Lincoln*, 9:125, 126–27; Marshall, *Private and Official Correspondence*, 5:8.

39. Welles, *Diary*, 2:95, 247; Thomas and Hyman, *Stanton*, 316; George S. Boutwell, *Reminiscences of Sixty Years of Public Affairs*, 2 vols. (New York, 1902), 2:90–93.

40. Brooks, *Washington in Lincoln's Time*, 170.

Chapter 20. "I begin to see it"

1. Dana, *Recollections*, 199; Grant, *Memoirs*, 2:276.

2. Rhodes, *History of the United States*, 4:464–66.

3. *B&L*, 4:541.

4. Meade, *Life and Letters*, 2:207.

5. Greeley to Lincoln, July 7 and 13, 1864, Lincoln Mss., LC-RTL; Thayer, *John Hay*, 1:174–75; Basler, *Works*, 7:443.

6. Thayer, *John Hay*, 1:178–79; Nicolay and Hay, *Lincoln*, 9:192–6; Greeley to Lincoln, August 8, 1864, Lincoln Mss., LC-RTL.

7. *B&L*, 4:495, 497; Couch to Stanton, July 7, 1864, Grant to Halleck, July 4 and 14, 1864, and Halleck to Grant, July 5, 1864, *ORA*, 37, pt. 2, 33, 59, 116, 301.

8. W. A. Croffut, ed., *Fifty Years in Camp and Field: Diary of Major-General Ethan Allen Hitchcock, U.S.A.* (New York, 1909), 463–64; Stanton to Curtin, July 7, 1864, *ORA*, 37, pt. 2, 115–16.

9. Grant to Halleck, July 9, 1864, Grant to Lincoln, July 10, 1864, and Lincoln to Grant, July 10 and 11, 1864, *ORA*, 37, pt. 2, 134, 155, 156–57, 191.

10. Brooks, *Washington in Lincoln's Time*, 173–75.

11. Brooks, *Washington in Lincoln's Time*, 175; S. P. Lee to James Doolittle, February 20, 1865, James R. Doolittle Papers, LC; Welles to S. P. Lee, July 14 and 19, 1864, *ORN*, 10:272, 284.

12. Thomas and Hyman, *Stanton*, 319–20.

13. *Hay Diary*, 209, 210.

14. Welles, *Diary*, 2:70; *Hay Diary*, 210; Dana to Grant, July 12 and 14, 1864, *ORA*, 37, pt. 2, 223, 302.

15. Beale, *Diary of Edward Bates*, 385; Grant to Halleck, July 14, 1864, *ORA*, 37, pt. 2, 301; Cyrus B. Comstock Diary, July 15, 1864, Cyrus Ballou Comstock Mss., LC; Halleck to Sherman, July 16, 1864, *ORA*, 38, pt. 5, 150–51.

16. Basler, *Works*, 7:439, 440.

17. Grant to Halleck, July 18, 1864, *ORA*, 37, pt. 2, 374.

18. Grant to Halleck, July 18, 1864, Halleck to Grant, July 21, 1864, and Grant to Lincoln, July 25, 1864, *ORA*, 37, pt. 2, 374, 408, 433–34.

19. Basler, *Works*, 7:456; D. McConaughy to Darius Couch and Governor Curtin, July 31, 1864, *ORA*, 37, pt. 2, 542–43.

20. Dana to Stanton, July 7, 1864, *ORA*, 40, pt. 1, 35–36.

21. Basler, *Works*, 7:469–70; Stanton to Halleck, July 27, 1864, *ORA*, 37, pt. 2, 463; Welles, *Diary*, 2:90; Grant to Halleck, August 1, 1864, *ORA*, pt. 2, 558.

22. Comstock Diary, August 4, 1864, Cyrus Ballou Comstock Mss., LC; Philip H. Sheridan, *Personal Memoirs of P. H. Sheridan*, 2 vols. (New York, 1888), 1:346–47; Lincoln to Grant, August 3, 1864, *ORA*, 37, pt. 2, 582.

23. Grant, *Memoirs*, 2:319–20; Sheridan, *Personal Memoirs*, 1:462–66.

24. Grant, *Memoirs*, 2:320–21; General Orders No. 240, August 7, 1864, and Grant to Sheridan, August 7, 1864, *ORA*, 43, pt. 1, 719.

25. Williams, *Lincoln and His Generals*, 333–34.

26. Chester G. Hearn, *Admiral David Glasgow Farragut: The Civil War Years* (Annapolis, Md., 1998), 170–71, 257–98; Farragut to Welles, August 27, 1864, and Farragut to Canby, September 5, 1864, *ORN*, 21:612, 626.

27. Butler to Lincoln, August 8, 1864, *ORN*, 21:440; Welles, *Diary*, 2:96, 98, 99, 100.

28. Dana, *Recollections*, 29; Boatner, *Civil War Dictionary*, 751.

29. Sherman, *Personal Memoirs*, 2:26, 28, 29.

30. Stanton to Sherman, May 20, 1864, *ORA*, 38, pt. 4, 260.

31. Sherman to Halleck, July 9, 1864, and Sherman to Grant, July 12, 1864, *ORA*, 38, pt. 4, 91, 123; Johnston, *Narrative*, 343–45.

32. J. B. Hood, *Advance and Retreat* (Secaucus, N.J., 1985), 127; Sherman, *Personal Memoirs*, 2:71, 104; Sherman to Halleck, September 3, 1864, *ORA*, 38, pt. 5, 777.

33. Nicolay to Therena Bates, August 21, 1864, Nicolay Mss., LC.

34. Sherman to Halleck, September 4, 1864, and Sherman to Halleck, September 3, 1864, *ORA*, 38, pt. 5, 777, 794; Basler, *Works*, 7:532, 533.

35. *Chicago Tribune*, September 5, 1864, quoted in Waugh, *Reelecting Lincoln*, 297; Basler, *Works*, 7:393.

36. Grant, *Memoirs*, 2:328; Richard O'Connor, *Sheridan the Inevitable* (Indianapolis, 1953), 200.

37. Nicolay and Hay, *Lincoln*, 9:305; Basler, *Works*, 8:13.

38. Basler, *Works*, 8:29; Sheridan Report, February 3, 1866, *ORA*, 43, pt. 1, 51–52.

39. Sheridan Report, February 3, 1866, *ORA*, 43, pt. 1, 52–54.

40. Basler, *Works*, 8:73–74.

41. Lincoln to Sheridan, November 8, 1864, Lincoln Mss., LC-RTL; Bates, *Lincoln in the Telegraph Office*, 67.

42. Basler, *Works*, 5:32, 185–86, 6:332–33, 496–97; 8:55–56.

Chapter 21. "What is the Presidency worth . . ."

1. Dana to J. S. Pike, August 8, 1864, quoted in Thomas and Hyman, *Stanton*, 321.

2. Basler, *Works*, 7:425–27; Hesseltine, *Lincoln and the War Governors*, 361–63.

3. Smith, *Francis Preston Blair Family*, 2:280–81; S. L. Barlow to Manton Marble, August 26, 1864, Manton Marble Mss., LC.

4. Weed to Seward, August 22, 1864, and Raymond to Lincoln, August 22, 1864, both in Lincoln Mss., LC-RTL.

5. Nicolay to Hay, August 25, 1864, Nicolay Mss., LC.

6. Nicolay to Therena Bates, August 28, 1864, Nicolay Mss., LC.

7. Brooks, *Washington in Lincoln's Time*, 180.

8. Nicolay and Hay, *Lincoln*, 9:251.

9. Nicolay and Hay, *Lincoln*, 9:255.

10. Nicolay and Hay, *Lincoln*, 9:257–58; Brooks, *Washington in Lincoln's Time*, 187.

11. Nicolay and Hay, *Lincoln*, 9:351.

12. Sears, *Civil War Papers of George B. McClellan*, 595–96.

13. Welles, *Diary*, 2:132, 135, 136.

14. Chase to Jay Cooke, September 8, 1864, Salmon P. Chase Papers, PHS; Weed to Seward, August 24, 1864, Lincoln Mss., LC-RTL.

15. Nicolay to Lincoln, August 30, 1864, Nicolay Mss., LC.

16. H. S. Elliot to Welles, September 3, 1864, Welles Mss., LC; Governor James T. Lewis to Greeley et al., September 7, 1864; Weed to Seward, September 10, 1864; and Chittenden to Lincoln, October 6, 1864, Lincoln Mss., LC-RTL.

17. Segal, *Conversations with Lincoln*, 337–38.

18. Hans L. Trefousse, *Benjamin Franklin Wade: Radical Republican from Ohio* (New York, 1963), 227–29; Henry Wilson to Lincoln, September 5, 1864, Lincoln Mss., LC-RTL.

19. McPherson, *Political History*, 426.

20. Basler, *Works*, 8:18; Francis P. Blair Sr. to Montgomery Blair, September 1864, Gist-Blair Mss., LC.

21. *Hay Diary*, 219; Blair to Lincoln, September 23, 1864, Lincoln Mss., LC-RTL.

22. Welles, *Diary*, 2:156–57; Nevins, *War for the Union*, 4:94–95, 104–5.

23. Basler, *Works*, 8:20; Welles, *Diary*, 1:469.

24. Emanuel Hertz, *Abraham Lincoln: A New Portrait*, 2 vols. (New York, 1931), 2:941.

25. Nicolay and Hay, *Lincoln*, 9:353–54.

26. Nicolay and Hay, *Lincoln*, 9:354n.

27. Basler, *Works*, 8:52–53n.

28. Kenneth M. Stampp, *Indiana Politics during the Civil War* (Indianapolis, 1949), 250–51; Cameron to Lincoln, October 19, 1864; and Chase to Lincoln, October 19, 1864, Lincoln Mss., LC-RTL; Sherman to Halleck, September 17, 1864, *ORA*, 39, pt. 2, 39, 396.

29. Grant to Stanton, September 13, 1864, *ORA*, ser. 3, 4:712–13.

30. Unsigned letter to Manton Marble, September 22, 1864, and G. W. Adams to Manton Marble, September 27, 1864, Manton Marble Mss., LC; Thomas and Hyman, *Stanton*, 328.

31. Basler, *Works*, 8:24; Thomas and Hyman, *Stanton*, 329–31.

32. Grant to Stanton, November 1, 1864, and Grant to Butler, November 3, 1864, *ORA*, 42, pt. 3, 470, 503; *Hay Diary*, 233.

33. Dana, *Recollections*, 261; *Hay Diary*, 231; Halleck to Francis Lieber, October 14, 1864, Francis Lieber Mss., HL.

34. *Hay Diary*, 229.

35. Basler, *Works*, 8:46.

36. McClure, *Abraham Lincoln*, 200–201.

37. Basler, *Works*, 8:58–59, 72.

38. Basler, *Works*, 7:506–7.

39. William F. Zornow, *Lincoln and the Party Divided* (Norman, Okla., 1954), 201; Hesseltine, *Lincoln and the War Governors*, 381.

40. Hesseltine, *Lincoln and the War Governors*, 381; Zornow, *Lincoln and the Party Divided*, 201.

41. Zornow, *Lincoln and the Party Divided*, 201, 204.

Chapter 22. "It shows . . . how *sound* and how *strong* . . ."

1. *Hay Diary*, 232–33.

2. Brooks, *Washington in Lincoln's Time*, 216.

3. Brooks, *Washington in Lincoln's Time*, 217–18; Nicolay and Hay, *Lincoln*, 9:376, 379; *Hay Diary*, 234.

4. Noah Brooks, *Mr. Lincoln's Washington: Selections from the Writings of Noah Brooks, Civil War Correspondent* (South Brunswick, N.J., 1967), 386.

5. Nicolay, *Lincoln's Secretary*, 216.

6. *Hay Diary*, 234–35.

7. Brooks, *Washington in Lincoln's Time*, 218–19; Brooks, *Mr. Lincoln's Washington*, 235; Basler, *Works*, 8:96, 100–101.

8. *Hay Diary*, 236.

9. Brooks, *Washington in Lincoln's Time*, 219; Sears, *Civil War Papers of George B. McClellan*, 618.

10. McPherson, *Political History*, 623; Rachel Sherman Thorndike, ed., *The Sherman Letters: Correspondence between General and Senator Sherman from 1837 to 1891* (New York, 1894), 241.

11. Grant to Stanton, November 10, 1864, *ORA*, 42, pt. 3, 581.

12. Brooks, *Washington in Lincoln's Time*, 221–22.

13. Brooks, *Washington in Lincoln's Time*, 222–23; Brooks, *Mr. Lincoln's Washington*, 387–88; Basler, *Works*, 8:100–101, 102n.

14. *Hay Diary*, 237–38.

15. Donald, *Inside Lincoln's Cabinet*, 254.

16. McClure, *Abraham Lincoln*, 140–41, 142.

17. Donald, *Inside Lincoln's Cabinet*, 256–59.

18. Nicolay and Hay, *Lincoln*, 9:393–94; "Interview with Foster" memorandum, October 23, 1878, Nicolay Mss., LC.

19. Beale, *Diary of Edward Bates*, 427–28; Bates to Lincoln, November 24, 1864, Lincoln Mss., LC-RTL; Nicolay and Hay, *Lincoln*, 344–35.

20. Basler, *Works*, 8:126–27; Beale, *Diary of Edward Bates*, 482–83.

21. Basler, *Works*, 8:154; Chase to Lincoln, December 6, 1864, Lincoln Mss., LC-RTL.

22. Nicolay to Therena Bates Nicolay, December 8, 1864, Nicolay Mss., LC.

23. Brooks, *Washington in Lincoln's Time*, 192–93, 195.

24. Sherman, *Memoirs*, 2:111; Halleck to Sherman, September 28, 1864, *ORA*, 39, pt. 2, 503.

25. Sherman to Thomas, October 20, 1864, *ORA*, 39, pt. 3, 377–78; Sherman, *Memoirs*, 2:152.

26. Grant to Sherman, November 1 and 2, 1864, and Sherman to Grant, November 2, 1864, *ORA*, 39, pt. 3, 576, 594, 595.

27. Sherman to Grant, November 6, 1864, and Thomas to Sherman, November 12, 1864, *ORA*, 39, pt. 3, 660, 756.

28. Sherman, *Memoirs*, 2:170.

29. Special Field Orders Nos. 119 and 120, November 8 and 9, 1864, *ORA*, 39, pt. 3, 701, 713–14.

30. Sherman, *Memoirs*, 2:178–79, 189–90; McClure, *Abraham Lincoln*, 238n; Members of Confederate Congress to People of Georgia, November 19, 1864, *ORA*, 44:869.

31. Grant to Sherman, December 6, 1864, *ORA*, 44:611–12, 636–37; Sherman, *Memoirs*, 2:206.

32. Sherman to Lincoln, December 22, 1864, *ORA*, 44:783; Segal, *Conversations with Lincoln*, 353.

33. Basler, *Works*, 8:148, 181–82.

34. Grant to Sherman, December 16, 18, and 27, 1864, *ORA*, 44:728–29, 740–41, 820–21; Sherman, *Memoirs*, 2:296.

35. Stanton to Grant, December 2 and 7, 1864, *ORA*, 45, pt. 2, 15–16, 84; Grant to Thomas, December 2, 6, and 8, 1864, *ORA*, 45, pt. 2, 17, 70, 97; Thomas to Grant, December 2 and 6, 1864, *ORA*, 45, pt. 2, 17–18, 70.

36. Grant to Stanton, December 7, 1864; Grant to Halleck and Halleck to Grant, December 8, 1864; Grant to Halleck, December 9, 1864, *ORA*, 45, pt. 2, 84, 96, 115–16.

37. Thomas to Grant, December 9, 1864; Halleck to Grant and Grant to Halleck, December 9, 1864, *ORA*, 45, pt. 2, 115, 116.

38. J. C. Van Duzer to Thomas Eckert, December 15, 1864, *ORA*, 45, pt. 2, 196; Bates, *Lincoln in the Telegraph Office*, 317.

39. Bates, *Lincoln in the Telegraph Office*, 318.

40. Bates, *Lincoln in the Telegraph Office*, 318; Grant to Thomas and Stanton to Thomas, December 15, 1864, *ORA*, 45, pt. 2, 195.

41. Basler, *Works*, 8:169; Williams, *Lincoln and His Generals*, 344–45.

42. Quoted in Thomas and Hyman, *Stanton*, 342.

Chapter 23. "It made my heart jump"

1. *B&L*, 4:642.

2. Welles to Porter, September 22, 1864, *ORN*, 21:657; Welles, *Diary*, 2:145–47.

3. *JCCW*, Fort Fisher Expedition, 2:4, 68; Welles, *Diary*, 2:209, 210.

4. *JCCW*, Fort Fisher Expedition, 2:10–11, 68, 72, 73, 84; Grant, *Memoirs*, 2:325; Grant to Porter, December 30, 1864, *ORN*, 11:394.

5. Basler, *Works*, 8:187; Grant to Lincoln, December 28, 1864, *ORA*, 42, pt. 3, 1087; Grant to Stanton, January 4, 1865, and General Orders No. 1, January 7, 1865, *ORA*, 46, pt. 2, 29, 60.

6. Welles, *Diary*, 2:223.

7. Hearn, *Admiral David Dixon Porter*, 285–303.

8. Basler, *Works*, 7:52; Carpenter, *Six Months*, 74–75.

9. Basler, *Works*, 7:172–73, 380.

10. Basler, *Works*, 8:149; Arnold, *Life of Lincoln*, 359–60.

11. Nicolay and Hay, *Lincoln*, 10:85, 86, 87n; Boutwell, *Reminiscences*, 2:36; Julian, *Political Recollections*, 251.

12. Basler, *Works*, 8:254–55.

13. Basler, *Works*, 7:429, 8:151–52.

14. Nicolay and Hay, *Lincoln*, 10:94–95; Basler, *Works*, 8:188.

15. Blair Report, January 1865, in Nicolay and Hay, *Lincoln*, 10:97.

16. Blair Report, January 1865, in Nicolay and Hay, *Lincoln*, 99–102, 105, 106; Jefferson Davis to Francis P. Blair, January 12, 1865, Lincoln Mss., LC-RTL.

17. Lincoln to Francis P. Blair Sr., January 18, 1865, Lincoln Mss., LC-RTL; Nicolay and Hay, *Lincoln*, 10:108–9.

18. Jones, *Rebel War Clerk's Dairy*, 2:384, 395.

19. *Southern Historical Society Papers*, 52 vols. (Millwood, N.Y., 1977), 4:214; Basler, *Works*, 8:246, 248.

20. Basler, *Works*, 8:250–52, 279, 281, 282; Thomas and Hyman, *Stanton*, 347.

21. Carl Sandburg, *Abraham Lincoln: The War Years*, 4 vols. (New York, 1939), 4:44–45.

22. Nicolay and Hay, *Lincoln*, 10:118–19; Basler, *Works*, 8:152, 279; Stephens, *Constitutional View*, 2:599–604.

23. Stephens, *Constitutional View*, 2:617–18.

24. Stephens, *Constitutional View*, 2:610–17; *Congressional Globe*, February 4, 1865, 595, 602; Basler, *Works*, 10:258, 270.

25. Welles, *Diary*, 2:237; Basler, *Works*, 8:260–61.

26. Nicolay and Hay, *Lincoln*, 10:136; Basler, *Works*, 8:261.

27. Basler, *Works*, 8:326.

28. Brooks, *Washington in Lincoln's Time*, 235; Welles, *Diary*, 2:251.

29. Brooks, *Washington in Lincoln's Time*, 236; Halleck to Francis Lieber, March 5, 1865, Francis Lieber Papers, HL.

30. Brooks, *Washington in Lincoln's Time*, 236–38; Welles, *Diary*, 2:252; McCulloch, *Men and Measures*, 373.

31. Basler, *Works*, 8:236–38; Nicolay, *Lincoln's Secretary*, 224, 225.

32. Basler, *Works*, 8:239; Noah Brooks, "Personal Reminiscences of Abraham Lincoln," *Scribner's Monthly* (March 1878): 678.

33. William H. Townsend, *Lincoln and His Wife's Home Town* (Indianapolis, 1929), 367.

34. Brooks, *Washington in Lincoln's Time*, 239; Basler, *Works*, 8:332–33.

35. Brooks, *Washington in Lincoln's Time*, 240.

36. Brooks, *Washington in Lincoln's Time*, 241; Chase to Mary Lincoln, March 4, 1865, Lincoln Mss., LC-RTL; Book of Isaiah, bk. 5, verses 27–28.

37. Brooks, *Washington in Lincoln's Time*, 241.

Chapter 24. "Now he belongs to the ages"

1. Basler, *Works*, 8:316, 320–21; Grant to Lincoln, February 26, 1865, *ORA*, 46, pt. 2, 704.

2. Special Field Orders, February 16, 1865, *ORA*, 47, pt. 2, 444; Sherman, *Memoirs*, 2:278–79.

3. Jones, *Rebel War Clerk's Diary*, 2:343–44.

4. Lee to Grant, March 2, 1865, *ORA*, 46, pt. 2, 824.

5. Lamon, *Recollections*, 250–51; Basler, *Works*, 8:330–31; Grant to Stanton and Grant to Lee, March 4, 1865, *ORA*, 46, pt. 2, 823–24, 825.

6. Stanton to Grant, March 3, 1865, *ORA*, 46, pt. 2, 802.

7. Grant to Lincoln and Lincoln to Grant, March 20, 1865, *ORA*, 46, pt. 2, pt. 3, 50; Thomas and Hyman, *Stanton*, 349–50.

8. Basler, *Works*, 8:372–73, 374; Penrose to Stanton, March 24, 1865, *ORA*, 46, pt. 3, 96; Badeau, *Military History*, 3:137–39.

9. Sherman to Grant, March 23, 1985, *ORA*, 47, pt. 2, 969; Nicolay and Hay, *Lincoln*, 10:165; Sherman, *Memoirs*, 2:324–26.

10. Basler, *Works*, 8:377, 381; Stanton to Lincoln, March 31, 1865, *ORA*, 46, pt. 3, 332.

11. Sheridan, *Memoirs*, 2:130–31; Grant, *Memoirs*, 2:621.

12. Basler, *Works*, 8:380–81, 382, 383, 384.

13. Grant, *Memoirs*, 2:459–61.

14. Stanton to Lincoln, April 3, 1865, Lincoln Mss., LC-RTL; Basler, *Works*, 8:385.

15. Bates, *Lincoln in the Telegraph Office*, 360–61.

16. Bates, *Lincoln in the Telegraph Office*, 361; Flower, *Edwin McMasters Stanton*, 262, 263.

17. Porter, *Incidents*, 294–95.

18. David Dixon Porter, *Naval History of the Civil War* (New York, 1886), 798; Randall, *Lincoln*, 4:346–47; Basler, *Works*, 8:386–87.

19. Dana, *Recollections*, 263–65; Sheridan to Grant, April 6, 1865, and Dana to Stanton, April 7, 1865, *ORA*, 46, pt. 3, 610, 619.

20. Basler, *Works*, 8:392, 388.

21. Seward, *Reminiscences*, 253.

22. Brooks, *Washington in Lincoln's Time*, 250; Welles, *Diary*, 2:278.

23. Brooks, *Washington in Lincoln's Time*, 251–52; Basler, *Works*, 8:393–94.

24. Brooks, *Washington in Lincoln's Time*, 252–55.

25. Basler, *Works*, 8:400–401.

26. Basler, *Works*, 8:402; Sherman, *Memoirs*, 2:326–27.

27. Basler, *Works*, 8:375–76, 396–97, 408–9, 410.

28. Flower, *Edwin McMasters Stanton,* 311.

29. Dana to Stanton, April 7 and 8, 1865, *ORA,* 46, pt. 3, 619, 655; Basler, *Works,* 8:389.

30. See Campbell's correspondence, April 7, 1865, *ORA,* 46, pt. 3, 656, 657.

31. Dana to Stanton, April 9 and 10, and Stanton to Weitzel, April 9, 1865, *ORA,* 46, pt. 3, 678, 684; Welles, *Diary,* 2:279.

32. Basler, *Works,* 8:405, 406–8; Flower, *Edwin McMasters Stanton,* 270–71.

33. Ord to Lincoln, April 14, 1865, *ORA,* 46, pt. 3, 748.

34. Flower, *Edwin McMasters Stanton,* 271–72.

35. Lamon, *Recollections,* 274–75; Cornelius Cole, *Memoirs* (New York, 1908), 214.

36. Badeau, *Military History,* 2:362; Bates, *Lincoln in the Telegraph Office,* 365–68; Otto Eisenschiml, *Why Was Lincoln Murdered?* (New York, 1939), 59, 61–62.

37. Eisenschiml, *Why Was Lincoln Murdered?* 59.

38. Flower, *Edwin McMasters Stanton,* 279.

39. Seward, *Reminiscences,* 259–60.

40. Welles, *Diary,* 2:282–83.

41. Schuckers, *Life of Chase,* 519; Lloyd Paul Stryker, *Andrew Johnson: A Study in Courage* (New York, 1929), 195.

42. Nicolay and Hay, *Lincoln,* 10:302.

BIBLIOGRAPHY

MANUSCRIPTS

Brown University, Providence, R.I.
    Hay, John. Diary and mss.
    Rosecrans, William S. Papers.
Dauphin County Historical Society, Harrisburg, Pa.
    Cameron, Simon. Mss.
Huntington Library, San Marino, Calif.
        Barlow, Samuel L. M. Papers.
    Lieber, Francis. Mss.
Illinois State Historical Library, Springfield, Ill.
    Grant, Ulysses S. Mss.
    Lincoln, Abraham. Mss.
Library of Congress, Washington, D.C.
    Blair, Francis Preston, et al., Gist-Blair Mss.
    Butler, Benjamin F. Mss.
    Cameron, Simon. Mss.
    Chandler, Zachariah. Mss.
    Chase, Salmon P. Diary and mss.
    Comstock, Cyrus Ballou. Diary and mss.
    Dahlgren, John A. Papers.
    Dana, Charles A. Mss.
    Doolittle, James R. Papers.
    Greeley, Horace. Papers.
    Heintzelman, Samuel P. Journal and mss.
    Hitchcock, Ethan Allen. Mss.
    Larned, Daniel Reed, Mss.
    Lincoln, Abraham. Mss., Robert Todd Lincoln Collection.
    McClellan, George B. Mss.
    Marble, Manton, Mss.
    Meigs, Montgomery C. Diary and mss.
    Nicolay, John G. Mss.
    Schurz, Carl. Papers.
    Seward, William H. Papers.
    Stanton, Edwin M. Papers.
    Stevens, Thaddeus. Papers.
    Toombs, Robert A. Mss.
    Trumbull, Lyman. Mss.
    Wade, Benjamin F. Papers.

Weed, Thurlow. Mss.
Welles, Gideon. Mss.
New York Public Library
Bigelow, John. Diary.
Bryant, William Cullen. Parke Godwin Papers.
Pennsylvania Historical Society, Philadelphia, Pa.
Blair, Montgomery. Papers.
Chase, Salmon P. Papers.
University of Rochester, Rochester, N.Y.
Seward, William H. Mss.

GOVERNMENT RECORDS

Official Records of the Union and Confederate Navies in the War of the Rebellion. 30 vols. Harrisburg, Pa.: Historical Times, 1987.

Report of the Joint Committee on the Conduct of the War. 8 vols. Washington, D.C.: Government Printing Office, 1863–66.

U.S. Congress. *Congressional Globe.*

War of the Rebellion: A Compilation of the Official Records of the Union and Confederate Armies. 130 vols. Harrisburg, Pa.: Historical Times, 1987.

BOOKS

Adams, Charles Francis. *Autobiography.* Boston: Houghton Mifflin, 1916.

Adams, Charles Francis, Jr. *Charles Francis Adams.* New York: Chelsea House, 1980.

Agassiz, George R., ed. *Meade's Headquarters, 1863–1865: Letters of Col. Theodore Lyman from the Wilderness to Appomattox.* Boston: Massachusetts Historical Society, 1922.

Annals of the War, Written by Leading Participants North and South. Edison, N.J.: Blue & Grey Press, 1996.

Arnold, Isaac N. *The Life of Abraham Lincoln.* Lincoln: University of Nebraska Press, 1994.

Badeau, Adam. *Military History of Ulysses S. Grant, from April, 1861 to April, 1865.* 3 vols. New York: Appleton, 1868–81.

Ballard, Colin R. *The Military Genius of Abraham Lincoln.* London: Humphrey Milford, 1926.

Bancroft, Frederic. *Life of William Seward.* 2 vols. New York: Harper & Bros., 1900.

Baringer, William E. *A House Dividing: Lincoln as President Elect.* Springfield, Ill.: Abraham Lincoln Assoc., 1945

———. *Lincoln's Rise to Power.* Boston: Little, Brown, 1937.

Barton, William E. *The Life of Abraham Lincoln.* 2 vols. Indianapolis: Bobbs-Merrill, 1925.

Basler, Roy P., ed. *The Collected Works of Abraham Lincoln.* 9 vols. New Brunswick, N.J.: Rutgers University Press, 1953–55.

Bates, David Homer. *Lincoln in the Telegraph Office.* New York: D. Appleton-Century, 1939.

Beale, Howard K. ed. *The Diary of Edward Bates, 1859–1866.* Washington, D.C.: Government Printing Office, 1933.

Bigelow, John. *Retrospections of an Active Life.* 5 vols. New York: Baker & Taylor, 1909–13.

Bigelow, John, Jr. *Chancellorsville.* New York: Konecky & Kentucky, 1995.

Blaine, James G. *Twenty Years of Congress from Lincoln to Garfield.* 2 vols. Norwich, Conn.: Henry Bill Publishing Co., 1884–86.

Boatner, Mark M., III. *The Civil War Dictionary.* New York: David McKay Co., 1959.

Boutwell, George S. *Reminiscences of Sixty Years of Public Affairs.* 2 vols. New York: McClure, Phillips, 1902.

Bradley, Erwin Stanley. *Simon Cameron, Lincoln's Secretary of War: A Political Biography.* Philadelphia: University of Pennsylvania Press, 1966.

Brooks, Noah. *Mr. Lincoln's Washington: Selections from the Writings of Noah Brooks, Civil War Correspondent.* Ed. P. J. Staudenraus. South Brunswick, N.J.: Thomas Yoseloff, 1967.

———. *Washington in Lincoln's Time.* New York: Century Co., 1896.

Butler, Benjamin F. *Autobiography and Personal Reminiscences of Major General Benjamin F. Butler: Butler's Book.* Boston: A. M. Thayer & Co., 1892.

Cain, Marvin R. *Lincoln's Attorney General: Edward Bates of Missouri.* Columbia: University of Missouri Press, 1965.

Carman, Harry J., and Reinhard H. Luthin. *Lincoln and the Patronage.* New York: Columbia University Press, 1943.

Carpenter, Francis B. *Six Months at the White House with Abraham Lincoln.* New York: Hurd & Houghton, 1866.

Catton, Bruce. *Grant Moves South.* Boston: Little, Brown, 1960.

———. *Grant Takes Command.* Boston: Little, Brown, 1969.

Chase, Salmon P. "Diary and Correspondence of Salmon P. Chase." *Annual Report of the American Historical Association for the Year 1902.* 2 vols. Washington, D.C.: Government Printing Office, 1903.

Chittenden, L. E. *Recollections of President Lincoln and His Administration.* New York: Harper & Bros., 1891.

Cole, Cornelius. *Memoirs of Cornelius Cole, Ex-Senator of the United States from California.* New York: McLoughlin Bros., 1908.

Colfax, Schuyler. *Life and Principles of Abraham Lincoln.* Philadelphia: J. B. Rodgers, 1865.

Cornish, Dudley. *The Sable Arm: Black Troops in the Union Army, 1861–1865.* New York: Harper's, 1966.

Cox, Samuel S. *Three Decades of Federal Legislation, 1855 to 1885.* Providence, R.I.: J. A. & R. A. Reid, 1885.

Crawford, Samuel W. *The Genesis of the Civil War: The Story of Sumter, 1860–1861.* New York: C. L. Webster & Co., 1887.

Crippen, Lee F. *Simon Cameron: Ante Bellum Years.* Oxford, Ohio: Mississippi Valley Press, 1942.

Croffut, W. A., ed. *Fifty Years in Camp and Field: Diary of Major-General Ethan Allen Hitchcock, U.S.A.* New York: Putnam's Sons, 1909.

Daddysman, James W. *The Matamoros Trade: Confederate Commerce, Diplomacy, and Intrigue.* Newark: University of Delaware Press, 1984.

Dana, Charles A. *Recollections of the Civil War.* Lincoln: University of Nebraska Press, 1996.

Dennett, Tyler, ed. *Lincoln and the Civil War in the Diaries and Letters of John Hay.* New York: Dodd, Mead & Co., 1939.

The Diary of a Public Man: Unpublished Passages of the Secret History of the American Civil War. Chicago: Abraham Lincoln Book Shop, 1945.

Dix, Morgan, ed. *Memoirs of John Adams Dix.* 2 vols. New York: Harper, 1863.

Donald, David Herbert. *Inside Lincoln's Cabinet: The Civil War Diaries of Salmon P. Chase.* New York: Longmans, Green & Co., 1954.

———. *Lincoln.* New York: Simon & Schuster, 1995.

Eisenschiml, Otto. *Why Was Lincoln Murdered?* New York: Halcyon House, 1939.

Faust, Patricia, ed. *Historical Times Illustrated Encyclopedia of the Civil War.* New York: Harper & Row, 1986.

Ferris, Norman B. *The Trent Affair: A Diplomatic Crisis.* Knoxville: University of Tennessee Press, 1977.

Fessenden, Francis. *Life and Public Services of William Pitt Fessenden.* 2 vols. Boston: Houghton Mifflin, 1907.

Flower, Frank A. *Edwin McMasters Stanton, the Autocrat of Rebellion, Emancipation, and Reconstruction.* New York: W. W. Wilson, 1905.

Ford, Worthington Chauncey. *A Cycle of Adams Letters, 1861–1865.* 2 vols. Boston: Houghton Mifflin, 1920.

Freeman, Douglas Southall. *R. E. Lee: A Biography.* 4 vols. New York: Scribner's, 1934–35.

Gibbon, John. *Personal Recollections of the Civil War.* New York: G. P. Putnam's Sons, 1928.

Gilmore, James R. *Personal Recollections of Abraham Lincoln and the Civil War.* Boston: L. C. Page & Co., 1898.

Godwin, Parke. *A Biography of William Cullen Bryant.* 2 vols. New York: D. Appleton, 1883.

Goodwin, Doris Kearns. *Team of Rivals: The Political Genius of Abraham Lincoln.* New York: Simon & Schuster, 2005.

Grant, Ulysses S. *Personal Memoirs of U. S. Grant.* 2 vols. New York: C. L. Webster & Co., 1886.

Gurowski, Adam. *Diary of Adam Gurowski.* 3 vols. Boston: Lee & Shepherd, 1862–66.

Halstead, Murat. *Caucuses of 1860: A History of the National Conventions of the Current Presidential Campaigns.* Columbus, Ohio: Follet, Foster & Co., 1860.

Hamlin, Charles E. *The Life and Times of Hannibal Hamlin.* Cambridge: Riverside Press, 1899.

Hanson, John W. *Historical Sketch of the Old Sixth Regiment of Massachusetts Volunteers during Its Three Campaigns.* Boston: Lee & Shepherd, 1866.

Hart, Albert Bushnell. *Salmon Portland Chase.* Boston: Houghton Mifflin, 1899.

Haupt, Herman. *Reminiscences of General Herman Haupt.* Milwaukee: Wright & Joys, 1901.

Hearn, Chester G. *Admiral David Dixon Porter: The Civil War Years.* Annapolis, Md.: Naval Institute Press, 1996.

———. *Admiral David Glasgow Farragut: The Civil War Years.* Annapolis, Md.: Naval Institute Press, 1998.

———. *Ellet's Brigade: The Strangest Outfit of All.* Baton Rouge: Louisiana State University Press, 2000.

———. *The Impeachment of Andrew Johnson.* Jefferson, N.C.: McFarland & Co., 2000.

Hebert, Walter H. *Fighting Joe Hooker.* Indianapolis: Bobbs-Merrill, 1944.

Helm, Katherine Helm. *The True Story of Mary, Wife of Lincoln.* New York: Harper's Bros., 1928.

Hendrick, Burton J. *Lincoln's War Cabinet.* Boston: Little, Brown, 1946.

Herndon, William H., and Jesse W. Weik. *Abraham Lincoln: The True Story of a Great Life.* 3 vols. Chicago: Belford-Clarke, 1890.

———. *Herndon's Life of Lincoln.* New York: Da Capo Press, 1942.

Hertz, Emanuel. *Abraham Lincoln: A New Portrait.* 2 vols. New York: Horace Liveright, 1931.

Hesseltine, William B., ed. *Civil War Prisons.* Kent, Ohio: Kent State University, 1962.

———. *Lincoln and the War Governors.* New York: Alfred A. Knopf, 1948.

Higginson, Thomas W. *Army Life in a Black Regiment.* Boston: Fields, Osgood & Co., 1870.

Hollandsworth, James G., Jr. *The Louisiana Native Guards: The Black Military Experience during the Civil War.* Baton Rouge: Louisiana State University Press, 1995.

Hollister, O. J. *Life of Schuyler Colfax.* New York: Funk & Wagnalls, 1886.

Hood, J. B. *Advance and Retreat.* 1959. Reprint. Secaucus, N.J.: Blue & Gray Press, 1985.

Horan, James D. *The Pinkertons: The Detective Dynasty That Made History.* New York: Crown Publishers, 1967.

Howard, Oliver O. *Autobiography of Oliver Otis Howard.* 2 vols. New York: Baker & Taylor, 1908.

Humphreys, Andrew Atkinson. *The Virginia Campaign of '64 and '65: Army of the Potomac and the Army of the James*. New York: Thomas Yoseloff, 1963.

Johnson, Robert U., and Clarence C. Buell, eds. *Battles and Leaders of the Civil War*. 4 vols. New York: Century Co., 1887–88.

Johnston, Joseph E. *Narrative of Military Operations Directed during the Late War between the States*. New York: D. Appleton, 1874.

Julian, George W. *Political Recollections, 1840 to 1872*. Chicago: Jansen, McClurg & Co., 1884.

Kelley, William D. *Lincoln and Stanton*. New York: G. P. Putnam's Sons, 1885.

King, Willard L. *Lincoln's Manager: David Davis*. Cambridge: Harvard University Press, 1960.

Lamon, Ward Hill. *The Life of Abraham Lincoln: From His Birth to His Inauguration as President*. Boston: Osgood & Co., 1862.

———. *Recollections of Abraham Lincoln, 1847–1865*. Lincoln: University of Nebraska Press, 1994.

Leech, Margaret. *Reveille in Washington*. New York: Harper's, 1941.

Macartney, Clarence E. *Lincoln and His Cabinet*. New York: Scribner's, 1931.

Marshall, Jessie Ames, comp. *Private and Official Correspondence of Gen. Benjamin F. Butler during the Period of the Civil War*. 5 vols. Norwood, Mass.: privately issued, 1917.

Marvel, William. *Burnside*. Chapel Hill: University of North Carolina Press, 1991.

McClellan, George B. *McClellan's Own Story: The War for the Union*. New York: C. L. Webster, 1887.

McClure, Alexander K. *Abraham Lincoln and the Men of War-Times*. 4th ed. Philadelphia: Times Publishing Co., 1892.

McCulloch, Hugh. *Men and Measures of Half a Century*. New York: Charles Scribner's Sons, 1888.

McPherson, Edward. *The Political History of the United States of America during the Great Rebellion*. Washington, D.C.: Philip & Solomons, 1865.

Meade, George Gordon. *The Life and Letters of George Gordon Meade, Major-General United States Army*. 2 vols. New York: Scribner's, 1913.

Mearns, David C., ed. *The Lincoln Papers*. 2 vols. Garden City, N.Y.: Doubleday, 1948.

Meneely, Alexander Howard. *The War Department, 1861*. New York: Columbia University Press, 1928.

Miers, Earl Schenk, ed. *Lincoln Day by Day*. 3 vols. Washington, D.C.: Lincoln Sesquicentennial Commission, 1960.

Monaghan, Jay. *Diplomat in Carpet Slippers: Abraham Lincoln Deals with Foreign Affairs*. Indianapolis: Bobbs-Merrill, 1945.

Moore, Frank A., comp. *The Rebellion Record*. 12 vols. New York: Van Nostrand, 1861–68.

Nevins, Allan. *Frémont, Pathmarker of the West*. New York: Appleton-Century, 1939.

———. *The War for the Union.* 4 vols. New York: Charles Scribner's Sons, 1959–71.

Nicolay, Helen. *Lincoln's Secretary: A Biography of John G. Nicolay.* New York: Longmans, Green & Co., 1949.

Nicolay, John G., and John Hay. *Abraham Lincoln: A History.* 10 vols. New York: Century Co., 1890.

———, eds. *Complete Works of Abraham Lincoln.* 12 vols. New York: Francis D. Tandy Co., 1905.

Niven, John. *Gideon Welles: Lincoln's Secretary of the Navy.* New York: Oxford University Press, 1973.

———. *Salmon P. Chase: A Biography.* New York: Oxford University Press, 1995.

O'Connor, Richard. *Sheridan the Inevitable.* Indianapolis: Bobbs-Merrill, 1953.

Owsley, Frank L. *King Cotton Diplomacy: Foreign Relations of the Confederate States of America.* 2nd ed. Chicago: University of Chicago Press, 1931.

Pease, Theodore C., and James G. Randall, eds. *The Diary of Orville Hickman Browning.* 2 vols. Springfield: Illinois State Historical Library, 1925–33.

Pennypacker, Isaac R. *General Meade.* New York: D. Appleton, 1901.

Piatt, Donn. *Memories of the Men Who Saved the Union.* New York: Belford, Clarke & Co., 1887.

Porter, David Dixon. *Incidents and Anecdotes of the Civil War.* New York: D. Appleton, 1885.

———. *Naval History of the Civil War.* New York: Sherman, 1886.

Porter, Horace. *Campaigning with Grant.* New York: Century Co., 1897.

Potter, David M. *Lincoln and His Party in the Secession Crisis.* Baton Rouge: Louisiana State University Press, 1995.

Pratt, Harry E., ed. *Concerning Mr. Lincoln: In Which Abraham Lincoln Is Pictured as He Appeared to Letter Writer's of His Time.* Springfield, Ill.: Abraham Lincoln Assoc., 1944.

Randall, J. G. *Constitutional Problems under Lincoln.* New York: D. Appleton, 1926.

———. *Lincoln the President.* 4 vols. New York: Dodd, Mead, 1946–55.

Raymond, Henry J. *The Life and Public Services of Abraham Lincoln .* New York: Derby & Miller, 1865.

Reid, Whitelaw. *Ohio in the War: Her Statesmen, Her Generals, and Soldiers.* 2 vols. Cincinnati: Wilstach, Baldwin & Co., 1868.

Rhodes, James Ford. *History of the United States from the Compromise of 1850 to the Final Restoration in 1877.* 7 vols. New York: Macmillan, 1896–1919.

Rice, Allen Thorndike, ed. *Reminiscences of Abraham Lincoln by Distinguished Men of His Time.* New York: North American Review, 1888.

Richardson, Albert D. *A Personal History of Ulysses S. Grant.* Hartford: American Publishing Co., 1868.

Richardson, James D. *A Compilation of the Messages and Papers of the Presidents, 1789–1905.* 11 vols. Washington, D.C.: Bureau of National Literature and Art, 1907.

Rusling, James F. *Men and Things I Saw in Civil War Days.* New York: Eaton & Mans, 1899.

Russell, William H. *My Diary North and South.* Boston: Burnham Publishers, 1863.

Sanborn, F. B. ed., *The Life and Letters of John Brown.* Boston: Little, Brown, 1891.

Sandburg, Carl. *Abraham Lincoln: The Prairie Years.* 2 vols. New York: Harcourt, Brace & Co., 1925–26.

———. *Abraham Lincoln: The War Years.* 4 vols. New York: Harcourt, Brace& Co., 1939.

Savage, John. *Life and Public Services of Andrew Johnson.* New York: Derby & Miller Publishers, 1866

Schouler, William. *History of Massachusetts in the Civil War.* 2 vols. Boston: Dutton, 1868–71.

Schuckers, Jacob W. *Life and Public Services of Salmon Portland Chase.* New York: D. Appleton, 1874.

Schurz, Carl. *The Reminiscences of Carl Schurz.* 3 vols. New York: McClure Co., 1907–8.

Sears, Stephen W., ed. *The Civil War Papers of George B. McClellan.* New York: Ticknor & Fields, 1989.

Segal, Charles M., ed. *Conversations with Lincoln.* New York: G. P. Putnam's Sons, 1939.

Seward, Frederick W. *Autobiography of William H. Seward.* Vol. 1 of Frederick W. Seward's *Seward at Washington.* New York: Derby & Miller, 1891.

———. *Reminiscences of a War-Time Statesman and Diplomat, 1830–1915.* New York: G. P. Putnam's Sons, 1916.

———. *Seward at Washington, as Senator and Secretary of State.* 2 vols. New York: Derby & Miller, 1891.

Sheridan, Philip H. *Personal Memoirs of P. H. Sheridan.* 2 vols. New York: C. L. Webster, 1888.

Sherman, William T. *Memoirs of General W. T. Sherman.* 2 vols. New York: D. Appleton, 1875.

Smith, Edward C. *The Borderland in the Civil War.* New York: Macmillan, 1927.

Smith, William E. *The Francis Preston Blair Family in Politics.* 2 vols. New York: Macmillan, 1933.

Soley, James R. *The Blockade and the Cruisers.* New York: Charles Scribner's Sons, 1883.

Southern Historical Society Papers. Vols. 3–4. Millwood, N.Y.: Kraus Reprint, 1977.

Stampp, Kenneth M. *Indiana Politics during the Civil War.* Indianapolis: Indiana Historical Bureau, 1949.

Stanwood, Edward. *A History of the Presidency from 1788 to 1897.* Boston: Houghton Mifflin, 1916.

Steele, Matthew F. *American Campaigns.* Washington, D.C.: U.S. Infantry Assoc., 1935.

Stephens, Alexander H. *A Constitutional View of the Late War between the States.* 2 vols. Philadelphia: National Publishing Co., 1868–70.

Stryker, Lloyd Paul. *Andrew Johnson: A Study in Courage.* New York: Macmillan, 1929.

Swinton, William. *Campaigns of the Army of the Potomac.* Secaucus, N.J.: Blue & Grey, 1988.

Tarbell, Ida M. *The Life of Abraham Lincoln.* 4 vols. Springfield, Ill.: Lincoln History Society, 1903.

———. *A Reporter for the Union: Story of Henry E. Wing, Soldier and Newspaperman.* New York: Book League of America, 1927.

Thayer, William Roscoe. *John Hay.* 2 vols. Boston: Houghton Mifflin, 1915.

Thomas, Benjamin P. *Abraham Lincoln.* New York: Alfred A. Knopf, 1952.

Thomas, Benjamin P., and Harold M. Hyman. *Stanton: The Life and Times of Lincoln's Secretary of War.* New York: Alfred A. Knopf, 1962.

Thompson, Robert Means, and Richard Wainwright, eds. 1918–19. Reprint. *Confidential Correspondence of Gustavus Vasa Fox, Assistant Secretary of the Navy 1861–1865.* 2 vols. Freeport, N.Y.: Books for Libraries Press, 1972.

Thorndike, Rachel Sherman, ed. *The Sherman Letters: Correspondence between General and Senator Sherman from 1837 to 1891.* New York: Charles Scribner's Sons, 1894.

Townsend, William H. *Lincoln and His Wife's Home Town.* Indianapolis: Bobbs-Merrill, 1929.

Tracy, Gilbert A., ed. *Uncollected Letters of Abraham Lincoln.* Boston: Houghton Mifflin, 1971.

Trefousse, Hans L. *Benjamin Franklin Wade: Radical Republican from Ohio.* New York: Twayne Publishers, 1963.

Usher, John P. *President Lincoln's Cabinet.* Omaha, Nebr.: Nelson H. Loomis, 1925.

Vallandigham, James L. *A Life of Clement L. Vallandigham.* Baltimore: Turnbull Bros., 1872.

Villard, Henry. *Lincoln on the Eve of '61.* Ed. Harold G. and Oswald Garrison Villard. New York: Alfred A. Knopf, 1941.

———. *Memoirs of Henry Villard, Journalist and Financier, 1835–1900.* 2 vols. Boston: Houghton Mifflin, 1904.

Warden, Robert B. *Account of the Private Life and Public Services of Salmon Portland Chase.* Cincinnati: Wilstach, Baldwin & Co., 1874.

Waugh, John C. *Reelecting Lincoln: The Battle for the 1864 Presidency.* New York: Crown Publishers, 1997.

Webb, Alexander S. *The Peninsula.* New York: Charles Scribner's Sons, 1881.

Weed, Harriet A. *The Life of Thurlow Weed, including His Autobiography and Memoir.* 2 vols. Boston: Houghton Mifflin, 1883.

Welles, Gideon. *Diary of Gideon Welles: Secretary of the Navy under Lincoln and Johnson.* 3 vols. Boston: Houghton Mifflin, 1911.

———. *Lincoln and Seward.* Freeport, N.Y.: Books for Libraries Press, 1969.

Werstein, Irving. *July, 1863: The Incredible Story of the Bloody New York City Draft Riots.* New York: Julius Messner, 1957.

White, Horace. *The Life of Lyman Trumbull.* Boston: Houghton Mifflin, 1913.

Whitney, Henry C. *Life on the Circuit with Lincoln.* Boston: Estes & Lauriat, 1892.

———. *Lincoln the President.* New York: Current Literature Publishing, 1909.

Williams, Kenneth P. *Lincoln Finds a General.* 5 vols. New York: Macmillan, 1949–59.

Williams, T. Harry. *Lincoln and His Generals.* New York: Alfred A. Knopf, 1952.

———. *Lincoln and the Radicals.* Madison: University of Wisconsin Press, 1941.

Wilson, James H. *The Life of Charles A. Dana.* New York: Harper's, 1907.

Woldman, Albert A. *Lincoln and the Russians.* Cleveland: World Publishing Co., 1952.

Zornow, William F. *Lincoln and the Party Divided.* Norman: University of Oklahoma Press, 1954.

ARTICLES

Brooks, Noah. "Personal Reminiscences of Abraham Lincoln." *Scribner's Monthly* (March 1878): 673–81.

Clement, Frank L. "Ward H. Lamon and the Dedication of the Soldiers' Cemetery at Gettysburg." *Civil War History* 31 (December 1985): 293–308.

Glonek, James F. "Lincoln, Johnson, and the Baltimore Ticket." *Abraham Lincoln Quarterly* 6 (March 1951): 255–71.

Nicolay, Helen. "A Candidate in His Home Town." *Abraham Lincoln Quarterly* 1 (September 1940): 1127–43.

Pratt, Harry E. "Simon Cameron's Fight for a Place in Lincoln's Cabinet." *Bulletin of the Abraham Lincoln Association* 49 (September 1937): 3–11.

Putnam, George Haven. "The Speech That Won the East for Lincoln." *Outlook* 130 (February 1922): 220–23.

Raymond, Henry W. "Excerpts from the Journal of Henry J. Raymond." *Scribner's Monthly* 19 (November 1879): 419–24.

Welles, Gideon. "Administration of Abraham Lincoln." *Galaxy* 23 (January 1877): 5–23, (February 1877): 149–59, (October 1877): 437–50, (November 1877): 608–24.

———. "History of Emancipation." *Galaxy* 14 (December 1872): 838–51.

Winchell, James A. "The Pomeroy Circular." *New York Times,* September 15, 1874.

NEWSPAPERS

Chicago Tribune
New York Evening Post
New York Herald
New York Times

INDEX